Wine Buying Companion For Dummies™

BUSINESS AND GENERAL REFERENCE BOOK SERIES FROM IDG

Quick Reference Card

Personal Shopping Record

Here's your opportunity to create your *own* wine reviews. Try a wine that we review in this book or one of your own finding; then write down the producer, wine name, appellation, vintage, and price and note your own rating and impressions of the wine. *Tip:* Copy this page before you start writing — we predict that you'll want to sample many more!

Remember that a wine's *appellation* refers to the area where the grapes were grown and sometimes includes the variety of grape used. If you're unsure of what information to put in each blank, ask your local wine merchant.

Producer: _____

Wine name: _____

Appellation: _____

Vintage: _____ **Price:** _____ **Your rating:** _____

Notes: _____

_____

_____

Producer: _____

Wine name: _____

Appellation: _____

Vintage: _____ **Price:** _____ **Your rating:** _____

Notes: _____

_____

_____

Producer: _____

Wine name: _____

Appellation: _____

Vintage: _____ **Price:** _____ **Your rating:** _____

Notes: _____

_____

_____

...For Dummies: Bestselling Book Series for Beginners

Wine Buying Companion For Dummies™

Quick Reference Card

Guide to Wine Grapes by Region

European wines, which are generally named after the region that produces the grapes rather than the variety of grape used, can be confusing. Unless you memorize all the wine laws of all the major European countries, you may not know what grape variety (or varieties) a particular wine is made from. Use the following chart to find out what grape varieties produce the most common types of European wine.

Region	Grape Varieties (Wine Names in Parentheses)
France	
Bordeaux	Cabernet Sauvignon, Merlot, and Cabernet Franc; Petite Verdot and Malbec (red Bordeaux); Sauvignon Blanc and Sémillon (dry white Bordeaux and Sauternes)
Burgundy	Pinot Noir (red Burgundy); Gamay (Beaujolais); Chardonnay (white Burgundy)
Champagne	Pinot Noir, Pinot Meunier, Chardonnay
Rhône Valley	*Red* — Syrah (Hermitage; Côte Rotie); Grenache, Mourvèdre, Syrah, others (Châteauneuf-du-Pape; Côtes du Rhône)
	White — Viognier (Condrieu); Roussanne, Marsanne (Hermitage Blanc)
Loire Valley	*Red* — Cabernet Franc (Chinon; Bourgueil)
	White — Sauvignon Blanc (Sancerre; Pouilly-Fumé); Chenin Blanc (Vouvray); Muscadet, also called Melon (Muscadet)
Alsace	Riesling; Gewurztraminer; Pinot Gris (Tokay-Pinot Gris); Pinot Blanc
Italy	
Piedmont	Nebbiolo (Barolo, Barbaresco, Gattinara); Barbera; Dolcetto
Tuscany	Sangiovese (Chianti; Brunello di Montalcino; Vino Nobille di Montepulciano)
Spain	
Rioja	Tempranillo; Garnacha (Rioja)

...For Dummies: Bestselling Book Series for Beginners

Praise For Wine Buying Companion For Dummies

"Communicating the characteristics of wines is an art in itself, and Mary and Ed have been able to do this in a clear and concise style. Their rating-system format emphasizes the subjectivity of wine evaluation and serves as a practical aid for the buyer."
— Dick Ponzi, Ponzi Vineyards

"A thirst-inspiring guide to the pleasures of wine."
— Kermit Lynch, Kermit Lynch Wine Merchant

"The authors are non-denominational missionaries of wine. They aren't concerned how you manifest your passion, but, as Joan Armatrading wrote, 'show some emotion.' When you put some of Mary-Ewing Mulligan's and Ed McCarthy's advice into play, I'm sure you will!"
— Roger Ormon, Brookline Liquor Mart

"*Wine Buying Companion For Dummies* solves many of the mysteries of finding and buying good wine values. You are sure to enjoy trying the numerous wine-and-food combinations that Ed and Mary recommend. I can't wait to try some of them myself."
— Philip H. Tenenbaum, President,
The Chicago Wine Company

"Ed and Mary have done it again! *Wine Buying Companion For Dummies* is the perfect source for wine lovers — novices and connoisseurs alike. The authors share their expertise in a clear, fun, and easy-to-follow format. A toast of J Sparkling Wine to the authors and readers of this fabulous book!"
— Judy Jordan, J Wine Company

"*Wine Buying Companion For Dummies* is as informative, insightful, and entertaining as their previous book. Having sold and/or tasted virtually all of the wines described in the book, I can attest that Mr. McCarthy's and Ms. Ewing - Mulligan's informative book will provide consumers with a trusted wine buying companion they should not be without."
— Jim Shpall, Applejack Liquors

"In Italy, wine is a part of our lives, and we have enjoyed it with food for years. I applaud Ed and Mary's information and their straightforward approach — everyone should enjoy wine with a meal!"
— Francesco Bolla, Bolla Wine Company

"Mary and Ed are experts who help their readers discover the pleasures of wine. [*Wine Buying Companion For Dummies*] is a great resource for anyone who enjoys wine."
— Angelo Gaja, Owner of Gaja Winery, Italy

"It is rare to find two people who are knowledgeable, passionate, and objective enough to understand individual preferences and have the ability to convey these perceptions with such style . . . take advantage of it!"
— Burt Williams, Williams & Selyem Winery

Praise for Wine For Dummies

"*Wine For Dummies* is complete and done in an agreeably relaxed style."
— Frank J. Prial, *The New York Times*

"*Wine For Dummies* offers clear advice and information about wine without a lot of fancy wine language."
— Jim Wood, *San Francisco Examiner* Food and Wine Critic

"A better and more entertaining introduction to wine would be hard to find. . . . Highly recommended."
— *Wine & Spirits Magazine*

Praise For Red Wine For Dummies & White Wine For Dummies

"*White Wine For Dummies* is an insightful reference guide for the beginning taster or the industry professional who has an appreciation of wine and wit."
— Lynn Penner-Ash, President/Winemaker, Rex Hill Vineyards, Inc.

"Finally a book that puts the spotlight exclusively on white wines! Thoroughly enjoyable and easy to read. Every white-wine drinker should read this."
— Terry Robards, Senior Managing Editor, *Wine Enthusiast Magazine*

"Everyone will enjoy reading *Red Wine For Dummies*. Its relaxed yet knowledgeable approach to a rather daunting topic will have novices and wine aficionados alike enjoying the book from cover to cover."
— Bruno Ceretoo, Chairman, Ceretto Winery, one of the most influential wine producers in Piedmont, Italy

™

References for the Rest of Us!™

5/97

WINE BUYING COMPANION FOR DUMMIES™

by Ed McCarthy
and Mary Ewing-Mulligan, MW

IDG Books Worldwide, Inc.
An International Data Group Company

Foster City, CA ♦ Chicago, IL ♦ Indianapolis, IN ♦ Southlake, TX

Wine Buying Companion For Dummies™

Published by
IDG Books Worldwide, Inc.
An International Data Group Company
919 E. Hillsdale Blvd.
Suite 400
Foster City, CA 94404
www.idgbooks.com (IDG Books Worldwide Web site)
www.dummies.com (Dummies Press Web site)

Library of Congress Catalog Card No.: 97-80185

ISBN: 0-7645-5043-8

Printed in the United States of America

10 9 8 7 6 5 4 3 2 1

1E/RZ/QZ/ZX/IN

Distributed in the United States by IDG Books Worldwide, Inc.

Distributed by Macmillan Canada for Canada; by Transworld Publishers Limited in the United Kingdom; by IDG Norge Books for Norway; by IDG Sweden Books for Sweden; by Woodslane Pty. Ltd. for Australia; by Woodslane Enterprises Ltd. for New Zealand; by Longman Singapore Publishers Ltd. for Singapore, Malaysia, Thailand, and Indonesia; by Simron Pty. Ltd. for South Africa; by Toppan Company Ltd. for Japan; by Distribuidora Cuspide for Argentina; by Livraria Cultura for Brazil; by Ediciencia S.A. for Ecuador; by Addison-Wesley Publishing Company for Korea; by Ediciones ZETA S.C.R. Ltda. for Peru; by WS Computer Publishing Corporation, Inc., for the Philippines; by Unalis Corporation for Taiwan; by Contemporanea de Ediciones for Venezuela; by Computer Book & Magazine Store for Puerto Rico; by Express Computer Distributors for the Caribbean and West Indies. Authorized Sales Agent: Anthony Rudkin Associates for the Middle East and North Africa.

For general information on IDG Books Worldwide's books in the U.S., please call our Consumer Customer Service department at 800-762-2974. For reseller information, including discounts and premium sales, please call our Reseller Customer Service department at 800-434-3422.

For information on where to purchase IDG Books Worldwide's books outside the U.S., please contact our International Sales department at 415-655-3200 or fax 415-655-3295.

For information on foreign language translations, please contact our Foreign & Subsidiary Rights department at 415-655-3021 or fax 415-655-3281.

For sales inquiries and special prices for bulk quantities, please contact our Sales department at 415-655-3200 or write to the address above.

For information on using IDG Books Worldwide's books in the classroom or for ordering examination copies, please contact our Educational Sales department at 800-434-2086 or fax 817-251-8174.

For press review copies, author interviews, or other publicity information, please contact our Public Relations department at 415-655-3000 or fax 415-655-3299.

For authorization to photocopy items for corporate, personal, or educational use, please contact Copyright Clearance Center, 222 Rosewood Drive, Danvers, MA 01923, or fax 508-750-4470.

is a trademark under exclusive license to IDG Books Worldwide, Inc., from International Data Group, Inc.

About the Authors

Ed McCarthy and **Mary Ewing-Mulligan** are two wine lovers who met at an Italian wine tasting in New York City's Chinatown in 1981. Two years later, they formally merged their wine cellars and wine libraries when they married. They have since co-authored four wine books (all for IDG Books Worldwide), taught dozens of wine classes together, tasted approximately 51,984 wines, run five marathons, and raised eight cats. Along the way, they have amassed more than half a century of professional wine experience between them.

Mary grew up in Pennsylvania and attended the University of Pennsylvania, where she majored in English literature. She got started in the wine business right out of college, by complete chance, when she accepted a position with the Italian Trade Commission. Today, her true love in wine is still Italian.

Ed, a New Yorker, graduated from City University of NY with a Master's degree in psychology. He taught high school English in another life, while working part-time in wine shops to satisfy his passion for wine and to subsidize his growing wine cellar. That cellar is especially heavy in his favorite wines — Bordeaux, Barolo, and Champagne.

Mary has spent half her professional career as co-owner and director of the International Wine Center in New York. There, she and Ed teach classes (both solo and jointly) for wine lovers and for professionals in the wine business. Ed also writes for *Wine Enthusiast Magazine,* and Mary is wine columnist for the *NY Daily News.*

In 1993, after five years of independent study, Mary became America's first — and only — woman Master of Wine (MW). There are only about 200 Masters of Wine in the world, including 14 in America.

When they aren't busy writing or teaching, Mary and Ed maintain a full schedule of continuing education by visiting the wine regions of the world, judging at professional wine competitions, and tasting as many new wines as possible. They admit to leading thoroughly unbalanced lives, in which their only non-wine pursuits are jogging and picnicking in the Italian Alps. At home, they wind down to the tunes of Bob Dylan and Neil Young, in the company of their feline roommates, La Tache, Léoville, Pinot Grigio, Brunello, Dolcetto, and Black & Whitey.

ABOUT IDG BOOKS WORLDWIDE

Welcome to the world of IDG Books Worldwide.

IDG Books Worldwide, Inc., is a subsidiary of International Data Group, the world's largest publisher of computer-related information and the leading global provider of information services on information technology. IDG was founded more than 25 years ago and now employs more than 8,500 people worldwide. IDG publishes more than 275 computer publications in over 75 countries (see listing below). More than 60 million people read one or more IDG publications each month.

Launched in 1990, IDG Books Worldwide is today the #1 publisher of best-selling computer books in the United States. We are proud to have received eight awards from the Computer Press Association in recognition of editorial excellence and three from *Computer Currents'* First Annual Readers' Choice Awards. Our best-selling *...For Dummies*® series has more than 30 million copies in print with translations in 30 languages. IDG Books Worldwide, through a joint venture with IDG's Hi-Tech Beijing, became the first U.S. publisher to publish a computer book in the People's Republic of China. In record time, IDG Books Worldwide has become the first choice for millions of readers around the world who want to learn how to better manage their businesses.

Our mission is simple: Every one of our books is designed to bring extra value and skill-building instructions to the reader. Our books are written by experts who understand and care about our readers. The knowledge base of our editorial staff comes from years of experience in publishing, education, and journalism — experience we use to produce books for the '90s. In short, we care about books, so we attract the best people. We devote special attention to details such as audience, interior design, use of icons, and illustrations. And because we use an efficient process of authoring, editing, and desktop publishing our books electronically, we can spend more time ensuring superior content and spend less time on the technicalities of making books.

You can count on our commitment to deliver high-quality books at competitive prices on topics you want to read about. At IDG Books Worldwide, we continue in the IDG tradition of delivering quality for more than 25 years. You'll find no better book on a subject than one from IDG Books Worldwide.

John Kilcullen
CEO
IDG Books Worldwide, Inc.

Steven Berkowitz
President and Publisher
IDG Books Worldwide, Inc.

Eighth Annual
Computer Press
Awards ≥1992

Ninth Annual
Computer Press
Awards ≥1993

Tenth Annual
Computer Press
Awards ≥1994

Eleventh Annual
Computer Press
Awards ≥1995

IDG Books Worldwide, Inc., is a subsidiary of International Data Group, the world's largest publisher of computer-related information and the leading global provider of information services on information technology. International Data Group publishes over 275 computer publications in over 75 countries. Sixty million people read one or more International Data Group publications each month. International Data Group's publications include: **ARGENTINA:** Buyer's Guide, Computerworld Argentina, PC World Argentina; **AUSTRALIA:** Australian Macworld, Australian PC World, Australian Reseller News, Computerworld, IT Casebook, Network World, Publish, Webmaster; **AUSTRIA:** Computerwelt Osterreich, Networks Austria, PC Tip Austria; **BANGLADESH:** PC World Bangladesh; **BELARUS:** PC World Belarus; **BELGIUM:** Data News; **BRAZIL:** Annuário de Informática, Computerworld, Connections, Macworld, PC Player, PC World, Publish, Reseller News, Supergamepower; **BULGARIA:** Computerworld Bulgaria, Network World Bulgaria, PC & MacWorld Bulgaria; **CANADA:** CIO Canada, Client/Server World, ComputerWorld Canada, InfoWorld Canada, NetworkWorld Canada; **CHILE:** Computerworld Chile, PC World Chile; **COLOMBIA:** Computerworld Colombia, PC World Colombia; **COSTA RICA:** PC World Centro America; **THE CZECH AND SLOVAK REPUBLICS:** Computerworld Czechoslovakia, Macworld Czech Republic, PC World Czechoslovakia; **DENMARK:** Communications World Danmark, Computerworld Danmark, Macworld Danmark, PC World Danmark, Techworld Denmark; **DOMINICAN REPUBLIC:** PC World Republica Dominicana; **ECUADOR:** PC World Ecuador; **EGYPT:** Computerworld Middle East, PC World Middle East; **EL SALVADOR:** PC World Centro America; **FINLAND:** MikroPC, Tietoverkko, Tietoviikko; **FRANCE:** Distributique, Hebdo, Info PC, Le Monde Informatique, Macworld, Reseaux & Telecoms, WebMaster France; **GERMANY:** Computer Partner, Computerwoche, Computerwoche Extra, Computerwoche FOCUS, Global Online, Macwelt, PC Welt; **GREECE:** Amiga Computing, GamePro Greece, Multimedia World; **GUATEMALA:** PC World Centro America; **HONDURAS:** PC World Centro America; **HONG KONG:** Computerworld Hong Kong, PC World Hong Kong, Publish in Asia; **HUNGARY:** ABCD CD-ROM, Computerworld Szamitastechnika, Internetto online Magazine, PC World Hungary, PC-X Magazin Hungary; **ICELAND:** Tolvuheimur PC World Island; **INDIA:** Information Communications World, Information Systems Computerworld, PC World India, Publish in Asia; **INDONESIA:** InfoKomputer PC World, Komputek Computerworld, Publish in Asia; **IRELAND:** ComputerScope, PC Live!; **ISRAEL:** Macworld Israel, People & Computers/Computerworld; **ITALY:** Computerworld Italia, Macworld Italia, Networking Italia, PC World Italia; **JAPAN:** DTP World, Macworld Japan, Nikkei Personal Computing, OS/2 World Japan, SunWorld Japan, Windows NT World, Windows World Japan; **KENYA:** PC World East African; **KOREA:** Hi-Tech Information, Macworld Korea, PC World Korea; **MACEDONIA:** PC World Macedonia; **MALAYSIA:** Computerworld Malaysia, PC World Malaysia, Publish in Asia; **MALTA:** PC World Malta; **MEXICO:** Computerworld Mexico, PC World Mexico; **MYANMAR:** PC World Myanmar; **NETHERLANDS:** Computer! Totaal, LAN Internetworking Magazine, LAN World Buyers Guide, Macworld Netherlands, Net, WebWereld; **NEW ZEALAND:** Absolute Beginners Guide and Plain & Simple Series, Computer Buyer, Computer Industry Directory, Computerworld New Zealand, MTB, Network World, PC World New Zealand; **NICARAGUA:** PC World Centro America; **NORWAY:** Computerworld Norge, CW Rapport, Datamagasinet, Financial Rapport, Kursguide Norge, Macworld Norge, Multimediaworld Norge, PC World Ekspress Norge, PC World Nettverk, PC World Norge, PC World ProduktGuide Norge; **PAKISTAN:** Computerworld Pakistan, Internetto online Magazine; **PANAMA:** PC World Panama; **PEOPLE'S REPUBLIC OF CHINA:** China Computer Users, China Computerworld, China InfoWorld, China Telecom World Weekly, Computer & Communication, Electronic Design China, Electronics Today, Electronics Weekly, Game Software, PC World China, Popular Computer Week, Software World, Software World, Telecom World; **PERU:** Computerworld Peru, PC World Profesional Peru, PC World SoHo Peru; **PHILIPPINES:** Click!, Computerworld Philippines, PC World Philippines, Publish in Asia; **POLAND:** Computerworld Poland, Computerworld Special Report Poland, Cyber, Networld Poland, Networld Poland, PC World Komputer; **PORTUGAL:** Cerebro/PC World, Computerworld/Correio Informático, Dealer World Portugal, Mac*In/PC*In Portugal, Multimedia World; **PUERTO RICO:** PC World Puerto Rico; **ROMANIA:** Computerworld Romania, PC World Romania, Telecom Romania; **RUSSIA:** Computerworld Russia, Mir PK, Publish, Seti; **SINGAPORE:** Computerworld Singapore, PC World Singapore, Publish in Asia; **SLOVENIA:** Monitor; **SOUTH AFRICA:** Computing SA, Network World SA, Software World SA; **SPAIN:** Communicaciones World España, Computerworld España, Dealer World España, Macworld España, PC World España; **SRI LANKA:** Infolink PC World; **SWEDEN:** CAP&Design, Computer Sweden, Corporate Computing Sweden, Internetworld Sweden, it.branschen, Macworld Sweden, MaxiData Sweden, MikroDatorn, Nätverk & Kommunikation, PC World Sweden, PCaktiv, Windows World Sweden; **SWITZERLAND:** Computerworld Schweiz, Macworld Schweiz, PCtip; **TAIWAN:** Computerworld Taiwan, Macworld Taiwan, NEW ViSiON/Publish, PC World Taiwan, Windows World Taiwan; **THAILAND:** Publish in Asia, Thai Computerworld; **TURKEY:** Computerworld Turkiye, Macworld Turkiye, Network World Turkiye, PC World Turkiye; **UKRAINE:** Computerworld Kiev, Multimedia World Ukraine, PC World Ukraine; **UNITED KINGDOM:** Acorn User UK, Amiga Action UK, Amiga Computing UK, Apple Talk UK, Computing, Macworld, Parents and Computers UK, PC Advisor, PC Home, PSX Pro, The WEB; **UNITED STATES:** Cable in the Classroom, CIO Magazine, Computerworld, DOS World, Federal Computer Week, GamePro Magazine, InfoWorld, I-Way, Macworld, Network World, PC Games, PC World, Publish, Video Event, THE WEB Magazine, and WebMaster; online webzines: JavaWorld, NetscapeWorld, and SunWorld Online; **URUGUAY:** InfoWorld Uruguay; **VENEZUELA:** Computerworld Venezuela, PC World Venezuela; and **VIETNAM:** PC World Vietnam. 3/24/97

Dedication

We dedicate this book to Susan Rusbasan, who gave so much of herself to the book, and to Sherry, whom we miss so much.

Acknowledgments

In preparation for writing this book, we tasted over 1,500 wines in six months. Even though the *Wine Buying Companion For Dummies* is our fourth wine book, it's our first wine-buying guide (with actual descriptions and recommendations of wines) and so we were treading on new ground. Fortunately for us, we had lots of help from good people, which enabled us to perform the minor miracle of getting this book published on time.

First, we thank the really outstanding group of people we work with at IDG, and gratefully acknowledge their invaluable assistance — CEO John Kilcullen, who is always encouraging our writing; Vice President and Publisher Kathy Welton, who first engaged us to write *Wine For Dummies;* our dear friend, Executive Editor Sarah Kennedy, who is constantly telling us "you can do it;" our project editor Shannon Ross, whose enormous patience and good judgment sustained us; and our very efficient copy editor, Tina Sims.

We thank Steve Etlinger, our agent and friend, who brought us to IDG in the first place, and who is always there for us.

We dearly thank and acknowledge Susan Rusbasan, to whom we have dedicated this book. Susan's incredible organizational skill in obtaining samples of wines, arranging all our wine tastings, and keeping track of all our tasting notes over a period of six intense months, was invaluable. The book literally could not have been written without her. Also, thanks to Susanne Bender for her special help.

We give special thanks and acknowledgment to our friend, wine consultant Steve Miller, for his help and advice. We recognize with gratitude Carol Sullivan of the German Wine Information Bureau, Jean-Louis Carbonnier of the Champagne Wines Information Bureau, and Dominic Nocerino of Vinifera Imports for their support.

The list of people in the wine industry who were kind enough to supply us with samples could go on for pages, and so we thank you all as a group and acknowledge your generous support. Please forgive us for not mentioning each of your names; we promise, at least, that we tried every one of your wines! We must nevertheless single out a few who went above and beyond the norm to give us access to wines we needed to taste: Bill Sciambi of Lauber Imports; Barbara Scalera and Lena Cammarota of Winebow; Kermit Lynch; Neal Rosenthal and Will Helburn of Rosenthal Wine Merchants; Kimberly Charles and Mary Ann Dancisin of Kobrand Corporation; Bobby Kacher and Virginia Sloan of Selected Fine Wines; Peter Koff MW of Fairest Cape Imports; Patrick Séré of Dreyfus-Ashby; Nancy Rugus of Vias Imports; Mary Marshall and Jen Jonas of Paterno Imports; Barbara Waits Juckett of Sager-Bell; Lisa Somogyi of Maison Marques & Domaines; Margaret Stern of M. Stern Communications; Marsha Palanci of Cornerstone Communications; Kathleen Talbert of Talbert Communications; Steve and Susan Deutsch of William Deutsch & Sons; Leah Karliner of William Grant; Jeff Pogash of Schieffelin & Somerset; Danielle Devoe and Nina Brøndmo of Clicquot, Inc.; Lars Leicht of Banfi; Mark Whitmore of Vineyard Expressions; the people of Martin-Scott; Matthew Green of Charmer Industries; Steve Metzler of Classic Wines from Spain; Odila Galer-Noël and Joe Janish of Frederick Wildman & Sons; Mitch Nathanson of Wine Markets International; Wilson-Daniels; Larry Soll; Shirley Alpert of the House of Burgundy; Joe Dressner and Kevin McKenna of Louis Dressner; Mike Petteruti of Palm Bay Imports; the people at Paramount Brands; John Gregory of Peerless Imports; Bob Shack and Frank D'Amico of Remy-Amerique; Kristen McDonough of Seagram Chateau & Estates; Lou Buonocolta of Trebon Wines & Spirits; Sam Levitas of Tricana Imports; the people of Athenee Imports; Chet Zeiger of Admiral Wine Merchants; Joao Oliveira of Tri-Vin Imports; Nina Zeiger of Organic Wine Company; Jim Galtieri of Pasternak Imports; Monica Elling of the Hungarian-American Business Bureau; and the people at Cazanove-Opici.

Thanks also to Elise and E.J. McCarthy and Cindy and David Tomarchio for their support and encouragement, and to our cats, La Tache, Léoville, Brunello, Dolcetto, PeeGee, and Black &Whitey, who provided much-needed diversion and helped us maintain perspective.

Contents at a Glance

Publisher's Acknowledgments

We're proud of this book; please send us your comments about it by using the IDG Books Worldwide Reader Response Card at the back of the book or by e-mailing us at feedback/dummies@idgbooks.com. Some of the people who helped bring this book to market include the following:

Acquisitions, Development, and Editorial

Project Editor: Shannon Ross

Aquisitions Editor: Sarah Kennedy, Executive Editor

Copy Editor: Tina Sims

Technical Editor: Patrick W. Fegan; Director, Chicago Wine School

Editorial Manager: Leah P. Cameron

Editorial Assistants: Donna Love

Acquisitions Assistants: Jill Alexander, Nickole Harris

Production

Project Coordinator: Valery Bourke

Layout and Graphics: Maridee V. Ennis, Sherry Gomoll, Drew R. Moore, Heather N. Pearson, Anna Rohrer, Brent Savage, M. Anne Sipahimalani, Kate Snell

Proofreaders: Christine Sabooni, Kelli Botta, Michelle Croninger, Joel K. Draper, Rachel Garvey, Rebecca Senninger, Karen York

Indexer: CZ Editorial Services

Special Help: Ann K. Miller, Editorial Coordinator; Linda S. Stark, Copy Editor

General and Administrative

IDG Books Worldwide, Inc.: John Kilcullen, CEO; Steven Berkowitz, President and Publisher

Dummies, Inc.: Brenda McLaughlin, Senior Vice President and Group Publisher

Dummies Technology Press and Dummies Editorial: Diane Graves Steele, Vice President and Associate Publisher; Kristin A. Cocks, Editorial Director; Mary Bednarek, Acquisitions and Product Development Director

Dummies Trade Press: Kathleen A. Welton, Vice President and Publisher; Kevin Thornton, Acquisitions Manager

IDG Books Production for Dummies Press: Beth Jenkins, Production Director; Cindy L. Phipps, Manager of Project Coordination, Production Proofreading, and Indexing; Kathie S. Schutte, Supervisor of Page Layout; Shelley Lea, Supervisor of Graphics and Design; Debbie J. Gates, Production Systems Specialist; Robert Springer, Supervisor of Proofreading; Debbie Stailey, Special Projects Coordinator; Tony Augsburger, Supervisor of Reprints and Bluelines; Leslie Popplewell, Media Archive Coordinator

Dummies Packaging and Book Design: Patti Crane, Packaging Specialist; Lance Kayser, Packaging Assistant; Kavish + Kavish, Cover Design

♦

The publisher would like to give special thanks to Patrick J. McGovern, without whom this book would not have been possible.

♦

Table of Contents

Introduction

*A*lmost as soon as each of us became seriously interested in wine — before we met each other, and long before we were published authors — friends and relatives who liked wine began asking us which wines they should buy. If we knew their tastes in food, and especially if we knew what types of wine they had already tried and what they thought of those wines, we could usually recommend wines that they liked. Otherwise, the best we could do was to tell them what *we* like and to suggest that they decide for themselves whether they agree with our taste.

We employ the same strategy here. This book is a collection of wines that we like and that we offer for your consideration. We can't guarantee that you'll like every wine that we like, or even a majority of them — but we promise that you'll have fun in the process of finding out.

The Purpose of This Book

Thousands of different wines line the shelves of wine shops and supermarkets across the U.S. No other type of food or beverage offers buyers such a confusing array of brands, flavors, styles, types, and price levels. Can you imagine having to choose from among 100 different types of bread? Such variety seems absurd — and yet many supermarkets stock as many as 200 different wines, and many wine shops stock thousands.

We happen to think that all this variety in wine is exciting; the sheer abundance of wines, each subtly, or not so subtly, different from the next, is one of the things that feeds our fascination with wine. But we realize that having so many choices can turn a simple beverage purchase into a big, complicated deal.

The purpose of this book is to shorten the playing field a bit by naming and describing specific wines for you to try — and, in that way, to make wine purchasing easier for you. Naturally, what's left when we shorten the field are wines that correspond to our personal taste.

Our purpose is also to excite you about wines that you've never tasted before, and to inspire you to try new wines — and, in that sense, to broaden your personal playing field. (If you always drink Cabernet and have never tried Pinot Noir, for example, we hope our enthusiasm for Pinot Noir will encourage you to try it.) The purpose of this book absolutely is *not* to dictate which wines you should drink.

About the Wines in This Book

The wines in this book — over 500 of them — are all wines that we like. (We like some of them more than others, naturally. And often one of us likes a wine more than the other does. Sometimes only one of us likes a wine enough to recommend it to you.) All these wines are also good wines, and many of them are truly great wines. But our criterion in selecting wines to include in this book is *how much we like them,* not how high in quality they are.

We emphasize this last point because we want you to understand that this book is not a definitive guide to the finest wines in the world. We don't believe that such a book can ever exist. After all, who could ever objectively determine the quality of thousands of wines without letting his or her personal likes and dislikes intrude in the judgment? Personal taste intervenes every time wine enters a human being's mouth, even if that person is a trained winemaker.

Anyway, the quality of a wine is ultimately less important than the *style* of the wine (that is, the general characteristics of the wine, or how the wine tastes) and how that style relates to your personal taste. A great red wine of the highest caliber might not taste good to white-wine lovers, for example, and a great full-bodied wine might not taste good to someone who favors lighter wines.

How we selected these wines

As our starting point for determining which wines to review in this book, we considered the hundreds of wines that we have known and loved over our years of wine tasting and wine drinking. We gathered samples of most of them and tasted the wines *blind,* that is, without knowing what each wine was. (We often knew the type of wine — for example, that it was an Italian red — but not the producer.) After each of us individually evaluated a group of wines, the two of us compared our notes on each wine and discussed the wines.

This process took many months. Our notes from these blind tastings, along with our previous experience with the various wines, form the basis for our descriptions of the wines in this book. In order to provide the most up-to-date wine descriptions possible, we don't review wines that we haven't tasted personally in the past 18 months, even if, in some cases, we know that we love the wines.

In choosing wines to review in this book, we aimed for a broad coverage of wine types, wine styles, and wine regions so that more readers could find in these pages wines that suit their tastes. Naturally, this coverage is not balanced, because the wines reflect our personal tastes.

We also aimed to cover different price ranges so that you can find everything from an $8 wine for a simple dinner to a $50 bottle worthy of your most special occasions. (However, in the interest of practicality, we set an upper limit of $50 a bottle for the wines we review.) Another goal in selecting the wines we review here was to include many wines that are widely available across the U.S.

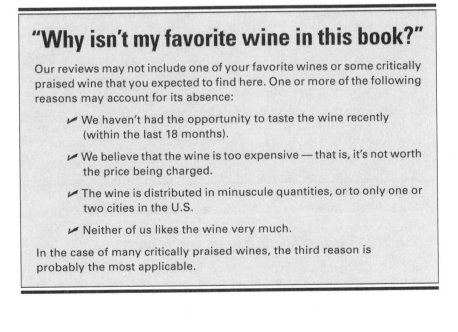

"Why isn't my favorite wine in this book?"

Our reviews may not include one of your favorite wines or some critically praised wine that you expected to find here. One or more of the following reasons may account for its absence:

- ✔ We haven't had the opportunity to taste the wine recently (within the last 18 months).

- ✔ We believe that the wine is too expensive — that is, it's not worth the price being charged.

- ✔ The wine is distributed in minuscule quantities, or to only one or two cities in the U.S.

- ✔ Neither of us likes the wine very much.

In the case of many critically praised wines, the third reason is probably the most applicable.

How we rate each wine

Each wine in this book carries a score that represents our measure of how much we like the wine. Most of the wines we review carry two scores: a score from Ed and a score from Mary. A wine that carries a score from only one of us suggests that the other one of us isn't crazy about that wine or, occasionally, that only one of us knows that wine well enough to feel comfortable recommending it. We each give our own score because we're two different people, each with our own tastes. Although we often agree, we don't always agree — just as you won't always agree with us.

We base our score for each wine on a potential high of 100 points, which is the most common scoring calibration used for wines in the U.S. (Because this book includes only those wines we recommend, you won't find any very low scores.) We express each score as a three-point range, for example, 85–87. Most wine critics and publications score wines with a single number, but we believe that pinning a single number on a wine is unrealistic. All sorts of variables come into play when we decide how much we like a wine. For example:

- ✔ One bottle of a wine can taste different from another bottle of the same wine, depending on how the bottles were stored or simply how the wine evolved in each bottle.

- ✔ The food we eat, the company we keep, our moods, and even the atmospheric pressure can influence how much we like a wine on a particular day.

- ✔ Even removing all those variables, two glasses of the same wine (from the same bottle, on the same day, with the same food, and so forth) can taste different if you taste them out of two different types of glasses.

As these variables shift, so does our score. By rating each wine with a three-point spread, we hope to reinforce the reality that each bottle of wine is a live performance, subject to variation.

Prices and availability of the wines

No such thing as a single, national, U.S. suggested retail price exists for wine. As an alcoholic beverage, wine is taxed by each of the 50 states, and each state regulates its sales. Differing state regulations result in different prices for the same product.

Each store also has its own system of determining a wine's shelf price. Even within a single state, the cost of a bottle of the same wine can easily vary by 25 percent, depending on whether you purchase it at a high-volume discount chain or a small, service-oriented, mom-and-pop operation.

In quoting a price for each wine we review, we use the New York State suggested retail price (rounded to the nearest dollar or half-dollar). Depending on where you purchase the wine, your cost could be less than the price we list — even considerably less. Or you might end up paying a little more for a bottle than the price we name.

If you decide to purchase certain wines that we review, searching around for the best price might be moot: Some wines are made in relatively small quantities and are therefore available only in fine wine shops in major cities. Other wines are available in most wine shops (or are available *to* the shop, if the buyer wishes to purchase them), and many wines are available in supermarkets, in those states that permit supermarkets to sell wine.

The Wine Language in This Book

In Chapter 18 of *Wine For Dummies,* we discuss the limitations of language in describing individual wines. The two main problems are that we don't all share a common vocabulary for describing taste, and that the experience of each wine is highly personal and subjective, occurring in the privacy of our own mouths.

We still stand by those thoughts. And yet, here we are, presuming to describe to you what 500 wines taste like, and presuming that our descriptions will be meaningful to you. What gives?

After many hours of thought and discussion about how to write wine descriptions that are clear and comprehensible, we came up with the following language and system of expression:

- ✔ We describe each wine in complete sentences. (Many wine descriptions just string adjectives together, but we feel that complete sentences communicate more effectively.)
- ✔ We limit the amount of technical language that we use to describe wines. Some technical terms (such as *tannin, acidity,* and *alcohol*) describe fundamental aspects of wine, and we believe that the use of such terms is unavoidable if the descriptions are to be truly useful. But we try to describe the *effect* of these aspects in any one wine — that the wine tastes *firm* because of its high tannin, for example, rather than mentioning tannin for tannin's sake.

✔ We define our wine-tasting terms in a glossary, which is Appendix C.

✔ We use terms in a consistent fashion throughout the book.

✔ We try to take a logical approach to describing the wines. Sometimes, we describe a wine by moving sequentially from the appearance to the smell to the mouth impression, as you would experience the wine "in person." More frequently, we describe the aromas and flavors of a wine together because both aspects of a wine are *olfactory* impressions (you "smell" flavors in your mouth); then we describe the wine's *basic taste* sensations (sweetness or dryness, acidity, and bitterness) and *tactile* sensations. (Refer to Chapters 2 and 18 of *Wine For Dummies* for a discussion of these terms.)

✔ We provide information on each wine that goes beyond the description of how it tastes so that you can understand something about the wine or the winery even if our tasting notes fail you.

✔ We write every wine description with a goal of *communicating* the wine to you.

How to Use This Book

You can carry your *Wine Buying Companion For Dummies* with you when you shop for wine or go to a restaurant, or you can browse through it for ideas of wine to buy before you shop or dine.

We hope that you will also refer to this book while you drink a wine that we review so that you can compare your own impressions of the wine with our impressions. By doing so, you can understand in what ways our tastes coincide with yours and in what ways they differ, and you can develop your own system of filtering our comments through your personal tastes. By reading as you taste, you can also gain a more visceral understanding of the terms we use to describe wine.

When you want to use this book as inspiration for wines to purchase, consider the following:

✔ Do you want a white wine, a red wine, or a bubbly wine?

✔ Do you want an inexpensive wine, or are you willing to spend more than $15 on a bottle?

✔ Is there a particular type of wine — such as California Chardonnay or Italian white — toward which you are gravitating?

✔ What's for dinner?

Depending on how you answer each question, different parts of this book will be useful to you. We describe each part in the following sections.

Part I: Seeing Red

The four chapters in this part of the book contain information about different types of red wines and reviews of many of our favorite red wines. Because we happen to favor red wines over white wines, this is a very substantial part of the book.

The first two chapters discuss red wines that sell for $15 or less. **Chapter 1** deals with inexpensive European red wines, and **Chapter 2** covers inexpensive red wines from the New World: the U.S., Chile, Argentina, Australia, and South Africa. **Chapter 3** covers European red wines (such as Bordeaux, Burgundy, Italy's best reds, and so forth) costing more than $15 a bottle, and **Chapter 4** discusses New World red wines costing more than $15 a bottle. (In Chapters 3 and 4, we limit our reviews to wines that cost under $50 a bottle.)

Part II: All Dressed in White

The four chapters in this part of the book cover white wines along the same lines as the chapters in Part I cover reds. **Chapter 5** discusses inexpensive European white wines, and **Chapter 6** discusses inexpensive New World whites. Pricier European white wines appear in **Chapter 7,** and costlier New World whites appear in **Chapter 8.** In this part, we also list our favorite rosé wines.

Part III: All Those Bubbles!

In **Chapter 9,** we review one of our favorite types of wine — true Champagnes (sparkling wines from the Champagne region of France). In **Chapter 10,** we describe our favorite non-Champagne sparklers, including sparkling wines from elsewhere in France, from other Old World wine countries, and from the New World.

Part IV: Appendixes

The pages that form this part of the book are likely to become dog-eared with use because the information contained here is so useful — at least we hope so!

- ✔ **Appendix A** offers suggestions of wines you might like to try, based on the wines you already know you like.

- ✔ **Appendix B** contains recommendations of wines that we think go well with various types of food.

✓ **Appendix C** is a glossary of wine-tasting (and smelling) terms. Here, we define all the terms we use to describe the wines we review, except for the really obvious words like *roses, lemon,* or *delicious.*

Icons Used in This Book

This icon indicates a wine that I (Mary) personally recommend. Perhaps Ed hasn't tasted this wine recently, or he doesn't feel as comfortable as I do in recommending it, or he simply doesn't like it. If you like one wine marked with this icon, your tastes might be similar to mine, and other wines marked "Mary's Choice" might be good bets for you.

When I (Ed) am really enthusiastic about a wine, and Mary isn't (or she doesn't know the wine as well as I do), we use this icon. If you weren't thrilled with a wine marked "Mary's Choice," maybe the wines marked "Ed's Choice" will be just what you're looking for.

A bargain's not a bargain unless you really like the dress, as they say. To our tastes, the wines we mark with this icon are bargains because we like them, we believe them to be of good quality, and their price is low compared to wines of similar type, style, or quality. Because we expect wines to have characteristics that are typical of their type, you can also interpret this logo as a badge of genuineness, as in "This Chablis is the real deal."

An unfortunate fact of life in the wine world is that some of the finest, most intriguing, most delicious wines are made in very small quantities. Naturally, such wines cost more than wines made in large quantities — but that's not the whole problem. The real frustration is that such wines have very limited distribution, and you can't always get your hands on a bottle even if you're willing to pay the price. We mark such wines with this icon, and hope that your search proves fruitful.

This icon indicates miscellaneous and sundry bits of good advice about storing wine, serving wine, enjoying wine, or even visiting wineries.

Part I
Seeing Red

In this part . . .

We love red wine. About four out of every five wines we drink are red, because red wines just seem right with many foods that we enjoy and because we love the range of styles that red wines encompass. Young or aged, spicy or fruity, light bodied or very full bodied, simple or serious — red wines fit the bill, no matter what the occasion.

What type of red wine suits your mood today? No matter how you answer, the four chapters in this part of the book can guide you to a red wine that meets your needs and tastes. We separate wines by cost: Chapters 1 and 2 cover inexpensive reds ($15 and under), and Chapters 3 and 4 discuss costlier reds (over $15). We also separate the wines in this part by their origin: We review reds from Europe (primarily France and Italy, but also Spain and Portugal) in Chapters 1 and 3, and reds from the New World (including the U.S., New Zealand, Australia, and South Africa) in Chapters 2 and 4. We like all the wines we review in this part (and in this whole book, for that matter!). We hope that you try a few and find some new favorite wines among them.

Chapter 1

Respecting Your Elders: Old World Red Wines for $15 or Less

. . . .

▶ Beaujolais beauties — and other affordable French reds

▶ The inexpensive side of *vino rosso italiano*

▶ Real values from Portugal and Spain

. . . .

*I*f, by some malicious twist of fate, the wines that we review in this chapter ended up being the only wines on earth . . . we'd actually manage just fine! Of course, we would miss white wine, and we'd definitely miss Champagne. Our lives would be a little drearier without the great, legendary (and more expensive) red wines of France and Italy to look forward to, and nothing could quite replace the high-end California Cabernets and Zinfandels we'd have to give up. But frankly, the wines we describe in the pages that follow are the wines we drink most often, day after day.

This chapter covers our favorite inexpensive French, Italian, Spanish, and Portuguese red wines. We arrange these wines by country, starting with France, and by region within each country.

Because these wines are from Europe, most of them are named after the place they come from — such as Bordeaux, Beaujolais, or Chianti — or have a combination grape-and-place name, such as Barbera d'Alba (the Barbera grape, grown in Alba), rather than a simple grape name, such as Merlot or Cabernet. (Refer to the Quick Reference Card at the front of this book for a listing of grape varieties used in major regions.) We list the vital information for every wine in this chapter according to this system:

   ✔ **The name of the producer:** This information is equivalent to the wine's brand name.

   ✔ **The wine name:** Most of the wines in this chapter are named after a place.

   ✔ **The wine's appellation:** In this chapter, the *appellation* (that is, the legal origin of the wine, the specific place from which the grapes came) and the wine name are often the same.

> When we group wines of more than one country in a single section, we indicate the country of origin in parentheses after each wine's appellation.
>
> ✔ **The approximate retail price of the wine:** This price can vary quite a lot according to what part of the country you're in and the type of store where you buy your wine. The price we use, the New York State suggested retail price, is likely to be a bit high if you shop in discount stores, if taxes are lower in your state, or if you buy in quantity.

In this chapter, and all throughout the book, we give each wine a rating, based on 100 points, to reflect how much we personally like each of the wines we recommend. (Naturally, we like all of them: That's why we're recommending them to you. But we feel even more strongly about some of these wines than others.)

The red wines we describe in this chapter represent such a range of styles (one reason why we could survive on them forever!) that we can't really generalize about them as a whole. Look for some regional generalizations at the beginning of each section.

Inexpensive French Red Wines

The words *wine* and *French* just seem to go together, especially when the color is red. We begin our red wine reviews with French wines for several reasons:

✔ Most of the important red wine grape varieties in the world were either born in France or became important in France — such as Cabernet Sauvignon, Merlot, Pinot Noir, Syrah, Cabernet Franc, and Gamay.

✔ Many of the world's most renowned red wines, including Bordeaux, Burgundy, Beaujolais, and Châteauneuf-du-Pape, come from France.

✔ France, along with Italy, is the world leader in wine production.

✔ Despite the popular myth that "all French wines are expensive," many of the great wine values in the world come from France.

Beaujolais: always fun, never expensive

Ah, Beaujolais! The very name suggests fun and frivolity. Aside from Champagne, Beaujolais is probably France's most famous wine. And why not? It's easy to drink, delicious, inexpensive, and easy to pronounce (just say *bo jho lay*). Some people accuse

Beaujolais of not being very "serious" (translation: deeply colored, very dry, and complex). But we don't always want to drink a serious wine. Sometimes — such as at parties, picnics, simple lunches, suppers, or warm-weather dinners — the occasion calls for easy to-drink wines, not wines for contemplation.

Most Beaujolais wines retail in the $7 to $15 price range. All Beaujolais wines are made from a single grape variety, Gamay (called *Gamay Noir* in the U.S.). California wines that are called Beaujolais don't really resemble true Beaujolais, and in most cases, they don't even come from the same Gamay grape variety. (In fact, recent changes in U.S. regulations prohibit the future use of the word *Beaujolais* on bottles of domestic wine.)

The Beaujolais district, where all Beaujolais wines come from, is actually a part of the Burgundy region in east-central France (known in French as Bourgogne, pronounced *boor guh nyeh*). Beaujolais occupies the southern third of Burgundy, with the city of Mâcon to the north and Lyon to the south.

Beaujolais wines are labeled in three different ways, according to where the grapes are grown:

- ✔ **Beaujolais:** The lightest-bodied wines, which come from the southern part of the Beaujolais district, are labeled simply *Beaujolais.* (The young, grapey wine called *Beaujolais Nouveau* that debuts each November generally falls into this category.) These wines cost about $7 to $8.

- ✔ **Beaujolais-Villages:** Fuller-bodied, more substantial wines that come from one or more of the 39 villages in the northern part of the region are labeled *Beaujolais-Villages.* They typically retail in the $10 to $12 price range.

- ✔ **Cru Beaujolais:** The finest quality Beaujolais wines, generally speaking, come from ten specific villages in the north. These wines carry their village name (such as Moulin-à-Vent or Juliénas) on their labels. Known as *cru* Beaujolais, these wines sometimes don't even have the word *Beaujolais* on their labels, except in small print. They usually retail in the $12 to $15 price range. (See Table 10-8 in Chapter 10 of *Wine For Dummies* for a complete description of the ten cru Beaujolais.)

Most Beaujolais wines come from large firms, such as Georges Duboeuf, Louis Jadot, Joseph Drouhin, and Louis Latour. But a few smaller producers, including those we mention in this section, do ship their excellent Beaujolais wines to the U.S.

The Beaujolais wines that we recommend are anything but simple: They are among the finest Beaujolais wines made today. We list our recommended wines alphabetically by the name of the producer.

Beaujolais-Leynes, Domaine Dalicieux

- ♪ **Producer:** Domaine Dalicieux *(dah lee s'yuh)*
- ♪ **Wine name:** Beaujolais-Leynes *(bo jho lay-lane)*
- ♪ **Appellation:** Beaujolais-Villages *(bo jho lay vee lahj)*
- ♪ **Price:** $10.50

For us, the name Domaine Dalicieux has been synonymous with quality for several years now. In a way, Domaine Dalicieux's wines are very un-Beaujolais-like, because they are dark, deep, and complex in flavor and are made to be ageworthy, unlike the many simple, quaffing wines carrying the Beaujolais label. The 1993 Domaine Dalicieux Beaujolais, from the village of Leynes (one of the 39 villages entitled to call its wines *Beaujolais Villages*), has incredible aromas of eucalyptus, menthol, spice, and strawberry. It's a dense, very concentrated wine with rich, ripe fruit character and some tannin, and yet it is supple and round enough to enjoy now. This is a serious wine that still has the vibrancy and personality of a Beaujolais.

Ed: 87–89   **Mary:** 92–94

Beaujolais-Villages, Domaine des Terres Dorées

- ♪ **Producer:** Domaine des Terres Dorées, of Jean Paul Brun
- ♪ **Wine name:** Beaujolais Villages, Cuvée a L'Ancienne
- ♪ **Appellation:** Beaujolais-Villages
- ♪ **Price:** $10

The Beaujolais-Villages wine from Domaine des Terres Dorées, made by Jean Paul Brun, is an excellent example of natural, old-fashioned winemaking. The 1995 Cuvée a L'Ancienne is a delicious, intensely flavored wine with a pronounced scent of cherries and ripe strawberry jam. Quite dry and firm for a Beaujolais, this wine has an intense, but not sweet, strawberry jam taste. A serious wine, this is our kind of Beaujolais!

Ed: 90–92   **Mary:** 85–87

Fleurie, Georges Duboeuf

- ♪ **Producer:** Georges Duboeuf *(doo buff)*
- ♪ **Wine name:** Fleurie ("Flower Label")
- ♪ **Appellation:** Fleurie
- ♪ **Price:** $14

In wine circles, Georges Duboeuf is known as "Mr. Beaujolais" because he ships dozens of Beaujolais wines, some of which are excellent, to the U.S. Our friend Jacques Capsouto (one of the three owner-brothers of Capsouto Frères, a French country restaurant in the Tribeca section of New York City that's one of our favorite hangouts) insists that Duboeuf's Fleuries are always among Duboeuf's best Beaujolais. This very dense, purple-red beauty is firm, rich, tannic, and full bodied for a Beaujolais, with flavors of tart, concentrated fruit. It will probably even improve with a year or two of aging.

Ed: 91–93   **Mary:** 86–88

Moulin-à-Vent, Domaine des Rosiers, from Georges Duboeuf

- ♪ **Producer:** Georges Duboeuf
- ♪ **Wine name:** Domaine des Rosiers, Moulin-à-Vent
- ♪ **Appellation:** Moulin-à-Vent
- ♪ **Price:** $14

The vineyards of Moulin-à-Vent make the most full-bodied and intense Beaujolais wines — so much so that many people consider these wines closer in style to a red Burgundy than to Beaujolais. (However, as with all Beaujolais wines, the grape is Gamay, not the Pinot Noir grape of Burgundy.) Duboeuf's Moulin-à-Vent is quite different from his other Beaujolais wines. It is fuller in body, more dense and concentrated, and also more tannic, because of oak aging. Strawberry-raspberry jam lurks in the aroma, and the taste is jammy, too. The 1995 vintage is delicious now and will certainly stay that way for a couple of years yet.

Mary: 88–90

St.-Amour, Domaine de la Pirolette, from Georges Duboeuf

- ♪ **Producer:** Georges Duboeuf
- ♪ **Wine name:** Domaine de la Pirolette, St.-Amour
- ♪ **Appellation:** St.-Amour
- ♪ **Price:** $13

St.-Amour is one of the ten villages that produce cru Beaujolais. Because of its name, St.-Amour is usually popular around St. Valentine's Day, but this particular wine is too good to drink just once a year! The Domaine de la Pirolette is a Beaujolais from a single estate. (Most Beaujolais wines are made from blends of several properties.) The 1995 is soft, rich, and intensely flavored, with notes of strawberries and cherries. It's serious enough for those in the know — and delicious enough for everyone. An outstanding Beaujolais.

Ed: 92–94   **Mary:** 86–88

Bordeaux reds that aren't pricey

Bordeaux is the most important wine region in the world, especially for its red wines. Among French wine regions, Bordeaux produces more serious wine than any other region. Internationally, the red wines of Bordeaux (which are made primarily from a blend of Cabernet Sauvignon, Merlot, and Cabernet Franc grape varieties) have served as a model for many New World countries, including the U.S.

The Bordeaux wine region is situated in southwest France, next to the Atlantic Ocean. The Gironde Estuary runs through this region, and the best vineyard areas are located near its banks. Bordeaux's four most important *districts* (subregions) are

- ✔ The Médoc district on the left bank of the Gironde
- ✔ The Graves/Pessac-Léognan district on the left bank of the Gironde
- ✔ The St.-Emilion district on the right bank of the Gironde
- ✔ The Pomerol district on the right bank of the Gironde

Bordeaux wines from the more gravelly Left Bank are dominated by Cabernet Sauvignon, while Merlot is the main grape variety in Right Bank Bordeaux.

Bordeaux wines have a reputation for being expensive, but actually only the famous-name wines (2 or 3 percent of the region's total, at most) are very pricey. Retail prices for Bordeaux wines actually start at about $6. (For more detailed information about Bordeaux wines, see *Wine For Dummies,* Chapter 10, or *Red Wine For Dummies,* also Chapter 10.)

The red Bordeaux wines we recommend in this chapter all represent good values. (We list our recommended wines alphabetically by the name of the producer.) They are wines that you can enjoy right now, even though they can age for a few years. For recommendations of more serious, ageworthy, over-$15 Bordeaux wines, turn to Chapter 3.

Médoc, Baron Philippe de Rothschild

> *𝄽* **Producer:** Baron Philippe de Rothschild
>
> *𝄽* **Wine name:** Médoc
>
> *𝄽* **Appellation:** Médoc
>
> *𝄽* **Price:** $10.50

The owners of the legendary Château Mouton-Rothschild bring you this inexpensive Bordeaux wine produced from grapes grown throughout the Médoc district rather than on any one château property. (This wine is part of a line of Bordeaux wines that each focus on a particular village or district of Bordeaux; the same company makes the good-value Mouton-Cadet wine, whose grapes come from throughout the large Bordeaux region.)

The 1994 Médoc shows classic, complex Bordeaux aromas and flavors of cedar, black currant fruit, ink, and spicy oak. This wine is medium bodied and has a cool, somewhat austere personality, probably reflecting a good deal of Cabernet in its grape blend. For the price, it offers a terrific way to experience the style of Bordeaux. We also like the 1995 Pomerol from the same producer — a softer, plumper wine from a district where the Merlot grape dominates — but that wine is twice the price of this one.

Ed: 86–88   **Mary:** 84–86

Michel Lynch Bordeaux Rouge

> ♪ **Producer:** Jean-Michel Cazes
> ♪ **Wine name:** Michel Lynch Bordeaux Rouge
> ♪ **Appellation:** Bordeaux
> ♪ **Price:** $9

This *generic* Bordeaux (meaning that its grapes come from the overall Bordeaux region rather than from any one district within the region) is made by the justifiably famous Jean-Michel Cazes, director of the hot Bordeaux properties, Château Lynch-Bages and Château Pichon-Baron. Maybe Cazes's expertise explains why this wine has been a smashing success since its first release a few years ago. Always well made and with considerable intensity of fruit, Michel Lynch is an excellent, reliable choice in the under-$10 Bordeaux category. The 1994 Michel Lynch is fairly tannic and full bodied, with substantial fruit and concentration — considering its price. But the tannins are soft, making the wine quite *forward* (that is, enjoyable in the near term). We suggest a steak or some hard cheese, such as cheddar, to balance the tannins in the wine.

Ed: 85–87   **Mary:** 85–87

Château Bel Air

> ♪ **Producer:** Château Bel Air, of Henri Martin
> ♪ **Wine name:** Château Bel Air
> ♪ **Appellation:** Haut-Médoc
> ♪ **Price:** $10

Château Bel Air is a very common name among Bordeaux wines — something like Smith or Jones in the U.S. This particular château is in the Haut-Médoc (the more important, southern part of the Médoc), and its wine is an absolute steal at $10. The 1993 Château Bel Air enters your mouth with a sweet impression of plump, rich fruit and then shows thick, rich texture and some minty tones on the finish. It's a substantial, chunky wine that could improve with a few more years of aging. We're both impressed by the price of this overachiever.

Ed: 88–90   **Mary:** 87–89

Château Cap de Faugères

- ♪ **Producer:** Château Cap de Faugères, of C. & P. Guisez
- ♪ **Wine name:** Château Cap de Faugères
- ♪ **Appellation:** Côtes de Castillon
- ♪ **Price:** $12

Corinne and Péby Guisez own an unusual property: the western half (where they grow grapes for the wine labeled Château Faugères) lies within the St.-Emilion district, while the eastern part (where they grow grapes for the wine labeled Château Cap de Faugères) is in the lesser-known Côtes de Castillon district. Naturally, their St.-Emilion wine — from the more famous appellation — costs 50 percent more than their fine Cap de Faugères! (In truth, there are slight differences in the soil, causing the Château Faugères to be the more intensely flavored of the two.) The 1993 Château Cap de Faugères is the readier to drink of the two. It has a classic Bordeaux lead-pencil aroma and is well balanced, smooth, rich, and easy to enjoy now, but it also will be good for four or five more years. Mary's notes say the wine "has guts and yet is soft and accessible."

Ed: 84–86   **Mary:** 87–89

Château de Cruzeau Rouge

- ♪ **Producer:** Château de Cruzeau, of André Lurton
- ♪ **Wine name:** Château de Cruzeau Rouge
- ♪ **Appellation:** Pessac-Léognan
- ♪ **Price:** $15

André Lurton has come to be associated with quality — for both his red and white wines — in the Pessac-Léognan district. We recommend both his red and white Château de Cruzeau. (Properties in this region commonly make both a red and a white wine.) For the red Cruzeau, a blend of 60 percent Cabernet Sauvignon and 40 percent Merlot, Ed's notes read: "Remarkable weight and substance for a Bordeaux in this price category." This wine has a spicy aroma, some tannin, and great balance. It will be even better in a few years.

Ed: 87–89   **Mary:** 85–87

Château Greysac

- ♪ **Producer:** Château Greysac
- ♪ **Wine name:** Château Greysac
- ♪ **Appellation:** Médoc
- ♪ **Price:** $12

Château Greysac has the advantages of wide distribution, an attractive price, and consistent reliability year after year. A substantial wine with good fruit and tannin, the 1994 Greysac could actually benefit from a bit more aging. Despite its significant tannins, however, this wine is fairly rich and soft, which signifies that it is also enjoyable for near-term drinking. A solid wine made in a rustic style, Château Greysac, which is usually about 50 percent Cabernet Sauvignon and 35 percent Merlot, along with other grapes, delivers satisfaction to Bordeaux lovers — at a reasonable price.

Ed: 84–86   **Mary:** 86–88

Château Saint Sulpice

- ♪ **Producer:** Château Saint Sulpice
- ♪ **Wine name:** Château Saint Sulpice
- ♪ **Appellation:** St.-Emilion
- ♪ **Price:** $9

Okay, okay. Not everyone likes vegetables, and not everyone likes what wine tasters call a "veggie" character in red wines. But if you do, you'll enjoy this medium-bodied, silky, harmonious wine from the St.-Emilion district of Bordeaux. Besides the fact that I like the flavor of the 1994 Château Saint Sulpice (some herbs thrown in with the veggie flavor), I find this wine very typical of St.-Emilion and of the Cabernet Franc grape that makes up a significant part of the grape blend there. Owning a few bottles of a well-balanced, easy-to-drink red wine like this is as practical as owning more than one black turtleneck.

Mary: 85–87

Rhône Valley values

As you travel south from the city of Lyon, the gastronomic capital of France, you enter the Rhône Valley, a source of many hearty red wines, as well as some full-bodied whites and dry rosés. Because the Rhône enjoys quite a warm and dry climate, the region's wines are more consistent from year to year than those of Bordeaux or Burgundy. In other words, Rhône wines have fewer "off" years.

We list our recommended wines alphabetically by the name of the producer. For more detailed information about Rhône wines, see our *Wine For Dummies,* Chapter 10, or our *Red Wine For Dummies,* Chapter 11.

Côtes du Rhône "Belleruche," Chapoutier

- **Producer:** M. Chapoutier *(sha poo too aye)*
- **Wine name:** Côtes du Rhône "Belleruche"
- **Appellation:** Côtes du Rhône
- **Price:** $11.50

Young Michel Chapoutier is the golden boy of the Rhône at the moment, having succeeded dramatically in turning around the wines of the company he and his brother took over from their father. The Chapoutier name on a bottle of Rhône wine today almost guarantees an intensely flavored wine infused with the character of its grapes. In the Rhône, of course, the character of the grapes is often very unfruitlike. For example, in the 1995 Côtes du Rhône of Chapoutier, which the winery calls "Belleruche," the aroma is as much smoky and burnt-rubbery as it is fruity, although some bright fruit flavor does come through in your mouth, as do meaty and earthy flavors. In fact, this wine is thick with flavor. It's quite dry, and it's supple in texture, despite its considerable tannin. If you try this wine and like it, be sure to check out our review of another Chapoutier wine in Chapter 3.

Ed: 85–87   **Mary:** 87–89

Côtes du Ventoux, Château Pesquie

🍷 **Producer:** Château Pesquie

🍷 **Wine name:** Côtes du Ventoux

🍷 **Appellation:** Côtes du Ventoux

🍷 **Price:** $9

The Côtes du Ventoux is directly east of the Côtes du Rhône; the wines from these two regions are very similar — in style and in price. Grenache is the dominant grape variety in the Côtes du Ventoux, but Syrah and other varieties are often used in the blend. The 1994 Château Pesquie has a deep, intense aroma of black pepper, and its somewhat subdued ripe fruit flavors are spiced up with plenty of black pepper. It's full bodied and tannic, with fleshy texture; its deep, inky flavors carry through to the wine's finish. Try it with a hearty beef or lamb stew.

Mary: 87–89

Vaucluse, Domaine de L'Ameillaud

🍷 **Producer:** Domaine de L'Ameillaud *(doh main deh lam eh yode)*

🍷 **Wine name:** Vaucluse *(voh kluse)*

🍷 **Appellation:** Vaucluse

🍷 **Price:** $8

Vaucluse is an area at the eastern edge of the Southern Rhône. Many good, inexpensive red wines come from Vaucluse, including this one from the Domaine de L'Ameillaud. The 1995 version of this wine is very dark red, dry, concentrated, and quite tannic, with typical Southern Rhône vegetal flavors, such as green olive. It is quite high in acidity and alcohol, but its substantial red-fruit flavors balance the wine. The wines of Vaucluse are excellent values. Try this one with hamburgers.

Ed: 85–87

Vacqueyras, Domaine des Amouriers

🍷 **Producer:** Domaine des Amouriers *(ah mor ee ay)*

🍷 **Wine name:** Vacqueyras *(vah kay rahss)*

🍷 **Appellation:** Vacqueyras

🍷 **Price:** $14

Vacqueyras and Gigondas *(jhee gohn dahs)* are two former Côtes du Rhône-Villages wines that "graduated" to independent appellations because their quality is considered superior to the wines of other villages of the Côtes du Rhône. Vacqueyras, being less known than Gigondas (although the wines are very similar), is usually the better value of the two. Grenache is the dominant grape variety in this Vacqueyras (60 percent), with 30 percent Mourvèdre and 10 percent Syrah. The 1994 Vacqueyras has subtle aromas of mint, herbs, and spice, with deep, dark, chunky fruit flavors accented by mint. It's a tannic but succulent wine with an inky, mysterious character. You can easily hold on to this wine for another five years, if you wish, but it's quite delicious right now.

Ed: 85–87   **Mary:** 89–91

Côtes du Rhône, Domaine Santa Duc

- **Producer:** Domaine Santa Duc
- **Wine name:** Côtes du Rhône
- **Appellation:** Côtes du Rhône
- **Price:** $10

Whenever anyone complains that French wines are too expensive, I say, "Try a Côtes du Rhône." They're plentiful, available almost everywhere, inexpensive, and generally of good quality. Although red Côtes du Rhône wines are usually made from a blend of several grape varieties, Grenache (a variety that makes hearty wines that are slightly high in alcohol) dominates. The 1995 Domaine Santa Duc Côtes du Rhône is a solid, serious, medium-weight wine with well-knit flavors and good fruit concentration. It's a gutsy, rustic wine that stands up to spicy food — try it with pizza. Drink this wine within three or four years of the vintage date.

Ed: 88–90

Crozes-Hermitage, Paul Jaboulet Aîné

- **Producer:** Paul Jaboulet Aîné
- **Wine name:** Crozes-Hermitage
- **Appellation:** Crozes-Hermitage
- **Price:** $13

The late Gérard Jaboulet, former head of the Paul Jaboulet Aîné company, is deservedly one of wine's most popular international figures, and his company's wines are fairly easy to find across the U.S. Of the two Crozes-Hermitage wines that Jaboulet makes, this particular wine is the more modest — and the less expensive. (We review the other wine, called Domaine Thalabert Crozes-Hermitage, in Chapter 3.) What I find so appealing about this wine is its unmistakable Rhonish character: the aroma and flavor of green olives and roasted fruits; the full-bodied, smooth-textured, not-too-fruity style; and the full-blown personality. Try the 1994 vintage with anything roasted or grilled, as long as the dish doesn't have any fruit flavors.

Mary: 87–89

Crozes-Hermitage, Vidal Fleury

- *!* **Producer:** Domaine J. Vidal Fleury
- *!* **Wine name:** Crozes-Hermitage
- *!* **Appellation:** Crozes-Hermitage
- *!* **Price:** $14

The venerable Rhône house of Vidal Fleury is now the property of Guigal, one of the hottest producers of the region today. Its wines are generally good values because Vidal Fleury's image is still somewhat that of a dusty, old-fashioned producer whom time has passed by — although the reality has changed. The 1991 Crozes-Hermitage of Vidal Fleury is pure Syrah (the grape which makes up this wine) right from the first whiff of rich, ripe fruit and the burnt-rubber-like aroma that is typical of the grape. This wine is rich with ripe flavors of black fruits and is smooth and supple in texture — a lovely, harmonious wine and very much a Rhône.

Mary: 89–91

Southern and southwestern France

Some of the best red wine values today are coming out of southern France — primarily, in the combined Languedoc-Roussillon *(lahn gweh doc roo see yon)* regions, the largest producer of wine in all of France. This region includes the specific zones of Corbières, Minervois, Fitou, and Costières de Nîmes, among others. In addition, numerous wines labeled with the appellation Vin de Pays d'Oc are made of grapes that can come from anywhere in the Languedoc-Roussillon region. Other good values are coming from the Provence region in the southeast and the wine zones of Cahors, Madiran, and Bergerac in the southwest.

We list our recommended wines in this section alphabetically according to the name of the producer.

Côtes du Roussillon, Château de Jau

~S CHOICE

- ♪ **Producer:** Château de Jau
- ♪ **Wine name:** Côtes du Roussillon *(coat du roo see yon)*
- ♪ **Appellation:** Côtes du Roussillon
- ♪ **Price:** $10

Smelling and tasting this wine from southern France (from the Roussillon region specifically), I imagine a big plate of vegetables, such as eggplant, zucchini, green and red peppers, and onions — all hot off the grill. The 1994 vintage of this wine would taste great with grilled vegetables because its aromas and flavors suggest black pepper, herbs, and other spicy things. And because the wine is medium bodied, dry, soft, supple, and easy to drink, it's not too serious for such a humble meal.

Mary: 87–89

Saint Chinian, Château Miquel–Saint Chinian

~S CHOICE

- ♪ **Producer:** Château Miquel–Saint Chinian
- ♪ **Wine name:** Saint Chinian
- ♪ **Appellation:** Saint Chinian
- ♪ **Price:** $8.50

We've never been to Saint Chinian, in the Languedoc region, but if the area looks anything like this wine tastes, it must be an earthy, rugged, raw-nature sort of place for hearty souls. The 1994 version of this medium-bodied, dry red wine is very dark, with an intense aroma of herbs and earthiness and an intense flavor, too. It packs a lot of personality of a rustic sort that won't be fazed by hearty meat dishes and strong cheeses. By the way, if you've ever heard wine tasters describe a wine as "funky," try this wine, and you'll know exactly what they mean!

Mary: 85–87

Minervois, Château d'Oupia

> ♪ **Producer:** Château d'Oupia
> ♪ **Wine name:** Minervois *(mee nair v'wah)*
> ♪ **Appellation:** Minervois
> ♪ **Price:** $8

The Minervois district — where Carignan, Cinsault, and Grenache are the principal red grape varieties — is potentially one of the greatest appellations for red wine in the Languedoc-Roussillon region. Château d'Oupia is a terrific example of the lusty red wines of the area. The 1995 Minervois has a deep purple-black color that foretells the massiveness of the wine. The wine's aroma suggests black pepper, spice, and black fruits, and its flavors are those of ripe, spicy, concentrated fruit. This is a very dry, chewy, concentrated wine that's surprisingly subtle in style, considering how big it is. We consider Château d'Oupia a really great value. Accompany it with something robust, such as steak, venison, or an ice-hockey match on television.

Ed: 91–93   **Mary:** 92–94

Cahors, Château Pech de Jammes

> ♪ **Producer:** Château Pech de Jammes
> ♪ **Wine name:** Cahors *(cah or)*
> ♪ **Appellation:** Cahors
> ♪ **Price:** $10

What a fine wine for this price! The 1989 Château Pech de Jammes has a particularly interesting, complex aroma suggesting lead pencil and a touch of tobacco. My notes read, ". . . a wine with some class . . . elegance and breed."
It is a well-balanced, medium-bodied, dry, supple wine with a tannic finish. Enjoy this wine now, perhaps with roast chicken or duck. It's an excellent $10 wine.

Ed: 89–91

Luc Sorin, Château Routas

> ♪ **Producer:** Château Routas
> ♪ **Wine name:** Luc Sorin

- ✔ **Appellation:** Côtes de Provence
- ✔ **Price:** $13

Two great things about Provence's Château Routas are, first, all of its wines are very good and, second, most of them sell for under $15. You can just taste the atmosphere of sunny Provence in this country red, with its aromatic, spicy, vegetal aroma and its delicious fruit flavors, well balanced by tannin. The 1994 Luc Sorin has plenty of stuffing; that is, it has a lot of substance — enough to hold up well to a duck or rich stew. Drink it over the next few years. With the 1995 vintage, this wine is re-named Agrippa, because former winemaker Luc Sorin is now preparing wine under his own name. We also like the Château Routas wine called Infernet Rouge ($10).

Ed: 90–92   **Mary:** 85–87

Corbières Réserve, "La Demoiselle," Domaine de Fontsainte

- ✔ **Producer:** Domaine de Fontsainte
- ✔ **Wine name:** Corbières Réserve, "La Demoiselle" *(day m'wah zel)*
- ✔ **Appellation:** Corbières *(kor bee air)*
- ✔ **Price:** $11.50

The Corbières district in the Languedoc region is the largest and perhaps the most important area for good red wine in the entire Languedoc-Roussillon. Domaine de Fontsainte makes both a Corbières and a Corbières Réserve ("La Demoiselle"), but the latter is clearly the finer of the two. The 1993 wine is a gutsy, grapey, southern French red wine with good fruit flavor and acidity — a rustic country wine that goes well with ham or pâté.

Ed: 85–87

Domaine Capion, of Philippe Salasc

- ✔ **Producer:** Domaine Capion
- ✔ **Wine name:** Domaine Capion
- ✔ **Appellation:** Vin de Pays de L'Hérault
- ✔ **Price:** $9

Contrary to traditional practice in southern France, Domaine Capion makes its red wines from *noble grape varieties* (that is, varieties that are known to produce great wine rather than merely good wine), such as Cabernet Sauvignon and Merlot. The 1993 Domaine Capion is a very dark-colored, big, tannic, gutsy wine that's still a bit rough. It's a big mouthful of wine that needs some rich food, such as a stew or cassoulet, to tame it. For all that, it's a classic southern French country wine.

Ed: 85–87

Syrah, Jean Balmont

- ♪ **Producer:** Jean Balmont
- ♪ **Wine name:** Syrah
- ♪ **Appellation:** Vin de Pays D'Oc
- ♪ **Price:** $7.50

Jean Balmont is a name to reckon with; this firm is making fine varietal wines at excellent prices. The 1995 Syrah has exuberant, herbal aromas and flavors, particularly mint and eucalyptus. Although it gives a sense of being a full wine because of its high alcohol, it's a bit austere because of high acidity and those herbal flavors. This is a very interesting country wine — a bit rustic in style — with lots of personality and presence. Try it with some roasted meats or hard cheeses. We also like the Jean Balmont Cabernet/ Merlot, a tannic red with vegetal and mint flavors, that sells for the same low price as this wine.

Ed: 84–86   **Mary:** 87–89

Cuvée Gourmande, Mas de la Dame

- ♪ **Producer:** Mas de la Dame
- ♪ **Wine name:** Cuvée Gourmande
- ♪ **Appellation:** Coteaux d'Aix-en-Provence
  (coh toh dex on pro vanhce)
- ♪ **Price:** $12

If you were spending *A Year in Provence* (as the book suggests) and drinking the local wines every day, this wine might be your Friday-night favorite — better than the rosés and simple reds you drink Monday to Thursday, but less expensive and complex than your weekend specials. The 1994 Cuvée Gourmande has classic southern France flavors of vegetables, herbs, and sun-drenched fruit, all expressed fairly intensely. But it's slightly more sophisticated than a mere "country" wine, with a civilizing touch of oak to dress it up.

Mary: 84–86

Italian Red Wines

You can find plenty of Italian red wines for less than $15 a bottle. Most wines from the south of Italy fall into this price range either because they are simple, unpretentious wines or because they are less famous than the wines from the northern regions. Northern and central Italian reds include some of the most famous types of wine in Italy, such as Chianti, Valpolicella, Barolo, and Brunello di Montalcino. Valpolicella tends to be inexpensive, and Chianti straddles the $15 line, with examples on both sides. But to find reviews of our favorite Barolo and Brunello di Montalcino wines, you have to turn to Chapter 3.

Northeastern Italy

Although northeastern Italy is a wine area of major importance, we don't review very many wines from that area in this section, for one simple reason — most of the more renowned wines from the northeast are white. (Turn to Chapters 5 and 7 for information on those wines.)

The red wines from the northeast fall into two major categories:

- ✔ **Varietally-labeled wines from the regions of Friuli-Venezia Giulia (in the extreme northeast) and Trentino-Alto Adige (south of Austria):** These wines tend to be medium bodied, and most of them are made from grape varieties that are well known internationally, such as Cabernet Sauvignon and Merlot.

- ✔ **Wines from the area surrounding the city of Verona, in the Veneto region:** These wines include Bardolino and Valpolicella, two types that are ubiquitous in Italian restaurants and are made from native Italian grape varieties that are virtually unknown outside that area.

Catullo Red, Bertani

- ! **Producer:** Bertani
- ! **Wine name:** Catullo Red
- ! **Appellation:** Vino da Tavola of Veneto
- ! **Price:** $12.50

This northeastern Italian wine is the child of a real mixed marriage of grape varieties. In addition to Corvina, Molinara, and Negrara grapes that are native to the Valpolicella area, where this wine is made, Catullo Red contains some Sangiovese (more common in central Italy than in the north) and Nebbiolo (usually grown only in the northwest of Italy, not the northeast). In the 1993 vintage, the combined effect is a full-bodied, thick-textured, gutsy red wine with lots of tannin. If you've ever wondered what critics mean when they call a wine "chewy" or say that a wine has a lot of "stuffing," tasting this wine can clear up any confusion. Catullo Red is impressive in its size and intensity.

Ed: 84–86 **Mary:** 85–87

Jago Valpolicella, Bolla

- ! **Producer:** Bolla
- ! **Wine name:** Valpolicella, Jago *(YAH go)*
- ! **Appellation:** Valpolicella
- ! **Price:** $13

Jago, Bolla's single-vineyard Valpolicella, is a much more sophisticated version of the winery's basic Valpolicella, which you can always find in any store for under $10. For us, the Jago is worth the extra few dollars: It offers all the best characteristics of Valpolicella, but at a notch higher in intensity. The 1996 Jago has fresh cherry aromas and the taste of fresh cherry fruit in a low-tannin, easy-drinking package. It's round, smooth, and delicious. This wine would be perfect to sip while sitting on the piazza in Verona, the wine's hometown, nibbling on a pizza from one of the trattorias that line the town square. If you can't make it to Verona, your backyard will do.

Ed: 86–88 **Mary:** 85–87

Tacchetto Bardolino, Guerrieri Rizzardi

> ❧ **Producer:** Guerrieri Rizzardi
> *(gwer ree AIR ee ritz ZAR dee)*
> ❧ **Wine name:** Tacchetto Bardolino *(tah KET toh)*
> ❧ **Appellation:** Bardolino
> ❧ **Price:** $10

Wine lovers can easily fall into the trap of enjoying ever bigger and more intense red wines, while forgetting the charms of lighter-bodied reds. When we feel that we're headed in that direction, we bring ourselves back down to earth by opening a bottle of this excellent Bardolino, cutting ourselves a few slices of hard Italian salami, and reveling in the simpler pleasures. This wine, from a vineyard named Tacchetto, has intense aromas and flavors of black pepper (which is why it's so good with salami!), tart cherry, dry tea, and tobacco. Tacchetto is crisp and dry, lively and fresh, and just bursting with personality. Buy it as young as you can find it so that you can drink the Tacchetto Bardolino when it's at its best — from 6 months to about 18 months after the harvest.

Ed: 88–90   **Mary:** 89–91

Villa Volpe Merlot, Volpe Pasini

> ❧ **Producer:** Volpe Pasini
> ❧ **Wine name:** Villa Volpe Merlot
> ❧ **Appellation:** Colli Orientali del Friuli
> ❧ **Price:** $9

The region of Friuli-Venezia Giulia (commonly known as *Friuli*) is one of the hip, happening places for Italian white wines. But some exciting red wines are made here, also. Some of Friuli's finest wines are coming from the Volpe Pasini estate in the Colli Orientali district. This progressive firm makes two lines of wines, and it labels its less expensive wines "Villa Volpe." Unlike some Merlots of northeastern Italy, which can be lean and austere, the 1994 Villa Volpe Merlot is fairly full bodied, with ripe cherry fruit and moderate tannin. If you're a Merlot lover, heed this rarity — a good Merlot for under $10! Try it with steak covered with tomato sauce and cheese.

Ed: 85–87

Lagrein Dunkel, Peter Zemmer

> ♪ **Producer:** Peter Zemmer
> ♪ **Wine name:** Lagrein Dunkel
> ♪ **Appellation:** Alto Adige
> ♪ **Price:** $12

In the beautiful Alto Adige region, the hillside vineyards are protected by mountains to the east, west, and north, giving the vineyards a warmer climate than you might expect. German is spoken here as commonly as Italian: Even some of the grape varieties, such as Lagrein Dunkel, and some of the producers, such as Peter Zemmer, have Germanic names. Lagrein is a grape variety seldom found outside of Alto Adige and neighboring Trentino, to the south. It produces very dark red, muscular, chunky wines with lots of tannin.

The 1994 Zemmer Lagrein has a rich, chocolate aroma with some coffee and spice; dry, ripe fruit flavor with a hint of mint; and a well-structured, medium- to full-bodied frame. At present, the tannins are a bit harsh, but with time, they will soften. This Lagrein can stand up well to rich foods and is a fine accompaniment to cheeses.

Ed: 86–88   **Mary:** 85–87

Piedmont's less expensive reds

The people of the northwestern Italian region of Piedmont love red wine. In fact, you rarely drink white wine when you visit this area — unless you happen to be in the vicinity of Gavi, which makes the best-known Piedmont white.

The everyday, less expensive wines of Piedmont come mainly from two grape varieties: Barbera and Dolcetto. Both grapes are grown in several zones within Piedmont, and the wines are named for the grape and the zone together, such as Dolcetto di Dogliani.

Almost all Dolcetto and Barbera wines are dry reds with slightly spicy flavor and tons of personality. Although Dolcetto is generally considered lighter in body than Barbera, it's also more tannic; the Barbera grape tends to be deficient in tannin but high in acidity. Try Barbera with anything tomatoey, and you discover that

Barbera's handicap is a real asset with food! Both wines are delicious when they're young, but most Barbera wines can handle many years of aging if they're well stored, whereas Dolcetto is best at two or three years of age.

In this section, we group the wines according to their type, such as Barbera or Dolcetto, and then list them alphabetically by producer.

Barbera d'Alba, Vietti

> ♪ **Producer:** Vietti
>
> ♪ **Wine name:** Barbera d'Alba
>
> ♪ **Appellation:** Barbera d'Alba
>
> ♪ **Price:** $15

We probably drink more Italian Barberas than any other type of wine. First of all, we love the wine; second, Barbera is not too expensive; and third, it goes well with the Italian food that we like — pasta, pizza, and so forth. Nowadays, many Barberas are over $15, but Vietti's basic Barbera d'Alba (formerly from the Bussia vineyard) is still an outstanding buy at around $15. (For a review of Vietti's more expensive Barbera Scarrone, see Chapter 3.)

The 1995 Vietti Barbera d'Alba has a rich, purple-red color; classic, tart cherry fruit; and the excellent acidity that makes it such a good partner with tomato-based dishes. The wine also has enough depth and concentration to accompany main courses such as Beef in Barolo or Veal Piccata. Barberas in good vintage years, such as 1995, can either be consumed in their youth or matured for up to 10 or 12 years; they *do* age well.

Ed: 88–90   **Mary:** 88–90

Dolcetto d'Alba, Renato Ratti

> ♪ **Producer:** Renato Ratti
>
> ♪ **Wine name:** Dolcetto d'Alba
>
> ♪ **Appellation:** Dolcetto d'Alba
>
> ♪ **Price:** $13

Renato Ratti, one of Piedmont's innovative winemakers, died prematurely about ten years ago, and today his son, Pietro, and his nephew, Massimo, nobly carry on his work. The 1995 Ratti Dolcetti d'Alba shows good depth of fresh, lively fruit and is firm and solid, moderately tannic, and quite dry, with fine concentration. It will keep well for two or three years. Try it with pasta, fresh tomatoes, mozzarella, and basil. Yummy!

Ed: 85–87   **Mary:** 84–86

Dolcetto d'Alba, Vietti

- ♪ **Producer:** Vietti
- ♪ **Wine name:** Dolcetto d'Alba
- ♪ **Appellation:** Dolcetto d'Alba
- ♪ **Price:** $14

Vietti is one of Piedmont's best producers, making not only great Barberas and Barolos but also one of the region's finest Dolcettos. The 1994 Vietti Dolcetto has aromas suggesting tobacco and chocolate. It is medium bodied, with lots of tannin and dense flavors of leather, earth, and spice. Drink this Dolcetto within two or three years (Dolcettos are best when consumed young — within five years of the vintage), preferably with a meaty pasta dish such as Tortellini alla Bolognese. (Vietti's newly available 1995 Dolcetto is even better than the 1994!)

Ed: 85–87   **Mary:** 85–87

Nebbiolo d'Alba, Abbona Marziano

- ♪ **Producer:** Abbona Marziano
- ♪ **Wine name:** Nebbiolo d'Alba
- ♪ **Appellation:** Nebbiolo d'Alba
- ♪ **Price:** $14

Nebbiolo d'Alba has a tough role to play in life. It's sort of the middle child: a wine meant to be enjoyed young, just like Barbera and Dolcetto, but made from the most important grape of Piedmont (Nebbiolo), just like the venerable Barolo and Barbaresco wines. The 1994 vintage from this producer veers more toward the serious side than the young-and-carefree personality. It's a full-bodied, smooth, sophisticated red with distinct herbal notes of eucalyptus and camphor in its flavor and aroma (an aroma very typical of Barolo). This wine also has an intriguing taste of lime peel. For a more easygoing wine from the same producer, try the very good Dolcetto d'Alba "Papa Celso."

Ed: 84–86   **Mary:** 86–88

Nebbiolo d'Alba, Stefano Farina

- **Producer:** Stefano Farina
- **Wine name:** Nebbiolo d'Alba
- **Appellation:** Nebbiolo d'Alba
- **Price:** $10

In these days of high wine prices, it's comforting to reach for a bottle of Stefano Farina Italian wine (the company sells Chianti as well as Piedmontese wines) and know that you are buying a well-made wine at a great price. Yes, Piedmont does have better producers, but few deliver such value for the money. After tasting this wine blind, I was shocked when I saw the price. Farina's 1993 Nebbiolo has good fruit character, lots of herbal aroma and flavor, and good structure. It is a wine that requires food; I suggest pasta with sausage and broccoli. Drink it within three or four years.

Ed: 85–87

Tuscany's best buys

The central Italian region of Tuscany is home to some of the greatest red wines in the world, as well as some excellent values. That's why you find many Tuscan red wines in this book, both here and in Chapter 3.

Most Tuscan red wines are based on the Sangiovese grape, a native Italian variety. Depending on exactly where this grape grows, how it is handled in the vineyard, and how its juice is vinified, Sangiovese in Tuscany can make every style of wine, from a pretty, little, light-bodied luncheon wine to a full-bodied, intense red of near-cosmic dimensions. In general, wines based on Sangiovese:

- Are crisp in acidity (read: great with food!)
- Are moderate in alcohol content
- Have aromas and flavors that can be described as dusty, nutty, and cherrylike

The most famous Tuscan red wines — all made primarily from Sangiovese — include simple varietally labeled Sangiovese, Chianti (and all its variations, such as Chianti Classico, Chianti Classico Riserva, and any other Italian wines named *Chianti*), Carmignano, Vino Nobile di Montepulciano, Rosso di Montalcino, Brunello di Montalcino, and some so-called super-Tuscan wines.

Because this chapter focuses on wines under $15, most of our recommendations are either Chianti or Rosso di Montalcino, which tend to be the two least expensive types of Tuscan red wine.

Santa Cristina Sangiovese, Antinori

- ♪ **Producer:** Marchesi Antinori
- ♪ **Wine name:** Santa Cristina Sangiovese
- ♪ **Appellation:** Vino da Tavola di Toscana
- ♪ **Price:** $9

When Mary and I wrote *Wine For Dummies,* we asked Piero Antinori to write the book's foreword because we respect him more than anyone else in the wine business. As head of a family firm that began in 1385, Piero Antinori has taken the Antinori winery to new heights. Even his least expensive red wine, the Santa Cristina Sangiovese (blended with 10 percent Merlot), is a pleasure to drink. The 1995 Santa Cristina is a bright, young colt, a true relative of the more serious Antinori Chianti thoroughbreds. It has tart-cherry aroma and flavor and is dry, intense, and medium bodied, with firm tannin and a lingering finish. Quite a good wine for $9! A light supper wine, it would be fine with pasta, pizza, or grilled chicken.

Ed: 88–90

Brusco dei Barbi

- ♪ **Producer:** Fattoria dei Barbi
  (faht toh REE ah day BAR bee)
- ♪ **Wine name:** Brusco dei Barbi
- ♪ **Appellation:** Vino da Tavola di Toscana
- ♪ **Price:** $11

Fattoria dei Barbi has long been one of the leading estates producing Brunello di Montalcino, Tuscany's most serious wine. Unfortunately, most good Brunellos cost over $40 today. But Barbi, as the winery is known, also makes a unique, old-style table wine from Sangiovese grapes, called Brusco dei Barbi, that's a terrific value. The wine is made by the *governo* process, a traditional Tuscan winemaking procedure that utilizes semidried grapes in addition to fresh grapes, thus contributing freshness as well as richness to the wine. The 1995 Brusco dei Barbi is a gutsy wine with intense fruit concentration — unusual in this price category. Its firm tannin is balanced by the depth of its fruit. Try it with a rich, spicy pasta, pork, or veal. The freshness of this wine makes it enjoyable now, but a couple years of aging won't hurt it.

Ed: 89–91   **Mary:** 84–86

Chianti Classico, Castello d'Albola

- **Producer:** Castello d'Albola
- **Wine name:** Chianti Classico
- **Appellation:** Chianti Classico
- **Price:** $9

The Chianti Classico zone has so many wineries (over 700, last we heard!) that we're never surprised to encounter a brand that's new to us. We first encountered the Castello d'Albola wines in the early 1990s, when the Seagram Classics Wine Company began importing them. We've been impressed with the consistency of quality, the wide availability of the wine, and the terrific value. Of course, we also like the *taste* of the wine! The 1994 has a textbook Chianti aroma and exuberant flavors of fresh, bright fruit (tart cherries, naturally), along with a slight tarry character. This wine is delicious now, but we suspect that it will develop nicely with two or three years of bottle age.

Ed: 91–93   **Mary:** 89–91

Chianti Classico, Castello di Brolio

- **Producer:** Castello di Brolio
- **Wine name:** Chianti Classico
- **Appellation:** Chianti Classico
- **Price:** $13

Castello, meaning "castle", is a common way of naming wine estates in Tuscany, but no other estate deserves the term quite as much as Brolio does. The Brolio property *is* a castle, once owned by the royal Ricasoli family and now, again, owned by a member of that family, Francesco Ricasoli, who bought back the historic estate from foreign ownership. The wines of Brolio, sadly mediocre for more than a decade, are now back on track and getting better with each vintage. But their prices haven't quite caught up yet with the new quality, making Brolio wines a particularly good value.

The 1994 Castello di Brolio Chianti Classico has fresh, lively aromas and flavors of tart cherries, along with a dusty, earthy scent that we find characteristic of wines based on the Sangiovese grape. This wine is medium bodied and fairly compact (as opposed to ample), with good concentration of its fruit character. We recommend drinking this Chianti young, while it's at its freshest; for a richer, weightier version that's capable of aging, try the excellent 1994 Chianti Classico Riserva of Brolio, about $20.

Ed: 84–86   **Mary:** 84–86

Chianti Classico Riserva, Castello di Volpaia

- ! **Producer:** Castello di Volpaia
- ! **Wine name:** Chianti Classico Riserva
- ! **Appellation:** Chianti Classico
- ! **Price:** $14

Year in and year out, Castello di Volpaia is one of our favorite Chianti wines. We like its crisp, spirited style. Situated high up in the hills of Radda in the Chianti Classico zone, Castello di Volpaia makes lean, dry, elegant Chianti wines — never too heavy and always with good acidity. The 1993 Chianti Classico Riserva has class and polish, with bright, focused cherry fruit and good concentration. It is harmonious and well balanced. Try it with steak or veal. You can enjoy this wine now, but it should keep well for another four or five years.

Ed: 89–91   **Mary:** 87–89

Rosso di Montalcino, Col d'Orcia

MARY'S CHOICE

- ! **Producer:** Col d'Orcia
- ! **Wine name:** Rosso di Montalcino
- ! **Appellation:** Rosso di Montalcino
- ! **Price:** $13

Eeny, meeny, miney, mo. Drink it now or age it slow? With this wine, either choice is correct. The character of fresh and dried cherry fruit in the 1994 vintage, and the round, supple style of the wine, make it delicious now (with food, all the better!). But the richness of tannin suggests that the wine will improve with a couple years of aging in the bottle. Whenever you drink it, you'll find it to be on the full side of medium bodied, a solid and gutsy wine. If you buy the 1995 vintage, do consider aging it a bit or aerate it about two hours in an open decanter before you drink it. This Rosso di Montalcino is serious stuff for the money!

Mary: 86–88

Chianti Classico "Isassi," Melini

- ! **Producer:** Melini
- ! **Wine name:** Chianti Classico, "Isassi" *(ee SAH see)*
- ! **Appellation:** Chianti Classico
- ! **Price:** $12.50

Melini is a huge operation, of a scale that you don't expect to find in the serene hills of the Chianti Classico zone. Maybe its size gives the winery a certain economy of scale, because the Melini wines are always among the most reasonably priced Chianti Classico wines that you can find. And you *can* find them, thanks to the winery's large production. Of course, a good price and easy availability mean nothing if the wine isn't good, but Melini covers that base as well. The 1994 "Isassi" is a soft, medium-bodied Chianti with aromas and flavors of ripe cherry. It's ready to drink now, while it's fresh and alive with flavor, and it probably won't benefit from age. We also like Melini's Chianti Classico Riserva called "Laborel," which sells for $14.50; it's a richer, fuller wine, although still elegant.

Ed: 86–88 **Mary:** 86–88

Chianti Colli Senesi, Poliziano

- ! **Producer:** Poliziano
- ! **Wine name:** Chianti Colli Senesi *(COH lee seh NAY see)*
- ! **Appellation:** Chianti Colli Senesi
- ! **Price:** $7.50

Wines labeled Chianti Colli Senesi come from vineyards in the hills around the medieval city of Siena. They're among the best buys of all Chianti wines. The remarkable Chianti of Poliziano, an estate better known for its more expensive Vino Nobile di Montepulciano wine, is an astonishing value; we seldom come across *any* red wines — not just Chianti — this good at this price. The 1995 Chianti Colli Senesi is dry and crisp, with the tart-cherry character, black pepper, and dusty tannins typical of Chianti. It's medium bodied, with very good concentration of fruit and the brightness and freshness that a young Chianti should have. Drink it within about three years of the vintage to enjoy its fresh exuberance.

Ed: 87–89   **Mary:** 87–89

Chianti Rufina, Renzo Masi

- ! **Producer:** Renzo Masi
- ! **Wine name:** Chianti Rufina
- ! **Appellation:** Chianti Rufina *(ROO fee nah)*
- ! **Price:** $7.50

Although they're not part of the more famous Classico district of Chianti, producers in the smaller Rufina district aren't jealous: They believe that their cooler microclimate gives them a more elegant and "finesseful" style of Chianti, which they like just fine. A terrific example of the Rufina style is this inexpensive Chianti from Renzo Masi. The 1995 vintage of this wine has everything we want in a young Chianti: plenty of fresh fruit flavor (cherries and plums); a light to medium body with crisp, refreshing acidity; and a delightful, vivacious personality. We suspect that the only reason this wine is so inexpensive is that it's not very well known yet in the U.S. Be the first on your block!

Renzo Masi also produces an excellent, but slightly more expensive, Chianti Rufina from grapes grown on his Fattoria di Basciano *(fah toh REE ah dee bah shee AH noh)* property. That wine carries the estate name, Fattoria di Basciano, along with the Masi name.

Ed: 89–91   **Mary:** 89–91

Chianti Classico, Rocca di Castagnoli

- *!* **Producer:** Rocca di Castagnoli
  (ROKE kah dee cah stah N'YOH lee)
- *!* **Wine name:** Chianti Classico
- *!* **Appellation:** Chianti Classico
- *!* **Price:** $15

Some Chianti producers seem determined to make as big and rich a Chianti as they possibly can — but not this winery. The 1993 Rocca di Castagnoli is a medium-bodied, very well balanced Chianti with good concentration of tart-cherry fruit. Every time we taste this wine, we find ourselves describing it as "pretty," but it's not frivolous or insubstantial. It's just real Chianti with nothing to prove. We like it with pasta dishes that aren't too rich, such as pasta with Amatriciana sauce (a slightly spicy tomato-and-bacon sauce).

Ed: 85–87   **Mary:** 85–87

Santedame Chianti Classico, Ruffino

- *!* **Producer:** Ruffino
- *!* **Wine name:** Tenuta Santedame Chianti Classico
- *!* **Appellation:** Chianti Classico
- *!* **Price:** $12

The Ruffino company, one of the most famous names in Chianti, now owns several wine estates throughout the Chianti Classico zone and produces a separate wine from each estate. Tenuta Santedame, from Ruffino's Santedame estate, is consistently one of our favorites. The 1993 vintage of this wine has surprising richness, concentration, and substance for its price. It's also very true to the style of Chianti, with dusty and nutty aromas, a vibrancy of cherry fruit, and a lovely subtlety of expression.

Ed: 91–93   **Mary:** 87–89

Chianti Montalbano, Capezzana

- ♪ **Producer:** Tenuta di Capezzana
  (teh NOO tah dee cah petz ZAH nah)
- ♪ **Wine name:** Chianti Montalbano
- ♪ **Appellation:** Chianti Montalbano
- ♪ **Price:** $9.50

The Chianti Montalbano district, directly west of Florence, is another of the lesser-known Chianti subregions. Here lies the magnificent estate called Villa di Capezzana (a former villa of the renowned Medici family). The Capezzana winery makes many fine Tuscan wines, but its Chianti Montalbano is probably the best value. Most Chianti wines that sell for under $10 taste like it — but the 1995 Capezzana Chianti Montalbano is a fine wine that tastes more expensive. It's well balanced, with fresh fruit flavor and crisp acidity. This lighter-styled Chianti reflects the relatively cool climate of the Montalbano district. Drink this wine within the next few years, perhaps with a light pasta dish or simple Veal Piccata.

Ed: 88–90

Two good values from Southern Italy

In reviewing Italian red wines under $15, another author may have numerous recommendations from the south of Italy. But taste is highly personal, and we prefer the wines from the north because they tend to have flavors of fresh fruit rather than flavors of cooked, baked, or stewed fruit, which southern wines tend to have. If your tastes differ from ours, by all means try the many inexpensive wines from southern Italy that are available in good wine shops. If your tastes coincide with ours, seek out the wines we recommend in this section.

Cannonau Riserva, Sella & Mosca

▌ ❗ **Producer:** Sella & Mosca
▌ ❗ **Wine name:** Cannonau Riserva *(cahn no NOW)*
▌ ❗ **Appellation:** Cannonau di Sardegna
▌ ❗ **Price:** $9

Cannonau, an ancient red grape variety related to Grenache, makes big, robust wines, and the 1992 Riserva of Sella & Mosca is a classic example. It has a fragrant, spicy, peppery aroma, similar to a good Southern Rhône red. The difference is that Cannonau is more powerful and sturdier than most Southern Rhône wines — especially in this price category. This Cannonau Riserva offers all the depth, concentration, and warm, ripe flavors that you can hope to find in an under-$10 wine. Try it with a game bird, such as pheasant or squab, or with rabbit. Drink this wine during the next couple of years. It is not an ager.

Sella & Mosca, one of the largest producers in Italy, also makes a non-riserva Cannonau, but stick with the riserva; it only costs about $2 more, and it's worth every penny.

Ed: 85–87   **Mary:** 84–86

"Maiana Rosso" Salice Salentino, Leone de Castris

▌ ❗ **Producer:** Leone de Castris
▌ ❗ **Wine name:** Salice Salentino "Maiana Rosso" *(my AH nah)*
▌ ❗ **Appellation:** Salice Salentino *(SAH lee chay sahl en TEE noh)*
▌ ❗ **Price:** $8

Salice Salentino has long been one of the most popular Italian red wines among value-conscious wine drinkers in the U.S. The wine comes from Puglia in southwest Italy — the so-called heel of the boot of Italy; breezes from the Mediterranean Sea and the altitude of the coastal vineyards have a cooling effect on the warm climate here. Two local grapes, primarily the Negroamaro with some help from Malvasia

Nera, make up Salice Salentino wines. The 1995 Maiana (from a very traditional producer, Leone de Castris) has a shoe-polish aroma that we associate with the Negroamaro grape, and its cooked-fruit flavors are typical in Southern Italian red wines. Despite its cooked-fruit, Southern character, the wine is fresh, grapey, and well balanced. It's a fine example of Salice Salentino. We suggest that you have it with a classic Southern Italian pasta dish, such as lasagna or ravioli with tomato sauce.

Ed: 86–88   **Mary:** 84–86

Good Buys from Portugal and Spain

Portugal and Spain have little in common with each other except that they share the Iberian Peninsula. Their wines also have little in common, except that the red wines of both countries tend to be made from native local grape varieties. As you may suspect, though, the Spanish grape varieties are completely different from the Portuguese grape varieties.

Spanish wines are generally easier to find in the U.S. than Portuguese wines, but most of our favorite Spanish wines cross the line into the over-$15 price category — and therefore appear in Chapter 3. Portuguese wines tend to be less expensive, but not many of them are broadly available in the U.S. For these reasons, the section that follows is a short one, combining the wines of Spain and those of Portugal.

Rioja Reserva, Marqués de Murrieta

- ♪ **Producer:** Marqués de Murrieta Ygay
  (mar KASE deh mor ree EH tah ee GAY)
- ♪ **Wine name:** Rioja Reserva
- ♪ **Appellation:** Rioja (Spain)
- ♪ **Price:** $13.50

In what wine region can you find a wine of world-class quality for under $15? One of the few places that comes to my mind is Rioja. And thanks to a revival in this most renowned of Spanish red wine regions, quality is now higher than ever. One leader in this quality revolution is Marqués de Murrieta. The 1992 Marqués de Murrieta has exceptional minty, eucalyptus aromas, and its flavors suggest ripe, herbal-scented fruit. It's a rounded, well-balanced, delicious wine with quite a long finish. Excellent quality here: Experience it with roast chicken, game birds, or Paella à la Valençiana. This wine — an outstanding value — should drink well for another ten years.

Ed: 91–93

Quinta de Parrotes

> ♪ **Producer:** Quinta de Pancas *(KEEN tah day PAHN cahs)*
> ♪ **Wine name:** Quinta de Parrotes
>   *(KEEN tah day pahr ROH tays)*
> ♪ **Appellation:** Alenquer (Portugal)
> ♪ **Price:** $7

Quinta de Pancas is one of the oldest wine estates in Portugal, dating back to the 1600s. Its traditional wine is Quinta de Parrotes, made mainly from the local grape called Castelão Frances, with 20 percent Cabernet Sauvignon added to appease the international market. The 1995 Quinta de Parrotes is a simple country wine that's medium bodied and flavorful with plump, ripe fruitiness. Its low tannin level suggests that this wine would be a good "party red" to quaff without contemplation. It's a wine to drink now rather than hold.

Ed: 88–90   **Mary:** 83–85

Cabernet Sauvignon, Quinta de Pancas

> ♪ **Producer:** Quinta de Pancas
> ♪ **Wine name:** Cabernet Sauvignon
> ♪ **Appellation:** Estremadura (Portugal)
> ♪ **Price:** $11

I'm of a mixed mind about wines like this — a Cabernet from Portugal, where Cabernet is not a traditional grape variety. Philosophically, I'd prefer to see Portuguese wines made from Portuguese grapes — but gustatorially, I like this wine just the way it is! In the 1995 vintage, the wine's ripe, concentrated fruit, herbal and spicy flavor accents, and firm tannin are typical of Cabernet. I'm not sure what characteristics of the wine say "Portugal," but when the roast beef is on the table and the dark red wine is poured into the wine glasses, who cares? A great buy.

Mary: 86–88

Coronas, Torres

- *Producer:* Torres
- *Wine name:* Coronas
- *Appellation:* Penedés (Spain)
- *Price:* $8.50

The remarkable Torres family makes so many wines (and all of them good!) that we confess to occasional confusion over which is which. This one, Coronas, comes in a Bordeaux-style bottle (a bottle with shoulders, as opposed to the sloping Burgundy bottle) and is made primarily from Spain's most important red grape variety, Tempranillo. In the 1994 vintage, this wine has a touch more finesse than the Sangre de Toro (another good, inexpensive Torres wine) and is a bit lighter in body and softer in tannin. You may notice some oaky character in the wine, but this is essentially a fruit-driven, ripe, supple red with cranberry-like flavor. Duck sounds good just now, doesn't it?

Mary: 85–87

Gran Sangre de Toro Reserva, Torres

- *Producer:* Torres
- *Wine name:* Gran Sangre de Toro Reserva
- *Appellation:* Penedés (Spain)
- *Price:* $12

Gran Sangre de Toro (blended 70 percent from Grenache and 30 percent from Carignan) is probably Torres's best under-$15 red wine. Although the 1993 version has an oaky aroma, its flavor is less oaky than the aroma leads you to expect. The wine is plump and fruity, supple, medium to full bodied (a bigger wine than the Sangre de Toro or Coronas), and tannic. This wine is still young and should drink well for several years. Try it with squab or similarly gamy dishes.

Ed: 85–87   **Mary:** 86–88

Chapter 2

New Kids on the Block: New World Red Wines for $15 or Less

. . . .

In This Chapter

▶ The unbridled flavor of real Zinfandel

▶ Mad Merlot mania

▶ Cabernet, Cabernet everywhere (and many a drop to drink)

▶ True value from Chile and Argentina

▶ South African discoveries

. . . .

*W*e Americans sip cappuccino and nibble on croissants, while French schoolchildren listen to the music of Kurt Cobain and munch Big Macs. But no matter how much the cultural lines have blurred, the wines of Europe and the wines of the rest of the world have remained stylistically distinct, at least so far. That's why we devote one chapter to inexpensive European red wines, and a separate chapter to inexpensive red wines produced outside of Europe, such as from America.

In wine circles, the wines of these non-European continents and countries are collectively referred to as *New World wines*. Some people think that this term is pure baloney (or bologna, as the case may be) because they don't believe that wines from countries so far away from each other can have any valid common ground. We disagree, however. We believe that New World wines share quite a few attributes, and that their common stylistic chord is distinct from the general style of European wines. We cover this ground in some detail in Chapter 12 of our book *Wine For Dummies*.

We begin this chapter with the wines of the U.S. and then move to South America, Australia, and South Africa. (New Zealand wines appear in Chapters 6 and 8 because our recommendations are all white wines.) Because grape variety is so central to the identity of New World wines, we group the wines of each country according to their grape variety.

We list the vital information for each wine in the following way:

- ✔ **The producer:** A wine's producer is the company that makes the wine. Most of the time, this company name is the brand name of the wine.

- ✔ **The wine name:** For New World wines, the wine name is usually a grape name.

- ✔ **The appellation of the wine:** This information tells you the geographic area in which the grapes for that wine grew. The appellation can be a small locale, such as Stags Leap District (a particular part of the Napa Valley in California), or a large area, such as California (meaning that the grapes grew in various parts of the state). When we group wines of more than one country in a single section, we indicate the country of origin in parentheses after each wine's appellation.

- ✔ **The approximate retail price of the wine:** Retail prices vary quite a bit, based on where you live and the type of store at which you buy your wine. We use New York State suggested retail prices, rounded to the nearest 50 cents.

U.S. Red Wines

Amazingly, 47 out of 50 states in the U.S. now make wine! We confess that we haven't gotten around to tasting the wines of all 47 yet (though we *have* been begging our editor to send us on a research mission to Hawaii for three years now). But even if we did have first-hand experience with all those wines, we couldn't report on so many wines in this small book.

In actuality, four states dominate fine wine production in the U.S.: California, Washington, Oregon, and New York. The giant, of course, is California, which accounts for about 88 percent of all wine made in the U.S (listed alphabetically by producer).

The most popular red wines in the U.S. are

- ✔ Cabernet Sauvignon
- ✔ Merlot
- ✔ Pinot Noir
- ✔ Zinfandel (Zinfandel, a red grape variety, is also made into a popular pink wine, which, strangely enough, is called *White Zinfandel.*)
- ✔ Blends made from Cabernet Sauvignon, Merlot, and/or Cabernet Franc

Unlike in Europe, where most wines are named for the place where the grapes grow (such as Bordeaux, Chianti, or Rioja), wines from the U.S. are usually named for their predominant grape variety, such as Cabernet Sauvignon or Merlot. Other American red wines — also named for grape varieties — are Syrah, Sangiovese, Cabernet Franc, and Petite Sirah.

In the sections that follow, we review our favorite U.S. red wines that sell for $15 a bottle or less.

Inexpensive Cabernet Sauvignon

We believe that, generally speaking, wines from the Cabernet Sauvignon grape and blends based on Cabernet Sauvignon are the best American wines, white or red. That doesn't mean that we don't love some of the really fine Pinot Noir wines from Oregon and California or some special Merlots from Washington and New York's Long Island. But if we had to select one wine as the U.S. ambassador to the United Nations of Wines, it'd probably be a Cabernet Sauvignon.

Cabernet Sauvignons — or *Cabs,* as they're called in the inner circles of wine — are typically deeply colored wines, with a good deal of tannin. Winemakers often add Merlot and/or Cabernet Franc — not only to enhance the wine's complexity but also to tone down the firm tannins of the Cabernet Sauvignon grape variety. Cabernet Sauvignon wines that are made from fully ripe grapes have aromas and flavors of black currants or cassis. For more information on Cabernet Sauvignon, see *Red Wine For Dummies,* Chapter 6, or *Wine For Dummies,* Chapters 9 and 12.

We recommend the following U.S. Cabernet Sauvignons in the $15-and-under category (listed alphabetically by producer).

Belvedere Cabernet Sauvignon

> ? **Producer:** Belvedere Winery
>
> ? **Wine name:** Cabernet Sauvignon
>
> ? **Appellation:** Dry Creek Valley
>
> ? **Price:** $12

Although Belvedere Winery is located in the Russian River Valley of Sonoma County, California, the company owns vineyards in Alexander and Dry Creek Valleys of Sonoma County as well. The 1994 Cab from Dry Creek Valley grapes is excellent and certainly one of the best Cabs yet from this value-conscious winery. Its aroma is spicy, fresh, bright, and slightly herbal. The wine is medium to full bodied and firm, with some minty flavors and good concentration. Still quite young, this Cab will even improve with a few years of aging. Quite remarkable for a $12 Cab!

Ed: 87–89   **Mary:** 87–89

Chateau Souverain Cabernet Sauvignon

- ! **Producer:** Chateau Souverain
- ! **Wine name:** Cabernet Sauvignon
- ! **Appellation:** Alexander Valley
- ! **Price:** $15

Beringer Estates has owned California's Chateau Souverain for more than ten years. During that time, Chateau Souverain has become one of the most consistently fine wineries in the $15-and-under category in the U.S. (although prices are inevitably creeping higher). The 1994 Souverain Cab has intense aromas of oakiness and black fruits. It's medium bodied, rich, velvety, and very flavorful, with soft flesh balanced by firm oak tannins. Somehow, it tastes "important;" only its fairly short finish prevents it from getting an even higher rating. Try it with a hearty stew or pot roast.

Ed: 85–87   **Mary:** 84–86

De Loach "Sonoma Cuvée" Cabernet Sauvignon

- ! **Producer:** De Loach Vineyards
- ! **Wine name:** "Sonoma Cuvée" Cabernet Sauvignon
- ! **Appellation:** Sonoma County
- ! **Price:** $15

De Loach Vineyards, in California's Russian River Valley, has been a steady performer for more than 20 years. The winery is probably best known for its fine Zinfandels, but frankly, its entire lineup of wines is exceptional. The 1995 "Sonoma Cuvée" Cabernet has an intense, delightful, berry fruit aroma and flavor, which makes the wine fresh and delicious. Its lively acidity ensures the wine a long life, but we're sorely tempted to drink it right now, especially if duck or roast chicken is on the menu.

Ed: 87–89   **Mary:** 87–89

Estancia Cabernet Sauvignon

- ♪ **Producer:** Estancia Estates
- ♪ **Wine name:** Cabernet Sauvignon
- ♪ **Appellation:** California
- ♪ **Price:** $14

We find it comforting to walk into a store and see Estancia on the shelf. In the $15 price category, few brands are as reliable as Estancia, vintage after vintage. The 1994 Estancia Cab is medium bodied and flavorful, with soft tannins and good concentration of berry fruit — a wine that deserves the word *delicious*. Enjoy this Cab now, perhaps with squab or quail, accompanied by wild rice with raisins and pine nuts.

Ed: 85–87 **Mary:** 84–86

Foppiano Cabernet Sauvignon

- ♪ **Producer:** Foppiano Vineyards
- ♪ **Wine name:** Cabernet Sauvignon
- ♪ **Appellation:** Russian River Valley
- ♪ **Price:** $12

Inflation has inflated the price of many a California wine these days, and escalating costs have escalated the problem. But a few old-time wineries, such as Foppiano Vineyards, continue to make fine wines without gouging the consumer. Now more than 100 years old, Foppiano has a secret weapon — 135 acres of prime vineyard land in the Russian River Valley district of Sonoma County. Foppiano's signature wine is Petite Sirah, but we've always enjoyed the winery's wonderful Cabernet Sauvignon, too. The 1993 Cab is full bodied, rich, and velvety, with ripe berry·fruit flavor. It is quite smooth in texture and yet has enough tannins to sustain it for several years. An exceptional Cabernet, this wine is a steal at this price. Try it with beef stew.

Ed: 88–90 **Mary:** 87–89

Hedges Cellars Cabernet/Merlot

- ♪ **Producer:** Hedges Cellars
- ♪ **Wine name:** Cabernet/Merlot
- ♪ **Appellation:** Columbia Valley
- ♪ **Price:** $10

Washington State wineries are making some of the best red wines in the U.S. At the new Hedges Cellars winery in Red Mountain (Yakima Valley), Tom Hedges is proving to the world that you can make a really fine red wine for $10. A blend of 67 percent Cabernet Sauvignon and 33 percent Merlot, this highly drinkable wine is a stunning value. Supple, smooth, and well balanced, it has an herbaceous, minty aroma, good texture, and lots of flavor. The Hedges 1995 Cab-Merlot blend is a wine to enjoy now, perhaps with hamburgers and French fries or with a juicy steak. And the good news is that there is enough of this wine to go around, *and* it's nationally distributed.

Ed: 90–92 **Mary:** 88–90

Mill Creek Cabernet Sauvignon

- ! **Producer:** Mill Creek
- ! **Wine name:** Cabernet Sauvignon
- ! **Appellation:** Sonoma County
- ! **Price:** $12

You might notice that we recommend more California Cabernets from Sonoma's wineries than from Napa's in this under-$15 category. The plain fact is that more real values exist in Sonoma, the cost of land being what it is in Napa. One great example of a Sonoma County value is this tasty Cab from reliable Mill Creek, a winery that has been in business for more than 30 years. The 1994 Cab is quite full bodied, with ripe fruit flavor, soft tannin, and a soft, velvety finish. Try it with a veal chop. It's perfect for drinking in the near future.

Ed: 84–86 **Mary:** 84–86

Pellegrini Vineyards Cabernet Sauvignon

- ! **Producer:** Pellegrini Vineyards
- ! **Wine name:** Cabernet Sauvignon
- ! **Appellation:** North Fork of Long Island
- ! **Price:** $14

Long Island's North Fork, in New York State, is home to quite a few good wines; unfortunately, quantities are small, and prices are often over $15. Pellegrini Vineyards is managing to keep prices sane with no sacrifice in quality. In five short years, Australian-born winemaker Russell Hearn has brought Pellegrini to the forefront of Long Island's wineries. The 1993 Cabernet has a spicy fruit flavor, a touch of oak, and hints of cedar and chocolate. This is a discreet wine, not a blockbuster, that should age well. Try it with lamb or roast beef.

Ed: 86–88

Renaissance Cabernet Sauvignon

> ✔ **Producer:** Renaissance Vineyard
> ✔ **Wine name:** Cabernet Sauvignon
> ✔ **Appellation:** North Yuba
> ✔ **Price:** $14

You mean you've never heard of North Yuba? Actually, the appellation is rather obscure because Renaissance Vineyard is the only winery using it. North Yuba is located in a remote area of the Sierra Foothills of northern California — a breathtaking setting, we're told. Renaissance has succeeded in making its wines, especially the Cabernet Sauvignons, better each year while managing to keep prices reasonable. The 1993 Cabernet is a mouthful of ripe, plush, thick fruit flavor. The wine has good concentration and should even improve with a few years' aging. Barbecued steaks or chicken go well with this wine.

Ed: 88–90   **Mary:** 89–91

St. Supéry Cabernet Sauvignon

> ✔ **Producer:** St. Supéry Vineyard *(san soo per ee)*
> ✔ **Wine name:** Cabernet Sauvignon
> ✔ **Appellation:** Napa Valley
> ✔ **Price:** $15

St. Supéry Vineyard in California is owned by the Skalli family of France, proprietors of the huge, extremely successful Fortant de France line of wines from southern France. The family applies the same philosophy to St. Supéry as it does to Fortant de France: Produce good, cleanly made wines at fair prices. Usually, St. Supéry Cabs are supple, low-tannin wines that are ready to drink when they're released. The winery's 1991 Cabernet is somewhat uncharacteristic, in that it is intensely flavored and moderately tannic — but it does have a sweet attack of ripe fruit on the palate. St. Supéry's Cab is so easy-drinking that you can serve it for parties or fancy picnics and rest assured that everyone will like the wine.

Ed: 84–86 **Mary:** 85–87

Villa Mt. Eden "Cellar Select" Cabernet Sauvignon

> ✦ **Producer:** Villa Mt. Eden
> ✦ **Wine name:** "Cellar Select" Cabernet Sauvignon
> ✦ **Appellation:** California
> ✦ **Price:** $12

How does Villa Mt. Eden do it? This Napa-based winery produces three Cabernet Sauvignons, and even the lowest-priced, large-volume "Cellar Select" Cab is darn good and a terrific value at $12. (Starting with the 1994 vintage, the name of this wine changes from "Cellar Select" to "California" Cabernet Sauvignon.) Kudos to winemaker Mike McGrath and to Stimson Lane (the folks in Washington State who bring you Chateau Ste. Michelle and Columbia Crest wines and who now own Villa Mt. Eden)! The 1993 "Cellar Select" has a soft, supple, creamy texture and aromas and flavors of plummy fruit and slightly spicy oak. Although the wine is full bodied, it's not extremely rich in flavor — but it is extremely likable. This is a Cabernet that Merlot lovers can enjoy.

Ed: 87–89 **Mary:** 86–88

Merlot madness

Bottled water, grunge clothing, fat-free food, retro disco, and Merlot. Get the drift? Merlot is a hot trend.

The problem with the Merlot trend is that, unlike most other trendy items, Merlot wine is an agricultural product. In order to make more Merlot, to feed the trend, you must plant more Merlot vines (usually in less-than-ideal regions for Merlot, because the best areas are already taken) or crank out more grapes from the vines you already have. Both options severely compromise the quality of the wine. And that compromise in quality severely limits the number of Merlot wines that we are willing to recommend.

If you enjoy Merlot, we don't mean to burst your balloon. Maybe you've been lucky enough to find a good Merlot (and maybe we're a bit overly cynical). If you aren't yet a Merlot drinker and want to try the wine, or if you're looking for a new brand, try the wines that we recommend in this section.

We must admit that when Merlot is good, it can be very, very delicious. Typical characteristics of a good-quality Merlot wine are deep color, full body, soft texture due to the relatively low tannin content of the grapes, and intense aromas and flavors of plums and, sometimes, chocolate. Merlot wine is somewhat similar to Cabernet wine (and Merlot often contains some Cabernet as a blending wine) in its weight and flavor, but Merlot is usually softer, rounder, and more generous in your mouth. Merlot is also less firm and less austere than Cabernet.

Because trends spawn demand and demand spawns price increases, the prices of California Merlot wines have gone through the roof. Wines that sold for $13 or $14 six months ago are now over $15. For our recommendations of more-expensive Merlots, turn to Chapter 4.

Chateau Julien Merlot Grand Reserve

> ♪ **Producer:** Chateau Julien
>
> ♪ **Wine name:** Merlot Grand Reserve
>
> ♪ **Appellation:** Monterey County
>
> ♪ **Price:** $10

Nowadays, good under-$15 U.S. Merlots have become as scarce as the bald eagle. We're happy to report that California's Chateau Julien Merlot is that rare bird! And this wine is well distributed throughout the U.S. The 1994 Chateau Julien has a fairly intense, plummy aroma and is rich and thick on the palate, with plummy Merlot fruit. A dry, medium-bodied, true-to-type Merlot, this wine is quite delicious right now, with attractive, easy-to-grasp flavors. Buy it while the price remains so attractive, and try it with roast chicken.

Ed: 87–89   **Mary:** 87–89

Foppiano Merlot

> ♪ **Producer:** Foppiano
>
> ♪ **Wine name:** Merlot
>
> ♪ **Appellation:** Russian River Valley
>
> ♪ **Price:** $12.50

In the Merlot department — just as in the Cabernet department — the Foppiano winery in California enjoys a strategic advantage over many other producers: It owns enough land to rigidly control the quality and cost of its wine. As a result, this Merlot is one of the best values in the category. Don't expect a lot of softness and plushness from this wine: The 1994 Foppiano is fairly tannic and firm for a Merlot. But it is also concentrated and rather intense in its flavors and, unlike almost every other Merlot at this price, is well made and decent.

Ed: 85–87   **Mary:** 84–86

Louis M. Martini Merlot

- **Producer:** Louis M. Martini
- **Wine name:** Merlot
- **Appellation:** North Coast
- **Price:** $12

The Louis M. Martini winery has a permanent place in the history of California Merlot because, in the early 1970s, it was the first to bottle Merlot as a varietal wine. (Until then, Merlot had been merely a silent blending partner, mainly for Cabernet.) Today, this winery still produces an honest, decent Merlot wine that's not overpriced. The 1994 Martini Merlot has good concentration, a thick and velvety texture, and ripe fruitiness. Its personality is a bit more earthy and country than cosmopolitan, so save the *magret de canard* for another night and have a burger instead.

Ed: 86–88   **Mary:** 85–87

Round Hill Napa Valley Merlot

- **Producer:** Round Hill
- **Wine name:** Merlot
- **Appellation:** Napa Valley
- **Price:** $14

This Napa Valley Merlot is a better (and costlier) wine than Round Hill's other Merlot (its "California" bottling), and we prefer the Napa Valley Merlot. The 1994 vintage offers all the softness, roundness, and suppleness that you want in a

Merlot, with lots of spicy fruitiness. If you're curious about why this whole Merlot trend exists, this wine might just tell you on the first sip.

Ed: 84–86   **Mary:** 84–86

Pinot Noir, when in doubt

We love Pinot Noir wines. They are so food-friendly that we often turn to them in those sticky food-and-wine pairing situations: when one of us has ordered squab and the other one is having the fish special, for example, or when we're just in doubt about which wine to drink. The low tannin in the Pinot Noir grape is probably one reason that Pinot Noir wine happily cuts across the lines between poultry, seafood, fish, vegetables, and red meat.

U.S. Pinot Noir wines delight us with their fresh, lively spirit and their unmistakable fruitiness. These wines are relatively light red in color and light to medium bodied. Pinot Noir wines generally have cherry, red-berry, or black-fruit flavors, but the flavors of the individual wines vary according to where the grapes are grown. For example, Pinot Noir wines from the Santa Barbara region in California often have strawberry or tomato-paste flavors, whereas those from Oregon more commonly exhibit black-fruit flavors, such as black cherry and blackberry. Whatever the flavors, Pinot Noir wines are elegant red wines, not blockbusters. They are as delicious to drink on their own as they are with food.

Because good Pinot Noir grapes are always scarce and in demand — just as Merlot grapes are nowadays — the prices of good American Pinot Noir wines fall into the over-$15 category more than they do the under-$15 range. We therefore can recommend very few under-$15 Pinot Noir wines that we consider worthwhile, from the U.S. or from around the world, for that matter. (See Chapter 4 for a larger selection of New World Pinot Noir wines in the over-$15 category.) For more information on Pinot Noir, see *Red Wine For Dummies,* Chapter 7, or *Wine For Dummies,* Chapters 9 and 12.

Estancia Pinot Noir

- ♪ **Producer:** Estancia Estates
- ♪ **Wine name:** Pinot Noir
- ♪ **Appellation:** Monterey
- ♪ **Price:** $14

You can count on reliable Estancia Estates to produce a good, affordable Pinot Noir in most vintages. The 1995 Estancia Pinot Noir, from the cool Monterey wine region, is surprisingly rich and intense for a Pinot at this price level. It has very pleasant raspberry fruit flavors, along with hints of eucalyptus and other herbs that offset the intense fruitiness of the wine and keep the fruit flavor from being excessive. This Pinot is a very enjoyable wine to drink now—and a good buy. Serve it with crab cakes. Delicious!

Ed: 87–89   **Mary:** 84–86

Napa Ridge Pinot Noir

- ♪ **Producer:** Napa Ridge
- ♪ **Wine name:** Pinot Noir
- ♪ **Appellation:** North Coast
- ♪ **Price:** $10

Napa Ridge is another successful California winery owned by Beringer Estates. (Elsewhere in this chapter, we recommend a wine from another Beringer property, Chateau Souverain.) And Napa Ridge's prices are the lowest of any of Beringer's wine estates. The 1995 Napa Ridge Pinot Noir has an intense, spicy-berry aroma, with soft, cherry fruit flavors, some tannin, and a slight impression of sweetness. Enjoy this Pinot Noir while it's young. It's a wonderful warm-weather red wine because it's light bodied and easy-drinking. Sip it on the porch while nibbling on some hors d'oeuvres.

Ed: 84–86   **Mary:** 85–87

Saintsbury "Garnet" Pinot Noir

- ♪ **Producer:** Saintsbury
- ♪ **Wine name:** "Garnet" Pinot Noir
- ♪ **Appellation:** Carneros
- ♪ **Price:** $14

California's Saintsbury, one of the most respected producers of Pinot Noir in the U.S., makes three fine, consistently reliable Pinot Noir wines. The "Garnet" bottling that we review here is the lightest bodied and the least expensive of the three. (The other two are the "Carneros" and the

"Carneros Reserve.") The 1995 Garnet is an easy-drinking Pinot Noir, with classic cherry and spicy strawberry flavors — typical of the style you can find in the Pinot Noir wines of the cool Carneros region. Try it with a light grilled fish or some mussels. It's a great Pinot Noir at this price. If you see it on the shelf, buy it — it sells out fast.

Ed: 86–88   **Mary:** 86–88

Willamette Valley Vineyards Pinot Noir

> ☞ **Producer:** Willamette *(will AM ette)* Valley Vineyards
>
> ☞ **Wine name:** Pinot Noir
>
> ☞ **Appellation:** Oregon
>
> ☞ **Price:** $15

Willamette Valley Vineyards, one of Oregon's largest wineries, is one of the few that's still able to make a decent Pinot Noir in the $15-and-under category. Its new winemaker, Joe Dobbes, has plenty of experience with Pinot Noir, and his contribution should be evident in the Pinot Noir wines from this winery, starting with the 1995 vintage. The 1995 Pinot has beautiful berry-cherry aromas and sweet, ripe cherry fruit flavors. It's a well-balanced, lighter style of Pinot Noir that can probably accompany lobster or crabs as well as salmon. Drink it while it's young and brimming with its delicious fruit.

Ed: 84–86

Zinfandel — a walk on the wild side

Over the past 20 years, a whole generation of wine buyers has experienced Zinfandel only (or mainly) as a slightly sweet, light-bodied pink wine known as *White Zinfandel.* If you count yourself in this group, you're in for a treat, because *real* Zinfandel is a delicious, versatile red wine. (If you're already one of the converted, we hope that you find a few new favorites among our selections.)

Zinfandel has been called "America's wine" because it's made almost exclusively in California — although the Zinfandel grape variety does have obscure European origins. Zinfandel wine usually has a dark ruby color and is typically full bodied, although it can be a lighter-bodied wine. Just like the Old West era, when

Zinfandel vines were first planted, Red Zinfandel has an untamed, exuberant nature, which exhibits itself as riotous wild-berry, spicy, and peppery flavors. Although Zin is generally a dry red wine the fruit flavors can be so intense that you get an impression of sweetness in the wine. (In the most full-blown versions, the alcohol content can be so high that it contributes to this impression of sweetness.)

Zinfandel is a versatile red wine, perfect for all kinds of food, including Italian, Asian, spicy Indian, and Mexican dishes. And no wine is better with charcoal-broiled or barbecued food than Red Zin.

Zin is made all over California, but some of the best Zinfandels come from Sonoma County, especially the Dry Creek, Alexander, and Russian River Valleys. And Zinfandels are not expensive: Many still cost less than $15. (We describe some excellent, over-$15 Red Zinfandels in Chapter 4.) For more information on Zinfandel, see *Red Wine For Dummies,* Chapter 7, or *Wine For Dummies,* Chapters 9 and 12.

Burgess Zinfandel

> ? **Producer:** Burgess Cellars
>
> ? **Wine name:** Zinfandel
>
> ? **Appellation:** Napa Valley
>
> ? **Price:** $13

Tom Burgess, a former pilot, is one of the really nice guys in the wine business. He's been making wine up on Howell Mountain in California's Napa Valley for 25 years now. Although most renowned for his ageworthy Cabernet Sauvignons, he also happens to make Zinfandel in a style that we enjoy. It's a dry, lean, firm, tannic style that's often referred to as *claret-style* Zin, meaning that the wine resembles a Bordeaux wine (which the British call "claret") or a Cabernet more than it does a ripe, lusty Zin. The 1992 Burgess Zin, although made in this claret style, is also quite rich, with lots of concentrated berry fruit flavor. It will age better than most Zinfandels if you care to age it; however, many wine lovers enjoy Zinfandel in its young berry fruit stage. Burgess's 1993 Zin has a somewhat softer, lusher style than the 1992 does. Try Burgess Zin with steak, a veal chop, or even swordfish.

Ed: 87–89   **Mary:** 87–89

Davis Bynum Zinfandel

> ♪ **Producer:** Davis Bynum Winery
> ♪ **Wine name:** Zinfandel
> ♪ **Appellation:** Russian River Valley
> ♪ **Price:** $12

We love Davis Bynum's Zinfandel. It has such bright, delicious, exuberant raspberry fruit aromas and flavors that we find ourselves finishing the entire bottle long before dinner is over! The 1993 Davis Bynum Zin typifies the Davis Bynum style — soft, cleanly made, easy-drinking, and delicious. Its good concentration of fruit character says quality, and the price says it's a super buy. This isn't a "serious" wine — just fun to drink. Try this wine with a simple pasta flavored with basil, mozzarella, and tomatoes.

Ed: 85–87   **Mary:** 85–87

De Loach Zinfandel

> ♪ **Producer:** De Loach Vineyards
> ♪ **Wine name:** Zinfandel
> ♪ **Appellation:** Russian River Valley
> ♪ **Price:** $13

De Loach Vineyards, in California's Sonoma County, produces several special, single-vineyard Zinfandels in the over-$15 category, but the winery's basic Zin is just fine. The excellent 1995 De Loach Zinfandel follows a very impressive 1994 rendition. The soft, ripe, generous 1995 Zin has plenty of raspberry and cherry fruit flavors, with some herbal accents. It's a supple, well-balanced wine with soft tannins that's perfect for near-term consumption. We like it best with roast chicken or grilled sausages.

Ed: 88–90   **Mary:** 88–90

Marietta Cellars Zinfandel

> ♪ **Producer:** Marietta Cellars
> ♪ **Wine name:** Zinfandel
> ♪ **Appellation:** Sonoma County
> ♪ **Price:** $14

When we think of excellent, inexpensive Red Zinfandels, one of the first names that comes to mind is Marietta. The 1994 Marietta Zinfandel has a deep, black ruby color and delectable, subtle berry aromas. The flavor is intense with berry fruit and herbal notes, especially eucalyptus — a bit ripe, sweet, and full blown, but totally delicious. A winner! Try this Zin with food that's flavorful enough to stand up to this wine, such as barbecued or grilled meats or pizza. Although you can drink this wine now, it will tolerate a few years of aging.

Ed: 92–94   **Mary:** 86–88

Ravenswood Sonoma County Zinfandel

- ⚑ **Producer:** Ravenswood
- ⚑ **Wine name:** Zinfandel
- ⚑ **Appellation:** Sonoma County
- ⚑ **Price:** $15

Ravenswood's winemaker and co-proprietor, Joel Peterson, is one of the world's most talented producers of Zinfandel. His lineup of single-vineyard Zinfandel wines (mainly available directly from the winery, phone 707-938-1960) is truly awesome; see the Zinfandel section in Chapter 4 for more on those wines. His Sonoma County Zinfandel — which is made from grapes not of a single vineyard but of various vineyards in Dry Creek, Alexander, and Sonoma Valleys, all in Sonoma County — is also consistently excellent, vintage after vintage. The 1994 Ravenswood Sonoma County Zin is a big, sturdy, full-bodied, ripe, rich Zin with a long finish. It's packed with intensely concentrated plum and blackberry fruit flavor and is firm with tannin. Try this wine with sturdy food, such as barbecued ribs or grilled steaks.

Ed: 87–89   **Mary:** 87–89

Seghesio Zinfandel

- ⚑ **Producer:** Seghesio Family Estates
- ⚑ **Wine name:** Zinfandel
- ⚑ **Appellation:** Sonoma County
- ⚑ **Price:** $12

The family-owned Seghesio winery in Sonoma County, California, produces well-crafted red wines in the Italian tradition. Seghesio's Zinfandels and Sangiovese-based wines are particularly renowned among knowledgeable, price-conscious wine drinkers. Although the winery does make a slightly more expensive Old Vine Reserve Zinfandel from fruit grown in Alexander Valley, Seghesio's more generic Sonoma County Zinfandel is just as good and a great value. The 1995 version is a classic Zin: very dark red, medium to full bodied, dry but soft and very fruity, with true ripe-berry flavors. Its fruitiness is balanced with good acidity and some herbal flavor. Try this Zin with pizza or any sort of pasta with tomato sauce (even the kind with hot pepper).

Ed: 86–88   **Mary:** 85–87

Wines from other grape varieties or blends

If you're looking for good value in domestic red wines, pay special attention to this section: The wines that don't carry the four most popular grape names often give you higher quality for the money than those that do.

Marietta Cellars Old Vine Red

- ❢ **Producer:** Marietta Cellars
- ❢ **Wine name:** Old Vine Red
- ❢ **Appellation:** Sonoma County
- ❢ **Price:** $10

This California wine sells out quickly because it has a big following, so if you see it on the shelf, grab it! The Marietta Cellars Old Vine Red is a deep-colored, rustic wine, most closely resembling a cross between Zinfandel and Petite Sirah (both of which it contains, plus Cabernet Sauvignon and Carignane). Crammed with earthy and black-peppery flavors and a suggestion of wild blackberries, the Old Vine Red is the perfect choice for barbecued or spicy cuisine; it stands up to almost any food that's not delicate. This lusty, full-bodied red wine is for drinking rather than for quiet contemplation. Old Vine Red is a nonvintage blend; the current release is called Lot #18.

Ed: 88–90

R.H. Phillips EXP Syrah

> ♪ **Producer:** R.H. Phillips
> ♪ **Wine name:** EXP Syrah
> ♪ **Appellation:** Dunnigan Hills
> ♪ **Price:** $12

The wines of R.H. Phillips are consistently a good value. From the winery's huge vineyard holdings in the Dunnigan Hills area of north-central California, the company makes numerous red and white wines, under several different labels; the EXP label (which is short for *explorateur*) is used only for wines made from what the winery calls Mediterranean grape varieties, such as Syrah. The 1994 EXP Syrah is all about texture: It's thick, soft, smooth, rich, and velvety — and yet it has enough firm tannin to keep it from being wimpy. It's so rich that it tastes a bit sweet. The 1995 vintage of this wine is similar, but it's a bit more tannic, crisper, and slightly more concentrated in its flavors.

Mary: 86–88

Wild Horse Trousseau

> ♪ **Producer:** Wild Horse Vineyards
> ♪ **Wine name:** Trousseau
> ♪ **Appellation:** Cienega Valley
> ♪ **Price:** $14

This wine from California's San Benito County is a real oddball because it's made from a grape variety, Trousseau, that is obscure not only in California but also in the world. (The home of the Trousseau grape is the Jura region of eastern France.) But, hey, we enjoy trying new and different things. When we tasted this wine from the 1994 vintage, we discovered flavors of cherry and a subtle aroma that suggested sweet cherry and herbs. Unlike so many red California wines, this wine is light bodied and crisp and has good length across the palate. Trousseau probably is not very easy to find, but if you see it, why not increase your grape variety vocabulary by trying a bottle?

Ed: 84–86   **Mary: 86–88**

Argentina and Chile Spell Value

Today, South American wines are enjoying a boom of popularity and appreciation among savvy wine drinkers in the U.S. These wines are easy to figure out because most of them are named for grape varieties, such as Cabernet Sauvignon or Merlot, just as California wines are. And the prices of South American wines are like yesterday's, compared to many California wines.

Cabernet Sauvignon and Merlot, South American style

The worldly Cabernet Sauvignon grape knows no borders: It grows just as happily in Chile or Argentina as it does everywhere else. The Cabernets we recommend here tend to be light- to medium-bodied wines, not extremely tannic or dry in texture (in other words, not very "serious" Cabs that need years of bottle-aging to become attractive). And yet they all deliver real Cabernet character for their price.

The Merlot grape isn't as good a traveler as the Cabernet Sauvignon grape because Merlot is a lot fussier about the types of soils and climates that it will tolerate. Grape experts claim that much of the Merlot that grows in Chile isn't really Merlot but rather an obscure variety called *Carmenère,* which local grape growers have mistaken for Merlot. When you buy a bottle of Merlot from Chile, you have no way of knowing which grape actually made the wine. But if it smells like Merlot and tastes like Merlot and you enjoy it, why be concerned about details? The wines that we recommend here all smell and taste like Merlot, and *we* like them (and their prices!). Hope you do, too.

In this section, we list our recommended wines alphabetically by producer, intermingling Cabernets and Merlots.

Carmen Cabernet Sauvignon Reserve

- **Producer:** Carmen Vineyards
- **Wine name:** Cabernet Sauvignon Reserve
- **Appellation:** Valle Central (Chile)
- **Price:** $14

The reserve bottling of a wine is typically oakier than the regular bottling from the same winery because wineries go to the expense of using more oak or newer oak for what they deem to be their better grapes. In Carmen's 1995 Reserve Cabernet Sauvignon, the spiciness of oak scents the wine and flavors it as well. But as in any well-made wine, you can find a concentration of ripe fruit to balance the oakiness. This is a fresh, modern style of wine that's slightly sweet from its ripe fruit, and very flavorful. What it lacks in elegance, it delivers in intensity. Ed also likes Carmen's regular (non-reserve) Cabernet, an $8 wine.

Ed: 87–89   **Mary:** 87–89

Casa Lapostolle Cabernet Sauvignon

- ♪ **Producer:** Casa Lapostolle
- ♪ **Wine name:** Cabernet Sauvignon
- ♪ **Appellation:** Rapel (Chile)
- ♪ **Price:** $9

The wines of Casa Lapostolle have been getting such good reviews from the critics ever since they hit the U.S. market in 1995 that we admit to feeling a bit redundant here. But yes, we like them, too. And why not? Michel Rolland, the French enologist and wine consultant who has the Midas touch when it comes to wine, has performed his magic here.

The 1995 Casa Lapostolle Cabernet has an intense aroma of spice and berry fruit and is very tasty, with lots of fruity and spicy flavors, a bit of oakiness, and an attractive lead-pencil character. We consider this wine to be on the full side of medium bodied. It's a bit heavier than most Chilean Cabs, and its flavors are a bit truer to the grape variety than many of its fellow Cabernets from Chile. This wine is definitely worth a try. (Another Casa Lapostolle Cabernet Sauvignon, Cuvée Alexandre, aged in 100 percent French oak barrels, is even richer and more complex than the regular Cab. But at $15 for the Cuvée Alexandre, we're recommending the standard Casa Lapostolle, a great buy at $9.)

Ed: 84–86   **Mary:** 87–89

Casa Lapostolle Merlot, Cuvée Alexandre

- **Producer:** Casa Lapostolle
- **Wine name:** Merlot Cuvée Alexandre
- **Appellation:** Rapel (Chile)
- **Price:** $15

Some critics claim that Casa Lapostolle's Cuvée Alexandre Merlot is Chile's greatest Merlot. We tend to agree, but you do have to like the aroma and taste of new oak, which dominates the wine when it's young. The dark purple color and the sweet, spicy, ripe aroma of the 1995 Cuvée Alexandre Merlot certainly do make an impression. The wine is medium to full bodied, with soft tannins, a velvety texture, and dense, concentrated fruit. A voluptuous wine, the Cuvée Alexandre is easy to enjoy now — with some beef, perhaps, or some aged sheep's milk cheese, such as Spanish manchego. But this Merlot is also built for aging, so it will still be fine in five to seven years. With time, the oak should integrate its flavors into the wine and play a more subtle role.

Ed: 87–89   **Mary:** 87–89

Concha y Toro Cabernet Sauvignon "Marques de Casa Concha"

- **Producer:** Concha y Toro
- **Wine name:** Cabernet Sauvignon "Marques de Casa Concha," Puente Alta Vineyard
- **Appellation:** Maipo (Chile)
- **Price:** $11

In a country that has practically been invaded by foreign winemakers and winery owners, Chile's Concha y Toro remains one of the oldies-but-goodies. This huge winery makes dozens of different wines, many of them carrying brand names other than the winery name itself — for example, its Trio brand or the unmistakably Latin-sounding brand, Walnut Crest. But our favorite Concha y Toro wines are consistently its high-end bottlings, like this single-vineyard Cabernet. This wine is somewhat old-fashioned, meaning that it's not a bright, fruity little number. The 1993 Cab is medium bodied and fairly lean (as opposed to rich), with noticeable tannin and what we call an inky flavor. We find that this wine has a certain rustic charm that we like in Cabernets. Because it's not very fruity, this Cab goes great with such dishes as beef stew or pot roast.

Ed: 84–86   **Mary:** 84–86

Errazuriz Merlot

- **Producer:** Errazuriz *(er RAH zuh reez)*
- **Wine name:** Merlot, El Descanso Estate
- **Appellation:** Curicó Valley (Chile)
- **Price:** $9.50

We are pleased to see South American wines being released for sale when they are very young and fresh. Experience seems to have made each year's wines better than the previous year's, and besides, we like the young and fresh style. The 1996 Errazuriz Merlot typifies that style: fairly pronounced aromas and flavors of cherry, plum, and chocolate; a medium body; and soft, supple texture. Drink it while it's young — from one to three years of age — to experience this style at its best. (We also like Errazuriz's Cabernet.)

Ed: 84–86   **Mary:** 86–88

Finca Flichman Cabernet Sauvignon, "Caballero de la Cepa"

- **Producer:** Finca Flichman
- **Wine name:** "Caballero de la Cepa" Cabernet Sauvignon
- **Appellation:** Mendoza (Argentina)
- **Price:** $9

This top-of-the-line Cabernet from the relatively small Finca Flichman winery tends to have some age by the time it's sold in the U.S. — but you wouldn't think so from tasting the wine. At 5$^{1}/_{2}$ years old, the 1991 vintage still had the deep purple color of a wine half its age, with vibrant blackberry fruit aroma and flavor to match. This isn't a complex Cabernet, but it delivers an amazing amount of fresh, intense fruit that's really delicious.

Ed: 85–87   **Mary:** 85–87

Navarro Correas Colecçion Privada Cabernet Sauvignon

- **! Producer:** Navarro Correas
- **! Wine name:** Cabernet Sauvignon, Colecçion Privada
- **! Appellation:** Mendoza (Argentina)
- **! Price:** $13

Navarro Correas is one of Argentina's elite wineries, and its Colecçion Privada (Private Collection) Cabernet Sauvignon is my favorite from this producer's stable. The 1991 vintage is a ripe, rich, full-bodied wine that cries for a charcoal-broiled steak to accompany it. You can enjoy this lush, concentrated wine now, but it's also capable of aging. To me, the Colecçion Privada typifies the new wave of well-made, balanced wines that are now emerging from Argentina.

Ed: 86–88

Terra Rosa Cabernet Sauvignon

- **! Producer:** Laurel Glen Vineyards
- **! Wine name:** Terra Rosa Cabernet Sauvignon
- **! Appellation:** Valle Central (Chile)
- **! Price:** $12

This wine carries a brand name and label that you might recognize as Californian, but it's made from grapes grown in the other place where California winemakers are heading these days: Chile. We liked the wine originally, when it was a California wine, and we still like it in the 1995 vintage, now that it's a Chilean wine. The common thread is Patrick Campbell, owner and winemaker of Laurel Glen Vineyards in Sonoma, a talented man whose tastes in wine apparently coincide perfectly with ours. This wine has more than a dollop of oakiness in its aroma and flavor, and its ripe, concentrated fruit balances its firm tannin nicely. If you want a fresh, lively, flavorful Cabernet that doesn't break the bank, give this wine a try.

Ed: 84–86   **Mary:** 84–86

Wines from other grape varieties or blends

We're not the bettin' kind, but if we were, we'd put our money on the Malbec grape as the exciting new thing from South America. This red grape comes from France, where it plays a major role in the wines of Cahors, in the southwest (not a region of major importance by international standards), and a minor role in the Bordeaux region, where it is usually blended with Cabernet and Merlot. (In other words, if you never heard of this grape before, don't beat yourself.)

In the warm, dry Mendoza region of Argentina, Malbec makes deeply colored, robust red wines that are considered some of that country's finest. Some producers also use Malbec as part of a Bordeaux-style blend based on Cabernet Sauvignon and Merlot. The Malbec spices up the blend, so to speak.

Mariposa Malbec

> ♪ **Producer:** Mariposa
>
> ♪ **Wine name:** Malbec
>
> ♪ **Appellation:** Mendoza (Argentina)
>
> ♪ **Price:** $8

It was snowing outside. We were happy to be indoors, warm and dry, sampling interesting new wines to our hearts' content and learning about Argentina and Chile from Randy Ullom, then-director of wine operations in South America for the hugely successful American wine company, Kendall-Jackson. (Ullom is now Kendall-Jackson's chief winemaker.) Without warning, he poured his 1996 Mariposa Malbec into our glasses. We loved the intense, spicy aroma and the berry, spice, and chocolate flavors. We commented on its full body, soft, thick texture, and good concentration of fruit. When he said "$8," we were even more impressed. Don't wait for a snowstorm to try it yourself.

Ed: 87–89   **Mary:** 87–89

Trapiche Malbec

> ♪ **Producer:** Trapiche
>
> ♪ **Wine name:** Malbec
>
> ♪ **Appellation:** Mendoza (Argentina)
>
> ♪ **Price:** $6

We're not recommending many wines at $6 or under in this book, but Trapiche's Malbec is definitely one worth recommending. Wine consultant (or should we say "genius"?) Michel Rolland is doing wonders with the Trapiche wines. The 1995 Malbec has a briary, spicy aroma with suggestions of honeysuckle and jasmine. (You're getting a lot for $6!) It's medium bodied, with soft, fruity, generous flavors and low tannin. This wine needs simple food, such as a grilled steak or pork loin, and is a great value.

Ed: 85–87   **Mary:** 83–85

Norton Privada Blend

ᵉᵈ'ˢ CHOICE

- ! **Producer:** Bodega Norton
- ! **Wine name:** Privada Blend *(pre VAH' dah)*
- ! **Appellation:** Mendoza (Argentina)
- ! **Price:** $14.50

Like many other California wineries, The Hess Collection has discovered new wine horizons in South America. The company is currently importing the wines of Argentina's Bodega Norton, a winery that was established in 1895. Norton's 1994 Privada, probably the winery's best wine, is a blend of Cabernet Sauvignon, Merlot, and Malbec, aged in new French oak. The wine's aroma is quiet, but we detect some chocolate and nutmeg, along with oakiness. It's a harmonious, well-balanced wine, with a lot of tannin (much of it from the oak), concentrated fruit flavor, and decent length. It will probably improve with a few years of aging. Try it with roast beef or some hard cheeses, such as cheddar or aged Gouda.

Ed: 88–90

Australia's Delicious Reds

We don't know if the Australian wine industry has an official motto, but we'd like to suggest "You've come a long way, baby!" We tasted our very first Australian wine less than 15 years ago; now, Australian wines are such a fixture in the U.S. that we can't talk about the wine market without mentioning the very good and very popular wines of Australia.

Australia's red wines are generally medium to full bodied, soft, and flavorful. Inexpensive Australian reds (unlike California reds) are often not oaky — and those that are made in oak often show herbal or sweet flavors of American oak rather than the toasty, smoky notes that French oak gives. The wines' flavors reflect their grape varieties. Syrah, which the Australians call Shiraz, is the most popular red grape, followed by Cabernet Sauvignon. Australia's law dictates that any wine with a single grape variety name must derive at least 85 percent from that grape.

For a selection of more-expensive Australian red wines, see Chapter 4. For more information on Australian red wines, refer to *Red Wine For Dummies,* Chapter 9, or *Wine For Dummies,* Chapters 9 and 12.

Peter Lehmann Shiraz

- **Producer:** Peter Lehmann
- **Wine name:** Shiraz
- **Appellation:** Barossa Valley
- **Price:** $11

The Barossa Valley is the home of some of South Australia's greatest red wines. There, Peter Lehmann operates a relatively small (by Australian standards) winery, producing quality wines. His best red wine is probably his Shiraz. The 1992 Peter Lehmann Shiraz has a nutty, sweaty aroma that also shows some raspberry-jam character. It's a smooth, earthy, very fruity wine that you can enjoy now or hold for a few years. Try it with hearty foods, such as veal stew.

Ed: 87–89   **Mary:** 86–88

Rosemount Diamond Label Cabernet Sauvignon

- **Producer:** Rosemount Estate
- **Wine name:** Cabernet Sauvignon (Diamond Label)
- **Appellation:** South Australia
- **Price:** $10

Of all Australia's large wineries, Rosemount Estate is one of the most successful at marketing its wines abroad — thanks to the combination of user-friendly wine style (soft, easy-drinking, well-priced wines that go well with food) and attractively labeled bottles. Rosemount's Diamond Label wines (so-named because the labels are — surprise! —

diamond-shaped) are particularly popular. Our favorite Diamond Label wine is the Cabernet Sauvignon. In the 1995 vintage, it's a soft, supple wine with a spicy oak aroma, exuberant black cherry and berry flavors, and low tannin. It's ready to drink now; try it with barbecued or grilled meats, such as steaks, hamburgers, or sausages.

Ed: 86–88   **Mary:** 84–86

Rothbury Estate Shiraz

- ❦ **Producer:** Rothbury Estate
- ❦ **Wine name:** Shiraz
- ❦ **Appellation:** South Eastern Australia
- ❦ **Price:** $9

This dry, full-bodied Shiraz, in the 1994 vintage, has subdued aromas and flavors that suggest green olive, leather, and grilled green vegetables. Despite its low price, this wine is not made in the fresh, bright-fruit style of most inexpensive Shiraz wines. Instead, it's rustic, gutsy, and also fairly tannic for an Australian wine. We enjoy this style of Shiraz, especially with grilled meats.

Ed: 87–89   **Mary:** 85–87

Sheldrake Shiraz

- ❦ **Producer:** Sheldrake
- ❦ **Wine name:** Shiraz
- ❦ **Appellation:** Western Australia
- ❦ **Price:** $13

Until recently, not many wines from the state of Western Australia were available in the U.S., but now more wineries from this relatively remote area are shipping their wines to the U.S. The Sheldrake wines are among the better values from Western Australia. The 1995 Sheldrake Shiraz has a spicy, grapey aroma, rather intense and exuberant. The wine is very soft and supple in texture and has a slight sweetness that's appealing. Because this wine is relatively subdued in its fruitiness, it's fairly versatile with food; try it with an "everything" pizza.

Ed: 86–88   **Mary:** 84–86

Taltarni Cabernet Sauvignon

> ! **Producer:** Taltarni Vineyards
> ! **Wine name:** Cabernet Sauvignon
> ! **Appellation:** Victoria
> ! **Price:** $15

In some ways, the wines of Taltarni go against the stylistic norm of Australian wines; they tend to be leaner, less exuberantly fruity, drier, and slightly more tannic. In other words, Taltarni wines are somewhat more European in style than Australian. (Perhaps not coincidentally, they are made by a Frenchman.) We like these characteristics and, therefore, count Taltarni among our favorite Aussie wineries. The 1992 Taltarni Cab is full bodied and dry, with firm tannin and tight, concentrated fruit flavor that shows itself on the finish. If you prefer soft reds, this wine may not be for you; but if you like character in your Cabernet, try a bottle. Serving Taltarni Cab with red meat or hard cheese softens the tannin considerably.

Ed: 84–86   **Mary:** 84–86

Tyrrell's Shiraz

> ! **Producer:** Tyrrell's Old Winery
> ! **Wine name:** Shiraz
> ! **Appellation:** South Australia
> ! **Price:** $12

The 1994 Tyrrell's Shiraz has a quiet aroma, but when you concentrate, you can catch unmistakable green pepper, leather, and burnt rubber notes — all typical of Syrah. The wine is dry but very flavorful, with more of that true-blue "Syrahness" and some charriness, probably from oak. Try drinking it with roasted lamb.

Mary: 85–87

South African Red Wines

South Africa grows most of the same red-wine grapes that are famous in Europe and America, including Cabernet Sauvignon, Merlot, Pinot Noir, and Syrah (which the South Africans call Shiraz). South Africa also boasts a unique red grape called

Pinotage, developed in that country by crossbreeding the Pinot Noir grape with Cinsaut, a Rhône Valley variety.

South Africa's red wines taste something like a cross between French red Bordeaux wines (with their characteristic leanness and subtlety) and Californian or Australian red wines (with their approachability and fleshy ripeness). But because such comparisons are never totally accurate, you might conclude that South African wines really have their own distinct personality.

For South African red wine recommendations in the over-$15 category, see Chapter 4. For more information on South African red wines, see *Red Wine For Dummies,* Chapter 9, or *Wine For Dummies,* Chapter 12.

Backsberg Estate Klein Babylonstoren

- *ℐ* **Producer:** Backsberg Estate
- *ℐ* **Wine name:** Klein Babylonstoren *(klane BAB eh lon stor en)*
- *ℐ* **Appellation:** Paarl
- *ℐ* **Price:** $12.50

Sidney Back, proprietor of Backsberg Estate, is an old-time veteran of the South African wine industry and one of its respected leaders. This wine is a blend of Merlot and Cabernet Sauvignon, in the red Bordeaux style. In the 1992 vintage, the wine has a dusty, plummy aroma, along with some smokiness and leathery notes. It's a generous wine, with vegetal and fruit flavors, soft texture, and an impression of depth that probably comes from the wine's high acidity. This wine *does* resemble a Bordeaux somewhat, but a fleshier New World version. Quite a wine for $12.50! Try it with lamb stew or a grilled steak.

Ed: 89–91   **Mary:** 88–90

Stellenryck Cabernet Sauvignon

- *ℐ* **Producer:** Stellenryck *(STEL len rick)*
- *ℐ* **Wine name:** Cabernet Sauvignon
- *ℐ* **Appellation:** Coastal Region
- *ℐ* **Price:** $15

Right from the first smell of the 1991 Stellenryck Cab, you catch a scent of mint, a note that resounds in the wine's flavor, giving the wine a bright, fresh character. The wine is medium bodied, dry, and fairly tannic, with velvety texture. Its great concentration of fruit character and its wonderful, long finish attest to its fine quality. We might enjoy this wine with leg of lamb, but we'd probably forgo the mint jelly, which would be too sweet for the wine.

Ed: 94–96   **Mary:** 87–89

Warwick Estate Cabernet Sauvignon

- ✔ **Producer:** Warwick Estate
- ✔ **Wine name:** Cabernet Sauvignon
- ✔ **Appellation:** Stellenbosch
- ✔ **Price:** $15

Warwick Estate is one of the newer stars on the South African horizon, with its first wines dating back only to 1984. This winery definitely makes some first-class wines. The 1991 Cabernet Sauvignon has the classic cassis and lead-pencil aroma of Cabernet. Its vivid flavor suggests berries, its texture is velvety, and the wine is very intense and distinctive. Warwick Estate is a winery to watch.

Ed: 91–93   **Mary:** 88–90

Zonnebloem Laureat

- ✔ **Producer:** Zonnebloem Wines *(ZONE eh blohm)*
- ✔ **Wine name:** Laureat
- ✔ **Appellation:** Stellenbosch
- ✔ **Price:** $10

Of the large range of red and white wines that Zonnebloem makes, this Bordeaux-style blend is our favorite. The complex aroma of the 1991 Laureat suggests tobacco, mint, leather, and a leafy character, like vegetation. The wine is medium bodied, with flavors of leather, ripe fruit, and chocolate. Instead of having the direct, exuberant fruitiness of a typical New World wine, Laureat is gentle and elegant in style, with all the complexity that comes from blending and aging. This wine is not widely available, but as they say, it's worth the search.

Ed: 88–90   **Mary:** 87–89

Chapter 3

Getting Serious: Old World Red Wines Over $15

. . . .

In This Chapter

▶ Great red Bordeaux wines, from $15 to $50

▶ Seductive, sensual red Burgundy

▶ The red wines of Tuscany and Piedmont

▶ Favorite Spanish and Portuguese picks

. . . .

*W*hen you pay $20 or $25 for a bottle of red wine, rather than only $8 or $12, what more do you expect to get for your money? More varietal character? (The Cabernet should taste more like Cabernet?) Better quality? The security of buying a good brand?

Those expectations are all valid, but we believe that a pricey wine should deliver another benefit: It should have the special character of the place from which it comes — not just *terroir* character (characteristics in the wine that result from the climate, soil, and other elements of the vine's growing conditions), but also a character deriving from the history, tradition, and culture of its birthplace. When we pay big money for a bottle of wine, we expect it to evoke a place and a time, and to be a link in a chain of nature that pre-existed us and will carry on long after we taste our last drop of wine.

We realize that we're laying some heavy expectations on what is, after all, just fermented grape juice. And sure, it's okay for a wine to be just delicious and nothing more. But when wine producers ask us to spend $25 for their wine, we're entitled to expect — and get — that special extra value.

Most of the wines we recommend in this chapter deliver that undefinable extra value. They are, for the most part, wines from classic European wine regions such as Bordeaux, Burgundy,

Barolo, the Chianti Classico zone, Montalcino, and Rioja. These regions have more than their share of winemaking tradition, which reflects in their wines.

We begin this chapter with the wines of France and then move on to Italy, Spain, and Portugal. We list the information on each wine in the following way:

- ✔ **The name of the producer:** This is the entity who makes the wine. Because most of the wines in this chapter are *estate-bottled* wines — that is, they are made from grapes grown in vineyards owned by the same family or company that makes the wine — the producer is responsible for growing the grapes as well as making the wine.

- ✔ **The wine name:** Most of the wines in this chapter are named for a place, either a wine region, a smaller district, a vineyard, or a specific estate. Some of the wine names in this chapter are the same as the producer names, especially for Bordeaux wines.

- ✔ **The wine's appellation:** The *appellation* (that is, the legal origin of the wine, the specific place from which the grapes came) and the wine name are the same for many wines in this chapter.

- ✔ **The approximate retail price of the wine:** This price can vary quite a bit, according to what part of the country you're in and the type of store where you buy your wine. The price we use, the New York State suggested retail price, is likely to be a bit high if you shop in discount stores, if taxes are lower in your state, or if you buy in quantity.

The Fine Red Wines of France

Over the past 200 years, France has probably produced more great red wines than any other country. Today, of course, France has no monopoly on fine red wine. But the legend of great French wine lives on in the privileged vineyards of the French countryside and in the rich heritage handed down from generation to generation of wine producers. When a bottle of French wine is outstanding, it's more than great wine: It is history, tradition, and culture in a bottle.

Three wine regions of France particularly excel at producing superb red wine:

  ✔ Bordeaux, in the west

  ✔ Burgundy, in eastern France

  ✔ The Rhône Valley, in southern France

Bordeaux is the largest of the three — which is fortunate for Bordeaux wine lovers. You may read some articles suggesting that Bordeaux wines are scarce and expensive, but that's true only for the most sought-after Bordeaux wines. Plenty of good — even great — Bordeaux is still available at all price levels.

Good Burgundy, on the other hand, does have a problem with availability. If you don't consider Beaujolais (which is technically a part of Burgundy but is really a different kind of wine; see Chapter 1), Burgundy produces only about 25 percent as much wine as Bordeaux. As a result, most good red Burgundies (the wines from the best producers) are expensive and difficult to obtain. In this section, we recommend some of our favorite red Burgundy wines that are more readily available and not exorbitant in price.

Red is definitely the dominant color throughout the Rhône Valley's wine districts. In general, even the best wines from the Rhône, with a few exceptions, are more readily available than those of Bordeaux or Burgundy, and their prices do not reach the outrageously high levels of the two more famous regions.

For more information on French red wines, see Chapter 1.

Bordeaux classics

The best Bordeaux wines have the capacity to age for decades. In general, the average life span of good Bordeaux wines from good vintages ranges from 20 to 50 years — and often, the wines don't even begin to evolve toward maturity until they are 10 to 15 years old. Because winemaking practices have changed somewhat over the years, young red Bordeaux wines are generally easier to enjoy today than they used to be. But the young wines are still mere shadows of the ultimate wine, lacking the amazing complexity of flavor that develops slowly in the bottle.

You can consume better Bordeaux wines from less-good vintages (such as 1984, 1987, or 1992) while they're young — that is, from the time they are released at 2 or 3 years of age until they are about 12 years old, depending on the wine and the particular vintage. The sidebar "Rating recent Bordeaux vintages" indicates the quality of recent vintages and gives a drinkability rating for the wines of each year.

Bordeaux styles range from soft and easy-drinking to austere, tannic, and concentrated, depending on the year the grapes were grown, the district in Bordeaux from which the grapes come, and the quality level of the finished wine. The typical, mid-range Bordeaux wine is medium bodied, dry, and fairly austere, with complex but subdued aromas and flavors of black currants, cassis, herbs, plums, vegetation, and cedar. It's reserved and subtle in style rather than effusively flavorful.

Rating recent Bordeaux vintages

Bordeaux is a large wine region. The two major districts on the Left Bank of the Gironde River, the Médoc and the Graves, have somewhat different climates than the districts on the Right Bank of the river (such as St.-Emilion and Pomerol), and the quality of the wine in a given year can sometimes vary from one side of the river to the other. Therefore, we sometimes give two different ratings for a vintage, according to the area. Check the key below the chart for an interpretation of the ratings.

Please do keep in mind that all vintage charts are only rough guides, providing general, average ratings of a vintage in a particular region. Some wines will always be an exception to the rating; for example, a few outstanding wine producers often find a way to make a good wine in a so-called poor vintage.

The ratings below cover the Bordeaux vintages, 1981–1995. For a more complete vintage chart, see Appendix D in *Red Wine For Dummies*.

Vintage	Médoc, Graves	St.-Emilion, Pomerol
1995	90+a	90+a
1994	90 a	90 a
1993	85−a	85−a
1992	75 c	75 c
1991	75 b	65 c
1990	95 a	95+a
1989	90 b	90 b
1988	85 a	85 a
1987	75 c	75 d

Vintage	Médoc, Graves	St.-Emilion, Pomerol
1986	90+a	85 b
1985	90 c	85 c
1984	70 d	65 d
1983	85 b	85+b
1982	95+b	95 b
1981	80 c	80 c

Key:

100 = Outstanding	a = Too young to drink
95 = Excellent	b = May be consumed now, but will improve with time
90 = Very good	
85 = Good	c = Ready to drink
80 = Fairly good	d = May be too old
75 = Average	+ = Even better than the number suggests
70 = Below average	− = Somewhat weaker vintage than the number suggests
65 = Poor	
50–60 = Very poor	

The following recommendations of $15 to $50 Bordeaux, listed alphabetically by producer, focus particularly on red Bordeaux wines in the $15 to $25 price range. These moderately priced Bordeaux wines are trickier to buy than the more expensive ones. After all, you don't have to be a genius to buy the famous-name, over-$25 Bordeaux wines; every wine retailer knows them and can point them out to you. (In case you really want to splurge, we conclude this section with a sidebar called "Recommended Bordeaux wines over $50.")

For more information about Bordeaux wines, see Chapter 1 of this book, Chapters 4 and 10 of *Red Wine For Dummies,* and Chapter 10 of *Wine For Dummies.*

Château l'Arrosée

> ✦ **Producer:** Château l'Arrosée *(lahr ro zay)*
> ✦ **Wine name:** Château l'Arrosée
> ✦ **Appellation:** St.-Emilion
> ✦ **Price:** $30

Château l'Arrosée is the Bordeaux for Burgundy lovers. It has the delicious cherry fruit flavor, soft tannins, and velvety texture more typical of red Burgundies than of Bordeaux wines. Its sweet, delectable, ripe fruitiness usually makes it irresistible to drink, even when the vintage is very recent. The 1993 rendition is typical l'Arrosée, with its dense, wonderfully rich aromas; flavors of oak, red fruits, and earth; and its soft, supple approachability that almost says to you, "Drink me now!" But it also does have enough depth and complexity to age well. (The wine from the 1994 vintage, in contrast, is unusually austere and powerful for this property; it will need at least five more years of aging.)

Ed: 90–92   **Mary:** 89–91

Château Clerc-Milon

> ✦ **Producer:** Château Clerc-Milon, of Baron Philippe de Rothschild
> ✦ **Wine name:** Château Clerc-Milon *(clair mee lohn)*
> ✦ **Appellation:** Pauillac
> ✦ **Price:** $28

We must confess that we have a special weakness for Bordeaux wines from the commune of Pauillac, which typically produces powerful and full-bodied Bordeaux with cedar and black currant aromas. The little-known Château Clerc-Milon, a Pauillac property adjacent to Mouton-Rothschild and owned by the same family, is one of our favorite Bordeaux wines. The 1994 Clerc-Milon is medium to full bodied, with rich, spicy, cedary aromas and black currant flavors. This wine will develop and become more complex with another ten or more years of aging.

Ed: 87–89   **Mary:** 87–89

Château La Dominique

> ! **Producer:** Château La Dominique
> ! **Wine name:** Château La Dominique
> ! **Appellation:** St.-Emilion
> ! **Price:** $35

We've been fans of Château La Dominique for many years because this estate has always been just what we want in an everyday Bordeaux — a soft, easy-drinking, well-made wine at a reasonable price. Unfortunately, La Dominique is no longer the tremendous bargain that it used to be. (Wasn't it only yesterday that it sold for $15 to $18?) The 1994 La Dominique, with about 75 percent Merlot in the blend, is tannic but well balanced, with some new-oak aromas and flavors of cassis, plum, and black currants. Its excellent concentration suggests that, even though you can enjoy the wine now, perhaps with roast beef, it will continue to develop for at least another five years.

Ed: 88–90   **Mary:** 87–89

Château Faugères

> ! **Producer:** Château Faugères of C & P Guisez
> ! **Wine name:** Château Faugères
> ! **Appellation:** St.-Emilion
> ! **Price:** $18

In Chapter 1, we recommend Château Cap de Faugères — a less expensive Bordeaux from the same couple who own Château Faugères. By contrast, this Bordeaux (simply called Château Faugères) is the family's best wine. The 1994 version has cedar and oak aromas and full, broad, cedary flavors. It's an old-style wine — tannic and solid — but with fleshy fruit to round it out. Have this substantial wine with a steak or other hearty entrée.

Ed: 87–89

Château Fourcas Hosten

> ! **Producer:** Château Fourcas Hosten
> ! **Wine name:** Château Fourcas Hosten
> ! **Appellation:** Listrac
> ! **Price:** $18

The 1994 Château Fourcas Hosten may be the best wine we've ever tasted from this property. Fourcas Hosten has undergone a steady improvement during the last decade, culminating in the 1994 wine. It has the classic Bordeaux lead-pencil aroma, as well as the scent of ripe fruit. This wine is concentrated, tannic, firm, and intense — a well-balanced, full-throttle wine, quite powerful and young right now. It really needs some time to tame down. Hold on to this very good Bordeaux until 2002 or 2004 before enjoying it. We look forward to good things from this château in the future.

Ed: 88–90   **Mary:** 88–90

Château Grand-Puy-Lacoste

> ! **Producer:** Château Grand-Puy-Lacoste, of Jean-Eugène Borie
> ! **Wine name:** Château Grand-Puy-Lacoste
> ! **Appellation:** Pauillac
> ! **Price:** $28

The Grand-Puy-Lacoste estate, owned since 1978 by Jean-Eugène Borie (proprietor of the renowned Château Ducru-Beaucaillou) and managed by his son, Xavier Borie, produces classic Pauillac. Its medium- to full-bodied, tannic, powerful wines are 70 percent Cabernet Sauvignon and are often surprisingly drinkable when young, but they also can easily age well for 20 or more years in good vintages. The 1994 Grand-Puy-Lacoste is a beauty, with classic lead-pencil and cassis aromas and flavors. It has plenty of tannin and rich, concentrated fruit characteristics. In our opinion, the 1994 Grand-Puy-Lacoste is the best wine from this estate since the great 1986 Grand-Puy-Lacoste. We'd hold on to this one.

Ed: 88–90   **Mary:** 86–88

Château Gruaud-Larose

> ♪ **Producer:** Château Gruaud-Larose, of Domaines Cordier
>
> ♪ **Wine name:** Château Gruaud-Larose *(groo ode lah rose)*
>
> ♪ **Appellation:** St.-Julien
>
> ♪ **Price:** $35.50

Château Gruaud-Larose has been one of the most consistent performers in Bordeaux over the past 20 years. The wine of this château is always dense, chunky, and tannic and typically needs some time to evolve. But the 1993 Gruaud-Larose is attractively drinkable now. It's a rich, intense wine with aromas and flavors of ripe black fruit, tobacco, and earth. Medium bodied, chewy, and complex, this wine has excellent concentration and a long, delicious finish. It's unusually precocious for this property, a wine to drink within the next three or four years, perhaps with lamb chops or other simple red meat.

Ed: 89–91   **Mary:** 87–89

Château Haut-Beauséjour

> ♪ **Producer:** Château Haut-Beauséjour, of Champagne Louis Roederer
>
> ♪ **Wine name:** Château Haut-Beauséjour *(oh boh say jhor)*
>
> ♪ **Appellation:** St.-Estèphe
>
> ♪ **Price:** $21

Just five years ago, the great Champagne house of Roederer purchased Château Haut-Beauséjour, located in the commune of St.-Estèphe in the Médoc district. The improved quality of the wine is already evident, especially in the 1994 vintage. The 1994 Haut-Beauséjour is a classic Bordeaux of the St.-Estèphe commune — the wines of St.-Estèphe being typically robust and tannic and sometimes a bit rustic in style. In the 1994 vintage, this wine has lots of concentrated, packed fruit character and will even be better if you can keep it for a few more years, so that some of the tannins can soften. For me, this wine is a winner, but keep in mind that I do love the sturdy Bordeaux style of St.-Estèphe wines.

Ed: 90–92

Château Lagrange

> ! **Producer:** Château Lagrange, of Suntory Corporation
> ! **Wine name:** Château Lagrange
> ! **Appellation:** St.-Julien
> ! **Price:** $25

Now is the time to buy Château Lagrange! The 1994 Lagrange has aromas of intense black-cherry fruit and new oak, with touches of chocolate, smoke, dill, and tobacco. It's medium bodied, with spicy, plump, ripe fruit flavors. The wine is quite tannic, but smooth, with very good concentration; you can see real depth and the trademark elegance of a St.-Julien-style Bordeaux shining through the oak. Hold on to this wine for at least five years. Lagrange's second wine, Les Fiefs de Lagrange (see the "Great seconds in Bordeaux" sidebar), was also very good in 1994 and 1993, and is ready to drink; it sells in the $15 to $17 price range.

Ed: 88–90   **Mary:** 87–89

Château La Tour-Haut-Brion

> ! **Producer:** Château La Tour-Haut-Brion, of Domaines Clarence Dillon
> ! **Wine name:** Château La Tour-Haut-Brion
> ! **Appellation:** Pessac-Léognan
> ! **Price:** $31

The Dillon family, the American owners of the great wine estates Château Haut-Brion and Château La Mission-Haut-Brion, both in the Pessac-Léognan subdistrict of Graves, also own the lesser-known Château La Tour-Haut-Brion. The 1994 La Tour-Haut-Brion has the characteristic Graves aromas of tobacco, smokiness, and coffee, along with earthy, deeply fruity, tobacco-like flavors. This rich, well-balanced Bordeaux has moderate enough tannins that you can enjoy the wine now, with a chunk of aged Gouda cheese and some crusty bread. If you choose to hold on to this wine, it will have no problem aging and developing for another 12 to 15 years.

Ed: 88–90   **Mary:** 88–90

Château Léoville-Barton

> ♪ **Producer:** Château Léoville-Barton, of Anthony Barton
>
> ♪ **Wine name:** Château Léoville-Barton *(leh oh veel bar tohn)*
>
> ♪ **Appellation:** St.-Julien
>
> ♪ **Price:** $38

Château Léoville-Barton has been a well-kept secret among Bordeaux lovers. While the winery's famous neighbor, Château Léoville-Las Cases, got all the attention, Léoville-Barton quietly made really fine Bordeaux and sold it in the $20 to $25 range. But the wine of Léoville-Barton has been so darn good lately that the inevitable has happened: The price is now about $38, and it's only going to get higher.

The 1994 Léoville-Barton has herbal, spicy, cedary aromas and is packed with concentrated, ripe cassis fruit flavor along with a touch of new oak. With at least 70 percent Cabernet Sauvignon in the blend, Léoville-Barton has the tannin and depth of a long-lived Bordeaux, perhaps more like a power-house Pauillac than a wine from St.-Julien. Buy this wine for your cellar and let it develop for 10 to 15 years. Who knows what its price will be by then!

Ed: 89–91   **Mary:** 89–91

Château Léoville-Poyferré

> ♪ **Producer:** Château Léoville-Poyferré *(leh oh veel p'wah feh ray)*
>
> ♪ **Wine name:** Château Léoville-Poyferré
>
> ♪ **Appellation:** St.-Julien
>
> ♪ **Price:** $28

Of the three St.-Julien estates whose names begin with the word "Léoville" (all once part of the same property 200 years ago), Poyferré had been the least consistent in quality. A couple of great wines in the early '80s (1982 and 1983) were followed by several ho-hum efforts throughout the '80s and early '90s. With the assistance of consulting *enologist* (wine technologist) Michel Rolland, the 1994 Léoville-Poyferré seems to have recaptured the estate's glory of the pre-World War II years. And fortunately, its price is reasonable. The wine has spicy oak, lead-pencil, and black currant aromas and flavors and is well balanced, with a firm tannic structure and rich, concentrated fruit character. Right now, the Poyferré is one of the few great classified growths from the Haut-Médoc that's still under $30 — but not for long! Preliminary reports suggest that the 1995 and 1996 Léoville-Poyferré will be even better (but at higher prices). Give the 1994 vintage a few years to develop.

Ed: 87–89   **Mary:** 87–89

The mad cost of 1995 and 1996 Bordeaux

Most of the prices in this section apply to Bordeaux wines of the 1994 vintage, the vintage that became available in 1997, and which is perhaps the last reasonably priced Bordeaux vintage. Judging by advertised prices for future purchases of 1995 and 1996 Bordeaux (which will be available in 1998 and 1999, respectively), wine drinkers will pay anywhere from 20 to 50 percent higher prices for the most sought-after 1995 Bordeaux, and 20 to 30 percent more for the 1996 wines than for the 1995 wines!

What has caused this madness? One reason is that preliminary reports indicate that both 1995 and 1996 are excellent vintages, the best since the great 1990 vintage. Another reason is that more wealthy buyers throughout the world, especially in new markets such as Asia and South America, seem to have emerged over the last few years, creating a demand for the most highly regarded Bordeaux and driving up the prices.

Our advice to you, if you enjoy good Bordeaux, is to buy some 1993 wines for current and near-term drinking and, especially, to buy some 1994 wines, a very good vintage, for laying away. Most of the better 1994 Bordeaux wines will benefit from ten or more years of aging (from their birth, in late 1994) to soften and develop. The best 1995 and 1996 Bordeaux wines will be not only extravagantly expensive but also difficult to obtain, judging by the current demand for them. The wines of some of the smaller properties in Pomerol have sold out already! We Bordeaux lovers are living in a "mad" time. Who knows when this Bordeaux buying frenzy will end?

Château Lynch-Bages

> ♪ **Producer:** Château Lynch-Bages, of Jean-Michel Cazes
> ♪ **Wine name:** Château Lynch-Bages *(lansh bahj)*
> ♪ **Appellation:** Pauillac
> ♪ **Price:** $42

Lynch-Bages has always been one of our favorite wines in Bordeaux. The 1994 Lynch-Bages is surprisingly forward for the vintage. It has spicy oak and ripe black currant aromas and flavors. The sweet, ripe, fleshy fruit character — in the typically rich style that we've seen from this château since the magnificent 1982 vintage — makes the wine easy to enjoy right now. Although you can surely drink the 1994 Lynch-Bages now, you can also cellar it if you wish. Judging by its past vintages, this well-structured Pauillac has no problem aging well for 15 to 20 years.

Ed: 88–90   **Mary:** 87–89

Château Montrose

> ♪ **Producer:** Château Montrose, of Jean-Louis Charmolüe
> ♪ **Wine name:** Château Montrose *(mohn't rose)*
> ♪ **Appellation:** St.-Estèphe
> ♪ **Price:** $40

We like Château Montrose because it's the classically styled St.-Estèphe Bordeaux — firm, earthy, intensely flavored, slow to mature, and lasting for decades. Montrose is not a Bordeaux for the faint-hearted. It typically is hard and austere in its youth, with plenty of tannin and extract. You need some roast beef or hard cheese, such as cheddar, to tame it down. But if you choose to cellar it, Montrose will reward you by aging beautifully. The 1994 Montrose has inky, spicy, rich, concentrated black currant and coffee aromas and flavors, with ripe tannins. The ripe fruit flavors will satisfy you if you drink the wine soon, but the wine's balance and depth ensure it a life of 20-plus years. The 1994 Montrose, unfortunately, may be the last wine from this property selling for under $50. The 1995 Château Montrose, possibly, and surely the 1996 vintage will break the $50 barrier.

Ed: 91–93   **Mary:** 90–92

Where have all the Pomerols gone?

Pomerols have been called the "Burgundies of Bordeaux" because their style — soft, luscious, round, and approachable — rather resembles red Burgundy wine. Most Pomerols have 75 to 80 percent Merlot (a soft, accessible wine) in their blends; the famous Château Pétrus is always at least 95 percent Merlot. Like Burgundian properties, most Pomerol wineries are very small, producing only a few thousand cases of wine annually. And like good Burgundies, good-quality Pomerols are always in demand, scarce, and expensive. We do mention four very fine Pomerols in our "Recommended Bordeaux wines over $50" sidebar, but even there, we limit our Pomerol recommendations because some are so high priced; for example, Châteaux Pétrus and Le Pin (pronounced *pan*) are in the $400 to $600 price range — per bottle, that is!

Yes, we do like Pomerols. But we're not reviewing many Pomerols in this book, because we don't want to frustrate you by recommending wines that are almost impossible to obtain or that don't represent good value.

Château de Moulin Rouge

- *?* **Producer:** Château de Moulin Rouge, of Pelon-Ribiero
- *?* **Wine name:** Château de Moulin Rouge
- *?* **Appellation:** Haut-Médoc
- *?* **Price:** $16

Bordeaux wines from the 1995 vintage are setting records for their high prices. But here's a 1995 Bordeaux that won't break the bank. Château Moulin Rouge is located just south of the St.-Julien district, and so you have a wine that resembles the more renowned St.-Julien wines, but at a lower price. We have seldom enjoyed a young Bordeaux at this price level as much as this one. The 1995 version has aromas of mint, wood, and fresh linen (a very clean wine!). It's a tannic, intensely flavored wine with lots of concentration and density. This solid wine is very young; we suggest that you hold on to it for at least a few years so that it can develop and soften.

Ed: 89–91

Mary: 88–90

Château Pichon-Baron

> *✦* **Producer:** Château Pichon-Longueville Baron, of AXA Millésimes
>
> *✦* **Wine name:** Château Pichon-Longueville Baron
>
> *✦* **Appellation:** Pauillac
>
> *✦* **Price:** $38

Château Pichon-Baron, as this wine is usually called, is a richly flavored, ripe, full-bodied, rather approachable Pauillac, about 75 percent Cabernet Sauvignon and 25 percent Merlot, much like Lynch-Bages — in style and grape varieties. (This property is run by the owner of Château Lynch-Bages.) Pichon-Baron differs from Lynch-Bages in weight; Pichon-Baron is the more powerful of the two.

The 1994 Pichon-Baron has spicy oak and cedary aromas, along with sweet cassis fruit flavors. It's a solid wine with some tannin and ripe fruit character. You can enjoy this wine right now, but it has enough depth and concentration to ensure its development for at least another 15 years.

Ed: 94–96   **Mary:** 90–92

Château Plince

> *✦* **Producer:** Château Plince, distributed by Jean-Pierre Moueix
>
> *✦* **Wine name:** Château Plince *(plahntz)*
>
> *✦* **Appellation:** Pomerol
>
> *✦* **Price:** $18

The scarcity of good Pomerols, plus their innate quality, has made them, on average, the most expensive Bordeaux wines of all: Very few decent Pomerols sell for under $20. Château Plince, distributed by the Moueix firm, is one of the few good inexpensive Pomerols. In the 1993 vintage, this wine has mild, inky, cedary aromas and smooth, supple texture. It's well balanced: soft and fleshy and yet crisp with acidity and moderate tannin. A light- to medium-bodied Bordeaux, it's a good choice to drink now.

Ed: 84–86   **Mary:** 87–89

Château Pontet-Canet

- ✦ **Producer:** Château Pontet-Canet, of Guy and Alfred Tesseron
- ✦ **Wine name:** Château Pontet-Canet
- ✦ **Appellation:** Pauillac
- ✦ **Price:** $25

Château Pontet-Canet is one of the real surprises in Bordeaux today. This rather large wine estate made "okay" wines for years. But owners Guy and Alfred Tesseron, father and son, recently decided to upgrade quality and, judging by the 1994 Pontet-Canet, have succeeded admirably. (And note that the price, fortunately, has not caught up with the quality yet.) The only other Pontet-Canet wines we've ever had that compare in quality to the 1994 wine. came from two great vintages — 1945 and 1961. The 1994 Pontet-Canet has incredibly dense, packed aromas and flavors of sweet, ripe black currants and new oak. This is a big, full-bodied, tannic, chunky blockbuster of a wine that will benefit from at least another 10 to 15 years of development. The 1994 Château Pontet-Canet reminds us why we love the Bordeaux wines of Pauillac.

Ed: 89–91   **Mary:** 87–89

Château de Clairefont

- ✦ **Producer:** Château Prieuré-Lichine
- ✦ **Wine name:** Château de Clairefont
- ✦ **Appellation:** Margaux
- ✦ **Price:** $17.50

The price of Château Prieuré-Lichine, a wine from the Margaux district, has risen to almost $30. Fortunately, the estate's "second" wine, Château de Clairfont, is almost on the level of the classified growth Prieuré-Lichine. (See the sidebars "Classified Bordeaux" and "Great seconds in Bordeaux" for explanations of *classified growth* and *second wine*.) As is the case with most second wines, the 1994 Château de

Clairefont has the advantage of being less tannic and readier to drink than the property's main wine. Very dark in color, the wine has cedary aromas and excellent concentration of fruit flavors. This is a serious mouthful of wine, with lots of depth and very high class at this price range. It's clearly the finest de Clairefont I've tasted since the wine's inception in 1979. I recommend it highly.

Ed: 90–92

Great seconds in Bordeaux

Many Bordeaux wine estates make a "second" wine. *Second wines* are usually wines made from grapes of an estate's younger vines, or they're wines that have just not made the final cut for the property's primary wine. Because the grapes for these second wines do come from the estate and the wines are made by the same winemaking team as the estate's first wines are, the second wines can give you a clear idea of the primary wine's style — as well as provide an excellent wine at a good price. A good second wine from a top Bordeaux estate is one of the great bargains of the region.

In our opinion, the five second wines listed here are not only Bordeaux's best seconds but also some of the best wines in Bordeaux. These wines all sell in the $25 to $35 price range — less than half (and in some cases, one-third) the price of the first, or primary, wine. They all warrant at least 87-90 points on our scale of preference:

Second Wine	Primary Wine	Appellation
Bahans-Haut-Brion	Château Haut-Brion	Pessac-Léognan
Carruades de Lafite	Château Lafite-Rothschild	Pauillac
Clos du Marquis	Château Léoville-Las Cases	St.-Julien
Les Forts de Latour	Château Latour	Pauillac
Pavillon de Château Margaux	Château Margaux	Margaux

"Classified" Bordeaux (authorized readers only)

Various phrases appear on the labels of some Bordeaux wines (especially those that cost over $15). Examples of such phrases are "Grand Cru Classé," "Premier Grand Cru Classé," "Cru Classé en 1855," "Cru Classé de Graves," "St-Emilion Grand Cru Classé," and "Cru Bourgeois." These phrases relate to the fact that three of the four major Bordeaux red-wine districts — the Médoc, Graves, and St.-Emilion — have classified the wines they produce into various categories of excellence. (Pomerol is the only major Bordeaux district without a classification system.) Bordeaux wines that have received such a classification are entitled to put that information on their labels — although not all of them do so. Wines with higher classification are known as Classified Growths; some lower classified wines are known as a Cru Bourgeois and are not considered classified growths. The words *growth* or *cru,* in Bordeaux-talk, mean "wine estate."

The classification of wines took place at different times for different districts of Bordeaux. The most famous classification, in 1855, was basically a Médoc classification for red wines; 61 wines (including one from the Graves district) were placed into five different categories. Today, these wines are still referred to as First Growths (the highest category), Second Growths, Third Growths, and so forth.

Of the more than 8,000 wine estates in Bordeaux, only about 600 have been singled out for a classification of merit. The relative scarcity of such classifications makes even the lowest of the rankings, such as "Cru Bourgeois" in the Médoc or "St.-Emilion Grand Cru" in St.-Emilion ("St.-Emilion Grand Cru Classé" is a higher category), quite an honor and distinction for the estates so recognized. For more information on the Bordeaux classifications (including a listing of the entire 1855 Classification), see Chapter 10 and Appendix A in *Wine For Dummies* and Chapter 10 in *Red Wine For Dummies*.

Château Rauzan-Ségla

- ***!*** **Producer:** Château Rauzan-Ségla
- ***!*** **Wine name:** Château Rauzan-Ségla
- ***!*** **Appellation:** Margaux
- ***!*** **Price:** $43

Château Rauzan-Ségla, one of the three great wine estates in Margaux (Château Margaux and Château Palmer are the others), is making great wines again after many years — decades, really — of serious underachievement prior to 1983. But rebuilding a reputation takes time. Wine lovers have only slowly caught on to the fact that Rauzan-Ségla has indeed returned to its former greatness. When the secret is totally out, we fear that the wine's price will zoom over $50. The 1994 Rauzan-Ségla (ranked second only to Château Pichon-Lalande at a recent blind tasting of 1994 Bordeaux wines at New York's International Wine Center) has aromas of spice, new oak, and tobacco, along with ripe, plump, black currant flavors. It's a rich, concentrated, tannic wine that, despite its intense flavors, has a smooth, supple quality, a characteristic of the Margaux commune. Hold on to the 1994 Rauzan-Ségla for at least another ten years so that it can soften and develop further.

Ed: 89–91   **Mary:** 88–90

Château Troplong-Mondot

- **Producer:** Château Troplong-Mondot, of Claude Valette and Christine Fabre-Valette
- **Wine name:** Château Troplong-Mondot *(troh lohn mohn doh)*
- **Appellation:** St.-Emilion
- **Price:** $48

I know that we're pushing the under-$50 envelope with the 1994 Troplong-Mondot — and the 1995 and 1996 vintages will surely break $50. But I'm convinced that Troplong-Mondot is not only the most improved wine estate in St.-Emilion, but one of the most improved in all of Bordeaux. The 1990 wine from this estate was one of the true stars of that great vintage, and the 1994 version is another success. The 1994 Troplong-Mondot has concentrated aromas and flavors of black fruit and new oak, with a distinct touch of licorice, which was also present in the fabulous 1990 wine. It's a rich, tannic St.-Emilion — very full bodied for this appellation. I highly recommend this wine, which really will benefit with another eight to ten years of cellaring.

Ed: 90–92

Recommended Bordeaux wines over $50

Expensive Bordeaux wines are among the greatest wines in the world. We list 15 outstanding but expensive (more than $50 a bottle) Bordeaux wines, without comment or score. They are all excellent wines and good values, considering their quality. Remember that we use New York State suggested retail prices; in some cases, if you shop around, you may be able to buy some of these wines at lower prices. Naturally, prices also vary from vintage to vintage, going up in the best years and dropping in less-good vintages.

We omit wines that we consider either too expensive or too difficult to obtain. This includes many Bordeaux wines from the Pomerol district, such as Châteaux Petrus, Lafleur, and Le Pin, and a few from St.-Emilion, such as Châteaux Ausone, l'Angélus, and Valandraud. The following wines are listed alphabetically.

Château	*Appellation*
Château Certan de May	Pomerol
Château Cheval Blanc	St.-Emilion
Château La Conseillante	Pomerol
Château Ducru Beaucaillou	St.-Julien
Château L'Evangile	Pomerol
Château Haut-Brion	Pessac-Léognan
Château Lafite-Rothschild	Pauillac
Château Latour	Pauillac
Château Léoville-Las Cases	St.-Julien
Château Margaux	Margaux
Château La Mission Haut-Brion	Pessac-Léognan
Château Mouton-Rothschild	Pauillac
Château Palmer	Margaux
Château Pichon-Lalande	Pauillac
Château Trotanoy	Pomerol

Vieux Château Gaubert Rouge

> - **Producer:** Vieux Château Gaubert
>   *(vee uh sha toh go bare)*
> - **Wine name:** Vieux Château Gaubert Rouge
> - **Appellation:** Graves
> - **Price:** $17

Many properties in the Graves district (directly south of the city of Bordeaux) make a Rouge as well as a Blanc wine. Vieux Château Gaubert is one such property. The 1994 Rouge has oaky, sweet, vanilla aromas, as well as flavors of plummy fruit and intense oak. This well-made wine has quite a bit of tannin and considerable depth — a sophisticated wine that's a good buy in this price range. Hold on to it for a few years so that its tannins can soften.

Ed: 84–86   **Mary:** 87–89

Burgundy's red beauties

We never understand those wine lovers who profess a love for the wines of Bordeaux *only* or for the wines of Burgundy *only;* we love both types of wine. Sure, they're vastly different wines: For starters, red Bordeaux is made mainly from Cabernet Sauvignon and Merlot grapes, whereas red Burgundy derives 100 percent from the Pinot Noir grape. Bordeaux tends to be subtle and restrained in its flavors and austere in texture; Burgundy is typically more flavorful, softer in texture, and more approachable. But both wines rank among the world's great, classic types of red wine. (We'd throw in some wines from Piedmont and Tuscany, as well, to complete the picture.)

The major problem that wine drinkers encounter in the pursuit of fine red Burgundies is that many of the finest wines are made in tiny quantities. Those wines are not only very expensive but also almost impossible to obtain by all but a few Burgundy cult devotees, who scoop them up as soon as the wines appear on the market. In Burgundy much more than in Bordeaux, a high percentage of the finest wines cost over $50 per bottle in wine shops.

In this section, we recommend some of our favorite red Burgundy wines that are generally available and also one Beaujolais wine, all of which are in the $15 to $50 price range. We list them alphabetically by producer. In a sidebar, we name the most consistently reliable Burgundy producers. Remember, the producer's name is *the* most important information for you to know when you select a Burgundy, more so than the wine's appellation or even the vintage. For more specific information on red Burgundy wines, see Chapter 10 in *Wine For Dummies* and Chapters 4 and 11 in *Red Wine For Dummies*.

Rating recent red Burgundy vintages

Between the Pinot Noir grape variety — the most fickle, difficult, fine wine grape in the world — and the variable climate in Burgundy, vintages do differ in Burgundy. In fact, the quality of the vintage is an extremely significant gauge of quality for a red Burgundy wine — second in importance only to the name of the producer. (See the sidebar "Great Burgundy producers" in this chapter.) Because some climate variation exists between the more northerly Côte de Nuits area and the Côte de Beaune area, we give vintage ratings for both subdistricts of the Côte d'Or. Vintage quality in the Côte Chalonnaise district tends to be similar to that of the Côte de Beaune, directly to its north; Beaujolais, the southernmost district of Burgundy, has less variation among vintages.

To interpret our vintage ratings, check the key below the chart. And please keep in mind that vintage charts are only a rough guide, providing a general, average rating of the vintage in a particular region. Some wines will always be an exception to the vintage rating; for example, a few outstanding wine producers often have the ability to make good wine even in a generally poor vintage. This exception is particularly true in the Burgundy region.

The following ratings cover the red Burgundy vintages from 1985 to 1995. For a more complete vintage chart, see Appendix D in *Red Wine For Dummies*.

Vintage	Côte de Nuits	Côte de Beaune
1995	90– a	90– a
1994	80+b	80+ b
1993	85+ a	85+ a
1992	75 b	80– b

Vintage	Côte de Nuits	Côte de Beaune
1991	85 b	70 c
1990	95–b	90 b
1989	85 b	85 b
1988	85– c	85– c
1987	85 c	80 d
1986	75–d	70 d
1985	85– c	85– c

Key:

100 = Outstanding

95 = Excellent

90 = Very good

85 = Good

80 = Fairly good

75 = Average

70 = Below average

65 = Poor

50–60 = Very poor

a = Too young to drink

b = May be consumed now, but will improve with time

c = Ready to drink

d = May be too old

+ = Quality higher than the number indicates

– = Slightly lower quality than the number indicates

Côtes de Nuits-Villages, Bertrand Ambroise

- ❢ **Producer:** Bertrand Ambroise
- ❢ **Wine name:** Côtes de Nuits-Villages
- ❢ **Appellation:** Côtes de Nuits-Villages
- ❢ **Price:** $24

Bertrand Ambroise is one of the bright, young producers in the Nuits St.-Georges area. In addition to his more expensive Burgundies, Ambroise makes a good Vieilles Vignes (old-vine) Bourgogne Rouge, about $15.50, and this Côtes de Nuits-Villages wine, made from 40-year-old vines. Wines labeled *Côtes de Nuits Villages* must come from certain designated villages in the Côtes de Nuits area; such Burgundies are a definite step up in quality from Bourgogne Rouge wines (which can come from anywhere in the Burgundy region), especially in the hands of a fine producer such as Ambroise.

His 1995 Côtes de Nuits-Villages has a tart red-fruit aroma with some oak, and concentrated red- and black-fruit flavors. It's a big, rich Burgundy, with pure, focused fruit character and a dry, tannic finish. Give this 1995 Côtes de Nuits-Villages a little time; it'll be awesome in two or three years.

Ed: 87–89   **Mary:** 89–91

Nuits St.-Georges Clos des Forets St.-Georges, Domaine de L'Arlot

- *? **Producer:*** Domaine de L'Arlot
- *? **Wine name:*** Nuits St.-Georges, Clos des Forets St.-Georges
- *? **Appellation:*** Nuits St.-Georges Premier Cru
- *? **Price:*** $32.50

Domaine de L'Arlot is a relatively young firm, compared with many wine producers in Burgundy, but it has established a solid reputation as a producer of stylish, elegant, well-balanced wines. The 1994 Nuits St.-Georges from the premier cru vineyard, Clos des Forets St.-Georges, has a wonderful intensity of bright cherry fruit in its aroma. Its flavor is still closed up tight, but not so tight that we can't detect fresh, raspberry fruit, good concentration, and spiciness — the latter characteristic a trademark of this house. This wine won't have any trouble lasting and improving for several years, provided that you store it properly.

Ed: 89–91   **Mary:** 89–91

Chambolle-Musigny Les Plantes, Domaine Bertagna

- *? **Producer:*** Domaine Bertagna
- *? **Wine name:*** Chambolle-Musigny Les Plantes
- *? **Appellation:*** Chambolle-Musigny Premier Cru
- *? **Price:*** $45

At a recent tasting of Domaine Bertagna's Burgundies, we were impressed with this estate's entire line, especially a 1993 Clos St. Denis grand cru (in the $65 to $70 price range) and this 1993 Chambolle-Musigny premier cru. The 1993 Les Plantes is a celestial Burgundy. It has wonderfully concentrated aromas of black fruits and intense black licorice, along with intense black-fruit flavors. It is quintessential

. Chambolle-Musigny Burgundy — elegant, silky, and lacy. It's not the fullest or richest Burgundy, but irresistibly soft and pretty. You can enjoy this outstanding wine now or save it for a few years.

Ed: 90–92   **Mary:** 91–93

Côtes de Nuits-Villages, Domaine Jean-Jacques Confuron

- **Producer:** Domaine Jean-Jacques Confuron
- **Wine name:** Côtes de Nuits-Villages
- **Appellation:** Côtes de Nuits-Villages
- **Price:** $25

The daughter of the late Jean-Jacques Confuron, Sophie Confuron Meunier, and her husband, Alain Meunier, have brought this domaine back to the forefront of outstanding Burgundies. The 1995 Côtes de Nuits-Villages has fragrant, sweet red-cherry fruit aromas, with accents of oak and cola. Its delectable flavor melds ripe red fruits, black fruits, and spicy oak. It's very smooth, supple, and well balanced — ready to enjoy right now.

Ed: 84–86   **Mary:** 87–89

Fixin Clos Napoleon, Domaine Pierre Gelin

- **Producer:** Domaine Pierre Gelin
- **Wine name:** Fixin Clos Napoleon *(feec san)*
- **Appellation:** Fixin Premier Cru
- **Price:** $27

The wines of Fixin, the northernmost village in the Côte de Nuits, are generally sturdy Burgundies that need time in the bottle to develop. That generalization is particularly true for Gelin's wine. The very youthful aromas and flavors of the 1994 Clos Napoleon — exuberant scents of herbs, eucalyptus, and wild strawberries and the intense, bright flavors of eucalyptus and herbs — suggest that the wine is still in the early stages of its development. Medium bodied and fairly tannic, this promising Burgundy is a taut, tight wine that needs a few years to smooth out its rough edges.

Ed: 84–86   **Mary:** 86–88

Great Burgundy producers

Great Burgundy wines are made by great Burgundy producers. Unfortunately, most of these producers have small vineyard holdings and can make only very small quantities — in some instances, 50 cases or less — of each of their rare gems in any given year. Naturally, these Burgundies are expensive and scarce.

We list the following outstanding producers of Burgundy in alphabetical order, and we name a few of their best wines. Just about all these wines are over $50, and in many cases over $100, a bottle. Often, only a few wine stores that specialize in fine Burgundies will carry these wines. (For a list of a few such stores, see Chapter 16 in *Wine For Dummies*.)

Producer	*Producer's Best Wines*
Domaine Bertrand Ambroise	Clos de Vougeot; Corton Les Rognets; Nuits-St.-Georges Les Vaucrains
Domaine Marquis d'Angerville	Volnay Clos des Ducs; Volnay Champans
Domaine Bertagna	Vougeot Clos de la Perrière; Clos St. Denis; Chambertin
Domaine Alain Burguet	Gevrey-Chambertin Les Champeaux; Gevrey-Chambertin Vieilles Vignes
Domaine Robert Chevillon	Nuits-St.-Georges Les St.-Georges; Nuits-St.-Georges Les Vaucrains
Domaine des Chézeaux	Griotte-Chambertin; Clos St.-Denis Vieilles Vignes
Domaine Chopin-Groffier	Clos de Vougeot
Domaine Jean-Jacques Confuron	Romanée St.-Vivant; Clos de Vougeot; Nuits-St.-Georges Aux Boudots
Domaine Claude Dugat	Griotte-Chambertin; Charmes-Chambertin
Domaine Dujac	Clos de la Roche; Bonnes Mares
Domaine René Engel	Grands-Echézeaux; Clos de Vougeot
Domaine Anne Gros	Richebourg; Clos de Vougeot

Producer	Producer's Best Wines
Domaine Haegelen-Jayer	Clos de Vougeot Vieilles Vignes; Echézeaux
Louis Jadot	Musigny; Chambertin Clos de Bèze; Romanée St.-Vivant; Beaune Clos des Ursules
Domaine Robert Jayer-Gilles	Echézeaux; Nuits-St.-Georges Les Damodes
Domaine Michel Lafarge	Volnay Clos des Chènes; Beaune Les Grèves
Domaine Dominique Laurent	Chambertin; Mazis-Chambertin; Grands-Echézeaux; Musigny; Bonnes Mares
Domaine René Leclerc	Gevrey-Chambertin Combe aux Moine
Domaine Leroy	Richebourg; Romanée St.-Vivant; Chambertin; Musigny
Domaine Hubert Lignier	Clos de la Roche; Charmes-Chambertin; Gevrey-Chambertin Les Combottes
Domaine Maume	Mazis-Chambertin; Charmes-Chambertin
Domaine Méo-Camuzet	Richebourg; Clos de Vougeot; Corton; Vosne Romanée Les Brûlées
Domaine Mongeard-Mugneret	Grands-Echézeaux; Richebourg
Domaine Albert Morot	Beaune Les Grèves; Beaune Les Cent Vignes; Beaune Les Bressandes
Domaine Jacques-Fréderick Mugnier	Musigny; Bonnes Mares; Chambulle-Musigny Les Amoureses
Domaine André Mussy	Beaune Les Epenottes; Pommard Les Epenots
Domaine Ponsot	Clos de la Roche Vieilles Vignes; Latricières-Chambertin; Griotte-Chambertin; Chapelle-Chambertin

(continued)

(continued)

Producer	Producer's Best Wines
Domaine Daniel Rion	Vosne-Romanée Les Beaux Monts; Nuits-St.-Georges Clos des Argillières
Domaine de la Romanée-Conti	Romané-Conti; La Tache; Richebourg
Domaine Joseph Roty	Mazy-Chambertin; Griotte-Chambertin
Domaine Emmanuel Rouget	Vosne-Romanée Cros Parantoux; Echézeaux; Vosne-Romanée Les Beaux Monts
Domaine Georges et Christophe Roumier	Musigny; Chambolle-Musigny Les Amoureuses; Bonnes Mares
Domaine Armand Rousseau	Chambertin; Chambertin Clos de Bèze; Gevrey-Chambertin Clos St.-Jacques
Domaine Christian Serafin	Charmes-Chambertin; Gevrey-Chambertin Les Cazetiers; Gevrey-Chambertin Vieilles Vignes
Domaine Tollot-Beaut	Corton; Corton Les Bressandes; Beaune Les Grèves
Domaine Louis et J.L.Trapet	Chapelle-Chambertin; Chambertin; Latricières-Chambertin
Domaine du Comte Georges de Vogüé	Musigny Vieilles Vignes; Bonnes Mares; Chambolle-Musigny Les Amoureuses

Beaune Clos des Ursules, Louis Jadot

- ❧ **Producer:** Louis Jadot
- ❧ **Wine name:** Beaune Clos des Ursules
- ❧ **Appellation:** Beaune Premier Cru
- ❧ **Price:** $36

We can think of no other large Burgundy house that has such a huge lineup of fine red Burgundies as that of Louis Jadot. And the Jadot wines are generally well distributed in all major cities. One of this firm's not-so-secret weapons is its very talented, tradition-oriented winemaker, Jacques Lardière. Under Lardière's guidance, the red Burgundies of Louis Jadot have improved substantially during the last decade. The 1994 Beaune Clos des Ursules has dense aromas and flavors of mint, spice, black fruits, and new oak. After blind-tasting several unremarkable Burgundies, Ed noted of this wine, "Finally, a Burgundy with good depth and concentration; complex and well balanced." Right now, the 1994 Clos des Ursules is somewhat tannic and firm; its impressive finish promises a good life ahead. (The 1995 wine, in contrast, has real Beaune character now: It's silky and spicy and a bit less tough than the 1994.)

Ed: 90–92   **Mary:** 87–89

Pitfalls in purchasing red Burgundy

Red Burgundy wines are often subjected to the same kind of storage that other, sturdier red wines receive, often spending months in warehouses or the back rooms of retail stores that are not temperature-controlled. But the risks of bad storage are greater for red Burgundies. Sustained temperatures of over 70°F will slowly kill any wine; in the case of red Burgundy or any other Pinot Noir wines, the deleterious effects of heat occur more rapidly. Most Burgundies cannot tolerate weeks — let alone months — of storage in temperatures over 70°F. Ideally, they should be stored in a cool, damp place, about 55°F but certainly not warmer than 65°F.

Because Burgundy is fragile, you should be careful where you buy your Burgundy. Fine wine stores, with temperature-controlled facilities, are your best bet. (We recommend some stores in Chapter 16 of *Wine for Dummies*.) You may have to pay higher prices in such stores than you would in large discount outlets, but those few extra dollars are well spent if they assure you a sound bottle of wine. In our experience, red Burgundy wines from large Burgundy firms are particularly susceptible to bad storage because these wines — being more widely available to the trade than the wines of very small producers — move through warehouses, transportation systems, and retail storage rooms that are not specifically geared to protecting fragile Burgundies.

Vosne-Romanée Les Beaux Monts, Louis Jadot

- **Producer:** Louis Jadot
- **Wine name:** Vosne-Romanée Les Beaux Monts
  (*vone-roh mah nay lay bo mont*)
- **Appellation:** Vosne-Romanée Premier Cru
- **Price:** $46

We love the Burgundies from the village of Vosne-Romanée, especially the premier cru and grand cru wines, which combine power and richness with elegance and wondrous, perfumed aromas. Grand cru Vosne-Romanée Burgundies are all well over $100, but many of the premier crus, such as this fine 1994 Les Beaux Monts from Jadot, are still under $50. This 1994 Vosne-Romanée is fragrant with aromas of black cherry, ripe blackberries, raspberries, and cranberries, with accents of cola and oak. It has a core of concentrated raspberry flavor that is currently masked by tannin. The solid fruit character and concentrated, powerful finish suggest that you should hold to this wine for three or four years, although it's tempting to drink now.

Ed: 85–87 **Mary:** 88–90

Bourgogne Hautes Côtes de Nuits, Jayer-Gilles

- **Producer:** Domaine Robert Jayer-Gilles
  (*roe bair jhai ay-jheels*)
- **Wine name:** Bourgogne Hautes Côtes de Nuits
  (*bor guh nyuh ote coat duh nwee*)
- **Appellation:** Bourgogne Hautes Côtes de Nuits
- **Price:** $29

Normally, $29 would be quite a lot to pay for a Burgundy with the simple appellation of Bourgogne Hautes Côtes de Nuits. (Wines from 18 villages in the western hills of the Côte de Nuits are entitled to use this name.) But in the hands of a fine producer such as Robert Jayer, cousin of the almost legendary, retired Burgundian winemaker, Henri Jayer, this wine rivals many producers' premier cru Burgundies. In the 1994 vintage, this wine has smoky, opulent aromas of coffee, ripe fruit, and oak, with an intriguing touch of cocoa, along with ripe berry fruit and coffee flavors. This isn't a particularly full-bodied wine, nor is it intensely concentrated, but it is nevertheless a thoroughbred Burgundy for its excellent

balance, smoothness, and suppleness. It's delicious right
now. Jayer-Gilles also makes a fine Bourgogne-Hautes Côtes
de Beaune, which we like almost as much.

Ed: 89–91   **Mary:** 86–88

Givry Clos du Cellier Aux Moines, Joblot

> ✔ **Producer:** Domaine Joblot *(jhoe blo)*
>
> ✔ **Wine name:** Givry, Clos du Cellier aux Moines
> *(jhee vree clo doo sel l'yah oh mwan)*
>
> ✔ **Appellation:** Givry Premier Cru
>
> ✔ **Price:** $25

If you're not a millionaire, an excellent strategy in purchasing
Burgundy is to focus on the wines of the lesser-known communes,
which cost less than those of the famous appellations, and to
seek out the best producers in each area. The village of Givry,
in the Côte Chalonnaise, is one such lesser-known area, and
Joblot is one such producer. The 1995 Givry of Joblot, from
the Cellier aux Moines vineyard, is a young, rather undeveloped
wine at this stage, with very little aroma other than some mint
and oak. The flavors are more accessible: black cherries,
herbs, and youthful grapiness, in tightly knit intensity. By the
middle of 1998, this wine should already have shed its
austerity and opened into a lovely, velvety Burgundy.

Ed: 84–86   **Mary:** 84–86

Beaune-Grèves, Michel Lafarge

> ✔ **Producer:** Domaine Michel Lafarge
>
> ✔ **Wine name:** Beaune-Grèves
>
> ✔ **Appellation:** Beaune-Grèves Premier Cru
>
> ✔ **Price:** $45.50

Michel Lafarge is known for Volnay wines more than for
wines from the commune of Beaune, but every wine from this
serious producer is top-notch. The 1994 Beaune-Grèves of
Lafarge has a subtle aroma of black fruits, with eucalyptus
and camphor emerging slowly. The ripeness of the black-fruit
flavor gives this full-bodied wine an impression of sweetness.
Smooth and round, this wine is delicious already.

Ed: 88–90   **Mary:** 88–90

Beaune Les Cent Vignes, Albert Morot

- **Producer:** Albert Morot
- **Wine name:** Beaune Les Cent Vignes
  (bone lay sant veen yeh)
- **Appellation:** Beaune Premier Cru
- **Price:** $31

The name of the producer is clearly the most important factor in choosing Burgundy, and the Albert Morot winery is one of the Côte de Beaune's stars. Françoise Choppin runs this winery, which produces six different Beaune premier cru Burgundies. The 1994 Beaune Les Cent Vignes has aromas of chocolate and new oak, along with herbal, cherry fruit, and oaky flavors. This very polished, pretty, sophisticated Burgundy is quite smooth despite its moderate tannin, and it has a good concentration of fruit. Enjoy this high-quality wine now, perhaps with roast chicken, or keep it for a couple of years.

Ed: 88–90   **Mary:** 90–92

Volnay Les Caillerets "Clos Des 60 Ouvrées," Domaine de La Pousse d'Or

- **Producer:** Domaine de La Pousse d'Or
  (doh mane deh la poose dor)
- **Wine name:** Volnay Les Caillerets, "Clos Des 60 Ouvrées" *(lay kye eh ray, clo day swah sahn oo vray)*
- **Appellation:** Volnay Premier Cru
- **Price:** $47.50

The word that's probably used most often to describe the wines of Volnay (now that everyone has abandoned the use of *feminine*) is *charming*. But this particular Volnay is typically fuller, richer, and less "charming" than other Volnays. The aroma of the 1994 version is closed-in and inexpressive at this stage, showing only the scent of oak, but black-cherry fruit and herbal notes are evident in the flavor. The wine is soft, round, and supple, with plenty more fruit character than tannin: the kind of Burgundy we love.

Ed: 86–88   **Mary:** 86–88

Côte de Nuits-Villages, Daniel Rion

> ♪ **Producer:** Domaine Daniel Rion & Fils
> ♪ **Wine name:** Côte de Nuits-Villages
> ♪ **Appellation:** Côte de Nuits-Villages
> ♪ **Price:** $23

We have found Daniel Rion's Burgundies to be consistently reliable over the years. For example, we recently enjoyed one of Rion's Burgundies from a so-called off vintage, 1984. Our experience with Rion's wines in both strong and weak vintages proves once again that the producer — and the winery's performance over the last decade — is the essential information for you to know when you buy Burgundy.

Rion's 1994 Côte de Nuits-Villages has aromas of spice, coffee, and really concentrated, intense red fruit. The wine is medium to full bodied, with rich, ripe plum and berry fruit flavors. It's a very attractive, chunky-styled, solid, young Burgundy but a bit closed right now. If you have a cool cellar, we suggest that you hold on to this well-made wine for three to five years, because we believe that it'll get even better.

Ed: 87–89   **Mary:** 87–89

Château de Rully Rouge, Antonin Rodet

> ♪ **Producer:** Antonin Rodet
> ♪ **Wine name:** Château de Rully Rouge
> ♪ **Appellation:** Rully
> ♪ **Price:** $19

The village of Rully, in the Côte Chalonnaise, makes slightly more white wine than it does red and is better known for its whites. But I enjoy Rully Rouge, too — especially because it's one of the more affordable types of Burgundy. Antonin Rodet's 1992 red Château de Rully is a delicious, ready-to-drink Burgundy, despite the winery's reputation of making a red wine that develops slowly. It has a rich, seductive aroma of black fruits, chocolate, and underbrush (a pleasantly musty scent, like autumn leaves) and a fairly pronounced flavor of blackberries and plums. The wine is soft, supple, and silky textured, with soft tannins. Terrific with salmon.

Mary: 89–91

Chambolle-Musigny, Roumier

- ♪ **Producer:** Domaine Georges et Christophe Roumier
- ♪ **Wine name:** Chambolle-Musigny
- ♪ **Appellation:** Chambolle-Musigny
- ♪ **Price:** $32.50

Roumier has long been one of our favorite producers in all of Burgundy. Plus, we've always loved the charming, elegant style of the Burgundies from the commune of Chambolle-Musigny. As a result, we find Roumier's wines, from the rare grand cru Musigny to the more available village-level Chambolle-Musigny, almost irresistible. The 1994 Chambolle-Musigny is incredibly fragrant, with ripe red fruit aromas, along with cherry-berry fruit flavors. It's harmonious and supple, our style of Burgundy — and yet its taut, focused fruit character suggests good potential to develop even further with a year or two of aging. At the risk of sounding corny, we describe this wine as glorious, yet gentle.

Ed: 89–91   **Mary:** 89–91

Juliénas, Domaine du Clos du Fief, of Michel Tête

- ♪ **Producer:** Domaine Michel Tête
- ♪ **Wine name:** Juliénas, Domaine du Clos du Fief
- ♪ **Appellation:** Juliénas *(jool yeh nass)*
- ♪ **Price:** $16

We realize that $16 is quite a bit to pay for a Beaujolais, but this single-vineyard cru Beaujolais (see Chapter 1 for an explanation of *cru Beaujolais*) from Michel Tête is quite special. The 1996 Clos du Fief has earthy, slightly spicy scents, but the wine's aroma is still a bit undeveloped right now. This wine is quite full bodied for a Beaujolais, with ripe, concentrated fruit flavors and a moderately long finish. It's an impressive, if somewhat ponderous, Beaujolais that will easily keep for a couple of years. If you want to drink it now, how does fried chicken sound with your Juliénas?

Ed: 85–87   **Mary:** 85–87

Aloxe-Corton Les Vercots, Tollot-Beaut

- **Producer:** Domaine Tollot-Beaut & Fils *(toh loh boh)*
- **Wine name:** Aloxe-Corton Les Vercots *(lay ver coh)*
- **Appellation:** Aloxe-Corton Premier Cru *(ah luhs cor ton)*
- **Price:** $37

Tollot-Beaut is one of the most well established wineries in Burgundy. You can usually depend on buying a well-made, reasonably priced Burgundy from this domaine. The 1994 Aloxe-Corton Les Vercots has delectable aromas of herbs, cherry, and red berry, along with some new oak, and its flavors are spicy and berry-like. Typical of the Burgundies from Aloxe-Corton, which are quite firm and tannic in their youth, this fine-quality wine is tannic now, but its concentration and lengthy finish suggest that it will be exceptional in three to five years. (We also like Tollot-Beaut's 1994 Chorey-Côte-de-Beaune, only $19.)

Ed: 88–90   **Mary:** 88–90

The Rhône Valley's Lusty Reds

With only a few exceptions, the madness of seriously escalating prices for fine wines has not yet reached the Rhône Valley or the other wine regions of southern France, such as Provence or the Languedoc-Roussillon, as it has Bordeaux and Burgundy. The Rhône Valley, in particular, is the region to explore if you want a world-class French red wine without having to break your kid's piggy bank.

The Rhône Valley has two distinctly different subregions, the Northern Rhône and the Southern Rhône. The Northern Rhône is much smaller, but it's the home of almost all the renowned, prestigious Rhône wines, as well as being arguably the world's finest wine region for Syrah-based wines. The only really well-known fine red wine in the Southern Rhône is Châteauneuf-du-Pape; the Southern Rhône is primarily the home of under-$15 Côtes du Rhône red wines.

For more specific information on the red wines of the Rhône Valley, see Chapters 4 and 11 in *Red Wine For Dummies* and Chapter 10 in *Wine For Dummies.* For our recommendations of Rhône and southern France red wines under $15, see Chapter 1.

Crozes-Hermitage Cuvée Louis Belle, Domaine Albert Belle

> ♪ **Producer:** Domaine Albert Belle
> ♪ **Wine name:** Crozes-Hermitage, Cuvée Louis Belle
> ♪ **Appellation:** Crozes-Hermitage *(crohz air mee tahj)*
> ♪ **Price:** $19.50

Albert Belle is making one of the most exciting Crozes-Hermitage wines we've ever had! Wines from this appellation normally don't come close in quality to their big brothers from the adjoining district, the great red Hermitage wines. But we'd stack Belle's 1994 Cuvée Louis Belle Crozes-Hermitage up against most Hermitages in a comparative tasting, confident that it would show well. It has deep, intense aromas of cocoa, vanilla, and black fruits, along with fresh black-fruit flavors of admirable concentration. This complex, tannic wine is full bodied but not massive, and it has a sleek, smooth texture. As great as it is now, it will only get better with a few more years of aging.

Ed: 92–94   **Mary:** 88–90

Gigondas, Les Hauts Montmirail of Daniel Brusset

> ♪ **Producer:** Les Hauts Montmirail, of Daniel Brusset
> ♪ **Wine name:** Gigondas
> ♪ **Appellation:** Gigondas
> ♪ **Price:** $24

Southern Rhône wines are not my thing, but every rule has its exceptions. The very first taste of Daniel Brusset's Les Hauts Montmirail Gigondas reveals what impressive concentration this wine has and indicates that this is not a casual country wine but a solid and important bottling. In the 1994 vintage, the wine has plenty of oaky character, evident in the aroma, flavor, and high tannin level of the wine. But it also has enough spicy, concentrated fruit character to measure up to the tannin, even if that fruit is somewhat buried now. This full-bodied, sturdy wine will benefit from a year or two of bottle age, but you can enjoy it now, preferably with a simply prepared red meat.

Mary: 89–91

Hermitage "La Sizeranne," M. Chapoutier

- ! **Producer:** M. Chapoutier
- ! **Wine name:** Hermitage, "La Sizeranne"
- ! **Appellation:** Hermitage
- ! **Price:** $45

Since young Michel Chapoutier took over the reins at the venerable Chapoutier firm, the wines here have been nothing short of outstanding. Probably his best wines are those from Hermitage. Chapoutier's 1995 Hermitage, called "La Sizeranne," has deep aromas of concentrated blackberry fruit, earth, and new oak, as well as rich fruit flavors layered with plenty of tannin. This very concentrated Hermitage will be best if it is cellared for at least 10 years so that it can fully develop. (An even more intense, complex Chapoutier Hermitage is the other-worldly "Le Pavillon," now over $100!)

Ed: 90–92   **Mary:** 91–93

Châteauneuf-du-Pape, Château Rayas

- ! **Producer:** Château Rayas
- ! **Wine name:** Châteauneuf-du-Pape
- ! **Appellation:** Châteauneuf-du-Pape
- ! **Price:** $50

Château Rayas has always been our favorite wine from the Southern Rhône. Amazingly, this wine is made entirely from the Grenache grape, with no help from the noble Syrah; it earns our vote as the greatest Grenache wine in the world. The 1994 Rayas has rich, spicy black-pepper and red-fruit aromas, and its flavors suggest raspberry, black cherry, and green pepper. This full-bodied, tannic, voluptuous wine is surprisingly supple even now, thanks to its soft tannins, but its concentrated finish suggests that the wine will develop further. We'd hold on to this dense powerhouse for at least another ten years.

Ed: 91–93   **Mary:** 89–91

Cornas La Louvée, Jean-Luc Colombo

> ✔ **Producer:** Jean-Luc Colombo
>
> ✔ **Wine name:** Cornas La Louvée *(lah loo vay)*
>
> ✔ **Appellation:** Cornas
>
> ✔ **Price:** $48

Jean-Luc Colombo has emerged in recent years as one of the best producers of Cornas, an often overlooked wine of the Northern Rhône made entirely from the Syrah grape. Colombo makes three Cornas wines: Cornas Terres Brûlées (about $33), Cornas Les Ruchets ($45), and Cornas La Louvée. The 1994 La Louvée is a great Cornas! It has aromas and flavors of ripe black fruits spiced with oak. Medium to full bodied and very well balanced, it's a rich, tannic, complex, very young wine with excellent concentration. This is classic Cornas, a wine for the future; we'd drink it in about five years, with a beef or lamb stew. Colombo's Cornas Les Ruchets is also excellent and easier to find.

Ed: 91–93   **Mary:** 88–90

Crozes-Hermitage Clos des Grives, Domaine Combier

> ✔ **Producer:** Domaine Laurent Combier
>
> ✔ **Wine name:** Crozes-Hermitage, Clos des Grives
>
> ✔ **Appellation:** Crozes-Hermitage
>
> ✔ **Price:** $25

We're excited to see up-and-coming young producers, such as Laurent Combier, making really high-class Rhône wines from an area such as Crozes-Hermitage, which can produce pedestrian wines in lesser hands. Combier makes a standard, very good Crozes-Hermitage, priced at $18, and the even better Clos des Grives, both made entirely from the Syrah grape. The 1994 Clos des Grives has smoky aromas and flavors, suggesting roasted meat and ripe black fruits. This dry, full-bodied, rich, well-balanced wine just cries "Syrah!" You can enjoy this beauty now, with barbecued strip steaks, or hold it; this wine should develop even further over the next five years.

Ed: 89–91   **Mary:** 89–91

Saint-Joseph Cuvée L'Amarybelle, Yves Cuilleron

> **✦ Producer:** Domaine Yves Cuilleron *(kwee leh ron)*
> **✦ Wine name:** Saint-Joseph, Cuvée Prestige L'Amarybelle *(lah mahr ee bell)*
> **✦ Appellation:** Saint-Joseph
> **✦ Price:** $25

In addition to producing one of the two best Condrieu wines (a white Rhône Valley wine from the Viognier grape), Yves Cuilleron makes both red and white wines from the lesser-known Saint-Joseph appellation in the Northern Rhône. His red 1994 Cuvée L'Amarybelle has rich aromas of black fruit, mint, black pepper, and leather, with meaty and leathery flavors. It's a firm but supple medium-bodied wine that is perfectly enjoyable now. It would be great with cheeseburgers and fries, but its quality deserves filet mignon. If you have difficulty finding Cuilleron's wines, call Neal Rosenthal Wine Merchants in New York, 212-249-6650.

Ed: 90–92   **Mary:** 89–91

Gigondas, Domaine du Gour de Chaule

> **✦ Producer:** Domaine du Gour de Chaule *(gore deh shole)*
> **✦ Wine name:** Gigondas
> **✦ Appellation:** Gigondas
> **✦ Price:** $16

A good Gigondas wine is one of the great bargains in the wine world. Although Grenache is the major grape variety in the wines of Gigondas, the 1993 Gigondas of the Domaine du Gour de Chaule clearly has a good dollop of Syrah in it. It has voluptuous aromas of black pepper, cherries, mint, and sweet potatoes. This wine makes you hungry! Full bodied, firm, and tannic, the Gigondas has velvety texture, outstanding balance, and a long finish. This very solid, intense wine really needs two or three years to open up; it should provide delicious drinking for many years after that. For now, it needs respect — and a good slab of beef or venison. If you have any difficulty finding it, call Neal Rosenthal Wine Merchants in New York, 212-249-6650, or the importer, Select Vineyards, 800-910-1990.

Ed: 95–97   **Mary:** 89–91

Crozes-Hermitage Domaine de Thalabert, Paul Jaboulet Aîné

- **Producer:** Paul Jaboulet Aîné
- **Wine name:** Crozes-Hermitage, Domaine de Thalabert
- **Appellation:** Crozes-Hermitage
- **Price:** $24

The most renowned wine in the entire Crozes-Hermitage district is the wine from Jaboulet's Domaine de Thalabert estate. (It's also one of the two truly great wines that Jaboulet produces, along with his superb Hermitage, La Chapelle.) The single-vineyard Thalabert is made from low-yielding, old Syrah vines, which accounts for its depth and intensity. The 1994 Domaine de Thalabert has aromas and flavors of very ripe fruit, some mint, some vegetal flavor typical of Syrah, and earthiness. It's medium to full bodied, complex, and well balanced. This rustic, old-style wine would have earned an even higher rating but for its over-ripeness in the 1994 vintage. Enjoy it with quail, squab, or duck confit. We also recommend Jaboulet's 1994 Gigondas "Pierre Aiguille," a robust wine from the Southern Rhône that's a terrific value at $19.

Ed: 86–88   **Mary:** 87–89

Saint-Joseph "Le Grand Pompée," Paul Jaboulet Aîné

- **Producer:** Paul Jaboulet Aîné
- **Wine name:** Saint-Joseph, "Le Grand Pompée"
- **Appellation:** Saint-Joseph
- **Price:** $21

Although I have never been a big fan of the wines from Saint-Joseph, I must admit that Jaboulet has hit a home run with his 1994 "Le Grand Pompée"! This is probably the best Saint-Joseph that I've ever tasted. It has rich black-fruit aromas and flavors, lots of tannin, and a long finish. This is a serious Syrah wine, as attested by the highly technical, professional comments in my notes, such as "WOW!" and "Yes!" Enjoy the wonderful, fleshy fruit flavors in this wine soon, perhaps with cheeseburgers.

Ed: 92–94

Côte-Rôtie, Joseph Jamet

 ❢ **Producer:** Joseph Jamet

 ❢ **Wine name:** Côte-Rôtie

 ❢ **Appellation:** Côte-Rôtie

 ❢ **Price:** $38

Joseph Jamet makes one of the richest, most powerful Côte-Rôtie wines. The 1994 Jamet has spicy, peppery, leathery aromas and the classic Côte-Rôtie herbal, green olive, and baked-fruit flavors. This dry, full-bodied wine has an appealing richness and liveliness that says, "Drink me now." We'd oblige that request within the next few years, with roast chicken or roast pheasant.

Ed: 90–92   **Mary:** 87–89

Italy's World-Class Reds

As two fanatics who have long loved Italian wine, we're sorry to see the escalating prices of Italy's best wines (not that they don't have company from French and Californian brands!). But we must admit that the quality of these wines supports their prices. Italy's best wines used to be bargains; now they are merely great wines that cost what great wines cost.

Italy's best wines are red. A disproportionate number of them come from two regions:

 ✔ Piedmont, in northwestern Italy, bordering France

 ✔ Tuscany, on the western coast of central Italy

A disproportionate number of Italy's red wines also come from just two grape varieties:

 ✔ The Nebbiolo grape of Piedmont

 ✔ The Sangiovese grape of Tuscany

Chapter 3 of _Red Wine For Dummies_ contains a description of these grape varieties. Generally speaking, Nebbiolo makes full-bodied, tannic red wines with earthy, herbal, and strawberry aromas and flavors; Sangiovese makes medium-bodied, supple red wines with herbal, nutty, and cherry aromas and flavors. Naturally, the style of any specific wine made from either of these grapes varies according to where the grapes grow and how the wine is made.

In this section, we review our favorite red wines from other parts of Italy as well as from Piedmont and Tuscany. We begin in the northeast and then move to Piedmont and to Tuscany.

When you try any of the wines we review in this section, remember that Italian wines, more than any other wines in the world, beg for food. (That's because the Italians themselves always serve wine at mealtime, and the wines are therefore made for food.) Especially if you are accustomed to drinking the soft, fruity red wines of California or Australia, your enjoyment and appreciation of these Italian wines will increase tremendously when you have them with a meal. Ironically, however, we don't give many specific food suggestions for the wines we review in this section: Most Italian wines are very flexible at the table.

Northeastern Italy

Some of the other parts of Italy that we cover in this chapter are easy to generalize about. Tuscany, for example, is a fairly compact, self-contained region with a single culture and a single dominant red grape variety. No such luck when it comes to northeastern Italy, however. That area encompasses three separate Italian regions, or states, several different cultures, various important red grape varieties, and three different languages!

Perhaps lumping the regions of Trentino-Alto Adige, Friuli-Venezia Giulia, and Veneto together is illogical, but it is a practical way of grouping our reviews of wines from northern Italy that don't come from Piedmont or Tuscany, the two regions we cover in more depth.

Because we don't have dozens of reviews in this section, we intermingle wines from the three different regions of northeastern Italy and simply list the wines alphabetically by producer.

Valpolicella Il Vegro, Brigaldara

- ♪ **Producer:** Brigaldara
- ♪ **Wine name:** Valpolicella, Il Vegro
- ♪ **Appellation:** Valpolicella Classico
- ♪ **Price:** $17.50

The Valpolicella zone, north of the city of Verona, makes wines that often get no respect, thanks to the many bland, characterless Valpolicellas on the market. Made primarily from a blend of three local grapes, Valpolicella is a light- to medium-bodied wine that's perfect for light dinners such as hamburgers, a light pasta dish, or pizza. Brigaldara makes an under-$10 Valpolicella and this more serious wine, from the Il Vegro vineyard. The 1993 Il Vegro is a fresh, crisp, dry wine with decent flavor concentration and lots of personality. It's the kind of wine that is very easy to drink — unlike heavy red wines from warmer-climate regions, or very oaky reds. Drink this wine when it's young and still fresh — within five years of the vintage.

Ed: 87–89   **Mary:** 87–89

Lagrein, Conti Martini

- ! **Producer:** Conti Martini
- ! **Wine name:** Lagrein
- ! **Appellation:** Trentino
- ! **Price:** $18.50

Conti Martini is an old family estate run by Lucia Cristina Martini. She specializes in the local red grape varieties, Teroldego Rotaliano and Lagrein Dunkel (better known today simply as Lagrein). The fairly obscure Lagrein grape variety makes dark-colored, robust wines, surprisingly full bodied for northeastern Italy.

The 1993 Conti Martini Lagrein has aromas and flavors that suggest chocolate, ripe cherry fruit, and tobacco. It has crisp acidity, good depth of flavor, and moderate tannins, along with great concentration of fruit character. This well-balanced wine, with its long, velvety finish, is of outstanding quality. I recommend holding on to the 1993 Lagrein for a few years. For food pairings, try a rich meat dish, perhaps beef or venison, or a rich cheese dish.

Ed: 89–91

Teroldego Rotaliano Vigneto Sgarzon, Foradori

- ! **Producer:** Foradori
- ! **Wine name:** Teroldego Rotaliano, Vigneto Sgarzon
- ! **Appellation:** Teroldego Rotaliano
  (teh ROLL day go roh tah lee AH noh)
- ! **Price:** $30

Any traditionalist who still associates females with sugar, spice, and everything nice will surely be surprised to learn that this intense, powerful red wine is made by a woman — and a young woman at that. Elisabetta Foradori makes some of the best wines of the Trentino area, in the region of Trentino-Alto Adige. She has devoted 70 percent of her family's vineyards to the Teroldego grape, a local variety that many considered inferior until she proved what terrific wines it can make when handled properly. The wine called Sgarzon is a single-vineyard Teroldego. The 1994 Sgarzon has intense, concentrated aromas and flavors of ink and some oak, with hints of toasted nuts, black pepper, and ripe fruit lurking below the surface. It's full bodied and solidly built, with velvety texture, but for such an intense wine, it's not very tannic. This wine is quite young yet and seems to need a year or two to open up.

Ed: 86–88   **Mary:** 87–89

Villa Barthenau Pinot Nero, Hofstätter

> *!* **Producer:** Hofstätter
>
> *!* **Wine name:** Villa Barthenau Pinot Nero, Vigna Sant' Urbano
>
> *!* **Appellation:** Alto Adige
>
> *!* **Price:** $48.50

The Hofstätter Villa Barthenau Pinot Nero (Pinot Noir) from the Sant' Urbano vineyard is by far the best Pinot Noir wine we've ever had from Italy. The 1993 Pinot Nero is a brilliant achievement. It has complex aromas of prunes, plums, damp earth, smoke, and green olives and intense, rich flavors of jammy red fruit, as well as the dead-leaf character reminiscent of a great French Burgundy. It is super-concentrated, with loads of depth and incredible length. If you're curious about how good an Italian Pinot Noir can be, check out this wine.

Ed: 92–94   **Mary:** 91–93

Piedmont's precious reds

The great red wines of Piedmont are truly in a class by themselves. Not only are they made from a grape variety that is almost exclusively theirs (Nebbiolo), but they also have a purity of flavor, an intensity, and a longevity that no other Italian wines have. (Brunello di Montalcino, a great Tuscan wine, is the only contender.)

The two great production zones for the Nebbiolo grape are Barolo and Barbaresco, two hilly areas on either side of the town of Alba. Barolo is the larger area and produces more wine; that wine is generally more powerful and somewhat fuller than the wine of Barbaresco. On the other hand, Barbaresco can claim to have more-elegant wines than Barolo — although still quite intense and powerful.

Besides Nebbiolo, the other important red grape of Piedmont for fine wine (and for plenty of everyday wine, too) is Barbera. Although this grape originated in Piedmont, it's now grown all over Italy. The finest Barbera wines in all the world come from Piedmont, however.

We describe our favorite Piedmont wines in alphabetical order according to the name of the producer. For more information on Piedmontese red wines, refer to Chapter 12 of *Red Wine For Dummies*.

Barolo Cannubi, Carretta

- ♪ **Producer:** Carretta
- ♪ **Wine name:** Barolo Cannubi
- ♪ **Appellation:** Barolo
- ♪ **Price:** $24.50

We can recommend very few Barolos for under $30, but Carretta's is a shining exception — and a "real deal." Apparently, the very traditional Barolos of Carretta aren't well known enough — yet! — to be able to command a higher price. Carretta's 1990 Barolo from the Cannubi vineyard has intense aromas and flavors of tar, dried herbs, licorice, mint, eucalyptus, and tobacco, along with tart-cherry fruit and mushrooms. It's a very fine, crisp, austere wine with real harmony and elegance, despite its guts and power. We'd hold on to the 1990 Carretta (the 1989 is equally good) for at least another five or six years, to let it develop further.

Ed: 92–94   **Mary:** 91–93

Barbaresco "Asij," Ceretto

- ♪ **Producer:** Ceretto
- ♪ **Wine name:** Barbaresco "Asij" *(ah SEE)*
- ♪ **Appellation:** Barbaresco
- ♪ **Price:** $24

Bruno Ceretto runs the business end of the winery; brother Marcello is the chief winemaker. Together, they've made the Ceretto winery one of the best in Piedmont, if not all of Italy. Ceretto makes an entire range of wines, including some great over-$50 Barolos and Barbarescos. Among his less-expensive wines, we like the Barbaresco "Asij," a wine that is fairly approachable, as well as readily available. The 1993 "Asij" has very fine aromas and flavors of herbs, tar, truffles, and spice; the tarry flavor, which is typical of the Nebbiolo grape that makes Barbaresco, really stands out. This medium-bodied, elegant, complex wine will probably reach peak drinkability in about three to five years, although it should last for at least ten years.

Ed: 88–90   **Mary:** 89–91

Dolcetto di Dogliani Briccolero, Chionetti

- ! **Producer:** Chionetti
- ! **Wine name:** Dolcetto di Dogliani, Briccolero *(bree coh LAY roh)*
- ! **Appellation:** Dolcetto di Dogliani *(doh l'yee AH nee)*
- ! **Price:** $18.50

This is no ordinary Dolcetto: In fact, it's one of the best Dolcettos we've ever tasted. We discovered this exceptional wine at Follonico Restaurant in New York, one of our favorite hangouts, when chef-owner Alan Tardi, a real wine buff, served it to us. Later, we included this wine in a blind tasting of Dolcetto wines, and it came out first, beating out many better-known Dolcettos.

Chionetti makes two Dolcetto wines, from the grapes of two different vineyards around the village of Dogliani: San Luigi, which sells for a dollar less than the Briccolero, and the Briccolero, which we slightly prefer. The 1995 Briccolero has spicy, black pepper, and dusty berry aromas and tart berry and cherry flavors. It's a tannic wine with lots of rich, spicy personality and an inner core of lively fruit. Dolcettos are best consumed within three or four years of the vintage.

Ed: 91–93   **Mary:** 91–93

Barbera d'Alba, Giacomo Conterno

- **Producer:** Giacomo Conterno
- **Wine name:** Barbera d'Alba
- **Appellation:** Barbera d'Alba
- **Price:** $22

Giovanni Conterno, the humble and highly respected man who makes the Giacomo Conterno wines, is the uncrowned "king" of Barolo. (We mention his wonderful Barolo wines in the sidebar "Great over-$50 Barolo and Barbaresco wines.") His winemaking talent extends to his Barbera d'Alba, which is a bit pricey for Barbera, but one of the best. The 1995 Barbera d'Alba has intense, voluptuous cherry fruit and strawberry jam aromas and tart, jammy fruit flavors. It's a really flavorful, delicious, very dry, crisp Barbera that you can drink now; we love Barberas with pizza (sausage and mushrooms, please) or a simple pasta with tomato sauce. The high acidity of Barbera wines suits them perfectly to tomato sauces.

Ed: 90–92   **Mary:** 89–91

Barbera d'Alba "Vignota," Conterno-Fantino

- **Producer:** Conterno-Fantino
- **Wine name:** Barbera d'Alba "Vignota"
- **Appellation:** Barbera d'Alba
- **Price:** $18

Conterno-Fantino is a relatively young operation with a fine, new winery on a hill above the sleepy town of Monforte d'Alba. Conterno-Fantino makes some wines traditionally and makes some in the more modern style — which often means using small, new barrels of French oak (called *barriques*) to age the wine. About 40 percent of the 1995 Barbera d'Alba "Vignota" has been aged in barriques. The wine has grapey and chocolatey aromas, along with rich, pronounced, spicy, tart cherry fruit flavors. This is a typical, rich young Barbera, quite delicious right now. We love Barberas with tomato-based pasta dishes or with pizza.

Ed: 90–92   **Mary:** 85–87

Barbaresco, Fontanafredda

> ♪ **Producer:** Fontanafredda
>
> ♪ **Wine name:** Barbaresco
>
> ♪ **Appellation:** Barbaresco
>
> ♪ **Price:** $22

The 1990 Fontanafredda Barbaresco, from a large, reliable producer whose wines are generally available, is a classic, old-style Barbaresco; it has lots of tannin and austere aromas and flavors of tar, eucalyptus, licorice, mint, and leather. This intense, full-bodied wine is well balanced between its acid and tannin firmness and its concentrated fruit richness. And what a great value for a Barbaresco from the great 1990 vintage! You can drink this fairly mature wine within the next three or four years. It would be great with a dish of tender beef braised in wine.

Ed: 93–95   **Mary:** 88–90

Barbera Sitorey, Angelo Gaja

> ♪ **Producer:** Angelo Gaja *(GUY ah)*
>
> ♪ **Wine name:** Barbera d'Alba Sitorey *(see toh RAY)*
>
> ♪ **Appellation:** Barbera d'Alba
>
> ♪ **Price:** $48

We certainly can't call this $48 Barbera a "real deal," but we can recommend it enthusiastically because the producer happens to be one of the greatest in the world. Angelo Gaja does not make ordinary wines; all his wines are works of art, in our opinion.

Gaja's 1993 Barbera Sitorey has the richness and harmony of a world-class wine, with the liveliness and delicious cherry fruit flavors of a Barbera. This round, elegant, medium-bodied wine has more depth and concentration than you would normally find in Barberas. You can enjoy the Sitorey now, or age it. Gaja's Barberas are so well made that they can live for 12 to 15 years without any problem.

Ed: 90–92   **Mary:** 89–91

Barolo and Barbaresco vintages

The Barolo and Barbaresco wine regions are close enough to each other geographically that the quality of each vintage tends to be similar in the two areas. In the following table, we rate the quality of vintages from 1995 back to 1982 and indicate the readiness of the wines from each vintage. Bear in mind, however, that our vintages ratings are merely general ratings for each vintage; great producers often find a way to make good wines in so-called average, or even poor, vintages.

Vintage	Rating	Vintage	Rating
1995	90 a	1988	90 a
1994	80 a	1987	80 c
1993	85 b	1986	85 c
1992	75– c	1985	95 b
1991	80+b	1984	65 d
1990	95+a	1983	75 c
1989	95+ a	1982	95 b

Key:

100 = Outstanding

95 = Excellent

90 = Very good

85 = Good

80 = Fairly Good

75 = Average

70 = Below Average

65 = Poor

\+ = Even better than the number rating

\– = Somewhat weaker than the number rating

a = Too young to drink

b = May be consumed now, but will improve with time

c = Ready to drink

d = May be too old

Barolo Brunate, Marcarini

- ? **Producer:** Marcarini
- ? **Wine name:** Barolo Brunate
- ? **Appellation:** Barolo
- ? **Price**: $41.50

Marcarini makes two Barolo wines: one from the Brunate vineyard and one labeled La Serra, after a special part of the

Brunate vineyard. Both are quite similar and are priced exactly the same. The 1993 Brunate, the currently available vintage, has very perfumed aromas and flavors of pungent white truffles (which grow in the area), tar, mint, damp earth, and tart cherry fruit. It's a rich, full, fairly intense wine with the characteristic soft, velvety tannins of a Barolo from the western part of the Barolo zone, where the Brunate vineyard is located. You can drink this smooth, supple Barolo now or within the next three or four years. (The Barolo Brunate is not Marcarini's only precocious wine; his other Barolos also are ready to drink sooner than those of many other producers.) We also recommend Marcarini's Brunate Barolo from 1992 and 1991, but we're less enthusiastic about the 1990 wine because Marcarini was changing winemakers then.

Ed: 90–92   **Mary:** 90–92

Barolo Monprivato, Giuseppe Mascarello

- ✔ **Producer:** Giuseppe Mascarello
- ✔ **Wine name:** Barolo Monprivato
- ✔ **Appellation:** Barolo
- ✔ **Price:** $34

A $34 bottle of wine might not seem a "real deal," but considering that other premium Barolo wines cost over $50, we believe that this wine is one of the best buys in this book. The Giuseppe Mascarello winery is one of the finest producers in the Barolo region, in our opinion, and in 1991 (a good, but not a great, vintage for Barolo), owner-winemaker Mauro Mascarello made one of the best Barolos of the vintage. His 1991 Barolo from the Monprivato vineyard has classic Barolo aromas and flavors of tar, bouillon, eucalyptus, camphor, mint, and coffee. It's a dry, austere, tannic wine, but the richness, depth, and complexity of flavor counterbalance the tannins; the intensity of the wine, in fact, is surprising for this vintage. You can enjoy this wine now or within the next few years, with a full-flavored meat dish, such as venison, wild boar, or roast beef. (Giuseppe Mascarello's other 1991 Barolo, Santo Stefano di Perno, is almost as good, and it's another great buy, at $31.)

Ed: 94–96   **Mary:** 95–97

Barolo, Pio Cesare

- **Producer:** Pio Cesare
- **Wine name:** Barolo
- **Appellation:** Barolo
- **Price:** $32

Wine-tasting wisdom maintains that great wineries find a way to make good wines in so-called *off vintages* — and Pio Cesare's 1992 Barolo is a case in point. This is a dry, austere, old-style Barolo with deep, intense aromas and flavors of violets, tar, leather, mint, and licorice. Surprisingly, for the rather weak vintage, the wine has deep, complex flavors and lots of depth. The 1992 Pio Cesare Barolo is still a very young, gutsy, tough wine with plenty of tannin, and it needs another eight to ten years to soften! To experience a really traditionally made Barolo, try the 1992 Pio Cesare.

Ed: 87–89   **Mary:** 87–89

Barbaresco "Torre," Produttori del Barbaresco

- **Producer:** Produttori del Barbaresco
- **Wine name:** Barbaresco, "Torre"
- **Appellation:** Barbaresco
- **Price:** $21

Produttori del Barbaresco is a co-op winery (as opposed to a small, private producer), and co-ops generally make fairly ordinary wine. However, the quality of the Produttori del Barbaresco wines is consistently solid, and their prices are always very reasonable. In good vintages, this winery produces six or seven single-vineyard Barbaresco wines. But in lighter years such as 1992, the winery's best grapes are blended into a single wine. The 1992 "Torre," a blended Barbaresco, is a pleasant, lighter-style, low-tannin Barbaresco that has the advantage of being ready to drink now. It has sedate aromas of pine and strawberries and a core of concentrated strawberry fruit flavors. This lean, elegant, dry Barbaresco should come alive with a rich, moist dish such as beef stew.

Ed: 85–87   **Mary:** 86–88

Great over-$50 Barolo and Barbaresco wines

Just as in Bordeaux and in Burgundy, many great Barolos and Barbarescos now cost over $50, and so we list them here, without comment. Although some producers sell at least one of their Barolo or Barbaresco wines for under $50, many of the elite producers — such as Angelo Gaja, Bruno Giacosa, Giacomo Conterno, Aldo Conterno, Bartolo Mascarello, and Luciano Sandrone — have no Barolo or Barbaresco wines under $50. We recommend the following producers and wines, listed in alphabetical order according to the producer:

Producer	*Wine(s)*
Ceretto	Barolo Bricco Rocche; Barbaresco Bricco Asili
Cigliuti	Barbaresco Serraboella
Aldo Conterno	Barolo Bussia Soprana; Barolo Vigna Cicala; Barolo Vigna Colonnello; Barolo Granbussia
Giacomo Conterno	Barolo Monfortino; Barolo Cascina Francia
Conterno-Fantino	Barolo Sorì Ginestra
Angelo Gaja	Barbaresco Sorì San Lorenzo; Barbaresco Sorì Tildin; Barbaresco Costa Russi; Barolo Sperss
Bruno Giacosa	Barbaresco Santo Stefano Riserva; Barolo Rionda di Serralunga; Barolo Falletto di Serralunga
Marchesi di Gresy	Barbaresco Cru Gaiun; Barbaresco Camp Gros
Bartolo Mascarello	Barolo
Pio Cesare	Barolo Ornato
Prunotto	Barolo Cannubi; Barolo Bussia
Giuseppe Rinaldi	Barolo Brunate (1990 vintage, over $50)
Luciano Sandrone	Barolo Cannubi Boschis
Paolo Scavino	Barolo Bric' del Fiasc'
Vietti	Barolo Villero Riserva; Barolo Rocche; Barolo Lazzarito; Barolo Brunate
Roberto Voerzio	Barolo Cerequio; Barolo Brunate; Barolo La Serra

Barolo Marcenasco, Renato Ratti

> ♪ **Producer:** Renato Ratti
> ♪ **Wine name:** Barolo Marcenasco
> ♪ **Appellation:** Barolo
> ♪ **Price:** $47

The Renato Ratti winery has two Barolo wines currently available: a lighter-bodied, very accessible 1992 Barolo (about $33) and the 1991 single-vineyard Marcenasco, which we clearly prefer. Ratti's Barolos are made in a relatively soft, more approachable style typical of the western part of the Barolo zone, where Ratti's vineyards lie. The 1991 Marcenasco has aromas and flavors of earth, tar, mushrooms, and strawberry fruit. Fresh and crisp, with very good concentration, it's a very pretty, drinkable Barolo that you can enjoy right now, with a mushroom risotto or with pasta with meat sauce. We would drink the 1991 Marcenasco within the next three or four years because it's not a long-lived style of Barolo.

Ed: 88–90   **Mary:** 87–89

Barolo Brunate, Giuseppe Rinaldi

> ♪ **Producer:** Giuseppe Rinaldi
> ♪ **Wine name:** Barolo Brunate
> ♪ **Appellation:** Barolo
> ♪ **Price:** $45

Giuseppe Rinaldi is a very traditional winemaker who makes Barolos in the same style as his father did — big, powerful, tannic, austere, long-lived wines, which take years to soften. We happen to love this style, but we realize that it's not for everyone or that perhaps it has to grow on you. Giuseppe Rinaldi's 1991 Barolo from the Brunate vineyard is a powerhouse wine for the vintage (although lighter than his magnificent 1989 and 1990). It has aromas of truffles, mint, strawberry jam, and coffee, along with fresh strawberry fruit flavors. This very concentrated, very rich Barolo has loads of tannin and acidity. This wine really needs another seven or eight years to develop and soften. (Rinaldi's 1990 Barolo Brunate is still available; because it costs over $50, we don't review it here, but we rate it 95–97.)

Ed: 93–95   **Mary:** 93–95

Barbaresco, Vietti

- ♪ **Producer:** Vietti
- ♪ **Wine name:** Barbaresco
- ♪ **Appellation:** Barbaresco
- ♪ **Price:** $25

Vietti is one of our very favorite wine producers in the world; we usually recommend Vietti's Barbera for everyday drinking and its Barolo for special occasions. But Vietti's 1991 Barbaresco is such a great value at $25 that we urge you to try it. (Most of Vietti's Barolos are over $50, and its Barbarescos over $35; the price reflects a lighter vintage.) The 1991 Vietti Barbaresco has classic aromas and flavors of the Nebbiolo grape, such as tar, eucalyptus, mint, and camphor. It's a dry, full-bodied, lean, tannic wine that is still very young and needs three or four more years to develop. A chunk of hard cheese or a rich beef dish will show this wine off nicely.

Ed: 87–89   **Mary:** 86–88

Barbera d'Alba Scarrone, Vietti

- ♪ **Producer:** Vietti
- ♪ **Wine name:** Barbera d'Alba, Scarrone
- ♪ **Appellation:** Barbera d'Alba
- ♪ **Price:** $22

Vietti's single-vineyard Barbera called Scarrone is in another league from the winery's regular Barbera d'Alba ($15) that we review in Chapter 1. The wine from Scarrone simply has more depth and intensity of flavor; in fact, we believe that it's one of the very best Barbera wines around. Unfortunately, only small quantities of Vietti Scarrone come into the U.S. (Vietti also makes an even more intense Barbera d'Alba Scarrone, "Vigna Vecchia," from the grapes of the vineyard's oldest vines. It sells for about $27, but it's even more difficult to find than the standard Scarrone.)

The 1995 Vietti Scarrone has aromas of tart cherry fruit, chocolate, spicy oak, herbs, and earth, and its tart, fresh cherry fruit flavors have spicy accents. It's a refreshing, focused wine, with richness, concentration of fruit flavor, great finesse, and the wonderful edge of acidity that Barbera should have: Barbera to the nth degree! Enjoy it now, with your favorite pizza or pasta, or keep it a while. Vietti's Barberas can age for ten or more years, but we tend to prefer Barberas when they're young and zippy.

Ed: 92–94   **Mary:** 90–92

Treasures from Tuscany

Any discussion of great Italian red wine invariably boils down to a contest between Piedmont and Tuscany — and which of those two regions wins the contest invariably depends on the personal taste of the people who are deciding.

We personally love the red wines of both areas. We find the pure, powerful flavors of Piedmont's finest wines incomparable, but again and again the wines of Tuscany tug at our hearts. We adore good Chianti in all its manifestations, especially Chianti Classico when it's young and sassy and Chianti Classico Riserva when it's aged to harmonious perfection. We love silky Carmignano and the young "Rosso" wines from the Montalcino and Montepulciano zones. And no wine is more exciting than a great bottle of Tuscany's Brunello di Montalcino (except, maybe, a great bottle of Piedmont's Barolo).

Although most Tuscan reds are based on the Sangiovese grape, they vary greatly in style. For example, some wine zones, such as the Montalcino area and the southern part of Chianti's classico district, naturally make fuller-bodied, more intense wines because grapes ripen more fully in those relatively warm pockets. Even within any specific part of Chianti, some winemakers produce more intense wines than their neighbors because they blend some Cabernet Sauvignon with their Sangiovese or because they age their wine in small barrels of French oak. Despite a single dominant red grape variety, the wines of Tuscany are definitely not monotonous.

In terms of quality, the red wines of Tuscany have never been better than they are today, thanks to a revitalization of the vineyards and a new dedication to quality on the part of the region's winemakers. In terms of price, plenty of Tuscan wines are still relatively affordable. We truly believe that Chianti is *the most affordable great red wine in the world today,* and it's the *only* great red that's still priced mainly between $12 and $18. The time has never been better to explore the fine red wines of Tuscany.

The wines that we review in this section are some of our very favorite Tuscan reds priced above $15. We list the wines alphabetically by producer, regardless of the type of wine.

"Tenute Marchese Antinori" Chianti Classico Riserva, Antinori

> ♪ **Producer:** Marchesi Antinori
>
> ♪ **Wine name:** "Tenute Marchese Antinori" Chianti Classico Riserva
>
> ♪ **Appellation:** Chianti Classico Riserva
>
> ♪ **Price:** $30

Of the five Chianti wines that Antinori produces, the "Tenute Marchese Antinori" is the finest, in both senses of that word: It is (in our subjective opinion) the highest in quality as well as the most elegant and "finesseful." The style of this wine has shifted gradually over the years, becoming less gentle and more intense but always maintaining its trademark grace. The 1993 version has very quiet aromas of dried tart cherries, nut meats, tar, and toasty oak. It's medium bodied and has good concentration of fruit as well as firm tannin, probably from oak. This wine already is pretty, but as it softens with bottle age, it should become even prettier as well as more complex in its flavor. We like this wine in every vintage; the 1994 (not yet released) is slightly richer than the 1993, for example, and the 1991 has begun to show some of the sweetening and softening effects of age. If you're looking for a refined dinner companion who will neither bore you nor overwhelm you, try this excellent wine. For about half the price, the 1993 Villa Antinori Chianti Classico Riserva is also very good.

Ed: 88–90   **Mary:** 89–91

Rosso di Montalcino, Argiano

> ♪ **Producer:** Argiano *(ar jee AH noh)*
>
> ♪ **Wine name:** Rosso di Montalcino
>
> ♪ **Appellation:** Rosso di Montalcino
>
> ♪ **Price:** $17

We've run hot and cold on the wines of Argiano over the years. But having been under a new owner since 1991 and a new winemaking consultant (Giacomo Tachis, one of Italy's very best) since 1988, the winery now seems to be in top form. Argiano's 1995 Rosso di Montalcino is so powerful that, in blind tastings, we sometimes mistake it for a Brunello, the more intense wine made in the same area. Nothing much is happening yet in the way of aromas with this young wine, but when you taste the wine, the action in your mouth is so intense that you may think that the wine should carry a warning label. The wine is not just full bodied; it's full everything: high alcohol, high tannin, high acid, and packed with ripe, concentrated fruit. The 1995 Rosso is brashly youthful now and should develop nicely in the bottle for five years or more, eventually becoming harmonious. For half the price of Argiano's Brunello, this Rosso di Montalcino gives you a good inkling of what power and intensity the wines of Montalcino can pack. (The 1991 Argiano Brunello, at $35, does happen to be terrific, however.)

Ed: 87–89   **Mary:** 88–90

Brunello di Montalcino, Caparzo

> ! **Producer:** Caparzo
>
> ! **Wine name:** Brunello di Montalcino
>
> ! **Appellation:** Brunello di Montalcino
>
> ! **Price:** $48

Caparzo's Brunello di Montalcino has been a favorite wine of ours for many years — even *before* that romantic lunch at the extraordinary restaurant La Chiusa in the Tuscan countryside, where the doting restaurant owner served us an unforgettable Caparzo Brunello. Actually, that particular bottle was Caparzo's single-vineyard bottling called La Casa, a great wine that's rather difficult to find and very expensive ($75). The regular Caparzo Brunello, which we review here, is also excellent. The 1991 Brunello has a very complex aroma suggesting earthiness, meatiness, mint, and dusty notes. The flavors are minty and austere, but the wine's texture is thick and chewy, and the combined impression is intense, rustic, and harmonious all at the same time. We bet that this wine will be super when it is ten years old. In the meantime, Caparzo's 1993 Rosso di Montalcino (from the La Caduta vineyard) is more approachable, and it's only $18.

Ed: 88–90   **Mary:** 90–92

Carmignano Riserva, Villa di Capezzana

- ♪ **Producer:** Tenuta di Capezzana, of Conte Contini Bonacossi
- ♪ **Wine name:** Villa di Capezzana Carmignano Riserva
- ♪ **Appellation:** Carmignano Riserva
- ♪ **Price:** $30

We recommend a less expensive wine from this producer in Chapter 1, but our very favorite Capezzana wine is the Carmignano Riserva. The wines of Carmignano traditionally contain about 10 to 15 percent Cabernet Sauvignon, along with Sangiovese, which tends to make them a bit fleshier than Chianti wines. The 1990 Carmignano Riserva from Capezzana has extraordinary mint and eucalyptus aromas and flavors, along with some coffee and charry oak. It's dry, full bodied, and very tannic at heart, and yet it tastes soft, round, and approachable on the surface. This very intense wine from a great vintage needs several years to develop; we believe that it has great potential.

Ed: 88–90   **Mary:** 88–90

Chianti Classico, Castellare di Castellina

- ♪ **Producer:** Castellare di Castellina
- ♪ **Wine name:** Chianti Classico
- ♪ **Appellation:** Chianti Classico
- ♪ **Price:** $16.50

The Tuscan estate called Castellare di Castellina, which boasts superior vineyards in Chianti's Castellina commune, has long been one of our favorite producers, not only for its outstanding super-Tuscan wine called I Sodi di San Niccolò (a real value at $37; see the sidebar "High-end super-Tuscans" in this chapter) but also for its Chianti Classico. The 1994 Castellare Chianti Classico has aromas of earth and leather, with earthy and tart cherry fruit flavors. It's a crisp, succulent Chianti with a velvety texture, good balance, and excellent concentration. You can enjoy this Chianti now, perhaps with a veal chop, or keep it for another two or three years.

Ed: 87–89   **Mary:** 84–86

Chianti Classico, Castello di Ama

- *!* **Producer:** Castello di Ama
- *!* **Wine name:** Chianti Classico
- *!* **Appellation:** Chianti Classico
- *!* **Price:** $18

Because the hilly, fairly large Chianti Classico zone encompasses many different altitudes and microclimates, there's no such thing as a typical style of Chianti Classico. But that reality doesn't stop me from thinking, when I taste the 1994 Chianti Classico of Castello di Ama, "Now *this* is what all young Chianti should be like!" The wine's dusty violet and cherry aroma is classic for classico, as is its very dry, tart cherry flavor. Medium bodied and full of personality, this wine has a zippy zing of acidity that makes it refreshing to drink in warm weather, but it also has a serious concentration of fruit character to hold the interest at serious dinners. Try it with turkey burgers or quail — and anything in between.

Mary: 92–94

Brunello di Montalcino, Castello Banfi

- *!* **Producer:** Castello Banfi
- *!* **Wine name:** Brunello di Montalcino
- *!* **Appellation:** Brunello di Montalcino
- *!* **Price:** $36

Castello Banfi is a newcomer to the Italian wine scene, having been founded only 20 years ago — and by Americans, no less! But this huge winery has earned respect all around. Its 1992 Brunello is a complex, serious Brunello with great richness and ripeness of fruit character and very impressive concentration. Despite the fact that the 1992 vintage was a weak one, this wine is very intense, with velvety texture and commendable balance. Although we can appreciate its greatness now, we know that the wine is just a shadow of what it will be with five or more years of aging. If you can't wait to try it, just be sure to accompany it with substantial but simple food, such as roasted lamb.

Ed: 92–94   **Mary:** 90–92

Chianti Classico, Castello di Fonterutoli

- ! **Producer:** Castello di Fonterutoli *(fon tay ROO toh lee)*
- ! **Wine name:** Chianti Classico
- ! **Appellation:** Chianti Classico
- ! **Price:** $16

Fonterutoli is the name of a hamlet where this small winery is situated, in the classico district of Chianti. The Mazzei family has made wine in that area since 1435, and the experience shows: Fonterutoli Chianti is consistently among our favorite Italian wines. The 1994 Chianti Classico has an impressive scent of dried cherries, eucalyptus, and nut meats (a very Chianti aroma) and a gentle flavor of herbs, dried fruit, and nuts. This isn't a very big wine, but it's quietly intense, with very focused and concentrated flavor and a soft, velvety texture. At $2^{1}/_{2}$ years of age, the wine is still quite young and will certainly sustain a few years of bottle age.

Ed: 88–90   **Mary:** 88–90

Chianti Classico Riserva, Castello di Monsanto

- ! **Producer:** Castello di Monsanto
- ! **Wine name:** Chianti Classico Riserva
- ! **Appellation:** Chianti Classico
- ! **Price:** $16

Monsanto, an estate owned since 1961 by Milanese textile producer Fabrizio Bianchi, makes some of Chianti's longest-lasting wines. (Its 1971 and 1975 vintages, for example, are both going strong.) Monsanto makes several wines, and its Chianti Classico Riserva Il Poggio, which comes from a single vineyard, is the gem. But we like Monsanto's regular riserva just as much, because it's less oaky and also less expensive. The 1993 riserva has perfumey, downright floral aromas of jasmine and honeysuckle, along with herbal notes. It's a rich, intense Chianti, combining suppleness and finesse with good extract and concentration. This fine Chianti has excellent balance and structure, and great length. Although you can drink the 1993 Monsanto now, we suggest that you hold it for a few years to let it develop further. This wine goes well with spicy pasta dishes, venison, or aged cheeses, such as Gouda.

Ed: 89–91   **Mary:** 88–90

Pinch-hitting for Castello Unavailable

Our local fine wine shop, Pop's Wines & Spirits in Island Park, New York, sells 112 to 115 different Chianti wines, and yet the store's manager, Jerry Martellaro, estimates that he carries only about half the brands available on the New York market. So many different brands of Chianti exist that retailers who are less fanatical than Jerry naturally end up carrying only a small percentage of the available wines.

If your local wine shop doesn't carry some of the wines we recommend in this section but does carry other brands of Chianti, consult this list of recommended producers, listed alphabetically. We find these Chianti wines to be reliable and generally good to great in quality:

Badia a Coltibuono
Carpineto
Castell'in Villa
Castellare di Castellina
Castello dei Rampolla
Castello di Ama
Castello di Brolio
Castello di Fonterutoli
Castello di Gabbiano
Castello di Volpaia
Cecchi (Villa Cerna)
Dievole
Fattoria di Felsina
Fontodi
Frescobaldi

Isole e Olena
Marchesi Antinori
Le Masse
Melini
Monsanto
Monte Vertine
Podere Il Palazzino
Renzo Masi
Ruffino
San Felice
San Giusto a Rentennano
Selvapiana
Villa Cafaggio
Viticcio

Chianti Classico, Castello dei Rampolla

- ✔ **Producer:** Castello dei Rampolla
- ✔ **Wine name:** Chianti Classico
- ✔ **Appellation:** Chianti Classico
- ✔ **Price:** $20

Personally, we enjoy and admire far too many Chianti Classico wines to proclaim a single favorite, but if we were forced at gunpoint to do so, Castello dei Rampolla's would make our short list. The 1994 Rampolla Chianti Classico has a quiet aroma suggesting herbs, chocolate, and some oak.

The wine is dry in texture and fairly tannic, but it has a solid foundation of fruit to balance the tannin and does have a certain finesse. All it needs is a year or two of bottle age to round itself out; all the right stuff is there.

Ed: 87–89   **Mary:** 88–90

Chianti Classico, Fattoria di Felsina

- ✔ **Producer:** Fattoria di Felsina *(FEL see nah)*
- ✔ **Wine name:** Chianti Classico
- ✔ **Appellation:** Chianti Classico
- ✔ **Price:** $20

Fattoria di Felsina is located in the warmer, southeast part of the Chianti Classico zone, where the Chianti wines tend to be more full bodied and powerful than those from the northern part of the zone. The 1995 Felsina Chianti Classico is a classic example of its area: It's a full-bodied, rich, concentrated Chianti with lots of latent strength. Still quite young, this wine has focused aromas of cherry fruit, with fresh, clean, tart berry fruit flavors. We'd give this beauty another two years to develop further, although it's impressive already.

Ed: 88–90   **Mary:** 89–91

Chianti Classico Riserva, Fontodi

- ✔ **Producer:** Tenuta Fontodi
- ✔ **Wine name:** Chianti Classico Riserva
- ✔ **Appellation:** Chianti Classico
- ✔ **Price:** $23

Two of the most esteemed wines from the well-run Fontodi estate are Vigna del Sorbo, a $36 single-vineyard Chianti Classico Riserva, and Flaccianello, a $45 Sangiovese aged in French oak. Fontodi's standard 1993 Chianti Classico Riserva is also a fine wine, with the tart cherry fruit aromas and flavors typical of Chianti, along with accents of new oak. This dry, full-bodied, firm wine is a brilliant, top-drawer Chianti in the new oak style. We'd give this exciting wine another year or two of aging so that it can develop further.

Ed: 89–91   **Mary:** 88–90

High-end super-Tuscans

If you begin exploring the red wines of Tuscany, sooner or later you come across a whole category of wines that we hardly mention in this chapter: the so-called super-Tuscan reds. These wines are expensive (generally over $50 a bottle), internationally styled wines. They're usually made from the Sangiovese grape, from Cabernet Sauvignon, or from a blend of both grapes, and they're usually aged in small, new barrels of French oak, which impart an oaky character to the wine. Super-Tuscan wines are almost always exciting, well-made wines, available only in small quantities. They invariably carry a *proprietary* name (a unique, privately-owned name). We list some of our favorite super-Tuscan wines here.

Producer	Super-Tuscan Wine
Castellare di Castellina	I Sodi di San Niccolò
Castello dei Rampolla	Sammarco
Marchese Incisa della Rocchetta	Sassicaia *(sah see KYE ah)*
Marchesi Antinori	Tignanello *(tee nya NEL loh)*; Solaia *(so LYE ah)*
Monte Vertine	Le Pergole Torte
Tenuta dell'Ornellaia	Ornellaia *(or nel LYE ah)*; Masseto
Il Palazzino	Grosso Sanese
San Giusto a Rentennano	Percarlo
Viticcio	Prunaio

Pomino Rosso, Frescobaldi

- ? **Producer:** Marchese de' Frescobaldi
- ? **Wine name:** Pomino Rosso
- ? **Appellation:** Pomino Rosso
- ? **Price:** $20

Hundreds of years ago, the Pomino zone was already renowned as a great wine area. Today, most Pomino wines, both red and white, are made by the Frescobaldi winery. We particularly enjoy Frescobaldi's Pomino Rosso, a wine that combines some Cabernet Sauvignon, Merlot, and even Pinot Noir with its dominant grape, Sangiovese.

The 1993 Pomino Rosso has a very dark red color; very ripe, plummy aromas with intense accents of new oak; and flavors that are both fruity and vegetal. It's a very serious, sophisticated, well-balanced, moderately tannic wine with an excellent concentration of fruit character. Ed considers it a "great wine" that you can enjoy now or hold for a few years.

Ed: 92–94   **Mary:** 86–88

Monte Vertine Riserva

- ✔ **Producer:** Fattoria di Monte Vertine
- ✔ **Wine name:** Monte Vertine Riserva
- ✔ **Appellation:** Vino da Tavola di Toscana
- ✔ **Price:** $37

In the early 1980s, Sergio Manetti, the owner of Monte Vertine, began naming his Chianti Classico simply Monte Vertine Riserva. He changed the name because he made his wine without any white grapes, which were then required by law in the blend of any wines with the name Chianti Classico. (Many other producers eliminated the white grapes and yet continued to call their wine Chianti Classico, but Manetti stubbornly adhered to the letter of the law.) Today, that law has changed, and Manetti could legally designate his Monte Vertine Riserva as a Chianti Classico — but to connoisseurs of Italian wine, the name Monte Vertine has come to carry far more weight than the Chianti appellation.

The 1994 Monte Vertine Riserva is still restrained in its aroma and flavor because it's very young, but it does show some of the tart cherry fruit that's typical of Chianti. The wine is medium to full bodied and very smooth, supple, and velvety in texture. We hesitate to use anthropomorphic language, but the best way to describe this wine is to compare it to a docile, civilized, sophisticated, and classy person who, nonetheless, has the underpinnings of a spirited personality. Enjoy it now or let it age for a few years. (We also love another Monte Vertine wine, the 1994 Il Sodaccio, which we sum up in just four words: real Sangiovese, real tradition.)

Ed: 88–90   **Mary:** 90–92

Chianti Classico Riserva, Nozzole

- ? **Producer:** Fattoria di Nozzole *(NOTZ zoh lay)*
- ? **Wine name:** Chianti Classico Riserva
- ? **Appellation:** Chianti Classico Riserva
- ? **Price:** $16.50

We must confess that we tend to take the Nozzole Chianti Classico Riserva for granted because it has been around for as long as we've been drinking wine, and we see it everywhere. Lately, however, we've begun to rediscover this wine, and we've found that it has been getting better and better. The 1993 version, for example, has a classic Chianti aroma of herbs and dried cherries and classic flavors of nuts and cherries, accented by oak. Like most Chiantis, this medium-bodied wine is relatively thin in texture and firm in acidity, but it shows impressive fruit concentration that most Chiantis would die for. We would prefer to drink the 1993 Nozzole Riserva in 1998 or 1999, but it's fine even now.

Ed: 89–91   **Mary:** 90–92

Ornellaia

- ? **Producer:** Tenuta dell'Ornellaia, of Lodovico Antinori
- ? **Wine name:** Ornellaia *(or nel LIE ah)*
- ? **Appellation:** Vino da Tavola di Toscana
- ? **Price:** $49

Lodovico Antinori, the founder and proprietor of the wine estate called Ornellaia, is the brother of Piero Antinori, who runs the famous Antinori operation. Ornellaia is situated in the Bolgheri area of western Tuscany, outside the Chianti zone. The vineyards of Ornellaia are dedicated almost entirely to Cabernet Sauvignon and Merlot rather than to Tuscany's own Sangiovese grape — a fact that might rub traditionalists the wrong way if the wine from those vineyards weren't so good.

The 1994 Ornellaia wine is young and still very closed now, but its rich, focused cherry and black currant fruit is evident beneath the wine's frame of oak and tannin. In fact, this wine is really packed with concentrated fruit, held in check for the moment by the oak. Unfortunately, purchasing this wine requires self-control and respect for the value of delayed gratification: We won't open a bottle again for two or three years, and we expect that the wine will improve in the bottle for another five to eight years. For more immediate pleasure, the estate makes a very good second wine called Le Volte, which sells for $17.50.

Ed: 92–94   **Mary:** 89–91

Brunello di Montalcino, Il Poggiolo

- ✔ **Producer:** Il Poggiolo, of Roberto Cosimi
- ✔ **Wine name:** Brunello di Montalcino
- ✔ **Appellation:** Brunello di Montalcino
- ✔ **Price:** $31

The late Roberto Cosimi's legacy of fine Brunello di Montalcino at decent prices is being carried out admirably by his son, Rudolfo, whose 1992 Brunello is currently available in the U.S. Although 1992 is a light vintage for Brunello, the 1992 wines have the advantage of being enjoyable fairly soon, unlike most Brunello wines. The 1992 Il Poggiolo has subtle, complex aromas and flavors, principally of spicy new oak and mint at this early stage of its development. Thickly textured, rich, and full bodied, this wine has great concentration of fruit character and a somewhat wild, rustic personality. The powerful, concentrated finish of the wine shows that it has the ability to improve with age; we would begin drinking it within the next two or three years, with a full-flavored meat or game entrée. A very impressive 1992: So much for vintage charts!

Ed: 93–95   **Mary:** 90–92

Rosso di Montalcino, Il Poggione

- ✔ **Producer:** Il Poggione *(poh gee OH nay)*
- ✔ **Wine name:** Rosso di Montalcino
- ✔ **Appellation:** Rosso di Montalcino
- ✔ **Price:** $18

Il Poggione is one of the most respected producers of Brunello di Montalcino. This winery's Rosso di Montalcino — its less expensive wine — is more elegant in style, that is, less intense and powerful, than many other wines of the area. The 1994 Rosso di Montalcino has an aroma of coffee and herbs and a relatively subdued flavor. Medium bodied and very dry, the wine has the rather lean and austere structure that's classic in Sangiovese-based wines, and it shows plenty of depth. By late 1998, the 1994 Rosso di Montalcino will probably be somewhat softer than it is now; in the meantime, a grilled lamb chop can do wonders for its drinkability.

Ed: 88–90   **Mary:** 90–92

Chianti Classico Riserva Ducale "Gold Label," Ruffino

MARY'S CHOICE

- ! **Producer:** Ruffino
- ! **Wine name:** Chianti Classico Riserva Ducale (Gold Label)
- ! **Appellation:** Chianti Classico Riserva
- ! **Price:** $26

Ruffino makes two wines called Riserva Ducale, both quite good and reliable from vintage to vintage. The two wines are distinguishable on the shelf by the color of their labels: One has a gold label, and the other, less expensive wine has a tan label. They are distinguishable in the glass by their intensity of flavor: The gold-label wine tends to be more concentrated and has some oaky character, while the tan-label wine is more gentle and harmonious, in the low-tannin style of a traditional Chianti. The 1990 Riserva Ducale "Gold Label" has aromas and flavors of mint, eucalyptus, and tart cherry fruit — fresh, delicate notes that provide a pleasant contrast to the wine's full, dense, intense body. Although the wine is firm with tannin, it manages to be harmonious and silky at the same time. Ruffino's Riserva Ducale wines have a long history of aging gracefully, but we wouldn't hesitate to drink this wine now.

Mary: 87–89

Brunello di Montalcino Pertimali, Angelo Sassetti

- ! **Producer:** Angelo Sassetti
- ! **Wine name:** Brunello di Montalcino, Pertimali
- ! **Appellation:** Brunello di Montalcino
- ! **Price:** $46

The Sassetti brothers, Livio and Angelo, had a feud and split their farm called Pertimali down the middle; as a result, you can now find two Brunellos called Pertimali, each carrying the name of one of the brothers. Both are fine wines, but we happen to have had more experience recently with Angelo's wine, which we review here. In the 1992 vintage, his Brunello di Montalcino is intensely perfumed and earthy. This voluptuous wine is still very tannic and has real depth and concentration and an incredible finish that goes on and on. We'd give this wine a few more years to develop. We also recommend Angelo Sassetti's Rosso di Montalcino, an intense, solid wine that's a fine value at $21.

Ed: 94–96   **Mary:** 87–89

Top Reds from Spain and Portugal

For economy's sake, we group the better red wines of these two very different wine-producing countries together in this section.

Although Portugal produces red wine up and down its length, most Portuguese reds are inexpensive, and many of them are unavailable or only spottily available in the U.S. We review two of the country's finest reds in this section; for recommended producers of Portugal's great, legendary fortified red wine, read the sidebar called "Port, as in Portugal" later in this chapter.

The battalion of Spanish red wines has traditionally been dominated by the wines of the Rioja region, our favorites of which we review here.

We list our recommended wines alphabetically by producer, regardless of the wine's country or region. For more information on Spanish and Portuguese reds, refer to *Red Wine For Dummies,* Chapter 12.

Rioja Gran Reserva "Imperial," Cune

- ✔ **Producer:** Cune (CVNE) *(COO nay)*
- ✔ **Wine name:** "Imperial" Gran Reserva Rioja
- ✔ **Appellation:** Rioja Gran Reserva (Spain)
- ✔ **Price:** $25

If we had to choose just one wine to represent the best of Rioja, Cune's "Imperial" Gran Reserva would be our candidate. It is the most classic Rioja in style, without any of the aging in new wood that many wine producers use today, even in traditional Rioja, to give their wines international appeal. Everyone calls this large wine firm *Cune* because its full name, Compañia Vinicola del Norte de España, is quite a mouthful and no one can pronounce its acronym, CVNE.

Red Rioja wines that are labeled *gran reservas* must be aged at least five years before release, but these wines can usually last for 20 to 30 additional years without any problem. The 1986 "Imperial" has lovely vanilla aromas, with some delicate herbal tones. It's smooth and firm, with leathery and concentrated fruit flavors. This well-structured wine has considerable depth and class, making it more exciting than most Riojas. We suggest that you accompany this Rioja with beef stew made with a lesser Rioja wine.

Ed: 92–94   **Mary:** 89–91

Barca Velha, A. A. Ferreira

> **Producer:** A. A. Ferreira
>
> **Wine name:** Barca Velha *(BAR cah VAY yah)*
>
> **Appellation:** Douro (Portugal)
>
> **Price:** $40

Unlike most of the world's great wines, Portugal's greatest dry red wine, Barca Velha, is known by only a few wine lovers outside of the Douro Valley in Portugal, where the wine is made. The Douro Valley is the home of the greatest *fortified* red wine in the world — Port. (*Fortified* wines are made by adding alcohol to the wine.) Ferreira makes Barca Velha from the same local grape varieties that make Port, but it vinifies Barca Velha as a dry, unfortified wine. Ferreira makes Barca Velha only in truly outstanding vintages — 1985 is the latest vintage available, 1978 before that, and 1964 before that!

The 1985 Barca Velha has deep, concentrated aromas of charry oak and raspberry fruit, and it has concentrated fruit flavors. The tannins are soft enough that you can drink the wine now, but the wine is so packed and concentrated and has such a long finish that we suggest that you hold on to the Barca Velha for a while. It will last for decades.

Ed: 90–92   **Mary:** 90–92

Castillo YGay Rioja Gran Reserva, Marqués de Murrieta

- **Producer:** Marqués de Murrieta
- **Wine name:** Castillo YGay Rioja, Gran Reserva Especial *(cah STEE yoh ee GAY)*
- **Appellation:** Rioja Gran Reserva (Spain)
- **Price:** $28

Marqués de Murrieta, one of the oldest Rioja wineries, has two very nice, aged Riojas available now: the 1989 Reserva Especial (about $16) and the even better 1987 Gran Reserva Especial, which is labeled with the traditional "Castillo YGay" name that the Murrieta firm uses for its oldest and best Riojas. The 1987 Gran Reserva has the sweet coconut aromas of American oak, which most traditional Rioja firms use to age their wines, and its rich fruit flavors are accented with coconut. Round and full bodied, this wine is an easy-drinking, nicely balanced Rioja. Although it will age well, you can enjoy the 1987 Gran Reserva now; it's great with paella or with chicken and rice.

Ed: 88–90

"Viña Monty" Rioja Gran Reserva, Bodegas Montecillo

- **Producer:** Bodegas Montecillo *(bo DAY gahs moan tay THEE yo)*
- **Wine name:** "Viña Monty" Rioja Gran Reserva
- **Appellation:** Rioja Gran Reserva (Spain)
- **Price:** $17.50

Bodegas Montecillo makes some of the most consistently reliable, reasonably priced Rioja wines. Its "Viña Cumbrero" Rioja Crianza is always a good buy at under $10. "Viña Monty" is the name of Montecillo's Gran Reserva, its Rioja wine that ages longer at the winery before being released for sale. The 1986 "Viña Monty" has rich, generous, smoky, leathery aromas and flavors. Medium bodied, smooth, and silky, this wine has an easygoing way about it, despite some firm oak tannin. A charcoal-broiled steak or London Broil would work fine with the 1986 "Viña Monty." (The 1987 "Viña Monty" is also now available and is just as good as the 1986 version.)

Ed: 86–88   **Mary:** 88–90

Rioja Reserva, Muga

- **Producer:** Bodegas Muga
- **Wine name:** Rioja Reserva
- **Appellation:** Rioja Reserva (Spain)
- **Price:** $15.50

Bodegas Muga is the least-known great Rioja estate. Its gran reserva, the 1987 Prado Enea (about $40) is one of Spain's great red wines. Muga's more readily available reserva, however, is a fine value. Of the two vintages of Muga Rioja Reserva now available, 1991 and 1992, we slightly prefer the 1991 wine. The 1991 Muga Reserva has rich cherry fruit and leathery aromas and flavors. It's a velvety, harmonious, traditionally made Rioja with good concentration. You can enjoy the 1991 Reserva now, perhaps with a grilled steak or some good Spanish manchego cheese, or keep it for a few more years; Muga Riojas age well.

Ed: 88–90   **Mary:** 88–90

Duas Quintas Reserva, Ramos-Pinto

- **Producer:** Ramos-Pinto
- **Wine name:** Duas Quintas Reserva
- **Appellation:** Douro (Portugal)
- **Price:** $18

We don't generally like red wines from very warm climates, such as Portugal's Douro Valley, because they tend to be overly alcoholic (due to excessive ripeness of the grapes) and to lack finesse. But Ramos-Pinto, a winery owned by Champagne Louis Roederer and primarily a producer of fortified Port wine, has managed to make a Douro red that shows good balance and restraint. The 1991 Duas Quintas Reserva is full bodied and fairly tannic, but its tannins are soft, and the wine is supple. True, the aromas and flavors do suggest the sun-baked fruit of a warm climate, but minty, herbal, and eucalyptus notes counterbalance the ripe fruitiness. Considering that 1991 is the first vintage of this wine and that Portugal's greatest red, Barca Velha also hails from the Douro, we plan to keep a keen eye on this wine.

Ed: 89–91   **Mary:** 88–90

Port, as in Portugal

Port is the world's great fortified red wine. The best Port — and some say the only true Port — comes from Portugal. All authentic Portuguese Port is now called *Porto,* a name derived from the harbor city of Oporto, in Portugal, from which Porto is shipped around the world. If you don't see the word "Porto" on the label, the wine is not from Portugal.

Porto is made from a combination of four parts red wine and one part neutral spirits, or alcohol. The alcohol is added to the red wine while the wine is still fermenting. The resulting increase in alcohol arrests the fermentation, leaving the "fortified" wine with some unfermented grape sugar in it. Because of this process, all Port wines are sweet and high in alcohol. Porto usually contains about 20 percent alcohol, compared with unfortified red wines, which contain about 11 to 14 percent alcohol.

Buying and serving Porto can be very complicated because so many different types exist. Prices range from about $10 a bottle, for the simplest type, to over $100 a bottle, for the highly regarded 1994 Vintage Portos. And depending on which type you buy, the wine can be ready to drink or can need 15 to 20 years of additional bottle aging.

The people who make Porto wines are among the most consistent producers of quality wine in the world. Some producers do stand out, however. We list our 25 favorite Porto producers in three categories, each in rough order of preference. The wines of producers in the first group tend to be a bit more expensive, especially their Vintage Porto wines.

Superb
Taylor Fladgate
Fonseca
Graham

Excellent
Dow
Smith Woodhouse
Cockburn *(COH burn)*

Very Good
Ramos Pinto
Warre
Quinta do Noval
Niepoort
Croft
Sandeman

Very Good (continued)
Quarles Harris
Quinta do Infantado
Quinta do Vesuvio
Ferreira
Quinta de la Rosa
Cálem
Churchill
Delaforce
Gould Campbell
Martinez
Osborne
Offley
Rebello Valente

Chapter 4

Coming of Age: New World Red Wines Over $15

· ·

In This Chapter

▶ Killer California Cabs and Merlots

▶ Zinfandel's finest moments

▶ Great Pinot Noir from Oregon and California

▶ Elite red wines from Washington and New York

▶ Great red wines from the Southern Hemisphere

· ·

*I*f the marketplace is any arbiter, the quality of red wines from California and other states must be at its highest level ever. (Actually, even a blind tasting by experts would support that fact!) Hundreds of domestic red wines sell for prices as high as $20 to $45 a bottle, with little resistance from wine drinkers. The most sought-after wines have no problem selling at even higher prices.

These elite red wines from California make up the bulk of this chapter. We also review expensive red wines from other U.S. states, as well as from Australia, Chile, Argentina, and South Africa — although hardly any of those wines climb to the price levels of California's reds.

Like most New World wines, the wines in this chapter are usually named for the grape variety from which they're made — and we group them according to their grape variety. However, several wines carry proprietary names rather than grape names, because they're blends of grape varieties, in the Bordeaux tradition; we review them in a separate section.

We list the vital information for each wine in the following way:

✔ **The producer:** This is the company that makes the wine, and most of the time, this company name is the brand name of the wine.

✔ **The wine name:** In most cases, this is a grape name, but sometimes it's a proprietary name. For these more expensive wines, the wine name often includes designations such as *reserve* (an unregulated term that usually indicates a higher quality than a winery's non-reserve version of the same wine) or the name of a single vineyard from which the grapes came.

✔ **The appellation of the wine:** This information tells you the official geographic area in which the grapes for that wine grew, which can be a small locale, such as Stags Leap District (a particular part of the Napa Valley in California), or a large area, such as California (meaning that the grapes grew in various parts of the state). When we review wines from two or more countries in the same section, we indicate the country in parentheses after the appellation.

✔ **The approximate retail price of the wine:** This price can vary quite a lot according to what part of the country you're in and the type of store where you buy your wine. We use the New York state full-list retail price for each wine.

Great Red Wines from the U.S.

In this section, we review our favorite U.S. red wines that sell for more than $15 a bottle. We group these wines according to grape variety, mingling wines from various states that are made from the same grape variety. Remember that the wines we list and describe here are simply some of *our* favorite wines; many other good and great U.S. red wines exist outside the realm of these personal choices. The rating that we give indicates how much we like the wine and isn't meant to be interpreted as a quality rating (although our impression of a wine's quality naturally is a factor in how much we like a wine). The descriptions explain the style of each wine so that you can identify those wines that seem to suit your own taste.

Cabernet Sauvignon

The current popularity of Merlot notwithstanding, we believe that Cabernet Sauvignon is the best type of red wine made in the United States. In fact, we believe that Cabernet is the country's best wine, period.

Classic Cabernet Sauvignon wines, as typified by California's finest examples, are dark in color and have intense, ripe fruit aromas and flavors, mainly berries and plums, sometimes accented with touches of chocolate, mint, and/or various herbs. The wines usually have spiciness and firm tannin from oak aging; they're full bodied, high in alcohol, tannic, and yet approachable when young. Their accessibility, their delicious, ripe fruit character, and their velvety texture have already made California Cabernet Sauvignons a classic style of wine despite the fact that they've really only been around for the last three decades.

For more detailed information on U.S. Cabernet Sauvignons, see Chapters 4, 6, and 8 in *Red Wine For Dummies* and/or Chapter 12 in *Wine For Dummies*. For our recommended U.S. Cabernet Sauvignons under $15 a bottle, see Chapter 2 of this book. We present our recommended $15 to $50 U.S. Cabernet Sauvignons in this section alphabetically, according to the producer.

Anderson's Conn Valley Vineyards Cabernet Sauvignon

- ❢ **Producer:** Anderson's Conn Valley Vineyards
- ❢ **Wine name:** Cabernet Sauvignon
- ❢ **Appellation:** Napa Valley
- ❢ **Price:** $35

Gus Anderson, one of the real nice guys in the wine business, and his son, Todd (the winemaker), have produced a string of very successful Cabernets throughout the '90s. They stress elegance and real integration of oak with the wine, perhaps more typical of Bordeaux than Napa Valley. Their 1994 Cabernet has aromas and flavors of ripe black fruits and subtle, spicy oak, with accents of coffee and chocolate, in a medium- to full-bodied frame. It has excellent balance, with a moderate level of tannin and good concentration of fruit. You can enjoy this wine even now, but we suggest that you keep it for about three years, to let it develop a bit more.

Ed : 90–92

Araujo Estate Cabernet Sauvignon, Eisele Vineyard

- ❢ **Producer:** Araujo Estate *(a ROUW ho)*
- ❢ **Wine name:** Cabernet Sauvignon, Eisele Vineyard *(ICE eh lee)*
- ❢ **Appellation:** Napa Valley
- ❢ **Price:** $48

The rather new and small winery called Araujo is making one of the great Cabs in the U.S. The magic here is Eisele Vineyard, clearly one of the outstanding Cabernet Sauvignon vineyards in the country. The 1993 Araujo Cab is one of those wines that, as soon as you taste them, make you smile and just say, "Wow! This is a wine!" Black currant dominates the aroma, complemented by a touch of chocolate. The ripe fruit flavors are dense, concentrated, and sweet. Already, the wine has exquisite balance and a long finish. You may be tempted to drink such a superb wine right now, but I recommend saving it for 15 to 20 years, when it should be even more thrilling. Because only a few thousand cases are made, I suggest that you get on Araujo Estate's mailing list by calling 707-942-6471. I haven't had the 1994 Araujo Cab yet, but I hear it's as good as, if not better than, the 1993 vintage.

Ed: 94–96

BV Private Reserve Cabernet Sauvignon

- ♪ **Producer:** Beaulieu Vineyard *(boh l'yuh)*, also known as BV
- ♪ **Wine name:** Cabernet Sauvignon, Georges de Latour Private Reserve
- ♪ **Appellation:** Napa Valley
- ♪ **Price:** $45

Beaulieu Vineyard, a winery founded in 1900 by Georges de Latour, boasts the longest continuously produced Cabernet Sauvignon in the U.S. The first Georges de Latour Private Reserve Cabernet was made in 1936, and it was still delicious 50 years later! Several vintages of this wine rank among the finest Cabernets ever made in the U.S. (the 1951, 1958, 1968, and 1970 come to mind), and the wine is still definitely in the elite group of California Cabernet Sauvignons. The 1993 wine has rich, seductive, spicy aromas, along with ripe flavors of black currants and a slight herbal/vegetal character, probably attributable to the type of oak used. It's a rich, full-bodied, flavorful Cabernet with very firm tannin balancing its ripe fruit, but it's quite young now. Like most past vintages of this wine, the 1993 Cab has the capacity to age for decades, if you desire to keep it. (BV also makes a lower-priced, consistently reliable Cabernet Sauvignon, the BV Rutherford, which retails for $17.50.)

Ed: 86–88   **Mary:** 90–92

Beringer Knights Valley Cabernet Sauvignon

- **Producer:** Beringer Vineyards
- **Wine name:** Cabernet Sauvignon, Knights Valley
- **Appellation:** Knights Valley
- **Price:** $20

Beringer Vineyards, one of the oldest and best wineries in the U.S., has always been known for its Cabernet Sauvignons, especially for its now-pricey ($60) Private Reserve. Beringer's less lofty Knights Valley Cabernet is a consistently reliable wine, the kind of Cabernet you can find everywhere and can always trust. (But we're a little disturbed that its full-list price has risen to $20.) Beringer's 1993 Cab from Knights Valley has aromas and flavors of cassis, sweet vanilla, woodiness, plummy fruit, and mint. It's a full-bodied mouthful of flavor, with firm tannins that are balanced by intense fruit character. Enjoy this wine now with a spicy meat entrée.

Ed: 86–88   **Mary:** 86–88

Cakebread Cabernet Sauvignon

- **Producer:** Cakebread Cellars
- **Wine name:** Cabernet Sauvignon
- **Appellation:** Napa Valley
- **Price:** $24

You have to love a winery with the unusual name of Cakebread. And when you meet the Cakebread family, you like the winery even more! (Visit in the off-season; this winery, on Highway 29 in Rutherford, is always crowded.)

The 1994 Cakebread Cabernet has aromas of blueberry and cedar, with touches of dill and mustard seed, along with berry fruit flavors. It's a soft, dense, thick Cabernet, quite Merlot-like in its ripe, plump fruit, and it has good depth. You can enjoy this Cabernet within the next few years. By the way, the Cakebreads make a superb Rutherford Reserve Cabernet Sauvignon that sells for about $42.

Ed: 88–90   **Mary:** 86–88

Chateau Montelena Cabernet Sauvignon, Calistoga Cuvée

- **Producer:** Chateau Montelena
- **Wine name:** Cabernet Sauvignon, Calistoga Cuvée
- **Appellation:** Napa Valley
- **Price:** $18

For many years, Chateau Montelena produced only one Cabernet Sauvignon wine, from grapes grown on its own vineyards. That wine, now called the Estate Cabernet, has become increasingly prized by collectors and is priced accordingly. Montelena's Calistoga Cuvée Cabernet has filled the gap at the everyday level, providing wine lovers with a less complex, less ageworthy wine that nevertheless is Montelena-style Cab.

The 1995 Calistoga Cuvée Cabernet is a full-bodied wine with inky, spicy aromas and flavors, velvety texture, and firm tannin — a fairly straightforward Cabernet. The 1994 wine is a bit lighter in body and more open, with berry and cassis flavors balancing the wine's firm tannin. In both vintages, this is a good, sturdy Cabernet at an honest price. (We both highly recommend the Chateau Montelena Estate Cabernet, about $43.)

Mary: 86–88

Clos du Val Cabernet Sauvignon Reserve

- **Producer:** Clos Du Val *(cloh du val)*
- **Wine name:** Cabernet Sauvignon, Reserve
- **Appellation:** Napa Valley
- **Price:** $24

In this case, a California winery with a French name is not a gimmick: Bernard Portet, a Frenchman, has been Clos Du Val's one and only winemaker since the winery was founded in 1970. The style of Cabernet Sauvignon here has always emulated that of Bordeaux wines (Bernard's father was the winemaker at Château Lafite-Rothschild); that is, the wines are elegant, subtle, austere when young, and full of finesse, rather than intense powerhouses. The 1994 bottling is typical of young Clos Du Val Cabs in that it's somewhat closed and inexpressive right now. Quiet aromas of spicy oak and coffee and some tart cranberry fruit flavors do show through, along with an impression of plenty of depth, good concentration, and a velvety texture. Actually, this wine is quite powerful for Clos du Val, because it's a child of the ripe 1994 vintage in Napa. This wine needs at least four or five years to develop and soften.

Ed: 88–90   **Mary:** 89–91

Columbia Cabernet Sauvignon, Red Willow Vineyard

- ♪ **Producer:** Columbia Winery
- ♪ **Wine name:** Cabernet Sauvignon, Red Willow Vineyard
- ♪ **Appellation:** Yakima Valley
- ♪ **Price:** $24

Columbia Winery is one of the pioneers of Washington State's young winemaking industry, and its innovative winemaker, British-born David Lake, has played a big role in the winery's success. In Lake's honor, Columbia's best wines are labeled "David Lake Series." Our favorite wine from this series is the Cabernet Sauvignon from grapes grown in Red Willow Vineyard. The 1993 version, with 15 percent Cabernet Franc blended in, has deep, complex aromas of earth, nuts, berries, nutmeg, vanilla, and mint, along with a real core of pure fruit flavor (mainly black currants) that hasn't quite unfolded yet. It's a well-balanced, medium-bodied wine, not a blockbuster, but solid and juicy. The Red Willow Cab is an exciting, intensely-wound wine that promises great things. We suggest that you cellar it for two or three years, but you may also enjoy it now. (We also recommend the 1994 Columbia "Milestone" Merlot, also made from grapes grown at Red Willow Vineyard.)

Ed: 88–90   **Mary:** 90–92

Ferrari-Carano Cabernet Sauvignon

- ♪ **Producer:** Ferrari-Carano Winery
- ♪ **Wine name:** Cabernet Sauvignon
- ♪ **Appellation:** Sonoma County
- ♪ **Price:** $25

Owners Don and Rhonda Carano and veteran winemaker George Bursick are at the top of their form with their elegant 1993 Cabernet Sauvignon, actually a blend of the five Bordeaux varieties, with Cab Sauvignon dominating. It has a full but sedate aroma of toasted almonds and charry oak as well as flavors of cassis and plums. This soft, thick, rich Cab will be enjoyable over the next few years, perhaps accompanied by a duck or flavorful lamb entrée.

Ed: 89–91   **Mary:** 90–92

Frog's Leap Cabernet Sauvignon

- ! **Producer:** Frog's Leap Winery
- ! **Wine name:** Cabernet Sauvignon
- ! **Appellation:** Napa Valley
- ! **Price:** $23

We like the understated winemaking style of Frog's Leap; its wines are usually elegant and well made, with clear expressions of the grape variety and without too much cumbersome oak. Having said that, we must admit that the 1994 Frog's Leap Cabernet Sauvignon is a blockbuster, an expression of the vintage, perhaps, more than the typical style of the winery. But we still love it; when you taste it, you'll see that this wine is hard not to love!

The 1994 Frog's Leap Cab has smoky, toasty aromas and ripe, rich fruit flavors. It's full bodied and plump, with firm tannin that sneaks up from the back of your mouth as you taste the wine; fortunately, the wine's rich fruit balances its acidity and tannin. This is a really serious Cabernet with velvety texture, impressive depth, and concentration. You can enjoy it within the next few years. Try this wine with grilled steak or sausages.

Ed: 92–94   **Mary:** 87–89

The Hess Collection Cabernet Sauvignon

- ! **Producer:** The Hess Collection
- ! **Wine name:** Cabernet Sauvignon
- ! **Appellation:** Napa Valley
- ! **Price:** $22

In a short time, The Hess Collection's Cabernet has become one of the most acclaimed and sought-after California Cabernet Sauvignons. The 1993 Hess Collection Cab has aromas of cinnamon and black fruits, along with very spicy flavor accents from oak. It's a firm, full-bodied, rather tough Cab with plenty of tannin and acidity and is relatively closed right now. This is a serious wine that's a bit too young for current drinking. Give it three to five years of aging to open and develop. (The winery also makes a lower-priced Cab, called Hess Select, which is a good value but doesn't have the intensity and concentration of the primary Cab.)

Ed: 87–89   **Mary:** 86–88

Paul Hobbs Cabernet Sauvignon, Hyde Vineyard

- ❢ **Producer:** Paul Hobbs Cellars
- ❢ **Wine name:** Cabernet Sauvignon, Hyde Vineyard
- ❢ **Appellation:** Napa Valley, Carneros
- ❢ **Price:** $40

Despite its good reputation, the Paul Hobbs Cabernet Sauvignon is a wine that we've hesitated to recommend in the past because production is small and the wines are difficult to obtain. We're making an exception for Paul Hobbs's 1994 Cab, however, because it's so darn good! Hobbs worked as a winemaker at Opus One and Simi before creating his own brand in 1991. The 1994 Hobbs Cabernet Sauvignon (this one's from Hyde Vineyard in Carneros; he makes another Cab from Liparita Vineyard in Howell Mountain, Napa) has aromas of ripe, plummy fruit with coffee nuances and an edge of oak; the flavors are of delicious, ripe, plump fruit. This is a real thoroughbred Cabernet, medium to full bodied and excellently balanced. The 1994 Hobbs Cab is so harmonious and generous that you can enjoy it now, perhaps with a platter of grilled meats and vegetables. But if you have the patience, the wine's tannin and acidity will enable it to live for well over a decade. (We also love the 1994 Paul Hobbs Pinot Noir from Carneros.)

Ed: 90–92   **Mary:** 88–90

Jordan Cabernet Sauvignon

- ❢ **Producer:** Jordan Vineyard
- ❢ **Wine name:** Cabernet Sauvignon
- ❢ **Appellation:** Alexander Valley
- ❢ **Price:** $32.50

Jordan Vineyard makes one of the most popular Cabernet Sauvignons in the U.S. — a top seller in wine shops and especially in restaurants. The Jordan style of Cabernet is typified by softness, elegance, and early drinkability, rather than by power — probably why the wine has earned so many fans. The 1993 Jordan Cab has berry fruit aromas and classic Cabernet flavors of cedar and lead pencil. The wine combines richness and sweet fruit with soft tannins. Drink this utterly pleasant wine in the near future; it's best when it's young. Merlot lovers will especially enjoy this soft Cabernet.

Ed: 86–88   **Mary:** 85–87

Kendall-Jackson Cabernet Sauvignon, Grand Reserve

- **Producer:** Kendall-Jackson
- **Wine name:** Cabernet Sauvignon, Grand Reserve
- **Appellation:** California
- **Price:** $42

Kendall-Jackson has been such a success story in California that it's difficult to believe that its wines have been around only for 15 years! K-J, as wine lovers often refer to the winery, makes a wide variety of wines, ranging in price from about $10 up to $60 (for the blended red wine called Cardinale).

The varietal wines in Kendall-Jackson's Grand Reserve Series are particularly good. The 1993 Cabernet Sauvignon is a power-packed wine. It's fragrant with black fruit and quiet oak scents, and it has deeply concentrated black-fruit and chocolate flavors. It's a big, full-bodied, ripe, intense Cab, soft enough to enjoy now, but it can age easily for another six to eight years, if you care to hold on to it.

Ed: 87–89   **Mary:** 88–90

Laurel Glen Cabernet Sauvignon

- **Producer:** Laurel Glen Vineyard
- **Wine name:** Cabernet Sauvignon
- **Appellation:** Sonoma Mountain
- **Price:** $34

Patrick Campbell, the thinking man's winemaker, has managed to push his Laurel Glen Cabernet Sauvignon to the very top echelon of Cabernets in the U.S. At a recent blind tasting of 1992 California Cabernets at the International Wine Center in New York, tasters ranked the Laurel Glen number one. The 1994 Laurel Glen Cabernet is very young and tannic right now (typical of young Cabs made from mountain-grown grapes), but its underlying, concentrated fruit character promises good things for the future. The wine has deep, quiet aromas, flavors of oak and cassis, excellent balance, and a long, fruity finish. A subtle Cabernet, it will be a great wine, but we advise patience so that it can develop — say, at least five years. Undoubtedly, it can live for at least two decades.

Laurel Glen's entire line of wines is excellent. If you have difficulty locating the 1994 Cabernet, or if it's a bit pricey for you (or if you don't feel like waiting around for it to develop!), try the Laurel Glen Counterpoint, at about half of the price of the winery's top Cab, or the Terra Rosa ($12) or the simply-named "Reds" ($8 to $9). All are really good values and well made.

Ed: 89–91   **Mary:** 89–91

L'Ecole No. 41 Cabernet Sauvignon

> ❢ **Producer:** L'Ecole No. 41 Winery
>
> ❢ **Wine name:** Cabernet Sauvignon
>
> ❢ **Appellation:** Columbia Valley
>
> ❢ **Price:** $27

This small winery, named for the historic French schoolhouse that it occupies, is located in the Walla Walla region of southeastern Washington State. Martin and Megan Clubb, the owners, have been making wine there since 1983, and their wines get better all the time. We especially like their Cabernet Sauvignons. The 1994 vintage, a 100 percent Cabernet Sauvignon blended from four separate vineyards in the Columbia and Walla Walla Valleys, has aromas of baked fruit, herbs, and new oak, along with intense fruit flavors. It's rich, velvety, and full bodied, with lots of depth and concentration. You can enjoy this full-flavored Cab now (perhaps with steak or venison), but it will age well for a few more years.

Ed: 87–89   **Mary:** 87–89

Great U.S. Cabernet Sauvignons and Cabernet blends over $50

The ranks of domestic Cabernet wines and Cabernet blends that sell for more than $50 a bottle have greatly increased in number over the last few years. This higher-priced category encompasses the very best Cabernet Sauvignons and Cab blends made in the U.S. today. We list some of our favorites of these wines alphabetically below; the winery name comes first in each listing, followed by the vineyard name or other designation that's part of the wine name, if any. Wines that have a proprietary name rather than the name "Cabernet Sauvignon" are indicated by the word "blend" in parentheses next to the name. (Otherwise, the wine is named Cabernet Sauvignon.) We omit from the list the wines of small, new wineries with tiny productions, because such wines are nearly impossible to obtain.

Cabernet Sauvignon/Blend	Appellation
Beringer Vineyards, Chabot Vineyard	Napa Valley
Beringer Vineyards, Private Reserve	Napa Valley
Caymus Vineyards, Special Selection	Napa Valley
Dalla Valle, Maya (blend)	Napa Valley
Dominus Estate	Napa Valley
Dunn Vineyards, Howell Mountain	Howell Mountain (Napa Valley)
Grace Family Vineyards	Napa Valley
Groth Vineyards, Reserve	Napa Valley
Harlan Estate	Napa Valley
Heitz Wine Cellars, Martha's Vineyard	Napa Valley
Joseph Phelps Vineyards, Backus Vineyard	Napa Valley
Joseph Phelps Vineyards, Insignia (blend)	Napa Valley
Kendall-Jackson, Cardinale (blend)	California
Niebaum-Coppola Estate, Rubicon (blend)	Napa Valley
Opus One (blend)	Napa Valley
Ridge Vineyards, Monte Bello Vineyard	Santa Cruz Mountains
Robert Mondavi Winery, Reserve	Napa Valley
Shafer Vineyards, Hillside Select	Stags Leap District (Napa Valley)
Silver Oak Cellars	Napa Valley
Stag's Leap Wine Cellars, Cask 23 (blend)	Napa Valley

Leonetti Cabernet Sauvignon

- *!* **Producer:** Leonetti Cellar
- *!* **Wine name:** Cabernet Sauvignon
- *!* **Appellation:** Columbia Valley
- *!* **Price:** $45

We debated a great deal about whether we should include Leonetti's Cabernet among our reviews. On the "pro" side, we love the wine; on the "con" side, you can't find it in your wine shop. Ultimately, our enthusiasm for the wine won out. Here's the problem: Winemaker-owner Gary Figgins makes only about 4,500 cases of wine a year, mainly Cabernet Sauvignon and Merlot, at his winery in Walla Walla, Washington. Thanks to great reviews, Leonetti wines have become among the most sought-after wines in the U.S., and only customers on the winery's mailing list can purchase them.

The Cab and the Merlot both represent the classic, intensely rich, voluptuous style of red wine that is so popular in the U.S. The 1994 Cabernet Sauvignon has an intense aroma of black currants, ink, and spicy oak, along with dense, packed flavors of black fruits. It's a fruity, delicious wine with a great balance of tannin, acidity, and fruit. This smooth, supple, sophisticated Cabernet is clearly capable of aging, but you can enjoy it even now. We tried a pre-release sample of the 1995 Leonetti Cabernet at the winery, and it will also be super. Leonetti's mailing list has a waiting list; if you've got the patience, write to Leonetti Cellar, 1321 School Ave., Walla Walla, WA 99362, and ask to be included on the waiting list.

Ed: 90–92   **Mary:** 90–92

Quilceda Creek Cabernet Sauvignon

- *!* **Producer:** Quilceda Creek Vintners
- *!* **Wine name:** Cabernet Sauvignon
- *!* **Appellation:** Washington
- *!* **Price:** $45

This Cabernet Sauvignon is so good that we feel obligated to mention it, even though the supply is small. Owner-winemaker Alex Golitzen had a pretty good teacher — his uncle, the grand old man of California wine, the late André Tchelistcheff. The 1993 Quilceda Creek Cabernet is a very dense wine, more closed than that of its friendly rival, Leonetti Cellar. It has intense aromas of blackberry fruit, along with deep, velvety, cassis flavors. It's a highly concentrated, complex Cabernet, with loads of tannin and acidity; it will certainly improve even further with a few more years of aging. The wine is a keeper and highly recommended for Cabernet lovers. If you have difficulty finding this wine, try phoning or faxing Quilceda Creek Vintners at 360-568-2389.

Ed: 91–93   **Mary:** 91–93

Rosenblum Napa Valley Cabernet Sauvignon

- ❢ **Producer:** Rosenblum Cellars
- ❢ **Wine name:** Cabernet Sauvignon
- ❢ **Appellation:** Napa Valley
- ❢ **Price:** $20

Kent Rosenblum, veterinarian by profession, winemaker by avocation (anyone who loves both animals and wine is our kind of guy!), has made his reputation in wine with his stunning series of red Zinfandels — about eight different Zins each year. But when you're good, you're good. And so I'm forced to recommend Rosenblum's Cabernet Sauvignon as well! The 1994 Cabernet from Napa Valley grapes has sweet, oaky aromas with soft, very rich, red- and black-fruit flavors. It's a hedonistic, voluptuous Cabernet, quite intense and young, but also soft enough to enjoy even now. I continue to be impressed with the 1994 California Cabernets; Napa Valley has apparently been particularly blessed in this vintage.

Ed: 90–92

Shafer Cabernet Sauvignon

- ❢ **Producer:** Shafer Vineyards
- ❢ **Wine name:** Cabernet Sauvignon
- ❢ **Appellation:** Stags Leap District (Napa Valley)
- ❢ **Price:** $28.50

The soil and microclimate in the Stags Leap District have such an effect on the style of Cabernets made there — soft, elegant wines, enjoyable when young — that tasters invariably assume that Merlot is blended into Shafer's Stags Leap District Cabernet. But John and Doug Shafer, father and son, will tell you (with a grin) that their wine is 100 percent Cabernet Sauvignon! If you want to see the effect of *terroir* (growing conditions) on wine, try a Shafer Cabernet next to one from another part of the Napa Valley. The difference is quite amazing.

The 1994 Shafer Cabernet has complex, ripe fruit, and herbal aromas, along with voluptuous, soft, fruit flavors. Despite the apparent softness, however, it's an intensely flavored, full-bodied, powerful wine that you can cellar for at least another ten years or so, if you wish. By the way, Shafer's other Cabernet Sauvignon, called Hillside Select, is even better than this very good one, but it now costs over $50.

Ed: 86–88 **Mary:** 86–88

Spottswoode Cabernet Sauvignon

- ✔ **Producer:** Spottswoode Vineyard
- ✔ **Wine name:** Cabernet Sauvignon
- ✔ **Appellation:** Napa Valley
- ✔ **Price:** $45

We're big fans of Spottswoode's Cabernet Sauvignon because we love its style — subtle, balanced, restrained, elegant, and ever more complex with age. (As you can surmise, we're not into bitingly tannic blockbusters.) Spottswoode is the Bordeaux lover's Cabernet Sauvignon. The 1994 Spottswoode Cabernet is really fragrant with aromas of black cherry and blackberry fruit and a touch of smoky bacon; its flavors are those of spicy, intense fruit. More voluptuous than usual because of the intensity of the 1994 vintage, this supple Cab nevertheless has lots of tannin and great depth, and needs time to develop. The 1994 Spottswoode is a serious Cabernet, and it extends one of the finest records for consistency of any of the California Cabernet Sauvignons.

Ed: 91–93 **Mary:** 89–91

Staglin Cabernet Sauvignon

- ✔ **Producer:** Staglin Family Vineyard
- ✔ **Wine name:** Cabernet Sauvignon
- ✔ **Appellation:** Rutherford
- ✔ **Price:** $37.50

Staglin Family Vineyard has some prized acreage in the heart of the so-called Rutherford Bench, a stretch of land known for its Cabernet Sauvignon grapes. The 1992 and 1994 Cabs from Staglin have been especially fine. The 1994 has intense, rich aromas and flavors of blackberry and tart cherry fruit, with some oakiness. Still firm and tannic, this oaky, concentrated wine should come around eventually. (The 1992 is drinking beautifully now.) We suggest that you hold on to it for two or three years, and then try it with lamb. (By the way, Staglin also makes one of the best Sangiovese wines in California.)

Ed: 90–92   **Mary:** 86–88

Stag's Leap Wine Cellars Cabernet Sauvignon

- **Producer:** Stag's Leap Wine Cellars
- **Wine name:** Cabernet Sauvignon
- **Appellation:** Napa Valley
- **Price:** $25

Stag's Leap Wine Cellars is one of the stars among Napa's wineries, and has been so for 25 years. (Careful: There's also a Stags' Leap Winery; note the different wording and the placement of the apostrophe in each name.) All Stag's Leap red wines are famous for their elegance, subtlety, and complexity, factors that reflect not only the *terroir* of the Stags Leap District, but also the philosophy of the winemaker. In the case of the Napa Valley Cabernet, however, the style derives from winemaker-owner Warren Winiarski, as the grapes are purchased from various Napa Valley vineyards rather than coming only from the winery's home district. The 1992 Stag's Leap Cab, Napa Valley, has an aroma of black currants, cedar, and charry oak that's wonderful enough to die for. It's a harmonious wine, with soft, supple, black-fruit flavors and a long, fine finish. You can drink it now or within the next several years.

Ed: 89–91   **Mary:** 89–91

Swanson Cabernet Sauvignon

- **Producer:** Swanson Vineyards
- **Wine name:** Cabernet Sauvignon
- **Appellation:** Napa Valley
- **Price:** $24

Swanson Vineyards is another winery blessed with prized Cabernet Sauvignon acreage in the renowned Rutherford Bench district of Napa Valley. (That area must also be very good for the Sangiovese grape, by the way, because Swanson's Sangiovese is one of the few standouts of this variety in California.) Young Marco Cappelli, the unassuming, refreshingly straightforward winemaker at Swanson, seems to be getting better and better results with each vintage. The 1994 Cabernet Sauvignon has deep, intense aromas of cassis, lead pencil, cedar, and smoky oak, along with ripe berry and cedar flavor. It's an elegant, extremely well-balanced Cabernet with moderate tannins and a core of intense fruit. We expect this wine to be perfect in two or three years.

Ed: 90–92   **Mary:** 89–91

Villa Mt. Eden Cabernet Sauvignon, Grand Reserve

> ♪ **Producer:** Villa Mt. Eden
>
> ♪ **Wine name:** Cabernet Sauvignon, Grand Reserve
>
> ♪ **Appellation:** Napa Valley
>
> ♪ **Price:** $20

We've been impressed with the steady improvement in quality at Villa Mt. Eden during the last few years. (We recommend Villa Mt. Eden's $12 California Cabernet in Chapter 2.) The 1993 Grand Reserve Cabernet has minty, oaky, and cola-like aromas along with sweet, ripe fruit flavors. It's full bodied, soft, very flavorful, and appropriately tannic, and it has lots of character. You can drink this wine soon; in fact, it begs for lamb!

Ed: 88–90   **Mary:** 86–88

Merlot from the U.S.

In Chapter 2, we lament the state of Merlot today: the over-produced, dilute wines that producers are pumping out of their Merlot vines to fill the huge demand for Merlot among wine drinkers. In this section, we introduce a different quality of Merlot: the richly-textured, plummy wines of the sort that were respon-sible for starting the Merlot craze in the first place.

The Merlots we review in this section are all fine wines, but they vary in style according to where their grapes grew and whether they contain any Cabernet Sauvignon in their blend (a fairly common practice in making Merlot). By reading our descriptions of the wines, rather than simply letting our scores guide you, you should be able to determine which of the wines are the style you prefer.

Bedell Cellars Merlot

- ! **Producer:** Bedell Cellars
- ! **Wine name:** Merlot
- ! **Appellation:** North Fork of Long Island
- ! **Price:** $16

Kip Bedell of Bedell Cellars has a reputation for making one of the best Merlots on Long Island, a young wine region that has already become one of the key players in the production of good U.S. Merlot. Bedell's 1994 Merlot is quite oaky: You can smell charry oak, and you can feel the firm, almost sharp tannin from the oak when you taste the wine. But this wine has good concentration of fruit character to balance out the oak. This massive Merlot is very young now; give it a year or two of age — or a chunk of hard cheese — and prepare to be impressed. If you come across the 1993 vintage of this wine, you'll find it softer and more approachable. The winery also makes a Reserve Merlot for $27.50, but for the money, we'll take the regular bottling.

Ed: 85–87   **Mary:** 88–90

Charles Krug Reserve Merlot

- ! **Producer:** Charles Krug Winery
- ! **Wine name:** Merlot, Reserve
- ! **Appellation:** Napa
- ! **Price:** $21

Charles Krug is a great old Napa Valley winery (established in 1861) whose wines experienced a dip in quality, but are now on the comeback trail. The style of the 1992 Charles Krug Reserve Merlot is very much steeped in Old World tradition rather than modern, fruit-oriented winemaking ideals. Wine tasters might describe the aroma and flavors as "barnyard" because they're earthy and pungent (a characteristic that some of us distinctly enjoy); they also show a bit of raspberry in the background. The wine is medium bodied, supple, and only moderately tannic — an easy-to-take sort of Merlot. Precisely because it's not oozing with fruitiness, this wine goes well with normal foods, such as pasta or casseroles that don't have fruity flavors themselves.

Mary: 84–86

Chateau Souverain Merlot

- ! **Producer:** Chateau Souverain
- ! **Wine name:** Merlot
- ! **Appellation:** Alexander Valley
- ! **Price:** $18

For approximately the past five years, the wines of Chateau Souverain have offered solid quality, a likable style, and excellent value. The 1995 Merlot is very soft, supple, and creamy, with ripe Merlot fruitiness as well as spicy aromas and flavors that derive from oak. It's a big, intensely flavored wine with a velvety texture. This smooth, well-balanced wine could be exactly what you're looking for in a Merlot to drink now: a very good wine from a very reliable producer.

Ed: 91–93   **Mary:** 88–90

Chateau Ste. Michelle Merlot, Cold Creek Vineyard

- ! **Producer:** Chateau Ste. Michelle
- ! **Wine name:** Merlot, Cold Creek Vineyard
- ! **Appellation:** Columbia Valley
- ! **Price:** $32

Washington's Chateau Ste. Michelle winery makes three or four single-vineyard Merlots and a good Columbia Valley Merlot (blended from the grapes of various vineyards; about $15 to $16). The winery also makes a Reserve Merlot for $40. The Cold Creek Vineyard Merlot — one of the single-vineyard wines — is our favorite because it's the best balanced of the group and because it integrates its oak better than the other Chateau Ste. Michelle Merlots do. The 1993 Cold Creek wine is 100 percent Merlot; it has intense, herbal, oaky aromas, along with intensely concentrated, plummy fruit flavors. Although a rich, big mouthful of wine, it's still the leanest and most austere of Chateau Ste. Michelle's Merlots, a trait that we value because it enables the wine to accompany food well. Give this important wine a few years to develop. (We also like the 1994 Cold Creek Vineyard Merlot best of this winery's five Merlots in the 1994 vintage, but it needs time to develop.) If you prefer a rich, voluptuous style of Merlot, however, we suspect that the 1994 Chateau Ste. Michelle Reserve could seduce you quite easily!

Ed: 91–93   **Mary:** 87–89

The allocation game

The game that wineries and wine distributors play to handle shortages of certain wines is called placing a wine *on allocation*. Wines that are on allocation are not available to just any store that wants to purchase them. In some cases, the wine is allocated to certain cities and not to others, and in some cases, the wine is allocated to restaurants and not to wine shops. Wineries sometimes favor restaurants over shops because having their wine on the wine list of good restaurants is considered prestigious. In addition, the wine sells more slowly in restaurants, thus stretching a small quantity of wine over a longer period of time.

If the wine you're looking for is on allocation, these are your only options:

✔ Find out from your retailer when the next vintage will arrive in the store and arrange to buy it.

✔ Try buying the wine from a store in another city.

✔ Try buying the wine directly from the winery.

✔ Drink the wine in restaurants.

✔ Hang in there; some wine industry forecasters predict that wine shortages will subside in the next few years.

Estancia Merlot

     ♪ **Producer:** Estancia Estates
     ♪ **Wine name:** Merlot
     ♪ **Appellation:** Alexander Valley
     ♪ **Price:** $17.50

Of all the wines from Estancia, we're most enthusiastic about the Merlot. Although the 1994 Estancia Merlot is soft, round, supple, and creamy — textbook Merlot characteristics — it's not a showy, seductive sort of wine. Its aroma is quiet, with hints of concentrated fruit, burnt chocolate, and charry oak; its flavors are similarly reserved. The wine has terrific concentration of rich fruit, but is understated now, in its youth. We don't quite understand how Estancia can sell such a good Merlot at such a reasonable price, but we're definitely not complaining!

Ed: 92–94   **Mary:** 91–93

Hargrave Vineyard Lattice Label Merlot

- ❢ **Producer:** Hargrave Vineyard
- ❢ **Wine name:** Merlot, Lattice Label
- ❢ **Appellation:** North Fork of Long Island
- ❢ **Price:** $16

Alex and Louisa Hargrave began the modern winemaking era on Long Island. In 1973, they purchased a potato farm in Cutchogue, and four years later released Long Island's first commercial wines, from grapes grown on their estate. Today, Hargrave Vineyard remains one of New York's best wineries. Its best line of wines is the "Lattice Label" series (a lattice pattern, resembling a trellis, is cut out of each label), which encompasses five wines, including a very good Cabernet Franc and an interesting Pinot Noir. The 1995 Merlot from this series is medium to full bodied, with aromas of bell peppers and inky, vegetal flavors. It has lots of depth and intensity, and an attractive velvety texture. The supple, relatively lean style of this wine makes it an ideal food wine; I suggest ratatouille or a platter of grilled summer vegetables with roasted potatoes.

Ed: 87–89

Matanzas Creek Merlot

- ❢ **Producer:** Matanzas Creek Winery
- ❢ **Wine name:** Merlot
- ❢ **Appellation:** Sonoma Valley
- ❢ **Price:** $43

The names Matanzas Creek and Merlot are inextricably linked in the minds of red wine lovers, not only because of the great Merlot wines that this winery has produced over the years but also because Matanzas Creek has dedicated itself to Merlot, making no other red wine. Its 1994 Merlot is as deep, dense, and black in color as a wine can be, setting you up for a truly intense Merlot experience — which the wine delivers. After a whiff of the dense, deep (but closed-in) aroma, you can taste plummy and spicy flavors that go deep into the wine, and you can feel the wine's rich texture and very firm tannin. "Quintessential California Merlot, at its deepest and richest," you might think — at least, that's what Ed thought. If your judgment instead is "a wine so intense and so young that it's impenetrable; the jury is still out," you're on Mary's wavelength.

Ed: 90–92   **Mary:** 86–88

Niebaum-Coppola Merlot

> ♪ **Producer:** Niebaum-Coppola Estate
>
> ♪ **Wine name:** Merlot, Francis Coppola Family Wines
>
> ♪ **Appellation:** Napa Valley
>
> ♪ **Price:** $25

Several years ago, filmmaker Francis Ford Coppola added a Merlot and a Zinfandel, among others, to his winery's repertoire; the new wines are known as Francis Coppola Family Wines. Rubicon, his mainly Cabernet Sauvignon blend, is still the star of the show at Niebaum-Coppola, but we also like the 1994 Merlot very much. Niebaum-Coppola's wines have always had that European touch to them. The 1994 Merlot has aromas reminiscent of a Bordeaux — lead pencil and cedar — along with plump, ripe, sweet, fruit flavors. It is concentrated and intense, but would go well right now with a veal dish in a rich tomato sauce. Enjoy this wine within the next few years.

Ed: 88–90   **Mary:** 89–91

Newton Vineyard Merlot

> ♪ **Producer:** Newton Vineyard
>
> ♪ **Wine name:** Merlot, "Unfiltered"
>
> ♪ **Appellation:** Napa Valley
>
> ♪ **Price:** $28

Newton Vineyard, on Spring Mountain in western Napa Valley, has long been one of California's leaders in producing Merlot; its first Merlots date back to 1978. Made from tough mountain-grown grapes, Newton Merlot is definitely not a wimpy wine. The 1994 Newton Merlot has black cherry and spice aromas, along with rich, deep plum, and black-cherry fruit flavors. It's a full-bodied wine with an extraordinary depth of flavor, Merlot at its deepest, densest, and richest. I recommend holding on to this beauty for a few years. This is a wine for Merlot lovers.

Ed: 90–92

Ravenswood Merlot, Sangiacomo Vineyard

- ♪ **Producer:** Ravenswood
- ♪ **Wine name:** Merlot, Sangiacomo Vineyard
  (san JHOCK oh mo)
- ♪ **Appellation:** Carneros
- ♪ **Price:** $25

We're big fans of Joel Peterson, winemaker and co-proprietor of Ravenswood. All of his wines are full of character and individuality. Ravenswood's Sangiacomo Vineyard Merlot is also consistently one of the country's best, in our opinion. The 1994 Sangiacomo has aromas of intensely spicy oak, earth, and ripe fruit, along with flavors of round, plump fruit, some oak, and even a touch of caraway seed. Its tannin and oakiness plus its very long finish suggest that this Merlot needs a few more years to soften and develop. But it will be a winner; to Mary, it's "the epitome of Merlot."

Ed: 90–92   **Mary:** 90–92

Swanson Merlot

- ♪ **Producer:** Swanson Vineyards
- ♪ **Wine name:** Merlot
- ♪ **Appellation:** Napa Valley
- ♪ **Price:** $24

Swanson Vineyards Merlot is probably the least-known of the better Merlots in California today. The 1994 Swanson Merlot has aromas of chocolate, cherry, and raspberry, along with ripe, lush, berry fruit flavors. It's a very rich wine, with wonderful, thick, soft texture, great balance, and a concentrated finish. (Swanson's 1995 Merlot, by the way, is quite tannic at this young age, but it clearly has potential.) You can drink the 1994 Merlot within the next few years.

Ed: 90–92   **Mary:** 90–92

Villa Mt. Eden Merlot, Grand Reserve

- **Producer:** Villa Mt. Eden
- **Wine name:** Merlot, Grand Reserve
- **Appellation:** Napa Valley
- **Price:** $18

We recommend several Villa Mt. Eden's wines in this book, for one simple reason: They are well-made, user-friendly wines. (Or is that two reasons?) The 1994 Merlot Grand Reserve has spicy, brambly fruit, and mineral aromas, along with earthy, oaky, and tart berry fruit flavors. It's an elegant, well-balanced wine with good concentration and a long finish. This Merlot is quite young now and needs about two years to develop. In its earthiness, it somewhat resembles a Bordeaux wine from France's Right Bank (where Merlot is the dominant grape).

Ed: 88–90   **Mary:** 87–89

Pinot Noir

The gamut of acceptable Pinot Noir styles is broad, encompassing light- to full-bodied wines; lightly oaked to oaky wines; vibrant, spicy wines to mellow, graceful wines; wines that are meant to be enjoyed young; and wines that are keepers. The one critical characteristic for a Pinot Noir wine is that it must reflect, in no uncertain terms, the grapes from which it was made rather than winemaking technique.

We describe some of our favorite U.S. Pinot Noir wines below in alphabetical order according to the producer, intermingling wines from California and Oregon, the two principal states for Pinot Noir production. We urge you to try one or two of these wines. No other red wine is quite like a good Pinot Noir. (For more information on Pinot Noir wines from the U.S., read the Pinot Noir sections in Chapters 7 and 8 of *Red Wine For Dummies*.)

Two extraordinary Merlots

Rather than frustrate you by overtly recommending two outstanding U.S. Merlots that are almost impossible to obtain, we mention them here, parenthetically, just in case you're fortunate enough to ever come across them:

- ✔ **Duckhorn Vineyards, Three Palms Vineyard Merlot, Napa Valley:** The Duckhorn is made in a big, tannic, concentrated style that usually takes years to mature, although lately it's been a bit softer and more accessible. The Three Palms Vineyard sells for about $34, but it's very difficult to find: Because of phylloxera damage to the vines and decreased grape production as a result, very little of this Merlot is being made right now.

- ✔ **Leonetti Cellar Merlot, Columbia Valley (Washington):** Leonetti Cellar makes only about 2,000 to 3,000 cases a year of its justifiably famous Merlot. (See our notes on Leonetti's Cabernet Sauvignon earlier in this chapter for information about the winery's mailing list.) The 1995 Merlot is a richly textured wine with a pure essence of concentrated Merlot fruit. It sells in the $40 to $45 range.

Adelsheim Pinot Noir, Elizabeth's Reserve

- ♪ **Producer:** Adelsheim Vineyard
- ♪ **Wine name:** Pinot Noir, Elizabeth's Reserve
- ♪ **Appellation:** Willamette Valley *(will AM et)*
- ♪ **Price:** $35

David Adelsheim was among the pioneers who decided that Oregon's Willamette Valley was a good place to grow Pinot Noir grapes; he founded his winery in 1971. David makes a good, standard Pinot Noir that sells for about half the price of this wine, but his Elizabeth's Reserve is special. In fact, it usually ranks among the U.S.'s best Pinot Noir wines. The 1994 Elizabeth's Reserve has aromas of raspberry fruit and chocolate, along with breathtakingly concentrated, pure raspberry fruit flavors. A full, rich Pinot Noir, the 1994

Elizabeth's Reserve is embryonic right now; give it two or three years to develop. It may turn out to be one of Adelsheim's all-time best Pinot Noir wines.

Ed: 90–92   **Mary:** 91–93

Amity Pinot Noir, Sunnyside Vineyard

> ✔ **Producer:** Amity Vineyards
> ✔ **Wine name:** Pinot Noir, Sunnyside Vineyard
> ✔ **Appellation:** Willamette Valley *(will AM et)*
> ✔ **Price:** $16

Myron Redford, proprietor of Amity Vineyards, is one of the "old-timers" in the relatively young Oregon wine business. He founded Amity in 1976, only six years after winemaking really began in Oregon.

The Sunnyside Vineyard is Myron's newest (and, for us, perhaps his best) current offering in Pinot Noir wines. The 1995 Sunnyside Pinot has delicate, fresh aromas of black fruits, with substantial, slightly tart, black cherry fruit flavor. This wine expresses pure, fresh fruit character, with none of the sweet fruitiness that you find in some Pinot Noir wines. The concentrated finish suggests that this wine has the substance to age a few years, but this finely tuned Pinot would be perfect now with a platter of fresh seafood.

Ed: 87–89   **Mary:** 86–88

Au Bon Climat Pinot Noir, "La Bauge Au-Dessus"

> ✔ **Producer:** Au Bon Climat
> ✔ **Wine name:** Pinot Noir, "La Bauge Au-Dessus" *(lah bojhe oh day soo)*
> ✔ **Appellation:** Santa Barbara County
> ✔ **Price:** $34

Owner-winemaker Jim Clendenon makes so many different Pinot Noir wines each year that keeping track of all of them is difficult. (He often makes four, but sometimes more.) His single-vineyard Pinot Noir wines, such as the "La Bauge Au-Dessus" from the famed Bien Nacido Vineyard in Santa Barbara, are made in small quantities, and so they might be difficult to find. Any Au Bon Climat Pinot Noir is worth trying, however, because Clendenon has a deft hand with this difficult grape variety. The 1995 "La Bauge Au-Dessus" is beautifully scented with rich, deep aromas of berries and some toasty oak, along with ripe fruit flavors. The wine is full bodied and has loads of depth and flavor concentration.

Ed: 89–91   **Mary:** 87–89

Calera Pinot Noir, Central Coast

> ❧ **Producer:** Calera Wine Company
> ❧ **Wine name:** Pinot Noir, Central Coast
> ❧ **Appellation:** Central Coast
> ❧ **Price:** $18

Josh Jensen, a Pinot Noir specialist, makes some great single-vineyard Pinot Noir wines from his home vineyards on remote Mount Harlan near California's Central Coast. But they're all in the $40 price range. From purchased grapes, he makes a very charming Central Coast Pinot Noir and sells it at less than half the price of his other Pinots. The 1995 Central Coast Pinot Noir has moderately intense, lively aromas of berry fruit and fresh herbs, with spicy, smoky, bacony, red cherry fruit flavors, accented with a charry oak character. It's a fresh, lively, medium-bodied Pinot Noir, with a typically delicious Pinot Noir-like, cherry fruit finish. A good buy from one of California's top Pinot Noir producers.

Ed: 87–89   **Mary:** 87–89

Dehlinger Estate Pinot Noir

> ❧ **Producer:** Dehlinger Winery
> ❧ **Wine name:** Pinot Noir, Estate
> ❧ **Appellation:** Russian River Valley
> ❧ **Price:** $24

Tom Dehlinger makes about five different Pinot Noir wines these days. The very good Estate bottling will be one of the relatively easiest to find, although these days — with really good Pinot Noir in high demand — any of Dehlinger's Pinots might be difficult to locate. The 1993 Estate Pinot Noir is made in the classic Russian River style: It has generous aromas of sweet cherry and berry fruit accented with spicy oak and the flavor of rich, thick, black-cherry fruit. It's a well-focused, balanced wine with crisp acidity and a rich finish. You can enjoy this wine now or within the next few years. Dehlinger clearly has emerged as one of the three or four best wineries for Pinot Noir in the Russian River Valley — a region that is, for many of us, *the* premium Pinot Noir area in the U.S.

Ed: 89–91   **Mary:** 88–90

Domaine Drouhin Pinot Noir

- **Producer:** Domaine Drouhin *(droo an)*
- **Wine name:** Pinot Noir
- **Appellation:** Oregon
- **Price:** $34

Robert Drouhin, director of the great Burgundy firm, Maison Joseph Drouhin, knew what he was doing in 1989 when he hired his daughter, Véronique, as winemaker at Oregon's only French-owned winery. Mother of three toddlers, Véronique has found the time to fashion one of the state's classiest and most dramatic Pinot Noir wines, especially impressive since the 1991 vintage. The 1994 vintage of this wine has reticent aromas of spicy oak and black fruit, along with rich, but compact and concentrated, fruit flavors. The hallmark of Domaine Drouhin's Pinot Noir is elegance, combined with a tight structure and a purity of fruit flavor; they're sort of the opposite of "blousy." Even in the super-ripe 1994 vintage, Domaine Drouhin has managed to achieve this style. Hold on to the 1994 bottle a few years so that it can develop further. (By the way, Domaine Drouhin introduced a reserve Pinot Noir, called Laurène, with the 1993 vintage; its full-list retail price is $45, and the wine is worth it. The awesome 1993 Laurène is one of the best Pinot Noir wines ever made in the U.S.)

Ed: 90–92   **Mary:** 90–92

Elk Cove Pinot Noir, La Bohème Vineyard

- **Producer:** Elk Cove Vineyards
- **Wine name:** Pinot Noir, La Bohème Vineyard
- **Appellation:** Willamette Valley *(will AM et)*
- **Price:** $26

You don't hear too much about Elk Cove Vineyards, but this winery has been quietly making some of the most elegant, understated Pinot Noir wines in the country — exactly the style of wine that we appreciate. (We vividly recall the stark contrast between a wonderfully restrained 1991 Elk Cove Pinot Noir La Bohème that we ordered in a Portland restaurant in 1996, and the wildly ripe 1994 Oregon Pinot Noir wines we'd tasted earlier that day.)

The Pinot Noir that Elk Cove makes from the La Bohème Vineyard is the winery's best Pinot Noir and is reasonably priced compared with other wineries' top-of-the-line Pinots. The La Bohème is not quite so elegant in 1994 as it is in other vintages, and yet it still shows delicacy of style and is fairly crisp for a 1994 Oregon Pinot Noir. The 1994 bottling is quite closed, with deep, brooding, strawberry aromas and a slight touch of oak, along with tart strawberry fruit flavors and really excellent concentration. Enjoy the La Bohème within the next few years, with a delicate seafood entrée.

Ed: 88–90   **Mary:** 88–90

Erath Pinot Noir Reserve, Weber Vineyards

- ✔ **Producer:** Erath Vineyards *(EE rath)*
- ✔ **Wine name:** Pinot Noir Reserve, Weber Vineyards
- ✔ **Appellation:** Willamette Valley *(will AM et)*
- ✔ **Price:** $25

Sometimes we become so fascinated by what's new or hot that we take the well-established, tried-and-true names for granted. Such is the case with Erath Vineyards (formerly known as Knudsen Erath). Dick Erath is a big, easy-going, likable guy, who has been making solid, reasonably priced Pinot Noir wines since 1972. (His standard 1995 Pinot Noir costs $12.) Because Erath Vineyards is now one of the larger wineries in Oregon, its wines are generally available. We believe that his Weber Vineyards Reserve is his current best Pinot Noir. The 1994 Weber Vineyards has deep, black-fruit, and earthy aromas, along with intensely concentrated fruit flavors; this is Erath's most complex wine. Give the 1994 Weber a few more years to develop. It might even warrant a higher rating then.

Ed: 88–90   **Mary:** 88–90

Étude Pinot Noir

> ♪ **Producer:** Étude Wines *(aye tude)*
> ♪ **Wine name:** Pinot Noir
> ♪ **Appellation:** Carneros (Napa)
> ♪ **Price:** $30

Tony Soter, owner of the Étude label, has been one of California's leading wine consultants for many years. Most of his work has been with Cabernet Sauvignon, but in 1984, he took on the challenge of the difficult Pinot Noir grape, making a Pinot Noir wine under his own label, from grapes grown in the cool Carneros region. Soter makes his Pinot Noir in a style that emphasizes finesse and delicacy rather than power. His wines have been particularly impressive since the 1991 vintage; the 1994 Étude Pinot Noir, for example, has clean, fresh, concentrated, spicy, raspberry aromas, along with intense raspberry fruit flavors. It's a medium-weight, dry, crisp, supple wine that you can enjoy now or over the next few years.

Ed: 88–90   **Mary:** 89–91

Eyrie Pinot Noir

> ♪ **Producer:** The Eyrie Vineyards *(EYE ree)*
> ♪ **Wine name:** Pinot Noir
> ♪ **Appellation:** Willamette Valley *(will AM et)*
> ♪ **Price:** $18

David Lett, owner-winemaker of The Eyrie Vineyards, was the first to make Pinot Noir in Oregon's Willamette Valley. He planted his vineyard in 1966 and made the first Pinot Noir in 1970. Lett's Pinot Noir wines are never heavy-handed blockbusters, but instead are made in a style that stresses elegance, finesse, and the character of the grape. The 1995 Eyrie Pinot Noir is a winner. It has that wonderfully complex Pinot aroma of raspberry and cherry fruit, with a touch of tomato. Its flavors of herbs and concentrated fruit are tight and precise. Enjoy this wine during the next two or three years, perhaps with grilled salmon.

Ed: 90–92   **Mary:** 89–91

King Estate Pinot Noir

- ✔ **Producer:** King Estate
- ✔ **Wine name:** Pinot Noir
- ✔ **Appellation:** Oregon
- ✔ **Price:** $20

King Estate, Oregon's largest winery, has made its finest Pinot Noir yet with the 1994 vintage. And the wine is generally available, both in the U.S. and abroad. The 1994 King Estate Pinot Noir is a polished, refined wine. It has compelling aromas of pure, tart cherry fruit, along with earthy, ripe fruit flavors. It is a solid, dry, and moderately tannic wine with good concentration. I recommend drinking the 1994 King Estate in about two years, accompanied by roast chicken or a game bird. (In addition to this $20 wine, the winery made small quantities of a very good 1994 Pinot Noir Reserve that costs about $35.)

Ed: 89–91

Robert Mondavi Pinot Noir, Carneros

- ✔ **Producer:** Robert Mondavi Winery
- ✔ **Wine name:** Pinot Noir, Carneros
- ✔ **Appellation:** Carneros
- ✔ **Price:** $26

Robert Mondavi's Pinot Noir Reserve (about $32) gets the most attention, and its standard Napa Valley Pinot Noir ($18 to $20) is probably the winery's most available Pinot. But we prefer the style of Mondavi's Carneros Pinot Noir. The Reserve is certainly the richest and the fullest of the Robert Mondavi Pinots, but it's also the heaviest and the oakiest. The Carneros Pinot Noir is the crispest, and the one that we believe goes best with food. The 1994 Carneros has a vanilla oak aroma and the spicy red fruit aromas and flavors typical of Pinots from this region. It's a smooth, supple, pleasant wine with good concentration of fruit character. You can enjoy the Carneros wine now and over the next few years.

Ed: 86–88   **Mary:** 86–88

Ponzi Vineyards Pinot Noir Reserve

- ❧ **Producer:** Ponzi Vineyards
- ❧ **Wine name:** Pinot Noir Reserve
- ❧ **Appellation:** Willamette Valley *(will AM et)*
- ❧ **Price:** $45

The 1995 Ponzi Vineyards Pinot Noir Reserve is an awesome wine. For us, it ranks with the 1994 Williams & Selyem Rochioli Vineyard as one of the two most impressive U.S. Pinot Noir wines that we've ever tasted. Dick and Nancy Ponzi call this their "25th Anniversary" wine, because Ponzi Vineyards was founded in 1970. Dick, a former mechanical engineer, is a multi-talented guy who has also been quite successful in the microbrewery business, but his heart has always been in wine. Nowadays, daughter Luisa is Dick's co-winemaker.

The 1995 Ponzi Reserve has smoky, rich aromas of black fruits and autumn leaves, along with deeply concentrated, classic Pinot Noir flavors of black fruits and dead leaves. It is full bodied and has amazing depth. Hold on to this beauty for about five years; it's too unevolved to drink now. (Ponzi's standard Pinot Noir is about $21 and is also very good.)

Ed: 94–96   **Mary:** 90–92

Rex Hill Vineyards Pinot Noir Reserve

- ❧ **Producer:** Rex Hill Vineyards
- ❧ **Wine name:** Pinot Noir Reserve
- ❧ **Appellation:** Willamette Valley *(will AM et)*
- ❧ **Price:** $41

Rex Hill Vineyards has made one of its finest Pinot Noir wines to date with its 1994 Reserve. Owner Paul Hart and his talented winemaker, Lynn Penner-Ash, have brought Rex Hill to the forefront of Oregon's wineries during the last few years. The 1994 Reserve has deep, complex aromas of black fruit and spicy oak, along with fleshy, black-fruit flavors. It's a powerful, full-bodied Pinot Noir that could use a few more years to develop. The standard Rex Hill Pinot Noir is also quite fine and a real bargain at $18.

By the way, if you spot any of Rex Hill's Archibald Vineyard Pinot Noir wines, in either the 1991 or 1992 vintage, grab it. At about $25, they are terrific; unfortunately, Rex Hill no longer has access to the fruit of this fine vineyard.

Ed: 90–92   **Mary:** 89–91

Sanford Pinot Noir, Central Coast

- ♪ **Producer:** Sanford Winery
- ♪ **Wine name:** Pinot Noir
- ♪ **Appellation:** Central Coast
- ♪ **Price:** $19

Richard Sanford, who has a background in geology, decided back in the early 1970s that the Santa Ynez Valley in the Santa Barbara region was the right spot for Pinot Noir. Today, Sanford Winery makes some of the most delicious, precocious Pinot Noir in California. (At least his standard Central Coast Pinot Noir is precocious; Sanford has a couple of single-vineyard Pinot Noir wines in the $27 to $32 price range that take time to develop.) The 1994 Sanford Central Coast Pinot Noir has sweet aromas and flavors of red and black fruit, with some earthiness. It's a rich, velvety Pinot Noir with lots of depth and good concentration of fruit. Enjoy this wine now, or in the near term, for lunch with a cold chicken salad.

Ed: 89–91   **Mary:** 85–87

Sokol Blosser "Redland" Pinot Noir

- ♪ **Producer:** Sokol Blosser Winery
- ♪ **Wine name:** Pinot Noir, "Redland"
- ♪ **Appellation:** Yamhill County
- ♪ **Price:** $35

Susan Sokol Blosser and Bill Blosser planted their vineyard in the Red Hills of Dundee, Oregon, in 1971 and founded Sokol Blosser Winery in 1977. Now they have one of the largest wineries in Oregon (30,000 cases annually), and their wines are in national distribution. The 1994 "Redland" (their name for their reserve bottling of Pinot Noir) is one of the finest Pinot Noir wines that Sokol Blosser has ever produced. It has rich, smoky, slightly spicy, understated aromas, along with ripe black-fruit flavors. This is a rich, crisp, well-made Pinot Noir that needs about two or three years to soften.

Ed: 89–91   **Mary:** 88–90

Wild Horse Pinot Noir, Central Coast

> ♪ **Producer:** Wild Horse Vineyards
>
> ♪ **Wine name:** Pinot Noir
>
> ♪ **Appellation:** Central Coast
>
> ♪ **Price:** $18

Owner-winemaker Ken Volk, whose winery is located in San Luis Obispo County, is a perfectionist; his entire line of wines is always well made and reasonably priced. The 1994 Central Coast Pinot Noir has attractive but unusual eucalyptus aromas, along with intriguing, tart red-fruit flavors. It's medium to full bodied and complex, with firm tannin and crisp acidity. You can enjoy your delicious Wild Horse now or within the next few years.

Ed: 91–93   **Mary:** 86–88

Three great Russian River Pinot Noir wines over $50

Three Pinot Noir wines from the Russian River Valley district of Sonoma are really special. But they are made in tiny quantities (so what else is new?), and their prices are quite high as a result. We like these wines so much that we rate them at 95 points or higher on a scale of 100.

- ✔ J. Rochioli Vineyard, West Block Vineyard (about $50)

- ✔ J. Rochioli Vineyard, East Block Vineyard ($60)

- ✔ Williams & Selyem Winery, Rochioli Vineyard ($60) (Williams & Selyem purchases grapes from Rochioli Vineyard to make this bottling.)

Try getting on the mailing list of these wineries if you want to experience these special Pinot Noir wines. You can contact Rochioli Vineyard by phone, 707-433-2305, or fax, 707-433-2358. Reach Williams & Selyem by phone, 707-433-6425, or fax, 707-433-6546.

Williams & Selyem Pinot Noir, Allen Vineyard

- ✦ **Producer:** Williams & Selyem Winery
- ✦ **Wine name:** Pinot Noir, Allen Vineyard
- ✦ **Appellation:** Russian River Valley
- ✦ **Price:** $42

The two sad facts about Williams & Selyem's Pinot Noir wines are that they are so much in demand and so small in production. You will seldom come across them, unless you're on the winery's mailing list or dining at certain restaurants in San Francisco or Healdsburg (the nearest town to the winery, in Sonoma County). If you're a Pinot Noir lover, you should make an effort to sample any Pinot Noir from this winery, because many wine critics consider them among the finest Pinot Noir wines in the U.S.

The 1994 Allen Vineyard Pinot Noir, from a vintage that was very good in the Russian River Valley (as was 1995), has woodsy, wild berry fruit aromas, along with enticing, rich, berry and cherry fruit flavors. Made in the complex, understated style of a great Burgundy, but with plump, Russian River fruit, this complex beauty could use a few more years of aging to develop. The Allen Vineyard wine is probably one of Williams & Selyem's two finest Pinot Noir, along with its Rochioli Vineyard bottling. The winery makes about 5,000 cases of nine or ten different Pinot Noir wines each year, but only the standard Russian River bottling is made in enough quantity (about 2,000 cases) that you can expect to find it in a few fine wine shops. To get on the winery's mailing list, call 707-433-6425.

Ed: 93–95   **Mary:** 92–94

Ken Wright Pinot Noir

- ✦ **Producer:** Ken Wright Cellars
- ✦ **Wine name:** Pinot Noir
- ✦ **Appellation:** Willamette Valley *(will AM et)*
- ✦ **Price:** $24

Ken Wright built a fine reputation for Panther Creek Cellars before selling that winery and starting his present operation. Based on the Pinot Noir from both wineries, Ken has become acknowledged as one of Oregon's leading winemakers. He makes five different single-vineyard Pinot Noir wines in tiny quantities that are almost impossible to obtain; this Willamette Valley bottling, his standard Pinot Noir, is more available. The 1994 Willamette Valley Pinot Noir has nutty aromas, with touches of olive and tobacco, along with spicy, concentrated black-fruit flavors. It's a smooth, harmonious, firm, rich wine with superb concentration of fruit and excellent length. Frankly, it's a real beauty! Enjoy this wine now or within the next few years.

Ed: 91–93   **Mary:** 92–94

Blended red wines and wines from other grapes

For reasons relating to quality or freedom of expression, some winemakers choose to create blended wines, which don't carry any grape name. Most of the wines we review in this section are blends. They carry *proprietary* names — names that the winery owners invented or chose, and have trademarked. Some blended wines use the name Meritage, which applies to a wine made from at least two of the five traditional grapes of France's Bordeaux region (Cabernet Sauvignon, Cabernet Franc, Merlot, Petit Verdot, and Malbec).

In this section, we also review U.S. wines that are made from grape varieties other than those covered elsewhere in this chapter. These wines include Syrah and Sangiovese. We intermingle these wines with the blended wines, listing them alphabetically by producer.

Bernardus "Marinus Red"

- **Producer:** Bernardus
- **Wine name:** "Marinus Red"
- **Appellation:** Carmel Valley
- **Price:** $36

Winemaker Don Blackburn is on the same wavelength as we are when it comes to wine style. His wines emphasize texture, harmony, and balance more than they do fruity aromas and flavors — and we're not members of the fruitiness camp, either. Blackburn's 1994 "Marinus Red" — a blend of 80 percent Cabernet Sauvignon, 19 percent Merlot, and a combined 1 percent Cabernet Franc and Malbec — has a deep aroma that suggests ink and sweet oak. The wine is full bodied, and it's so rich that it almost seems sweet. It also has good depth of flavor (a sensation that the flavor goes down deep rather than being all on the surface) and is very well balanced — a very good, graceful wine.

Ed: 88–90   **Mary:** 89–91

Cain Cuvée

> ♪ **Producer:** Cain Vineyards
> ♪ **Wine name:** Cain Cuvée
> ♪ **Appellation:** Napa
> ♪ **Price:** $18

Cain Vineyards makes two blended red wines from the five Bordeaux grape varieties: this less expensive wine and the pricier ($40 to $45) wine called Cain Five. We like both of them, but we're particularly impressed with the quality-for-dollar value of this Cain Cuvée. The 1993 version has deep aromas and flavors that are classically Bordeaux-like: ink and tobacco, with some vegetal notes. It's supple and smooth in texture, with plenty of concentrated richness of the grapes but not too much hard tannin. This intense wine is a bit mysterious, by which we mean that when you taste it, you get the sense that there's more going on than meets the tongue. You can enjoy this wine now, but it will probably remain just as good for another three or four years.

Ed: 88–90   **Mary:** 90–92

Carmenet Moon Mountain Estate, "Vin de Garde Reserve Selection"

> ♪ **Producer:** Carmenet *(car meh nay)*
> ♪ **Wine name:** Moon Mountain Estate Meritage, "Vin de Garde Reserve Selection"
> ♪ **Appellation:** Sonoma Valley
> ♪ **Price:** $37

This wine is as big and intense as its name is long — and much easier to like than its name is to understand. The Carmenet Winery makes several red wines from grapes grown on its Moon Mountain Estate. Some of the wines have varietal names, such as *Cabernet Franc,* and some of them are called *Meritage* to designate them as a blend of Bordeaux grape varieties. But the winery's best wine is its "Vin de Garde Reserve Selection" (the French phrase means a wine to lay away for long aging).

The 1990 version of this wine, with seven years of age on it already, shows some attributes of age — such as a roasted coffee aroma and a (quite pleasant) sort of sweat-like aroma that older red wines can develop. But it still has plenty of youthful energy, in the form of a strong minty character, and a wallop of tannin that hits in the back of your mouth. Not that the wine is hard and tough, however: in fact, it's rich, with very ripe fruit character and real softness and smoothness of texture until the tannin speaks up. It's a lot of wine — and worth the trouble of getting through that long name.

Ed: 85–87   **Mary:** 87–89

Chateau St. Jean "Cinques Cépages"

- ⚘ **Producer:** Chateau St. Jean
- ⚘ **Wine name:** "Cinques Cépages" *(sank say pahj)*
- ⚘ **Appellation:** Sonoma
- ⚘ **Price:** $25

Although probably best-known for its Chardonnays, Chateau St. Jean also makes excellent red wines, including the "Cinques Cépages" (which translates to "five grape varieties"), so-called because it's a blend of the five Bordeaux grape varieties: Cabernet Sauvignon, Cabernet Franc, Merlot, Malbec, and Petite Verdot (although Cabernet Sauvignon dominates, making up more than 75 percent of the blend). The blend from the 1993 vintage has a dense aroma that's closed now, except for some herbal notes. The first impression in the mouth is the sweetness of intense, ripe fruit flavors followed by an impression of fairly soft tannins. "Cinques Cépages" is a very concentrated, round Cab blend that's perfect for near-term drinking.

Ed: 88–90

DeLille Cellars "Chaleur Estate Red"

- ⚘ **Producer:** DeLille Cellars
- ⚘ **Wine name:** "Chaleur Estate"
- ⚘ **Appellation:** Yakima Valley
- ⚘ **Price:** $32

If we had to name Washington State's best winery, DeLille Cellars would be one of our strongest contenders. Right now, this winery is making two of the best wines in the U.S. — one red and one white. Both wines are called Chaleur Estate, and both are Bordeaux-type blends. (Our review of the white wine appears in Chapter 8.) The 1994 "Chaleur Estate Red" is 65 percent Cabernet Sauvignon, 25 percent Merlot, and 10 percent Cabernet Franc. Winemaker Chris Upchurch makes this stylish wine in the manner of a Bordeaux from St.-Julien or Margaux, with elegance and perfect balance. The 1994 "Chaleur Estate" has aromas of black currants, chocolate, and some new oak, along with subdued flavors of cedar, chocolate, and cassis. This supple, sophisticated, harmonious wine has lots of complexity and could easily be mistaken for a fine Bordeaux. Serve it now with lamb or hold on to it for four or five years; it will probably even get better.

Ed: 92–94   **Mary:** 91–93

Geyser Peak Shiraz

- ! **Producer:** Geyser Peak
- ! **Wine name:** Shiraz
- ! **Appellation:** Sonoma County
- ! **Price:** $18

Although this wine is made from the Syrah grape in California, it carries the Australian name for Syrah: Shiraz. The reason for this cultural incongruity is probably that Geyser Peak's head winemaker, Darryl Groom, is Australian. The 1994 Shiraz is a hedonistic wine, terrifically flavorful and intense, with tons of sweet oak aroma and flavors and a ripe, lush fruitiness. Smooth, supple, velvety, and deep, this wine makes people sit up and take notice when they taste it. Even though we both agree that it's not our sort of wine (too ripe and lush), we like it anyway. That's a crowd-pleaser for you!

Ed: 89–91   **Mary:** 89–91

Leonetti Cellar Sangiovese

- ! **Producer:** Leonetti Cellar
- ! **Wine name:** Sangiovese
- ! **Appellation:** Walla Walla Valley
- ! **Price:** $45

True to his Italian roots, master winemaker Gary Figgins (whose mom was born a Leonetti) is debuting a Sangiovese wine, based on the major grape of Chianti, with the 1995 vintage. Although not quite so impressive as Leonetti Cellar's Cabernet Sauvignon or Merlot (how many wines are?), the 1995 Leonetti Sangiovese is still quite a bit better than most other Sangiovese wines now made in California. It has dusty aromas of cherry candy and charred oak, along with lush, ripe, red-berry fruit flavors. It's a solid, flavorful wine but very tannic at present; we recommend giving it a few years to age. (For information about getting on Leonetti's mailing list, see our Leonetti Cellar Cabernet Sauvignon notes, earlier in this chapter.)

Ed: 87–89   **Mary:** 86–88

Qupé Syrah, Bien Nacido Vineyard

> ♪ **Producer:** Qupé Vineyards *(cue pay)*
> ♪ **Wine name:** Syrah, Bien Nacido Vineyard
> ♪ **Appellation:** Santa Barbara County
> ♪ **Price:** $24

We're not generally impressed with California's efforts with the Syrah grape and other varieties from the Rhône Valley in France, but we find Qupe's Syrah to be right on target and a terrific wine. (Owner Bob Lindquist happens to be one of the earliest producers of Syrah in his state.) The 1995 Qupé Syrah, from grapes grown in the Bien Nacido vineyard, has subdued aromas and flavors that smell and taste much better than they read (and are typical of the Syrah grape), such as cooked green pepper and other vegetables, black pepper, burnt rubber, and ink, with a little mocha thrown in. This wine is full bodied, and its tannin is soft, making for a smooth, supple, and big wine. We can imagine it going well with a simple roast, a stew, or a vegetarian casserole.

Ed: 89–91   **Mary:** 86–88

Sakonnet Cabernet Franc

> ♪ **Producer:** Sakonnet Vineyards *(sah CON net)*
> ♪ **Wine name:** Cabernet Franc
> ♪ **Appellation:** South East New England
> ♪ **Price:** $21

Not many wineries make a varietal Cabernet Franc. This grape, an erstwhile blending partner to Cabernet Sauvignon and Merlot, can perform well on its own when it's grown in the right climate, such as in the cool Rhode Island region where Sakonnet Vineyards is located. The 1994 Cabernet Franc, with a bit of Merlot and Cabernet Sauvignon blended in, has an inky, oaky aroma. It's a well-balanced, medium-bodied wine with good acidity, the classic, Cabernet Franc vegetal flavors, and a pleasant finish. Try it with barbecued or grilled steaks.

Ed: 88–90

Seghesio Sangiovese "Vitigno Toscano"

- ❥ **Producer:** Seghesio Family Estates *(seh GAY see oh)*
- ❥ **Wine name:** Sangiovese, "Vitigno Toscano" *(vee TEE nyoh tos CAH noh)*
- ❥ **Appellation:** Alexander Valley
- ❥ **Price:** $17

The Seghesio Family traces its winemaking roots in Sonoma back to 1902, but it's been bottling wine under its own label only since 1985. We have been less than thrilled with most of the Sangiovese wines made in California today, but Seghesio's "Vitigno Toscano," 100 percent Sangiovese, is clearly one of the few successes. (It actually resembles Italian Sangiovese!) This wine is less well known and less expensive than the Seghesio wine called Chianti Station, a mainly Sangiovese wine with some Cabernet Sauvignon blended in, and yet we prefer the "Vitigno Toscano."

The 1994 Sangiovese has tart cherry fruit aromas, along with clean, fresh, cherry fruit flavors. It's a medium-bodied wine with moderate amounts of acidity and tannin. The wine clearly gets better with age, when it loses some of its oak influence, as a 1991 "Vitigno Toscano" proved to us. Try it with a tomato-based pasta with meat sauce.

Ed: 88–90   **Mary:** 88–90

Swanson Sangiovese

- ❥ **Producer:** Swanson Vineyards
- ❥ **Wine name:** Sangiovese
- ❥ **Appellation:** Napa Valley
- ❥ **Price:** $24

Swanson Vineyards and Seghesio Family Estates produce two of the best Sangiovese wines in California today. (Staglin Family also makes a good Sangiovese, but it's well over $50 a bottle.) Interestingly, all three have an Italian heritage. In the case of Swanson, the winemaker, Marco Cappelli, is Italian-American. The 1995 Swanson Sangiovese, with 5 percent Cabernet Franc blended in, has aromas of cherries, with touches of coffee and tar; chocolate and cherry fruit flavors; and a thick, velvety texture. It is delicious now, but can use a few years of aging to develop. Try it with grilled veal chops or grilled swordfish.

Ed: 88–90   **Mary :** 87–89

Swanson Syrah

> ? **Producer:** Swanson Vineyards
>
> ? **Wine name:** Syrah
>
> ? **Appellation:** Napa Valley
>
> ? **Price:** $25

Swanson Vineyards is producing not only one of California's best Sangiovese wines but also one of its best Syrahs. Swanson's Syrah, made from 100-year-old vines, resembles a northern Rhône wine more than it resembles a California Syrah. The 1995 Syrah, perhaps the winery's best yet, has fascinating aromas of coffee, smoky oak, and green vegetables, along with bacon and black-fruit flavors. It's an intense, tannic, young wine — almost animalistic — with loads of depth and character. The Swanson Syrah is a must-buy for Syrah lovers, but we suggest holding on to it for a few years. It goes well with game, such as venison, or with roast pork.

Ed: 90–92   **Mary:** 91–93

Zinfandel

Zinfandel is a wonderfully versatile grape, capable of making inexpensive wines that are delicious and easy to enjoy (see our reviews in Chapter 2) as well as serious, first-rate, expensive, great wines that are delicious and easy to enjoy.

Because of the grape's irrepressible fruitiness, even the most expensive, most elite Zinfandels are not dry, austere wines. Zinfandels can even give the impression of sweetness to some wine drinkers. This fruity character is ideal for many of the foods that Americans eat every day. Zinfandel easily crosses the line from Tex-Mex to grilled foods to barbecue (even the real stuff!) to Thanksgiving turkey with yams on the side. Just don't pair it with meek foods, because they'll be blown away by Zin's unrestrained flavor.

Elyse Zinfandel, Howell Mountain

- *♪* **Producer:** Elyse Vineyards
- *♪* **Wine name:** Zinfandel, Howell Mountain
- *♪* **Appellation:** Howell Mountain (Napa Valley)
- *♪* **Price:** $20

Elyse has been a red Zinfandel specialist since the brand began in 1987. The winery makes three different Zinfandels, but the one from Howell Mountain is the clear standout for us. The 1995 Howell Mountain has fairly subdued aromas of black fruit, with a touch of chalkiness and oak, along with really concentrated, very rich, black-fruit flavors. This truly majestic wine has excellent balance, velvety texture, and incredible depth. Ed considers this wine "the Rolls Royce of Zins." Because the tannins are fairly soft, surprisingly so for a Howell Mountain wine, you can drink the 1995 Elyse now, perhaps with barbecued sausages, but it'll certainly age well for five or six years.

Ed: 95–97   **Mary:** 87–89

Ferrari-Carano Zinfandel

- *♪* **Producer:** Ferrari-Carano Winery
- *♪* **Wine name:** Zinfandel
- *♪* **Appellation:** Sonoma County
- *♪* **Price:** $18

Ferrari-Carano makes a superb Zinfandel. Its 1994 Zin has rich, intense aromas of strawberry, cranberry, and spice. It's a smooth, full-flavored, full-bodied Zin, fairly high in alcohol, with all sorts of wonderful black cherry, plum, cedar, and blackberry flavors on its rather long finish. Ferrari-Carano Zin is a concentrated wine that can age for several years — if you can wait. You can expect it to go well with steak, roast beef, or a selection of hard cheeses.

Ed: 88–90   **Mary:** 88–90

Franus Zinfandel, Brandlin Ranch

> ♪ **Producer:** Franus Winery
> ♪ **Wine name:** Zinfandel, Brandlin Ranch
> ♪ **Appellation:** Mt. Veeder (Napa Valley)
> ♪ **Price:** $18

Peter Franus, another Zinfandel specialist, makes two fine Zinfandels: the Brandlin Ranch, with grapes from over-70-year-old vines on Mt. Veeder, and the George Hendry Vineyard Zin. We slightly prefer the bigger of the two, the Brandlin. The 1994 Brandlin Ranch has aromas of rich black fruit, vanilla, and smoky oak, along with spicy, black-peppery, berry fruit flavors. It has the depth and concentration to last for the long haul, but frankly, we like our Zinfandels young, when they have all that delicious berry fruit. If you live on the West Coast of the U.S., you may be able to find Franus Zinfandels in wine stores; otherwise, we suggest that you call the winery, 707-945-0542, to be placed on the mailing list.

Ed: 89–91   **Mary:** 86–88

Frog's Leap Zinfandel

> ♪ **Producer:** Frog's Leap Winery
> ♪ **Wine name:** Zinfandel
> ♪ **Appellation:** Napa Valley
> ♪ **Price:** $20

Any winery that has a motto like "Time's fun when you're having flies" and inscribes the word *Ribbit* on its corks has precisely the right attitude for making Zinfandel — which should always be a fun wine. We've long been big fans of Frog's Leap Zinfandel. We're still enjoying the 1990 Zin for its elegant, supple, medium-bodied style and its plum, berry, and dill flavors. The 1994 Frog's Leap Zinfandel is more typical of the ripe 1994 vintage: It's a lush, velvety, delicious Zin that's more suitable for current drinking than for aging. But even in ripe vintages, the Frog's Leap Zinfandels don't hit you over the head with their intensity of flavor; instead, they accompany your food in a well-behaved manner, as any good animal companion would. (Try it with anything except frog legs.)

We like the 1995 Frog's Leap Zin best of all. It has a minty aroma and flavor that lends a note of elegance to the wine's full-bodied, firm, concentrated style. The 1995 Frog's Leap is not just great Zinfandel — it's great wine. It should age beautifully, if you can keep your hands off it. (We're not sure that we can.) Our rating is for the 1995 vintage of this wine.

Ed: 90–92   **Mary: 94–96**

Grgich Hills Zinfandel

> ♪ **Producer:** Grgich Hills Cellar *(GUR gitch)*
> ♪ **Wine name:** Zinfandel
> ♪ **Appellation:** Sonoma County
> ♪ **Price:** $21

Grgich Hills Cellar is best-known for its Chardonnays, but I've always been a big fan of its Zinfandels. Although his winery is in Napa, Croatian-born Mike Grgich, winemaker and co-owner, makes his Zinfandel from grapes grown in Sonoma, where all the old Zinfandel vines are. The 1994 Grgich is my idea of a great Zinfandel; it has the lively acidity (a Grgich Zin trademark) that I crave in Zinfandel, because it counterbalances the ripe fruit character that you typically find in these wines. This wine has aromas of mint and spicy oak, along with berry and black-fruit flavors. Unlike Grgich's elegant Chardonnays, his Zin is a rather coarse, rustic wine, but that's fine with me. It goes well with spicy Asian cuisine or barbecued meats.

Ed: 91–93

Kendall-Jackson Zinfandel, "Vintner's Reserve"

> ♪ **Producer:** Kendall-Jackson
> ♪ **Wine name:** Zinfandel, "Vintner's Reserve"
> ♪ **Appellation:** California
> ♪ **Price:** $18

The least expensive wines of Kendall-Jackson — the range of wines labeled Vintner's Reserve — have had a stormy relationship with me. Sometimes, I find them too easy, even a little sweet, and I resent the fact that they're not more serious. But other times, I find the wines delicious and admirably made.

The 1995 K-J Zinfandel has caught me more than once on a good day. It has a dense, tight aroma of berries and oak. It's full bodied, supple, and harmonious, but it has some herbal flavor to give it a touch of austerity. This wine has good concentration of fruit character, especially on the finish, and a sense of depth. It's not tannic or firm enough to be called powerful, but it's too interesting to be dismissed as easy.

Mary: 90–92

Niebaum-Coppola Zinfandel, "Edizione Pennino"

> ♪ **Producer:** Niebaum-Coppola Estate Winery
>
> ♪ **Wine name:** Zinfandel, "Edizione Pennino"
> *(eh deez zee OH nay pen NEE noh)*
>
> ♪ **Appellation:** Napa Valley
>
> ♪ **Price:** $22

Francis Ford Coppola's taste in wines is as good as the wonderful films he's directed. Niebaum-Coppola's top-of-the-line wine, Rubicon, a Cabernet blend, is spectacular, but we also enjoy his very good Zinfandel, Edizione Pennino (named for Coppola's maternal grandmother). The 1994 Edizione Pennino has peppery and raspberry aromas, along with earthy, ripe berry fruit flavors. It's medium bodied and ready to drink now. We suggest that you accompany it with some grilled cheeseburgers or sausages, in the unpretentious Italian way of enjoying good wine.

Ed: 88–90

Mary: 88–90

A. Rafanelli Zinfandel

> ♪ **Producer:** A. Rafanelli Winery
>
> ♪ **Wine name:** Zinfandel
>
> ♪ **Appellation:** Dry Creek Valley
>
> ♪ **Price:** $16

David Rafanelli's Zins are always dry wines and never show the exaggerated style of a wine made with over-ripe fruit. Other trademarks of Rafanelli Zinfandels: They're always cleanly made, they're never exuberantly fruity, and they have a precision and purity of fruit that at least partially reflects expert winemaking at work.

The 1994 Rafanelli Zin has rich, smoky, berry fruit aromas, along with raspberry and cherry fruit flavors. It's a dry, crisp, medium-bodied wine with firm oak tannin. Not a flashy Zin, it's just a solid, well-made, old-style wine that goes well with food. Because of its fairly high acidity, it's great with pizza or any tomato-based dish. Or you can keep this wine for five or six years; Rafanelli's Zinfandels age very well. Rafanelli wines (he also makes a good Cabernet Sauvignon) are obtainable mainly through his mailing list; call 707-433-1385.

Ed: 89–91   **Mary:** 90–92

Ravenswood Zinfandel, Dickerson Vineyard

> ♪ **Producer:** Ravenswood
>
> ♪ **Wine name:** Zinfandel, Dickerson Vineyard
>
> ♪ **Appellation:** Napa Valley
>
> ♪ **Price:** $21

Ravenswood's Joel Peterson makes about eight Zinfandels, ranging from his simple, inexpensive (about $12) "Vintner's Blend" to five superb, single-vineyard Zins, in the $20 to $24 price range. Our favorite is usually his Old Hill Zinfandel, but that one is always the most backward, requiring many years of cellaring. The Dickerson Vineyard Zin — the only Ravenswood single-vineyard Zinfandel whose grapes are from Napa rather than Sonoma — is, in comparison, usually the most precocious of Ravenswood's single-vineyard Zinfandels.

The aroma of the 1994 Dickerson Zin displays plenty of mint and eucalyptus, plus spicy, berry fruit; its flavors include mint and ripe raspberry fruit. You can enjoy it soon with flavorful food, such as barbecued spareribs. If you're feeling a little reckless, try it with some bitter-chocolate cake. (It works, believe it or not; it's that raspberry fruit!) Although the Dickerson is Ravenswood's most accessible single-vineyard Zinfandel, it can age as well as the others — ten years or more, if you'd like to hold on to it. Ravenswood's single-vineyard Zinfandels are available mainly through the winery's mailing list; call 707-938-1960.

Ed: 90–92   **Mary:** 90–92

Ridge Geyserville

- ***Producer:*** Ridge Vineyards
- ***Wine name:*** Geyserville
- ***Appellation:*** Sonoma County
- ***Price:*** $22

About eight or nine years ago, Paul Draper, winemaker at Ridge Vineyards — and one of the most respected men in the wine business — decided to count his vines at his most renowned Zinfandel vineyard, Geyserville, in Sonoma's Alexander Valley. When he discovered that only about 62 percent were Zinfandel vines (the rest were mainly Petite Sirah and Carignane), Draper removed the Zinfandel name from the wine's label. (California law requires at least 75 percent of the named grape variety in the bottle.) Technically, therefore, Geyserville is not a Zinfandel, but a blend. Nonetheless, it remains our favorite whatever-you-call-it Zinfandel-like wine from Ridge; Draper also makes four "legitimate" Zinfandels.

The 1994 Geyserville has intriguing aromas of herbs (eucalyptus and rosemary), pepper, smoke, and leather, along with concentrated, sweet, ripe black-fruit flavors. It's dry and full bodied, with firm tannins and a long finish, but it's supple enough to enjoy even now. Since the 1990 vintage, Geyserville has become drinkable sooner, and yet its balance and depth suggest that it will have the staying power for which it has become renowned. Personally, we'd hold on to this wine for six to eight years.

Ed: 92–94

Mary: 92–94

Rosenblum Zinfandel, Contra Costa County

- ***Producer:*** Rosenblum Cellars
- ***Wine name:*** Zinfandel, Contra Costa County
- ***Appellation:*** Contra Costa County
- ***Price:*** $17

Kent Rosenblum, a veterinarian, is an amazing man. Besides running his practice, he finds time to make eight or nine Zinfandels every year, all of them good, plus a score of other wines. Like Ravenswood's, the single-vineyard Zins from

Rosenblum Cellars are made in small quantities; your best bet in getting them is to call the winery (510-865-7007), but we do spot some of them in wine shops at times.

Rosenblum's Contra Costa County Zin and his Sonoma Old Vines Zin are more available. The 1995 Contra Costa Zin has ripe, jammy fruit aromas, with some herbal and oaky touches, as well as herbal, jammy, and berry fruit flavors. It's a solid, well-built wine with plenty of firm tannin and herbal, spicy flavors to keep its jammy fruit in line. As to its ageworthiness, we can attest to the fact that Rosenblum's Zins age extremely well. Try this wine, or any Rosenblum Zin, with simple grilled meats or a ratatouille.

Ed: 87–89   **Mary:** 89–91

Elite Red Wines from Chile and Argentina

Both Chile and Argentina have ideal conditions for growing red-wine grapes, and the wines of Chile and Argentina have never been as good as they are today. And they're destined to get even better during the next few years. In the meantime, wine prices are still low in both countries. Their best, most expensive red wines, some of which we recommend here, are between $15 and $26. We could not talk of such low prices for any other country producing fine red wines, with the possible exception of South Africa.

We include wines from both Chile and Argentina in the following list. The wines are in alphabetical order according to the name of the producer. For our recommendations of red wines under $15 from these two countries, see Chapter 2.

Catena Malbec, Lunlunta Vineyard

> ✔ **Producer:** Catena
> ✔ **Wine name:** Malbec, Lunlunta Vineyard
> ✔ **Appellation:** Mendoza (Argentina)
> ✔ **Price:** $20

The Malbec grape, a minor grape of Bordeaux and a major grape of the Cahors region in southwest France, is the grape variety for fine red wines in Argentina. Although we've had some mediocre Malbecs from Argentina, the most exciting

Argentine wines we've tasted have also been Malbecs. The 1994 Malbec made by Bodegas Esmeralda — part of the large Catena wine company — from grapes grown in the Lunlunta Vineyard, represents one of our exciting Malbec experiences. This wine is opaque purple-red in color (Malbec is typically very dark) and has intense, dense aromas of chocolate, mint, and oak. The wine is packed with dense flavors of ripe fruit, sweet oakiness, and chocolate. It's full bodied and shows plenty of tannin (also typical of Malbec), but the tannin doesn't get in the way of the rich fruit flavor. This wine is a good buy because Malbec is not exactly a type of wine that wine drinkers are thronging to the stores to buy (yet).

Ed: 88–90   **Mary:** 88–90

Concha y Toro Cabernet Sauvignon, "Don Melchor"

- **Producer:** Concha y Toro *(CONE cha ee TORE oh)*
- **Wine name:** Cabernet Sauvignon, "Don Melchor," Puente Alto Vineyard
- **Appellation:** Maipo Valley (Chile)
- **Price:** $26

Of all the wines that the huge Concha y Toro winery makes — under its own label and other labels, such as Walnut Crest — the Don Melchor Cabernet is the winery's finest. In fact, we've always considered this wine to be the finest red wine in all of Chile. The 1994 Don Melchor is as black and inky as a wine can be, with very intense aromas of ink, hay, wet earth, and leather. The wine is full bodied, dry, and rich, with subdued flavors suggesting earthiness, ink, and ripe fruit. Although it's rich, this wine has rather mouth-drying tannin from oak. The Don Melchor can age quite well for five years or more, we suspect, but you can also enjoy it now, especially with a manly dish such as a saddle of lamb.

Ed: 90–92   **Mary:** 89–91

Errazuriz Cabernet Sauvignon, "Don Maximiano"

- **Producer:** Errazuriz *(ay RAH sue rees)*
- **Wine name:** Cabernet Sauvignon, Don Maximiano *(max ee me AH noh)*
- **Appellation:** Aconcagua Valley (Chile)
- **Price:** $26

If you taste this wine side-by-side with the normal Cabernet Sauvignon bottling of Errazuriz, you can see the family resemblance; for example, both wines are strong expressions of the fruit character of the Cabernet Sauvignon grape. The more expensive Don Maximiano, the winery's Estate Reserve, is more intensely concentrated, however, and, at the same time, more subtle and sophisticated than the winery's regular Cabernet. The 1993 Don Maximiano Cabernet has an intense, almost opulent, aroma of briary fruit and ink, suggesting a very youthful wine. It has flavors of cassis (typical Cabernet) and spicy oak, a soft fleshiness of texture, and yet very firm tannin, probably from oak. The real differences between this wine and the regular bottling will probably show themselves over time; this wine will develop a rich complexity of flavor, while the less expensive wine becomes less interesting. One thing that we like about this wine is its potential: We'd be happy to drink it now, but we'd prefer to wait three to five years.

Ed: 86–88 **Mary:** 85–87

Weinert Merlot

- ! **Producer:** Bodega Weinert (*VINE ert*)
- ! **Wine name:** Merlot
- ! **Appellation:** Mendoza (Argentina)
- ! **Price:** $16

The first wines from Argentina that ever impressed us were made by Bernardo Weinert, a dignified man with a keen instinct for fine wine. His 1993 Merlot has complex aromas and flavors of ink, bramble fruit, and vegetal notes. It's a well-balanced, classy wine in the lean, austere style of Merlot (rather than the plump, rich style), with the softness typical of wines made from this grape variety. (We also like Weinert's 1992 Cabernet Sauvignon, a bigger and richer wine than his Merlot.)

Ed: 88–90 **Mary:** 84–86

Top Red Wines from Australia

If you enjoy California's red wines, you'll probably like Australian reds, too (or vice versa). Wines from both regions tend to be robust, fruit-driven, cleanly made, precocious, and approachable, the latter thanks to the soft tannins in the wines; in fact, soft tannins are a trademark of Australia's wines.

When Australian wines first became popular in the U.S, in the mid-1980s, Australia played the card of affordability and shipped mainly its inexpensive red and white wines to the U.S. Prices have risen, but the Australian wines that you tend to see on the shelves of wine shops and supermarkets are still the inexpensive ones, for the most part. The wines that we recommend in this section are among the exceptions: the elite of Australian reds. We present these wines alphabetically by producer. For our recommendations of Australian red wines under $15, see Chapter 2.

Cape Mentelle Cabernet Sauvignon

- ⚑ **Producer:** Cape Mentelle
- ⚑ **Wine name:** Cabernet Sauvignon
- ⚑ **Appellation:** Margaret River
- ⚑ **Price:** $22

We're very fond of Cabernets from the Margaret River wine region in Western Australia, which tend to taste less opulent, as if their flavors were more under control, than most other Australian red wines. The Cape Mentelle winery is a real star in this region, and the fine Cape Mentelle Cabernet is one of the region's best wines. The 1992 Cape Mentelle Cab has an aroma that's more suggestive of barnyard (pungently earthy) than fruit — quite an atypical aroma for an Australian wine — but ripe, black fruit emerges in the flavor. The wine is full bodied and firm with tannin that's surprisingly intense for Australian wine — an earthy, rustic sort of Cabernet that's as intriguing as it is fine quality and good-tasting. But throw a steak, not a shrimp, on the barby for this one.

Ed: 84–86   **Mary:** 88–90

Evans & Tate Cabernet-Merlot

- ⚑ **Producer:** Evans & Tate
- ⚑ **Wine name:** Cabernet-Merlot, "Barrique 61"
- ⚑ **Appellation:** Western Australia
- ⚑ **Price:** $17.50

If we had to describe the 1995 Evans & Tate Cabernet-Merlot in just one word, we'd say it's solid, because it's a big wine with a great deal of substance. The rather dense aromas and flavors of this wine suggest black pepper, oak, and mint. Although this flavorful wine is plump, smooth, and rich in texture, it has plenty of stuffing, and its oakiness takes a back seat to its fruit character — a real plus in our book. Also, the wine has none of the candied fruitiness we often find in New World wines, another plus. You can enjoy it now and for the next couple of years.

Ed: 86–88   **Mary:** 86–88

Henschke Shiraz-Cabernet-Malbec

> ! **Producer:** Henschke *(HEN shkey)*
>
> ! **Wine name:** Shiraz-Cabernet-Malbec
>
> ! **Appellation:** Barossa
>
> ! **Price:** $24

Henschke is one of the top wineries in Australia, particularly known for its Shiraz wine called Hill of Grace, which is made from 130-year-old vines and costs almost as much in dollars as the age of its vines. The wine that Henschke blends from Shiraz (the Syrah grape of the Rhône Valley in France), Cabernet, and Malbec is somewhat less exalted in quality than that wine, but it's nevertheless a very good wine — and far more affordable! Like all of Henschke's reds, the Shiraz-Cabernet-Malbec blend is very deeply colored; it has rather subdued but fascinating aromas of charred meat and wild berries, as well as ripe flavors of juicy fruit. This full-bodied, flavorful wine is relatively dry, considering its ripe fruitiness. It's firm with tannin but not overly tannic, and it shows good depth of flavor. The concentration of fruit that this wine shows on its finish suggests that it can age for a few years without a care.

If you come across any of Henschke's other reds — such as the Mount Edelstone Shiraz from the Keyneton Vineyard — don't hesitate to buy them; this is a very reliable producer.

Ed: 89–91   **Mary:** 87–89

Mitchelton Cabernet Sauvignon Reserve

- *MARY'S CHOICE*
  - **Producer:** Mitchelton
  - **Wine name:** Cabernet Sauvignon Reserve
  - **Appellation:** Victoria
  - **Price:** $20

I've enjoyed many wines from Mitchelton over the years, both red and white. A case in point is the 1993 Cabernet Sauvignon Reserve, a very deeply colored, sweetly perfumed, highly flavorful, super-rich wine. Although I tend to judge such rich wines with some suspicion — tasting carefully to determine whether the wine is just all fluff and flavor or whether it has some substance behind its delicious exterior — the Mitchelton Cabernet survives my scrutiny. It's full bodied, thick with minty flavor, and supple in texture — and it has plenty of stuffing. You can serve this with confidence at a dinner party, knowing that your guests will love it.

Mary: 90–92

Penfolds "Bin 389" Cabernet-Shiraz

- **Producer:** Penfolds
- **Wine name:** Cabernet-Shiraz "Bin 389"
- **Appellation:** South Australia
- **Price:** $19

Large quantity of production and high quality of product coincide less often in the wine business than we would wish, but that combination is a regular occurrence for the Penfolds wines. The Penfolds wine called "Bin 389," a blend of Cabernet Sauvignon and Shiraz (Syrah) wine, is not only a very fine wine but also widely available — and at a very fair price. The 1993 "Bin 389" has an intense, dense aroma of ripe fruit, earthiness, and butterscotch and equally intense flavors of black cherries and earth. Full-bodied and firm with tannin, this wine is very young; it will reward aging by softening in texture and showing increased complexity of flavor. If you like powerful red wines that are bristling with youthfulness, you can enjoy this wine now, probably all the more so with some simply prepared red meat.

Ed: 88–90   **Mary:** 88–90

Rosemount Estate Cabernet Sauvignon Reserve

- ♪ **Producer:** Rosemount Estate
- ♪ **Wine name:** Cabernet Sauvignon Reserve
- ♪ **Appellation:** Coonawarra
- ♪ **Price:** $22

Rosemount's inexpensive "Diamond Label" Cabernet Sauvignon is one of the terrific values in Australian wine (see Chapter 2) and a great everyday Cabernet. This reserve Cabernet is a step up in quality and subtlety, and yet it's true to Rosemount's typically soft, very fruity style of red wines. The 1994 reserve has a lovely aroma that's dusty and minty, along with intense, minty flavor accents. The wine is medium to full bodied, rich, and supple, with soft tannins but enough acidity to keep the wine lively-tasting. Above all, it sings with delicious, fresh fruit. If most serious Cabernets are a bit too austere for you, try this one.

Ed: 86–88   **Mary:** 87–89

Taltarni Shiraz

- ♪ **Producer:** Taltarni Vineyards
- ♪ **Wine name:** Shiraz
- ♪ **Appellation:** Victoria
- ♪ **Price:** $16.50

Taltarni's 1994 Shiraz is dry, firm, fairly lean, and rather austere for an Australian wine (which probably explains why we like it; to us, over-ripeness is a cardinal sin of wine). It has smoky and charry oak aromas and old-fashioned, unfruity flavors that are earthy and vegetal. If you enjoy sweet, lush red wines, the restrained Taltarni Shiraz may be too austere for you. But we find that this style goes far better with food — perhaps a hearty stew.

Ed: 85–87   **Mary:** 84–86

Elite Red Wines from South Africa

We didn't plan to review as many South African red wines in this chapter as we actually do review. But when we checked our tasting notes to identify wines that we've enjoyed in the past and then retasted many of those wines for a fresh opinion, we had so many favorites that we had to expand this section.

In the end, providing a few extra reviews is probably a good decision (we rationalized!) because many of these South African wines are small-production items that are available only here and there across the U.S. At least with nine wines as candidates, your odds of finding one of them are better.

With one exception, all the wines in this section are either Cabernet Sauvignons or blends that incorporate Cabernet and other Bordeaux grape varieties, such as Merlot or Cabernet Franc. We list these wines alphabetically by producer. For our recommendations of South African red wines under $15, see Chapter 2.

Glen Carlou "Grand Classique"

- ✔ **Producer:** Glen Carlou
- ✔ **Wine name:** "Grand Classique" Blend
- ✔ **Appellation:** Paarl
- ✔ **Price:** $17

One of the most interesting impressions a wine can deliver, in our opinion, is a sense of point-counterpoint: flavors or elements of the wine that balance each other out, back and forth, as you taste the wine. Glen Carlou's 1993 "Grand Classique" — a Bordeaux-style blend of Cabernet Sauvignon, Merlot, and Cabernet Franc — performs just like that. It's a full-bodied wine with lots of tannin that's firm but soft at the same time; it has enough acidity to create a rather dry, rough texture, but the wine also gives you a profound sense of ripe, round fruit character that's almost the opposite of rough. The "Grand Classique" is a gutsy wine with real character, but it deals in innuendo more than aggression. And the aroma: ripe, plummy fruit and a touch of mint. You get the impression that if you could just smell deeply enough, you'd find a buried treasure. Does this sound like great wine, or what?

Ed: 86–88   **Mary:** 88–90

Grangehurst Cabernet-Merlot Reserve

- **Producer:** Grangehurst Winery
- **Wine name:** Cabernet-Merlot Reserve
- **Appellation:** Stellenbosch
- **Price:** $30

Simply put, this is the most exciting wine that I've ever had from South Africa. I believe that South Africa has jumped higher in the quality of its red wines in the last ten years than any other country in the world, as the existence of this five-year-old winery demonstrates. The Grangehurst Cabernet-Merlot Reserve, 76 percent Cabernet Sauvignon and 24 percent Merlot, is Grangehurst's flagship wine. In the 1994 vintage, it's intensely fragrant with mint and has rich black-fruit and mint flavors. It has an amazingly rich, velvety texture, as well as considerable depth, firm tannin, and outstanding balance. If I hadn't known it was a South African wine, I would've mistaken this super-impressive Cabernet Sauvignon-Merlot for an expensive Bordeaux, such as Château Margaux. It's delicious right now, but it's capable of aging for eight to ten years, at least.

Ed: 96–98

Grangehurst Cabernet Sauvignon

- **Producer:** Grangehurst
- **Wine name:** Cabernet Sauvignon
- **Appellation:** Stellenbosch
- **Price:** $26

Only five years old, Grangehurst is producing wines that are already internationally acclaimed. The 1993 Cabernet Sauvignon of Grangehurst has a deep crimson color and a deep, deep aroma suggesting cedar, mint, and some earthiness. It has an excellent concentration of dark, rich fruit and is an intense, quietly powerful wine. I'd like to be a little more explicit, but as with many great wines, this Cabernet is difficult to describe.

Mary: 90–92

Hamilton Russell Pinot Noir

- ♪ **Producer:** Hamilton Russell Vineyards
- ♪ **Wine name:** Pinot Noir
- ♪ **Appellation:** Walker Bay
- ♪ **Price:** $16

Hamilton Russell Vineyards has been producing South Africa's best Pinot Noir wine since 1981. As the country's most southerly vineyard, it has the cool climate necessary for this challenging grape variety. The 1995 Hamilton Russell Pinot Noir has tart cherry and black-fruit aromas with a whiff of dead leaf, along with flavors of tart cherry and some stewed fruit. It's a delicately flavored, light-bodied wine with flavors that are on target for this grape variety. This style of Pinot is perfect with a light summer lunch or dinner; a delicate fish or seafood would be a good accompaniment to the wine.

Ed: 86–88   **Mary:** 85–87

La Motte Estate Cabernet Sauvignon

- ♪ **Producer:** La Motte Estate
- ♪ **Wine name:** Cabernet Sauvignon
- ♪ **Appellation:** Franschhoek Valley (Paarl)
- ♪ **Price:** $17

La Motte Estate winemaker Jacques Borman, who has made several working trips to Bordeaux, fashioned an outstanding Cabernet Sauvignon in 1991. The wine has aromas of deep, ripe black-currant fruit, along with ripe black-fruit flavors. It is supple with soft, ripe tannins and has great depth, complexity, and concentration of fruit. Ed sums up the wine by saying, "The whole package here." Mary says, "A really, really great wine in its understatement; so much there and yet so gently, quietly, agreeably!" Its long, concentrated finish suggests that you can hold this beauty for several more years, if you wish. But it's so delicious that we'd have a tough time keeping the cork in the bottle.

Ed: 93–95   **Mary:** 92–94

Meerlust Cabernet Sauvignon

> **Producer:** Meerlust Estate
>
> **Wine name:** Cabernet Sauvignon
>
> **Appellation:** Stellenbosch
>
> **Price:** $19

When we write that the red wines of South Africa seem to have one foot in the Old World of winemaking and one foot in the New, Meerlust Estate is often our subconscious inspiration. Meerlust's reds are never as freshly fruity as Australian or Californian wines, but they seem almost sweet with fruit compared to many a red Bordeaux. The 1991 Meerlust Cabernet Sauvignon, for example, has rustic aromas and flavors of earth and ink and a firm, gutsy personality, but it also has an attractive sweetness from its ripe grapes and its fairly high alcohol. To us, this wine is almost quintessentially Cabernet grown in a warm climate, somewhere between traditional and modern. (We're also great fans of Meerlust's "Rubicon," a Bordeaux-style blend that, in many vintages, is one of the best wines of all South Africa.)

Ed: 88–90   **Mary:** 90–92

Plaisir de Merle Cabernet Sauvignon

> **Producer:** Plaisir de Merle
>
> **Wine name:** Cabernet Sauvignon
>
> **Appellation:** Paarl
>
> **Price:** $19.50

Plaisir de Merle is the showpiece winery of the gigantic Stellenbosch Farmers Winery, South Africa's largest private wine firm. Winemaker Niel Bester — together with Paul Pontallier, winemaker of Château Margaux and consultant to Plaisir de Merle — is now making one of the best Cabernet Sauvignons in South Africa. The 1994 Plaisir de Merle Cabernet has intriguing aromas of mint, coffee, and fresh milk, with ink and ripe cassis flavors. It's full bodied, smooth, supple, and rich, but quite tannic — profound, intense Cabernet. You can enjoy the 1994 Plaisir de Merle Cabernet now, but it should only get better with a few more years of development.

Ed: 88–90   **Mary:** 91–93

Rozendal

- ♪ **Producer:** Rozendal Farm
- ♪ **Wine name:** Rozendal
- ♪ **Appellation:** Stellenbosch
- ♪ **Price:** $22.50

Kurt Ammann runs a country inn and restaurant on the outskirts of Stellenbosch, and manages to make some wine, which he simply calls Rozendal, on his estate. It's mainly a Merlot wine (80 percent), with 20 percent Cabernet Sauvignon. The 1994 Rozendal has seductive aromas of chocolate, prunes, and cassis, along with ripe, concentrated fruit flavors. This is a rich, complex, and velvety wine with firm tannins that counterbalance the wine's sweet, ripe fruit. Full-bodied and intense, it's made in a powerful style. The Rozendal has years of life ahead of it; we'd hold on to this very impressive wine for a few years.

Ed: 92–94   **Mary:** 88–90

Simonsig "Tiara"

- ♪ **Producer:** Simonsig Estate
- ♪ **Wine name:** "Tiara"
- ♪ **Appellation:** Stellenbosch
- ♪ **Price:** $22

Simonsig Estate, one of the largest wineries in South Africa, is especially known for its Pinotage (a red South African grape variety) and its Shiraz. But equally impressive is its "Tiara," a blend of 78 percent Cabernet Sauvignon, 18 percent Merlot, and 4 percent Cabernet Franc. The 1993 "Tiara" has aromas of mint and cedary oak, along with mint and berry flavors. It has plenty of depth and tannin, which outweighs the fruit right now. But the minty flavor gives a freshness and a coolness to this dry, full-bodied wine, relieving the heaviness of the tannin. We like this wine's potential, and recommend holding on to it for two or three years.

Ed: 85–87   **Mary:** 84–86

Part II
All Dressed in White

In this part . . .

*E*ven though we drink a good deal of red wine, we know from experience that a cool, crisp white wine is often the perfect choice. Some foods — such as seafood, fish, poultry, and vegetables — just go better with white wine than with red. And no matter what's on the table, when the weather is warm and sultry or when we want something easy-drinking to sip, white wines are ideal.

This part of the book features reviews of our favorite white wines, ranging from the popular Chardonnay to lesser-known delights such as Riesling, Gewürztraminer, Pinot Gris, Sauvignon Blanc, and Sémillon. We divide the wines in this part by cost: Chapters 5 and 6 deal with less-expensive white wines, and Chapters 7 and 8 cover white wines in the $15 to $50 price range. We also divide the chapters according to origin: Reviews of European white wines (including French, German, and Italian wines) appear in Chapters 6 and 8, and reviews of white wines from New World countries (such as the U.S., South Africa, Australia, and New Zealand) appear in Chapters 5 and 7. We hope that, among our recommendations in these four chapters, you find several white wines that are just right for you.

Chapter 5

Where It All Started: Old World White Wines for $15 or Less

A funny thing happened to white wines on the way to America: The rich spectrum of white-wine grapes that exists in Europe got downsized by the U.S. market, leaving dozens of deserving grapes with no place in corporate American winedom. Two grapes (Chardonnay and Sauvignon Blanc), for the most part, had to bear the entire burden of production in the U.S. Fortunately for the downsized grapes (and for adventurous wine drinkers), Europe's winemakers still cherish diversity among white wines.

The white wines that we review in this chapter come from France, Italy, Germany, Austria, Spain, and Greece. They range in style from dry, crisp, light-bodied whites to *off-dry* (slightly sweet) wines brimming with charm, to full-bodied whites with the richness of sun-baked fruit. These wines represent a wide range of grape varieties (*including* Chardonnay and Sauvignon Blanc), and they offer a whole world of white wine to explore.

Like most European wines, the wines that we cover in this chapter tend to be named for the place where the grapes grow, such as Saint-Véran or Soave, rather than for the grape variety or varieties that make up the wine. Two notable exceptions are the wines of Germany and those of France's Alsace region, which carry grape variety names.

We group the wines in this chapter according to their country of origin, and then by their region of production. We start with France because . . . well, because French wines have always been the leaders of Europe. Then we move to German and Italian whites. Finally, we list our under-$15 white wine recommendations from other European countries, which we group together because we review only a few wines from each country.

We list the vital information for each wine in the following way:

- ✔ **The producer:** The name of the company that makes the wine (the *producer*) is usually considered the brand name of the wine.

- ✔ **The wine name:** For most of the wines in this chapter, the wine name is the place where the grapes grow, but sometimes it's a grape name, instead.

- ✔ **The appellation:** The *appellation* is a necessary and legal part of the wine label, intended to tell you where the grapes that make up the wine came from and other technical information about the wine, such as whether it qualifies for special designations such as *reserve.* For wines with place names, the appellation is repetitive: The appellation is the wine name, and the wine name is the appellation. For wines with grape names, the appellation gives you additional information about the wine. When we review wines from more than one country in the same section, we indicate the country in parentheses after the appellation.

- ✔ **The approximate retail price of the wine:** This price can vary greatly according to where you live and the type of store where you buy your wine. We use New York State suggested retail prices, rounded to the nearest half dollar.

France, Home of Vin Blanc

Just about every wine region in France makes white wine — even regions that specialize in red wine, such as the Rhône Valley or Bordeaux. France's greatest white wines cost well over $15 a bottle, but plenty of good, $15-and-under French white wines are out there on retail shelves.

We cover the white wines of France according to the region they come from, arranging the major regions alphabetically.

The Alsace advantage

The wines of the Alsace *(ahl zahss)* region of France are unique among the white wines of the world. For one thing, they are made from grape varieties (such as Riesling, Pinot Gris, and Gewurztraminer) that don't grow elsewhere in France. Also, Alsace wines are generally drier and fuller in body than German wines made from the same grape varieties. Wines from Alsace are not oaky, like most California whites. And, of course, they are the only wines in the world that have the flavor of Alsace — a sort of minerally, spicy character that underlies many of the wines from the Alsace region, almost regardless of grape variety.

Although Alsace wines are becoming better known and appreciated in the U.S., they are still less popular than they deserve to be, which means that you can find some good values. The prices are not extremely low, but the quality is high for the price, relative to many other types of white wine.

All Alsace wines come in tall, slim, green bottles. And, with the exception of a few blended wines, every Alsace wine also carries the name of the grape variety from which it was made as well as the regional name Alsace.

Be sure not to serve Alsace whites very cold, which causes them to taste austere and stand-offish. When these wines are merely chilled (about an hour in the refrigerator should do the trick), as opposed to ice cold, their richness comes through much more clearly.

We recommend some of our favorite Alsace wines in this section, listing them alphabetically by producer. For more information on Alsace wines, refer to *White Wine For Dummies,* Chapters 4 and 11.

Gewurztraminer Bollenberg, Lucien Albrecht

- **Producer:** Lucien Albrecht
- **Wine name:** Gewurztraminer Bollenberg
- **Appellation:** Alsace
- **Price:** $14

I used to associate the smell of Gewurztraminer wine with lychee fruit, but somewhere along the way, the wine began to remind me more of roses. Now the scents of Gewurztraminer and roses are so intertwined in my neural wiring that when I recently smelled a rose, I remarked how it much it smelled like Gewurztraminer! The 1994 Gewurztraminer of Lucien Albrecht, from grapes grown in the Bollenberg vineyard, has an intoxicating aroma of rosewater. Typical of Gewurztraminer, the wine is full blown and generous, even a bit fat and very slightly sweet — a big, soft, plump wine that's ripe with the flavor of its grapes. To balance the richness of the wine, I suggest roast pork or a mild, soft cheese.

Mary: 86–88

Pinot "Blanc de Blancs," Léon Beyer

- ! **Producer:** Léon Beyer *(lay on buy ehr)*
- ! **Wine name:** Pinot "Blanc de Blancs"
- ! **Appellation:** Alsace
- ! **Price:** $11.50

Alsace wine producers consider Pinot Blanc to be their ambassador, the wine that converts wine drinkers into fans of Alsace wines for life. The "ambassador" is armed with a naturally appealing personality — relatively light body, crispness, and easygoing, unassertive flavor — but these days, it often sports a bit of sweetness, too, just for good measure. Fortunately, a few producers, such as Léon Beyer, still make a truly dry Pinot Blanc. Beyer's 1995 Pinot Blanc is medium bodied and firm, with typical Alsace intensity. It has some floral and fruity character, but the flavors are essentially steely and austere. Try this wine with just about any poultry, soup, or sandwich. The Léon Beyer Riesling is also tops.

Ed: 85–87   **Mary:** 86–88

Tokay-Pinot Gris, Léon Beyer

- ! **Producer:** Léon Beyer *(lay on buy ehr)*
- ! **Wine name:** Tokay-Pinot Gris
- ! **Appellation:** Alsace
- ! **Price:** $14.50

We like the style of this producer: dry, lean, and firm wines that accompany food very well. Of all Beyer's wines, however, the Tokay-Pinot Gris is probably the richest, simply because such is the nature of the Pinot Gris grape variety in Alsace. The 1995 Beyer Pinot Gris has broad aromas and flavors suggestive of white truffles (the mushroom, not the chocolate) — quite appealing to anyone who has cultivated a taste for that delicacy. The wine is dry, rich, and fairly flavorful: Besides the white truffles, it suggests floral notes and peaches. Expect this Tokay-Pinot Gris to be delicious with pork, veal, or any other full-flavored white meat.

Ed: 84–86   **Mary:** 84–86

Riesling, Trimbach

> ♪ **Producer:** Trimbach
> ♪ **Wine name:** Riesling
> ♪ **Appellation:** Alsace
> ♪ **Price:** $15

"Trimbach's wines are very trim" is what we tell our students to describe the style that cuts across all the wines this producer makes; "nothing huge or flamboyant here." Of three Rieslings that Trimbach makes, the basic Riesling described here is the least expensive and the least compelling, but it's still quite good. The gentle aroma of the 1994 Trimbach Riesling combines tart apples, a floral scent, and mineral notes. The flavors echo tart fruit and minerals, the texture is fairly soft and welcoming, and the wine is dry. If you have a cool place to store this wine, you can let it age a year or more before you drink it. Whether you drink it young or aged, expect this wine to taste terrific with roast pork.

Ed: 84–86   **Mary:** 84–86

Sylvaner "Cuvée Oscar," Clos St. Landelin

> ♪ **Producer:** Clos St. Landelin *(clo sant lahn deh lan)*
> ♪ **Wine name:** Sylvaner, "Cuvée Oscar"
> ♪ **Appellation:** Alsace
> ♪ **Price:** $12

The Sylvaner grape variety is widely planted in Alsace, but its wines are far less popular than other Alsace wines, probably because this grape lacks the distinctiveness of Alsace's other varieties. But when it's made right, Sylvaner can be very attractive, and its price is definitely right. "Cuvée Oscar" is a particular bottling of Clos St. Landelin Sylvaner. The 1994 "Cuvée Oscar" is quite dry and well balanced between its high alcohol level and its crisp, refreshing acidity. This wine shows good concentration of very ripe fruit and a slight suggestion of honey flavor. Try this wine with fish in a rich sauce or with soft French cheeses. If you haven't tried a Sylvaner, "Cuvée Oscar" is a good first choice.

Ed: 85–87

Bordeaux's basic whites

White Bordeaux wines are based on the Sauvignon Blanc grape, usually with some Sémillon blended in. Sauvignon alone usually makes a light-bodied, crisp wine, but Sémillon changes the whole picture, giving weight, richness, and a bit of "fat" to the bony Sauvignon frame. The least expensive wines are usually unoaked and, as a result, have much less flavor intensity than Sauvignon Blanc-based wines from California — but also more flexibility with food. The higher the price of a white Bordeaux wine, the greater the chance that it has been made in oak barrels, giving it richness and more flavor.

We describe some of our favorite inexpensive white Bordeaux wines in alphabetical order by producer.

Mouton-Cadet Blanc

⚑ **Producer:** Baron Philippe de Rothschild

⚑ **Wine name:** Mouton-Cadet Blanc
   (*moo tahn cah day blahnck*)

⚑ **Appellation:** Bordeaux

⚑ **Price:** $9

Mouton is one of the most famous names in the whole world of wine, thanks to the legendary red Bordeaux wine, Château Mouton-Rothschild (see Chapter 3). The wine called Mouton-Cadet — which comes in a red or white version (*rouge* or *blanc,* as they say in French restaurants) — is legally related to the legendary Mouton in that it's made by the same company. Genetically, however, the two wines are not related, because the Mouton-Cadet grapes don't come from the same privileged plot of earth that produces the grapes that make Mouton-Rothschild. The Mouton name has certainly contributed to the enormous success of the Mouton-Cadet wines over the years, but the wines themselves (even the white one) are good, reliable, and worthy of that success. The 1995 Mouton-Cadet Blanc is a light-bodied, crisp white wine that's fresh, clean, and relatively neutral in flavor. Even if this wine cost as much as $12 a bottle, we would still consider it a good value. Mouton-Cadet Blanc is a fine candidate for your all-purpose "house" white.

Ed: 85–87   **Mary:** 85–87

Michel Lynch Bordeaux Blanc

> ♪ **Producer:** Jean-Michel Cazes
> ♪ **Wine name:** Michel Lynch Bordeaux Blanc
> ♪ **Appellation:** Bordeaux
> ♪ **Price:** $9

The Bordeaux appellation on this wine indicates that its grapes come from vineyards throughout the large Bordeaux region, not from vineyards in a single district such as Pessac-Léognan or Graves. Probably because of this technically lesser pedigree, the Michel Lynch Bordeaux Blanc is a terrific value — and despite its lesser pedigree, the wine is quite good. The same people who make the prestigious red Bordeaux, Château Lynch-Bages, make this white wine. The 1995 Michel Lynch Blanc is medium bodied and fairly rich in flavor and texture, suggesting honey. Although it's not a fruity wine, this wine does have a slight apricot flavor. This wine strikes me as a bit majestic in personality — a grown-up wine, not a fruity adolescent.

Mary: 87–89

Château de Cruzeau Blanc

> ♪ **Producer:** Château de Cruzeau
> ♪ **Wine name:** Château de Cruzeau Blanc *(crew zoh)*
> ♪ **Appellation:** Pessac-Léognan *(pays sac lay oh nyan)*
> ♪ **Price:** $14

In quality and style, this wine from the high-quality Pessac-Léognan district of Bordeaux has more in common with the over-$15 white Bordeaux wines we describe in Chapter 7 than it does with the inexpensive wines. Château de Cruzeau Blanc has all the smoky-toasty aromas, flavors, and textural richness that oak aging gives. An attractive lemony character accompanies the oaky aroma and flavor, and the wine is relatively full bodied. The 1994 Château de Cruzeau is so delicious at 2¹/₂ years of age that any further bottle age seems an unnecessary frustration. Drink it now, savor its richness, wallow in it!

Ed: 88–90   **Mary:** 89–91

Château de Quantin Blanc

- ♪ **Producer:** Château de Quantin
- ♪ **Wine name:** Château de Quantin Blanc *(kawhn tan blahnk)*
- ♪ **Appellation:** Pessac-Léognan
- ♪ **Price:** $10

André Lurton owns Château de Quantin, as well as Château de Cruzeau and several other wine estates in Bordeaux. (His name appears in small print on the labels.) His white wines are generally so good that his name has become synonymous with quality white Bordeaux wine. Fortunately, most of Lurton's wines are reasonably priced. The 1994 Quantin Blanc has a quiet aroma with just a slightly honeyed character. It's dry and rather full bodied, with supple flesh and an almost creamy texture, and yet it has a firm backbone of acid that gives the wine crispness. The flavor is subtle — some lemon, some apple, and some earthiness — but all of it discreet. This combination of characteristics at this price spells best buy.

Ed: 84–86   **Mary:** 87–89

White Burgundy

The word "Burgundy" (or, as the French say, *Bourgogne*) suggests the color red. Although it's true that more red Burgundy wines exist than white, it's also true that many of the best white wines in the world are white Burgundies.

In the inexpensive arena, white Burgundy is not an exalted category, but one in which you can, nevertheless, find good wines with character and pedigree. Instead of coming from the very best vineyard areas of Burgundy, such as the Côte d'Or (see the sidebar "White Burgundy made easy"), these good-value Burgundies tend to be made from grapes that grow in the less famous districts of the Burgundy region.

What unites most white Burgundies, from the plebian to the patrician, is the grape variety. Practically all white Burgundies are made from the Chardonnay grape. This fact might surprise you, because almost no French white Burgundies — except, perhaps, some of the most ordinary — have the word "Chardonnay" on the label. (After all, anyone anywhere can grow Chardonnay and name the wine Chardonnay, but only a grape grower in the village of Meursault, for example, can claim to make Meursault wine.)

We review some of our favorite inexpensive white Burgundy wines in this section, organizing the wines alphabetically by producer. For more information about white Burgundy, see Chapter 10 in either *White Wine For Dummies* or *Wine For Dummies.*

White Burgundy made easy

The Burgundy region is situated in eastern France, directly north of Lyon and a few hours' drive southeast of Paris. Four distinct districts, listed here from north to south, are involved in the production of white Burgundy:

- **Chablis:** Wines from this area are crisp, minerally, light to medium bodied, and generally unoaked. They're excellent with fish, especially shellfish.

- **Côte d'Or, particularly its Côte de Beaune subdistrict:** Wines from this most renowned district are medium to full bodied and usually fermented and aged in oak barrels. Their flavors are often reminiscent of hazelnuts, almonds, vanilla, apples, or honey. Some important wine names are Montrachet, Meursault, Corton-Charlemagne.

- **Côte Chalonnaise:** Wines from this area are medium bodied, with earthy flavors. Some of Burgundy's best bargains ($12 to $25) come from such Chalonnaise villages as Mercurey, Rully, Montagny, Givry, and Bouzeron.

- **Mâcon:** Wines from this area are light to medium bodied, and their prices range from $7 or $8 to over $30. The least expensive wines from this district, such as Mâcon-Villages or Saint-Véran, are unoaked; the more expensive Pouilly-Fuissé wines are often aged in oak.

Bourgogne-Aligoté, Jayer-Gilles

- **Producer:** Domaine Robert Jayer-Gilles (*jhai ay jheel*)
- **Wine name:** Bourgogne-Aligoté (*ah lee go tay*)
- **Appellation:** Bourgogne-Aligoté
- **Price:** $12.50

Although almost all white Burgundy wines are made from Chardonnay, wines labeled Bourgogne-Aligoté are made from a completely different grape variety, Aligoté, which tends to be higher in acidity and less rich than Chardonnay. The 1995 Bourgogne-Aligoté produced by Jayer-Gilles has the typical freshness and crispness of Aligoté. Its smoky aroma is interlaced with herbal and floral notes, and its moderately intense flavors suggest lemon and lime. This medium-bodied wine shows good concentration of fruit character and very good quality. It would be a great apéritif wine with seafood and shellfish or with fairly delicately flavored hors d'oeuvres.

Ed: 87–89   **Mary:** 86–88

Mâcon-Charnay Les Chenes, Manciat-Poncet

- **Producer:** Domaine Manciat-Poncet
  (*mahn see ah pon say*)
- **Wine name:** Mâcon-Charnay Les Chenes
  (*mah kon shar nay lay chen*)
- **Appellation:** Mâcon-Villages
- **Price:** $11.50

If white wine descriptors such as *gutsy* and *characterful* make you salivate, this wine should definitely go onto your shopping list. The 1995 Mâcon-Charnay (named after one of the specific villages in the Mâcon-Villages area) of Manciat-Poncet is not an elegant or sophisticated wine, but it delivers plenty of flavor and character for less than $12. The aroma of this wine is rather intense with scents of lemon, minerals, and nuts. The wine is full bodied, with earthy, mineral flavors, as well as the slight nuttiness that comes from aging a wine on the *lees*, the solid deposits of fermentation. Not only is this wine real Mâcon: It's also real value.

Ed: 84–86   **Mary:** 87–89

Chablis, Moreau

- ! **Producer:** J. Moreau et Fils
- ! **Wine name:** Chablis Moreau
- ! **Appellation:** Chablis
- ! **Price:** $15

We love a good, crisp, minerally French Chablis. No wine goes better with shellfish — especially oysters — than Chablis. Unfortunately, decent Chablis wines under $15 are now very difficult to find. But the firm of J. Moreau et Fils, the largest privately owned producer in the Chablis district, still makes a basic Chablis for about $15. Moreau produces its Chablis without using oak barrels, so the fruit character dominates the wine. The 1995 Moreau Chablis has pleasant floral and minerally aromas, with a suggestion of green apple, and also a very subtle flavor of green apple. It's light bodied, dry, crisp, and fresh, with ripe fruit character that balances the wine's acidity. A sound, well-made Chablis with a nice finish, this wine is a pleasure to drink. Where are the oysters?

Ed: 89–91

Mâcon-Igé, Domaine des Roches

- ! **Producer:** Domaine des Roches *(doh mane day rohsh)*
- ! **Wine name:** Mâcon-Igé *(mah kon ee jhay)*
- ! **Appellation:** Mâcon-Igé
- ! **Price:** $12

The Mâcon area produces far more white wines under $15 than any other district in Burgundy. Some good-value wines are labeled Mâcon-Villages, an appellation that means their grapes come from any of 43 specific villages in the Mâcon area. Sometimes, the actual village name appears on the label as part of the wine name, as in this Mâcon-Igé. (Other examples are wines labeled Mâcon-Lugny or Mâcon-Viré.) In the 1995 vintage, this wine has a spicy aroma and quiet flavors of ripe lemons and ripe apples. It's dry and quite full bodied, yet elegant and well balanced by its crisp acidity. We recommend serving this Mâcon as an apéritif wine for hors d'oeuvres, or with a light fish entrée, such as fillet of sole or flounder.

Ed: 84–86   **Mary:** 84–86

Saint-Véran, J.J. Vincent

> ♪ **Producer:** J.J. Vincent
> ♪ **Wine name:** Saint-Véran *(san veh ran)*
> ♪ **Appellation:** Saint-Véran
> ♪ **Price:** $8.50

Saint-Véran wine, from the Mâcon district of Burgundy, is usually a notch higher in quality than most Mâcon-Villages wines. The 1993 Saint-Véran from J.J. Vincent is a dry, moderately flavorful, gutsy white, more rustic in style rather than elegant and refined. We like the way it feels in the mouth, combining a soft, creamy texture with high acid crispness.

Mary: 84–86

Loire Valley values

For the most part, Loire Valley white wines are made entirely from a single grape variety and are not fermented or aged in new oak barrels. Thus, they have the pure flavor of their grapes, without any ancillary toasty or woody character from oak.

The wines called *Muscadet,* made from the Melon grape, tend to be an excellent value because they represent a fairly unpopular style of wine — being not only crisp, dry, and austere but also relatively neutral in aroma and flavor (as opposed to the vaguely sweet, strongly flavored California Chardonnays, for example). The Muscadet wines from the better producers do have an intriguing earthiness and appley fruit character, however. If you like dry, crisp whites, you may find some pleasant surprises among our Muscadet recommendations.

Based entirely on the Sauvignon Blanc grape, the wines of Sancerre and Pouilly-Fumé are dry, medium bodied, and crisp and can have fascinating mineral notes in their aromas and flavor. Because these wines aren't rich or oaky, their flavors are relatively subdued and easy to overlook — especially if the wine is very cold. But the best wines reveal plenty of flavors-in-hiding if you give them the chance.

Some Loire Valley wines come from a third grape variety, Chenin Blanc, but those wines don't happen to rank among our favorites, and we don't review any in this section. We do review several Muscadets (arranged alphabetically according to the producer) because we enjoy them, and they almost always cost less than $15.

Most of the best Sancerre and Pouilly-Fumé wines are priced higher than $15 a bottle, and we review several of those wines in Chapter 7. In this section we review one Pouilly-Fumé whose price sits right on the $15 line.

Muscadet, Château du Cléray

- **Producer:** Château du Cléray *(cleh ray)*
- **Wine name:** Muscadet de Sèvre-et-Maine Sur Lie *(sev'r et mehn suhr lee)*
- **Appellation:** Muscadet de Sèvre-et-Maine
- **Price:** $10

The popular myth "French wines are expensive" is simply not true if you disregard Burgundy and the most sought-after Bordeaux and Rhône wines. For example, you can still buy some very good Muscadets for under $10 — such as Château du Cléray, an estate-grown wine from a property owned by Sauvion et Fils, a company that makes other Muscadets as well. The 1995 Château du Cléray has a subtle aroma of earth and apple, and when you taste it, you can notice a slight prickle on your tongue, along with the flavor of tart apple. The wine is dry, crisp, medium bodied, and relatively flavorful and has enough complexity to please a serious wine taster. Drink this terrific warm-weather wine in its youth, preferably with some clams, mussels, or oysters.

Ed: 86–88   **Mary:** 87–89

Getting "Sur Lie" with you

The best Muscadets come from the Sèvre-et-Maine district, named for two rivers that flow through the area. The wines are often labeled Sur Lie, which literally means "on the lees." (*Lees* are the fine grape solids and dead yeast cells that precipitate to the bottom of the tank after fermentation.) The phrase "Sur Lie" refers to the traditional practice of bottling the Muscadet wine directly from the tank, where it is still "on its lees," so that the wine can be in contact with its lees as long as possible. The lees contribute flavor complexity to the wine, preserve the wine's delicacy and freshness, and cause a small amount of carbon dioxide to remain in the wine — which can give the wine a slight effervescence.

Muscadet Clos des Allées, Luneau-Papin

> ♪ **Producer:** Domaine Pierre Luneau-Papin
>
> ♪ **Wine name:** Muscadet de Sèvre-et-Maine Clos des Allées, Vieilles Vignes *(clo days ahl lay, vee ay vee nyeh)*
>
> ♪ **Appellation:** Muscadet de Sèvre-et-Maine
>
> ♪ **Price:** $12

The Luneau-Papin firm produces several different Muscadet wines, each wine distinguished from the next either by the specific area from which its grapes come or by particular winemaking techniques. The Muscadet called Clos des Allées comes from grapes grown on old vines *(vieilles vignes)* in a vineyard of the same name as the wine. The 1995 Clos des Allées is a fairly rich Muscadet, with citrus fruit, floral, and mineral aromas and flavors. Its ripe, rich character is balanced by a lively acidity of the sort that you expect in a Muscadet.

Ed: 86–88

Muscadet Cuvée du Millenaire, Marquis de Goulaine

> ♪ **Producer:** Marquis de Goulaine *(mar kee deh goo lan)*
>
> ♪ **Wine name:** Muscadet de Sèvre-et-Maine, Cuvée du Millenaire (Black Label)
>
> ♪ **Appellation:** Muscadet de Sèvre-et-Maine
>
> ♪ **Price:** $11

This wine, often referred to as Goulaine's Black Label Muscadet, is the finer and more expensive of two Muscadet bottlings from this respected producer, whose family interest in wine dates back more than 1,000 years. In the 1994 vintage, this wine has a fairly intense, minerally aroma with a hint of ripe apples. It is dry and austere in flavor, is rather full bodied for a Muscadet, and has a wonderful crispness of acidity that brings the wine to life. If you drink this wine very cold, it tastes overly austere and flavorless; however, if you chill it down just a little (no more than an hour in the refrigerator) and serve it in a large wine glass, its subtle qualities emerge.

Ed: 84–86   **Mary:** 88–90

Pouilly-Fumé, Domaine de St. Laurent l'Abbaye

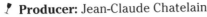

MARY'S CHOICE

- **Producer:** Jean-Claude Chatelain
- **Wine name:** Pouilly-Fumé, Domaine de St. Laurent l'Abbaye
  (poo ee foo may doh mane deh san lo rahnt lab aye ee)
- **Appellation:** Pouilly-Fumé
- **Price:** $15

This Pouilly-Fumé wine ranks near the top of my list of always-reliable white whites, not only for its taste but also because it's fairly easy to find. In the 1995 vintage, the wine has a broad but fairly subdued aroma with earthy and minerally notes. Its flavors of concentrated lemon and apricot are quite intense, and its body is fairly full and plump for a Pouilly-Fumé, although it's well balanced by tart acidity. This is not a typical Pouilly-Fumé, but a good one, nevertheless.

Mary: 86–88

Germany, Where White Wine Is Golden

In the universe of white wines, Germany is a galaxy unto itself. The number and array of white wines produced in Germany are huge, the styles of wine are different from those of other countries, and even the grape varieties are, in many cases, unique to Germany.

Because the country's cool climate is better suited to growing white grapes than red, most of the wine produced in Germany is white. The climate is so cool, in fact, that most of Germany's wines are very low in alcohol (from about 9 to 11.5 percent, compared to a range of about 12.5 to 14 percent in countries or regions with warmer climates, such as California) and they are usually very light bodied. Despite the current trend toward heavily oaked white wines in many other countries, Germany's whites are generally unoaked; instead of smoky, toasty aromas and flavors, they usually have fruity flavors.

The star of the German white wine galaxy is Riesling, a grape variety that experts generally acknowledge to be one of the two greatest white grapes in the world. (Chardonnay is the other.) This assessment is based on Riesling's ability to produce wines of outstanding quality. Rieslings make up the bulk of our recommendations in this section.

Because of the intricacies of German wine law, every wine we review has not only a grape name and a place name (for inexpensive wines, often the name of a region; for finer wines, a vineyard name) but also an indication, as part of the wine name, of the ripeness level of the grapes at harvest. Words or abbreviations indicating ripeness level of the wines we review include the following:

- **QbA:** Short for Qualitätswein *(KAHL ee tates vine)*, indicates a relatively low level of ripeness
- **Kabinett:** Indicates a higher ripeness level

For more information on these terms, and on German wine in general, refer to Chapter 12 of *White Wine For Dummies* or Chapter 11 of *Wine For Dummies.* For reviews of German wines costing more than $15, turn to Chapter 7 of this book.

Forster Riesling QbA, Dr. Bürklin-Wolf

- **Producer:** Dr. Bürklin-Wolf
- **Wine name:** Forster Riesling
- **Appellation:** Forster QbA
- **Price:** $14

In Chapter 7, we review a single-vineyard Riesling wine from Dr. Bürklin-Wolf. But this wine, labeled simply Forster Riesling, comes not from the grapes of a single vineyard but from the grapes of various vineyards in the vicinity of the town of Forst, in the Pfalz *(fahllz)* wine region. The 1995 Forster Riesling has an aroma of smokiness and ripe citrus fruit, more orange than grapefruit. The wine is fairly full bodied and soft for a German wine, with terrific concentration of ripe orange and tangerine flavor at its core. Fruity, off-dry, and richly flavored, this wine would go great with all sorts of foods that are difficult with other wines, such as Eggs Benedict (or anything else with hollandaise sauce), chef salad, or spinach salad with bacon and hard-boiled eggs.

Ed: 88–90   **Mary:** 88–90

Müller-Thurgau QbA Trocken, Castell

- **Producer:** Castell
- **Wine name:** Müller-Thurgau Trocken *(moo ler TER gow)*
- **Appellation:** Franken QbA
- **Price:** $13

The Müller-Thurgau grape occupies a huge amount of vineyard land in Germany, but much of the wine made from it is simple, ordinary stuff that's blended into very inexpensive, off-dry wines. In the Franken region, however, Müller-Thurgau makes crisp, minerally, light-bodied wines that are often dry. Castell's 1995 Müller-Thurgau Trocken is an extremely dry, crisp wine. (*Trocken* means dry.) Its aroma is smoky and spicy (like white pepper, with a hint of cinnamon), and its flavors suggest green apples and minerals. This medium-bodied wine has enough concentration and character to actually improve for a year or two; in the meantime, it tastes particularly good with smoked fish, such as smoked trout.

Ed: 86–88   **Mary:** 86–88

Riesling QbA, Diel

- ♪ **Producer:** Schlossgut Diel
- ♪ **Wine name:** Riesling
- ♪ **Appellation:** Nahe QbA
- ♪ **Price:** $13.50

Diel is one of the leading producers in the Nahe (pronounced *NAH heh*) region, an area known for the intricacy of its Riesling wines. Diel's Riesling QbA is an uncomplicated wine, blended from the grapes of his various vineyards rather than from a single vineyard. In the 1994 vintage, this wine has a classic Riesling aroma of mineral, slate, and a whiff of what we call "fusel," an attractive scent that's a bit like diesel fuel. The wine is fruity, soft, and off-dry (slightly sweet), with lemon and mineral flavors and a strong backbone of acidity to counterbalance the sweetness. Flavorful and vibrant, Diel's QbA Riesling is a pleasure to drink.

Ed: 87–89   **Mary:** 85–87

Ockfener Bockstein Riesling Kabinett, Dr. Fischer

- ♪ **Producer:** Dr. Fischer
- ♪ **Wine name:** Ockfener Bockstein Riesling Kabinett
- ♪ **Appellation:** Ockfener Bockstein Kabinett
- ♪ **Price:** $13

This wine from the Ockfener Bockstein vineyard, in the Mosel-Saar-Ruwer region of Germany, has always been a favorite, simply because it's so easy to like. Words such as *pretty* and *charming* are apt descriptors for Dr. Fischer's 1995 Ockfener Bockstein Kabinett. This wine is fairly light bodied and off-dry, with aromas of coconut and mixed fruits and flavors of minerals and earth. It's fresh, bright, and gentle — a terrific accompaniment to creamy vegetable soups and mild cheeses such as Monterey Jack.

Ed: 86–88   **Mary:** 85–87

Riesling Kabinett, Dr. Loosen

✔ **Producer:** Dr. Loosen *(LOH sen)*

✔ **Wine name:** Riesling Kabinett

✔ **Appellation:** Mosel-Saar-Ruwer Kabinett

✔ **Price:** $14

The single-vineyard Riesling wines of Ernst Loosen run as high as $40 a bottle, depending on the vineyard and the ripeness of the grapes. This less expensive Riesling Kabinett, which is not from a single vineyard, provides a taste of the fine winemaking for which Loosen is admired, but at a lower price and with a simpler name. Loosen's 1995 Riesling Kabinett has an utterly lovely aroma that combines herbs, tart apples, roses, and raw ginger root. The wine is light bodied and off-dry, with delicate herbal and floral flavors. Because this wine is so strikingly delicious, the temptation to open a second bottle is strong; fortunately, with only 7.5 percent alcohol, this wine won't wipe you out the way a Chardonnay with 13 percent alcohol could. Enjoy this wine with delicate foods.

Mary: 86–88

Niersteiner Brückchen Riesling Kabinett, Strub

✔ **Producer:** J.u.H.A. Strub

✔ **Wine name:** Niersteiner Brückchen Riesling Kabinett

✔ **Appellation:** Niersteiner Brückchen Kabinett

✔ **Price:** $14

This single-vineyard wine comes from the Rheinhessen region of Germany, from a well-regarded producer. I particularly enjoy this wine in the 1995 vintage for the contrasts it shows. It's slightly sweet, but crisp with acidity at the same time; it's rather full bodied, but restrained and not over-blown. This wine has aromas and flavors of grapefruit, nuts, smoke, and dry earth. Although it's off-dry, the wine is so crisp and refreshing that even those who insist on dry wines are likely to enjoy it.

Mary: 87–89

Italy's Food-Friendly White Wines

As recently as 10 to 15 years ago, we hardly ever turned to Italy for _any_ white wines, let alone less expensive whites. Of course, Italy produced excellent _red_ wines, but her _white_ wines in those days could be described in one word — _blah_ (translation: neutral, dilute, and characterless).

Happily, an amazing transition has occurred in Italy during the last decade or so. Changes have come about mainly for three reasons: dramatic, worldwide advances in winemaking technology, major advances in viticultural knowledge, and Italian wine producers' desire and need to compete on the world market of white wine. Now, some of the best white wines in the world come from Italy, especially its three northeastern regions:

- ✔ Friuli-Venezia Giulia _(free OO lee veh NET zee ah JOO lee ah)_, also known simply as Friuli
- ✔ Trentino-Alto Adige _(tren TEE no-AHL toe AH dee jhay)_
- ✔ Veneto _(VEH neh toe)_

But quality white wine production is not limited to these three regions. Better white wines are being made throughout all of Italy — and when you consider that Italy leads the world in wine production, we're talking about a lot of wine!

For more information on Italian white wines, see Chapter 13 in _White Wine For Dummies_ or Chapter 11 in _Wine For Dummies_.

Northern Italy

The northeastern corner of Italy is the country's premier area for the production of white wines (although plenty of red wine is produced there, too). That area consists of three political regions, similar to states; two of these regions (Friuli-Venezia Giulia, in the far northeast, bordering Slovenia and Austria, and Trentino-Alto

Adige, farther west but also bordering Austria) are considered particularly important areas for high-quality white-wine production. The third region, the Veneto, in the middle, is home to one of Italy's most famous white wines, Soave *(so AH vay)*.

Although every Italian wine carries a place-name as part of its full identity, many wines from the northeast are *varietal* wines, named for the grape variety that makes them. The grape varieties whose names are most likely to appear on labels of northeastern Italian wines exported to the U.S. are the following:

- ✔ Pinot Grigio (known as *Pinot Gris* outside of Italy)
- ✔ Chardonnay
- ✔ Sauvignon (known elsewhere as *Sauvignon Blanc*)
- ✔ Pinot Bianco (also called *Pinot Blanc*)
- ✔ Tocai Friulano (a native grape of Friuli)

(For more information on the first four of these grape varieties, refer to *White Wine For Dummies,* Chapter 3.)

The other regions of northern Italy also produce white wine, but that wine seldom reaches the quality peaks of the northeastern Italian wines. We review one white wine from Piedmont in this section, but all of our other recommendations are from the northeast.

Stylistically, the inexpensive wines of northern Italy are usually light bodied or medium bodied, unoaked, dry, and crisp, with rather neutral aromas and flavors. They are wines to consume young because freshness is their primary virtue. Because wines from northeastern Italy are not assertive and flavorful, they tend to go well with all sorts of food.

We review our recommended northern Italian whites alphabetically according to producer.

Soave San Vincenzo, Anselmi

- ❢ **Producer:** Anselmi
- ❢ **Wine name:** Soave Classico San Vincenzo
- ❢ **Appellation:** Soave Classico
- ❢ **Price:** $11

Roberto Anselmi is a Soave specialist who produces several different versions of Soave from grapes grown in his own vineyards — one wine from a single vineyard, another that's barrel-fermented (a practice not customary in the Soave area), and another in a dessert-wine style. Anselmi's Soave labeled San Vincenzo is his basic Soave, plain and simple. We love it because it shows what an important contribution the raw material (good quality grapes) makes to the ultimate quality of any wine. The aromas and flavors of Anselmi's 1996 Soave Classico San Vincenzo show a stony, minerally, nutty, tart apple, and slightly lemony character. The wine is dry, crisp, and medium bodied (but fairly rich for Soave), with excellent concentration of flavor and a finish that has the attractive bitterness typical of Soave. Like most Soaves, this wine is easy to drink with all sorts of food (try fried calamari) and doesn't demand any particular attention. But it does *deserve* the attention.

Ed: 86–88   **Mary:** 87–89

Pinot Grigio, Marco Felluga

> ! **Producer:** Marco Felluga
> ! **Wine name:** Pinot Grigio *(PEE noh GREE gee oh)*
> ! **Appellation:** Collio
> ! **Price:** $13

Pinot Grigio is probably Italy's most popular white wine now. Unfortunately, much of the lower-priced stuff calling itself Pinot Grigio is really mediocre. That's why it's a real pleasure to come across a really fine one, such as the 1995 Marco Felluga, for less than $15! This classy wine has earthy, steely aromas that suggest a wine with character. It's quite full bodied, with mineral and tart apple flavors, high acidity, and good flavor concentration. I'm surprised at the price, because the wine tastes expensive. Try it with a full-flavored fish or shellfish dish, such as lobster.

Ed: 88–90

Castelcosa Grigio, Franco Furlan

> ! **Producer:** Franco Furlan
> ! **Wine name:** Castelcosa Grigio
> ! **Appellation:** Vino da Tavola della Venezia Giulia *(VEE no da TAH vo la, veh NET zee ah JOO lee ah)*
> ! **Price:** $14.50

Franco Furlan's estate-bottled wines are called Castelcosa, the estate name, and they come in tall bottles with artistic, bright-yellow strip labels — which, unfortunately, can give you some difficulty in reading the vintage or even the wine name. Castelcosa Grigio is Furlan's Pinot Grigio; in the 1995 vintage, this wine has a very floral aroma and rich, honeyed flavors. Dry and medium bodied, it has good concentration and is somewhat richer than most Pinot Grigio wines. It's a good wine to serve with hors d'oeuvres, especially little fishy things. Drink it young.

Ed: 84–86   **Mary:** 85–87

Soave Costeggiola, Guerrieri-Rizzardi

> ♪ **Producer:** Guerrieri-Rizzardi
> *(gwer ree AIR ee ritz ZAR dee)*
>
> ♪ **Wine name:** Soave Classico Costeggiola
> *(coh stay JOE lah)*
>
> ♪ **Appellation:** Soave Classico
>
> ♪ **Price:** $9

The Soave called Costeggiola comes from a hilltop vineyard of the same name, where some volcanic soil and fairly old vines give a special character to the traditional grapes of Soave. We admire this wine because it's fruitier and more substantial than most Soaves and it shows good concentration of flavor. In the 1996 vintage, the Costeggiola has aromas and flavors of nuts, minerals, apples, and cherries. The wine is dry, medium bodied, and atypically flavorful for a Soave, with good persistence of flavor in its finish. Because of its nutty flavor, we plan to serve this wine with a buttery, lemony Fillet of Sole Almondine.

Ed: 86–88   **Mary:** 86–88

Soave Monte Grande, Prà

> ♪ **Producer:** Fratelli Prà
>
> ♪ **Wine name:** Soave Classico, Monte Grande
>
> ♪ **Appellation:** Soave Classico
>
> ♪ **Price:** $15

Owned by the Prà brothers, Monte Grande is a steep, south-facing single vineyard with volcanic soil. This site is considered an unusually good location for growing the grapes for

Soave. Both the soil and the southern exposure of the vineyard encourage ripeness in the grapes, resulting in a particularly full-bodied Soave wine. Prà's 1995 Monte Grande Soave, in fact, is a rich wine. Although the wine's smoky, flinty, honeyed, and appley aromas and flavors are delicate and discreet, the wine's texture is rich and smooth, quite unlike the thin texture that's unfortunately all too common in Soave. The Prà brothers also make a very good $12 Soave that's not a single-vineyard wine.

Ed: 88–90   **Mary:** 89–91

Traminer di Faedo, Pojer e Sandri

> ! **Producer:** Pojer e Sandri *(PO yer ay SAHN dree)*
> ! **Wine name:** Traminer di Faedo
>   *(TRAH mee ner dee fah AY doh)*
> ! **Appellation:** Trentino
> ! **Price:** $15

Mr. Pojer and Mr. Sandri grow grapes and make wine in the Trentino hills, about 1,000 feet in altitude. Their whites tend to be unoaked, crisp wines with fresh, delicate flavors — although their Sauvignon, which I particularly enjoy, is quite rich. My favorite Pojer e Sandri wine is the Traminer (made from Traminer grapes) di Faedo (the town where their winery is located). In the 1995 vintage, this wine has a very gentle aroma of roses, the telltale sign of the Traminer grape. Medium bodied and dry, the wine has broad, earthy flavor, decent concentration, fairly high alcohol for an Italian white, and good length. I could happily sip this wine on a summer evening without food or with a spicy chicken stir-fry.

Mary: 87–89

Tocai Friulano, Sant'Elena

> ! **Producer:** Sant'Elena *(sant EL eh nah)*
> ! **Wine name:** Tocai Friulano *(toh KYE free oo LAH noh)*
> ! **Appellation:** Isonzo
> ! **Price:** $13.50

Maybe one reason we decided, years ago, that Pinot Grigio wines from northeastern Italy were boring was that we were already in love with the wines made from another grape,

Tocai Friulano. We find Tocai Friulano wines, such as this wine from Sant'Elena, far more interesting. The 1995 Sant'Elena Tocai Friulano shows its stuff as soon as you pour it, through an intense honeyed and floral aroma. Its flavors of citrus, almonds, vegetal notes, and earthiness run the gamut of Tocai's repertoire. The wine's combination of slightly oily texture and very crisp acidity teases and provokes exactly as a Tocai Friulano should. The Sant'Elena Tocai Friulano begs for food, anything from fresh mozzarella with red peppers, to salami, to pasta with cream sauce.

Ed: 87–89   **Mary:** 86–88

Moscato d'Asti Cascinetta, Vietti

> ♪ **Producer:** Vietti
>
> ♪ **Wine name:** Cascinetta Moscato d'Asti
> *(cah she NET tah mohs CAH toh DAHS tee)*
>
> ♪ **Appellation:** Moscato d'Asti
>
> ♪ **Price:** $12

We don't know anyone who doesn't love Moscato d'Asti. Just like the sparkling wine called *Asti,* the light-bodied, utterly charming wine called Moscato d'Asti is made from Muscat grapes grown in the Asti area of the Piedmont region. But instead of being sparkling, this wine is what the Italians call *frizzante,* lightly bubbly. The 1996 Cascinetta Moscato d'Asti of Vietti has irresistible floral-peachy aromas and flavors of Muscat grapes. It's not truly a dry wine (Moscato d'Asti never is); at only about 7 percent alcohol, it's barely wine, for that matter. We love it for brunch, with scrambled eggs, fresh fruit, bacon, and croissants. Just be sure that the bottle you buy is as fresh as possible; this wine is really at its best only for about the first 18 months after its September harvest.

Ed: 87–89   **Mary:** 87–89

Chardonnay, Peter Zemmer

> ✔ **Producer:** Peter Zemmer
>
> ✔ **Wine name:** Chardonnay
>
> ✔ **Appellation:** Alto Adige
>
> ✔ **Price:** $9

We complain elsewhere in this book about the dearth of good Chardonnays in the under-$15 price range — yet here's one at under $10! The Alto Adige region is renowned for its fine white wines. The people of this area speak German as often as Italian because many residents are of Austrian origin — which explains the less-than-Italian sound of Peter Zemmer's name! We've found all Peter Zemmer's white wines to be reliable and well priced. The 1995 Chardonnay has an extremely fresh, fragrant aroma (like clean linen), with some minerally components. It's a dry, full-bodied, full-flavored wine, with pronounced minerally, earthy tones. The finish shows some complexity and concentration. A great buy!

Ed: 84–86   **Mary:** 87–89

Central Italy

Although the white wines of northeastern Italy lend themselves to certain generalizations, the wines of central Italy do not. Many different white grape varieties grow in isolated pockets of central Italy, leading to an array of unique wines. A grape such as Verdicchio, for example, grows only in the Marche region, and the Vernaccia grape grows mainly in the San Gimignano zone of Tuscany.

If we could generalize at all about the white wines of central Italy, we would comment on the predominance of the dull Trebbiano grape variety, which makes light-bodied wines with neutral flavors. But, as you can imagine, those wines don't figure heavily among our favorite inexpensive Italian whites.

Castello della Sala Sauvignon Blanc, Antinori

> ⚑ **Producer:** Marchesi Antinori
> ⚑ **Wine name:** Castello della Sala Sauvignon Blanc
> ⚑ **Appellation:** Umbria
> ⚑ **Price:** $11

The great Tuscan wine firm of Antinori also has a wine estate, called Castello della Sala, in Orvieto, in the Umbria region. Antinori now makes two inexpensive varietal wines there, a Chardonnay and this Sauvignon Blanc. The 1996 Sauvignon Blanc has the unmistakable mark of its grape variety, which shows in its herbal and flinty aroma and its herbal, green-grass flavor. Like any good Sauvignon Blanc (in our opinion), this light-bodied wine has plenty of fresh, zingy personality and loads of flavor. If we're having pasta, we'll make a light butter-and-herb sauce to go with this wine. Enjoy this wine while it's young and don't chill it too much.

Ed: 86–88   **Mary:** 84–86

Verdicchio Cuprese, Colonnara

> ♪ **Producer:** Colonnara
>
> ♪ **Wine name:** Verdicchio dei Castelli di Jesi Classico, Cuprese *(coo PRAY say)*
>
> ♪ **Appellation:** Verdicchio dei Castelli di Jesi Classico *(ver DEE key oh day cah STEL lee dee YAY see)*
>
> ♪ **Price:** $13.50

Of two Verdicchio wines that the large Colonnara winery produces and ships to the U.S., the single-vineyard Verdicchio called Cuprese is the more exciting. The 1995 Cuprese has an extremely delicate (and unusual) aroma of hazelnuts and toasted almonds, and its moderately intense flavors include honey, earthiness, and nuts. When you take a taste of this wine, it comes on full and generous at first and then begins to focus itself in your mouth, showing a slightly oily texture and, ultimately, a zippy, crisp acidity. The crispness and the character of this wine are both compelling. We like to drink it practically at room temperature because we find the interplay of its crispness and richness more interesting when the wine is not cold.

Ed: 87–89   **Mary:** 89–91

Verdicchio, Fazi-Battaglia

> ♪ **Producer:** Fazi-Battaglia *(FAH zee-bah TAH l'yah)*
>
> ♪ **Wine name:** Verdicchio dei Castelli di Jesi *(ver DEE key oh day cah STEL lee dee YAY see)*
>
> ♪ **Appellation:** Verdicchio dei Castelli di Jesi
>
> ♪ **Price:** $8

Fazi-Battaglia is back. This famous wine firm in the Marche *(MAR kay)* region had floundered for a while in the last decade, suffering from the usual problem of Italian white wine: overproduction of grapes, resulting in lesser-quality wine. A few years ago, the firm hired one of Italy's finest wine consultants, Franco Bernabei. The proof is now in the pudding, so to speak: The 1995 Verdicchio is a smashing success! We believe that you'd find it difficult to buy a better white wine for this price. The wine has a fresh, delicate aroma, with suggestions of lime, pine, and green apple. This Verdicchio is dry and full bodied, with earthy, minerally flavors, a slightly oily texture, and an almost salty character, suggesting the sea. (The grapes do grow near the seacoast.) This is *the* perfect fish wine. Drink it while it's young and fresh.

Ed: 85–87   **Mary:** 85–87

Vermentino La Cala, Sella & Mosca

> ♪ **Producer:** Sella & Mosca
> ♪ **Wine name:** Vermentino di Sardegna, La Cala
> ♪ **Appellation:** Vermentino di Sardegna
> ♪ **Price:** $7.50

Sella & Mosca is not only the island of Sardinia's largest winery but also one of the largest wine estates in Italy. The firm makes two wines from the Vermentino grape variety; this single-vineyard Vermentino di Sardegna, called La Cala, is the better one. The 1996 La Cala has a very light, fresh, clean, flowery aroma, with a suggestion of lemon; the flavor is similar, along with some pear character. Dry, crisp, and very light bodied, Vermentino La Cala is wonderful with a platter of fresh seafood — but enjoy it while it's young, preferably within a year of its vintage date.

Ed: 87–89

Other European White Wines

White wine is produced all through Europe, and each country boasts special white wines that are important locally. But apart from France and Italy (the two largest wine-producing nations on earth) and Germany (a true world power for white wines), Europe doesn't produce many white wines that are commercially significant in the U.S.

Nevertheless, the wine that we end up enjoying the most is often the surprise wine, the wine from an unknown grape variety or an unconsidered region. In this section, we review a few white wines from unusual sources:

- ✔ **Spain:** A warm country far better known for its red wines than its whites

- ✔ **Austria:** A country whose excellent dry white wines are only now beginning to be available to U.S. wine drinkers

- ✔ **Greece:** A country whose wine image is weak for both red and white wines but which is beginning, ever so quietly, to establish itself as a serious European wine land (2,000 years after the fact!)

We list our recommended wines alphabetically by producer.

Albariño, Martin Codax

- ✔ **Producer:** Bodegas de Vilariño-Cambados
- ✔ **Wine name:** Martin Codax Albariño
- ✔ **Appellation:** Rias Baixas *(REE ahs BYESH ahs)*, (Spain)
- ✔ **Price:** $15

Some of our friends call us acid freaks because we have such a bias toward lean, crisp, high-acid white wines. Maybe that bias explains why the wines made from the high-acid Albariño grape in cool, damp northern Spain, along the Portuguese border, hold such an appeal for us. We don't recommend these wines across the board, because not all of them are well made. But we have found several that we recommend quite enthusiastically, such as this Martin Codax Albariño. The 1996 Martin Codax Albariño has an intense, penetrating aroma of grapefruit and red berries (the latter quite unusual in a white wine), along with moderately intense flavors of the same fruits. Medium bodied and fairly dry, this wine has a silky softness of texture, crisp acidity, and very good concentration of fruit character. This fine wine can accommodate many types of food, but if you happen to be in a Spanish restaurant, why not order the seafood paella?

Ed: 87–89   **Mary:** 87–89

Grüner Veltliner, Höpler

- **Producer:** Höpler
- **Wine name:** Grüner Veltliner Trocken (Dry)
- **Appellation:** Burgenland (Austria)
- **Price:** $9.50

The Grüner Veltliner grape is the most planted grape variety in Austria, but its best wines are anything but common. This inexpensive bottling of Grüner Veltliner is quite good, with grapefruit, floral, apple, and vegetal aromas; a dry, firm, crisp style coupled with a full body; and good persistence of flavor. Considering that this wine sells for less than $10 a bottle in the 1995 vintage, we hope that it piques your curiosity. It's worth a try.

Ed: 86–88   **Mary:** 87–89

Foloi, Mercouri Estate

- **Producer:** Mercouri Estate
- **Wine name:** Foloi
- **Appellation:** Peloponnese (Greece)
- **Price:** $8.50

This wine is made from the Rhoditis grape, a pink-skinned variety that makes plenty of undistinguished base-wine for distilling but that, in the right climate, can produce quality white wine. The 1995 Foloi Mercouri has a very distinctive but subtle aroma that suggests almond paste and flowers. The wine is dry, full bodied, and rich, with flavors of mint, flowers, and honey. This exotic wine makes us wish we were outdoors somewhere beautiful, with a plate of black olives and little Greek sausages.

Ed: 83–85   **Mary:** 85–87

Rueda, Marqués de Riscal

- **Producer:** Marqués de Riscal
- **Wine name:** Rueda *(roo AY dah)*
- **Appellation:** Rueda (Spain)
- **Price:** $7.50

The Marqués de Riscal winery, of Spain's famous Rioja region, pioneered the production of fresh, modern white wines (as opposed to Sherry-type wines) in the nearby Rueda region in the 1970s. Rueda wines are made primarily from a grape called Verdejo *(ver DAY ho)*, which is indigenous to the region. The 1995 Marqués de Riscal Rueda has floral and fruity aromas and flavors, recalling pears, peaches, and orange blossoms. It's light bodied and flavorful, apparently off-dry (slightly sweet) when you first taste it, but finishing dry — a pleasant, all-purpose wine that's easy to enjoy. Marqués de Riscal Rueda is widely available.

Ed: 85–87   **Mary:** 83–85

Viña Esmeralda, Torres

> ♪ **Producer:** Torres
>
> ♪ **Wine name:** Viña Esmeralda
>
> ♪ **Appellation:** Penedés (Spain)
>
> ♪ **Price:** $13

We have always enjoyed Torres's Viña Esmeralda, for two simple reasons: It's unusual and it's delicious. Wine lovers who hear that this wine is a blend of Muscat and Gewurztraminer grapes are likely to conclude that it's extremely flavorful (which it is) and that it's sweet (which it definitely is not!). Viña Esmeralda is dry but very fruity, refreshing, and delightful. The 1996 Viña Esmeralda has an exuberant aroma of flowers and fruit, with a hint of spicy white pepper. Its flavors are a fresh fruit medley of peaches, apples, and oranges. This light-bodied wine would be ideal to serve as the first wine in a multicourse meal, with prosciutto ham and melon or with baby shrimp and avocado. Like all Torres wine, Viña Esmeralda is widely available.

Ed: 86–88   **Mary:** 85–87

Chapter 6

Young and Free: New World White Wines for $15 or Less

. . . .

In This Chapter
▶ Chardon-opoly
▶ Pinot Gris, Pinot Blanc, Pinot delicious
▶ Sauvignon Blanc from Washington and California
▶ Exotic white wines from the Southern Hemisphere

. . . .

*W*hen we first became interested in wine, we had some very romantic ideas about it. We imagined that most wines were made by hardworking, talented guys (we use the term *guys* literally because very few women were winemakers 25 years ago!) who blended their wines in cool, damp cellars full of wooden barrels. The first time we visited a large modern winery and saw gleaming stainless steel tanks lined up shoulder to shoulder, each of them about three stories high, we realized that at least some wine-making had more in common with the modern dairy business than it did with our romantic notions of dark cellars and cobwebs.

In reality, technology is a key player in the production of many wines today, especially inexpensive white wines. Freshness is a prized trait in inexpensive whites, and achieving freshness is a much surer bet when computers precisely regulate the pressure exerted upon grapes to extract their juice, and fermentation tanks automatically cool down the juice when its temperature rises above a preset point. Although red wines can also benefit from sophisticated winemaking technology, white wines as we know them today — fresh, fruity, and clean — simply would not exist without such technology.

Countries such as the U.S. and Australia, two of the protagonists in this chapter, don't have a monopoly on winemaking technology, but in many ways, they have been leaders in the field of high-tech, scientific technique. (Lacking the ingrained winemaking traditions that European countries have, the U.S. and Australia have generally emphasized winemaking science, instead.) Thanks to the influence of technology, the less expensive white wines of the U.S. and Australia usually have a fresh, fruity character and a vividness of flavor. The white wines of South Africa, South America, and New Zealand are similarly clean and fruit-driven.

Most of the wines in this chapter carry the name of the dominant grape variety from which they were made. About half the wines in this chapter are named *Chardonnay*, because wines based on the Chardonnay grape dominate the white-wine market these days. This chapter also features wines made from the somewhat popular Sauvignon Blanc grape, as well as a few wines based on grapes that are real bit players in the market, such as Pinot Gris, Gewurztraminer, Chenin Blanc, and Pinot Blanc.

We begin this chapter with the wines of the U.S.; then move to Australia and New Zealand; and finally, South Africa. Because grape variety is so central to the identity of New World wines, we group the wines of each country according to their grape variety.

We list the vital information for each wine in the following way:

- ✔ **The producer:** This is the company that makes the wine. Most of the time, this company name is the brand name of the wine.

- ✔ **The wine name:** For New World wines, the wine name is usually a grape name.

- ✔ **The appellation of the wine:** This information tells you the geographic area in which the grapes for that wine grow, which can be a small locale, such as Russian River Valley (a particular part of Sonoma County in California) or a large area, such as California (meaning that the grapes grow in various parts of the state rather than in one specific locale). Every wine must carry a geographic appellation. When we review wines from two or more countries in the same section, we include the name of the country in parentheses.

- ✔ **The approximate retail price of the wine:** This price can vary quite a lot according to what part of the country you're in and the type of store where you buy your wine. We base our prices on the current New York State retail price.

U.S. White Wines

Most of the wines sold in the U.S. are (a) domestic, (b) inexpensive ($15 or less, by our definition), and (c) white. Although interest in red wine is stronger than ever, and red wine sales are growing in the U.S., inexpensive domestic white wine is still the strongest sales category.

But the wines in this category present problems to wine drinkers who enjoy simple, honest, inexpensive, dry white wine. Recent price hikes by California wineries have pushed many wines across the $15 line (sometimes, *way* across). Much of what's left under $15 is either sweet (never mind if the label says "dry"; that term is subjective and not regulated by law) or overoaked.

Our advice? Veer off the mainstream: Try white wines from lesser-known grape varieties that are not in as much demand as popular wines like Chardonnay. Try a Pinot Gris from Oregon, for example; you can still find good Pinot Gris wines for under $15. (Of course, if Pinot Gris ever attains the popularity of our current prom queen, California Chardonnay, *its* prices may skyrocket, as well.)

In this section, we review those inexpensive white wines that we personally enjoy the most; we find them to be well made, relatively food-friendly, and good values. These wines include several Chardonnays, as well as miscellaneous white wines from other grapes. For more information on U.S. white wines, see Chapters 6, 7, and 8 in *White Wine For Dummies*. For our recommendations of U.S. white wines that are over $15, see Chapter 8 of this book.

Chardonnay all the way

Chardonnay is the single best selling type of wine in the U.S. Having emerged only within the last 30 years or so, Chardonnay's enormous popularity is a relatively recent phenomenon in the slow-moving world of wine. Although Chardonnay first caught on in California, it has spread to the vineyards of such states as Washington, Oregon, New York, Virginia, Connecticut, and Texas.

Unfortunately, Chardonnay may have become too popular for its own good. High-quality Chardonnay grapes — grapes from the best growing regions — are now extremely expensive, driving up the price of the better wines. Many winemakers are forced to take shortcuts in an effort to produce inexpensive Chardonnays, and the results aren't always successful. Too often, less expensive Chardonnays are too oaky, too sweet, and too high in alcohol.

We recommend some $15-and-under Chardonnays from producers who have succeeded in making well-crafted wines with some character. We list our recommended Chardonnays alphabetically according to the name of the producer. For reviews of Chardonnays that cost more than $15, see Chapter 8.

Chateau Souverain Chardonnay

> ⚲ **Producer:** Chateau Souverain
>
> ⚲ **Wine name:** Chardonnay
>
> ⚲ **Appellation:** Sonoma
>
> ⚲ **Price:** $15

Chateau Souverain, one of the Beringer Estates wineries, continues to make consistently fine wine throughout its entire line. But we wonder how long this well-made Chardonnay will remain in the $15-and-under category, because the price has been creeping up. In the 1995 vintage, the wine has an attractive oaky aroma and ripe, peachy flavor. It's full bodied and firm, with crisp acidity. This wine is relatively dry and full of character compared to most California Chardonnays. Try it with grilled vegetables and grilled chicken.

Ed: 85–87   **Mary:** 84–86

Canoe Ridge Vineyard Chardonnay

> ⚲ **Producer:** Canoe Ridge Vineyard
>
> ⚲ **Wine name:** Chardonnay
>
> ⚲ **Appellation:** Columbia Valley
>
> ⚲ **Price:** $13

Canoe Ridge Vineyard is one of the newest wineries situated in the small but excellent Walla Walla wine region in southeast Washington. However, this Chardonnay was born in the vineyards of the vast Columbia Valley. The 1995 version, fermented in mainly new-oak barrels, has a nutty aroma and fresh, creamy, rich flavors of pear, peach, and green apple. Because the style of this wine is fresh and lively, we suggest that you drink it while it's young, perhaps with salmon or shellfish.

Ed: 86–88   **Mary:** 84–86

Dr. Konstantin Frank's Vinifera Wine Cellars Chardonnay

> ♪ **Producer:** Dr. Konstantin Frank's Vinifera Wine Cellars
> ♪ **Wine name:** Chardonnay
> ♪ **Appellation:** Finger Lakes
> ♪ **Price:** $13

Dr. Konstantin Frank, a Russian immigrant, was the great pioneer of fine wines in New York State's Finger Lakes region, and his son, Willy, is carrying on the family tradition admirably. The 1995 Frank Chardonnay has a subtle aroma and flavors that suggest apple fruit. It's a lean, fresh, light- to medium-bodied Chardonnay, ever so slightly sweet, with crisp acidity and some discreet oaky flavor. We enjoy this restrained style of Chardonnay and hope that you will, also. Try it with freshwater fish, such as trout.

Ed: 87–89   **Mary:** 85–87

Estancia Chardonnay, Pinnacles Vineyard

> ♪ **Producer:** Estancia
> ♪ **Wine name:** Chardonnay, Pinnacles Vineyard
> ♪ **Appellation:** Monterey County
> ♪ **Price:** $13

Estancia wines always do so well in our blind tastings that we're never surprised when we pull off the paper bag and see an Estancia label. Estancia's 1995 Chardonnay, which comes from the Pinnacles Vineyard in California's Monterey County, tastes important, certainly as if it costs over $15. The wine has a spicy, honeyed, oaky aroma; it's soft, generous, and fairly dry, with ripe fruit flavors. The texture is creamy, soft, and unctuous, and yet the wine has the firmness of oak — a classic American Chardonnay. We salute Estancia's owners, the well-regarded Franciscan Vineyards, for producing wines of this quality at these prices.

Ed: 88–90   **Mary:** 87–89

Foris Vineyards Chardonnay

- **Producer:** Foris Vineyards
- **Wine name:** Chardonnay
- **Appellation:** Rogue Valley (Oregon)
- **Price:** $10

We're big fans of Foris Vineyards, a winery located in southern Oregon's Rogue Valley. Winemaker Sarah Powell definitely has a fine touch with Chardonnay, making it in a dry, medium-bodied, discreetly oaked style. Her 1994 Chardonnay has appley, minerally flavors and a richness that comes from extended contact with the *lees* (yeast deposits) during fermentation and aging in French oak barrels. A wine with crisp acidity and good depth of fruit, the Foris Chardonnay is perfect with grilled chicken sandwiches.

Ed: 87–89   **Mary:** 87–89

Geyser Peak Chardonnay

- **Producer:** Geyser Peak Winery
- **Wine name:** Chardonnay
- **Appellation:** Sonoma County
- **Price:** $13.50

Ever since 1989, when Australian winemaker Darryl Groom began making the wines at Geyser Peak Winery, the quality of the Geyser Peak wines has improved steadily, to the point that this brand is now one of the most reliable wine brands in California. The 1996 Geyser Peak Chardonnay typifies the fresh, flavorful style that has proven so popular for the winery. This wine sports aromas of melon and smoke and has succulent flavors of lemon and apple. It's full bodied and high in alcohol, with crisp, balancing acidity. Because this wine is so flavorful, you need to match it with equally flavorful food, such as chicken satay with a spicy peanut sauce.

Ed: 86–88   **Mary:** 85–87

Lamoreaux Landing Chardonnay

- ! **Producer:** Lamoreaux Landing
- ! **Wine name:** Chardonnay
- ! **Appellation:** Finger Lakes
- ! **Price:** $15

We hesitate to recommend the wines of small-production wineries, because we realize that you may have difficulty finding such wines. But in this case, allow us to make an exception. Lamoreaux Landing is one of the truly fine wineries in the Finger Lakes region of New York State; it's clearly making a Chardonnay that can compete on the world market. The 1994 Lamoreaux Landing Chardonnay has a subtle, smoky-oak aroma and tart apple flavors. It's a very crisp, refreshing, well-balanced wine with a long finish — a fine, intriguing Chardonnay. (The winery's telephone number is 607-582-6011.)

Ed: 90–92   **Mary:** 85–87

Mill Creek Vineyards Chardonnay

- ! **Producer:** Mill Creek Vineyards
- ! **Wine name:** Chardonnay
- ! **Appellation:** Dry Creek Valley
- ! **Price:** $12

Mill Creek is one of those low-profile wineries that continues to make good wines at extremely reasonable prices. The winery's 1995 Chardonnay has an oaky aroma, with some ripe apricot and peach flavors. It's a lively wine with firm acidity and a pleasant finish. A decent wine like this, at this price, restores our confidence in California Chardonnays. We recommend it with grilled fish or seafood.

Ed: 85–87   **Mary:** 83–85

Millbrook Chardonnay

- ! **Producer:** Millbrook Vineyards
- ! **Wine name:** Chardonnay, New York State
- ! **Appellation:** New York State
- ! **Price:** $12.50

The success Millbrook Vineyards has had with several different kinds of wine proves that fine wines can come from the Hudson Valley, north of New York City. However, the 1995 Millbrook Chardonnay carries not a Hudson Valley appellation but a New York State appellation, because its grapes come from three wine regions within New York State — half from the Hudson Valley, and the balance from the Finger Lakes region and Long Island. This wine has an attractive, smoky, nutty aroma and subdued appley, smoky flavors that are closer to a Burgundian Chardonnay in style than to a Californian. This balanced wine — with a creamy texture, some complexity, and an earthy finish — is a fine value. Try it with a platter of mussels or clams.

Ed: 85–87   **Mary:** 88–90

The Monterey Vineyard Classic Chardonnay

- ✦ **Producer:** The Monterey Vineyard
- ✦ **Wine name:** Classic Chardonnay
- ✦ **Appellation:** Monterey County
- ✦ **Price:** $7

The Monterey Vineyard in California has been a source of decent, low-priced wines for many years now. The 1995 Classic Chardonnay has a pleasant appley and oaky aroma, and is soft and full bodied. It's an easy-drinking wine with fairly simple flavors, a wine to serve with finger food at large gatherings and parties.

Ed: 84–86   **Mary:** 84–86

Palmer Vineyards Estate Chardonnay

- ✦ **Producer:** Palmer Vineyards
- ✦ **Wine name:** Estate Chardonnay
- ✦ **Appellation:** North Fork of Long Island
- ✦ **Price:** $12

Winemaker Dan Kleck is doing good things at Palmer Vineyards in New York State, and fortunately, his wines are available nationally as well as abroad. The 1995 Estate Chardonnay has a broad, earthy, mushroomy aroma with a suggestion of lemon, as well as an intriguing array of flavors, including ripe apple and melon. This full-bodied, soft, creamy, generous wine is quite easy to drink on its own. On the other hand, it can accompany lobster quite well.

Ed: 84–86   **Mary:** 84–86

Rodney Strong Sonoma County Chardonnay

- ✔ **Producer:** Rodney Strong Vineyards
- ✔ **Wine name:** Chardonnay
- ✔ **Appellation:** Sonoma County
- ✔ **Price:** $12.50

We periodically organize wine competitions in which we judge a couple hundred wines of the same type (such as Chardonnay) and try to identify the best wines at various price levels. The Rodney Strong wines are perennial winners because they deliver more quality than most other wines of similar price.

The winery makes three California Chardonnays, and the Sonoma County bottling is the least expensive. (The other two Chardonnays include one with the appellation of Chalk Hill and one that's called Reserve.) We recommend the simple Sonoma County Chardonnay because we find it to be unusually good for the price. In the 1994 vintage, this wine has aromas of apple, orange peel, flowers, and oak, and its fresh flavors suggest ripe apples and oak. It's a soft, medium-bodied wine with creamy texture, vivid fruitiness, and concentrated flavor — a straightforward Chardonnay that manages to avoid the two common excesses of California Chardonnay: high alcohol and too much oak.

Ed: 85–87   **Mary:** 85–87

Wente Central Coast Chardonnay

- ✔ **Producer:** Wente Vineyards *(WEN tee)*
- ✔ **Wine name:** Chardonnay
- ✔ **Appellation:** Central Coast
- ✔ **Price:** $12

Wente Vineyards is one of California's pioneer wineries, established in the previous century and now run by the fourth generation of Wentes. Maybe because the brand is so well established or maybe because the winery is somewhat off the beaten track — in the Livermore Valley area rather than in Napa Valley or Sonoma County — the wines tend to be very fairly priced. The 1995 Wente Chardonnay from the Central Coast (the winery also makes a Chardonnay with the appellation of Arroyo Seco) has a quiet aroma of oak and herbs and flavors that suggest bitter orange peel and lemon. Dry, firm, and crisp, this wine shows good concentration of fruit. It's not a come-hither sort of Chardonnay, but rather a cool, stand-offish, solid wine that works far better with food than most Chardonnays do.

Ed: 85–87   **Mary:** 85–87

Wines from other grape varieties and blends

Devoting one large section in this chapter to U.S. Chardonnays and another section to "other U.S. white wines" is as disturbing to us as walking into a music store and finding one large section for country western (or opera or jazz, for that matter) and another section for "other music." But because so many brands of Chardonnay are available, and because the wine is so popular, Chardonnay has a near-monopoly in the field of U.S. white wines.

By mustering together all our recommended inexpensive non-Chardonnays in one section, we figure we can at least create the illusion that you can find as many non-Chardonnays as Chardonnays in the U.S. aisle of your wine shop. We hope that you'll try a few of them and discover that they go great with folk rock, classical jazz, country, rock 'n roll, rhythm and blues, and show tunes.

We list the wines in this section alphabetically by producer, regardless of the type of wine.

Alderbrook Gewurztraminer, Saralee's Vineyard

- ♪ **Producer:** Alderbrook Winery
- ♪ **Wine name:** Gewurztraminer, Saralee's Vineyard (*gah VERTZ trah mee ner*)
- ♪ **Appellation:** Russian River Valley
- ♪ **Price:** $9

Most Gewurztraminers made in the U.S. are too sweet or too dilute, or both! In some cases, perhaps, the grape grows in the wrong area. Alderbrook, a winery in California's Dry Creek Valley, purchases its Gewurztraminer grapes from cool, nearby Russian River Valley, clearly a good move. The 1996 Alderbrook Gewurz has the classic, perfumey aroma of fresh roses and the typically pungent flavor of fresh lychee fruit, with an attractive undercurrent of bitterness on the finish. The wine is really fresh and flavorful and a wonderful example of this variety. Made in an off-dry style, this wine does have a slight touch of sweetness. Try it with any kind of spicy Asian cuisine.

Ed: 86–88   **Mary:** 86–88

Arbor Crest Sauvignon Blanc, Bacchus Vineyard

> ♪ **Producer:** Arbor Crest Wine Cellars
>
> ♪ **Wine name:** Sauvignon Blanc, Bacchus Vineyard
>
> ♪ **Appellation:** Columbia Valley
>
> ♪ **Price:** $9

The Sauvignon Blanc wines produced in Washington State are invariably less expensive than those of California and often have more varietal character. The 1995 Arbor Crest has a fresh, lemony aroma and delicious, quite intense, lemony fruit flavor. This is a succulent, lively wine, and yet it's full and creamy. It's a well-balanced, well-made Sauvignon Blanc (with 3 percent Semillon added to round it off). We suggest oysters or clams to accompany it.

Ed: 85–87   **Mary:** 85–87

Barnard Griffin Semillon

> ♪ **Producer:** Barnard Griffin Winery
>
> ♪ **Wine name:** Semillon *(sem ee yon)*
>
> ♪ **Appellation:** Columbia Valley
>
> ♪ **Price:** $10

Semillon wine has not really caught on yet in the U.S., except possibly with the residents of Washington State, where most of the best Semillons are produced. Barnard Griffin's co-proprietors, husband-and-wife Rob Griffin and Deborah Barnard, specialize in making fine white wines, including one of the country's best Semillons. Their 1994 Semillon has a full, intense, slightly smoky aroma, with a suggestion of oak that carries over to the taste. The wine's classic melon and fig flavors are typical of Semillon. This dry, full-bodied wine has a viscous texture. For a delicious combination, try this wine with Cornish game hens or squab.

Ed: 86–88   **Mary:** 86–88

Bethel Heights Pinot Gris

- ✔ **Producer:** Bethel Heights Vineyard
- ✔ **Wine name:** Pinot Gris
- ✔ **Appellation:** Willamette Valley *(will AM et)*
- ✔ **Price:** $13.50

Because wines from the Pinot Gris grape are a relatively new type of wine for most Oregon wineries, many winemakers are still exploring the possibilities of this grape, and various styles of Pinot Gris wine abound. Bethel Heights, which in 1996 produced Pinot Gris for the third time, is making the wine in a dry, medium-bodied, relatively soft, unoaked style. The 1996 Bethel Heights Pinot Gris has somewhat earthy aromas and flavors, with just a slight suggestion of apple and pear. A pleasant note of honey emerges on the finish. Serve this wine with any sort of food in the delicate to moderately flavorful range.

Ed: 86–88   **Mary:** 85–87

Daniel Gehrs Dry Chenin Blanc "Le Chenière"

- ✔ **Producer:** Daniel Gehrs
- ✔ **Wine name:** Dry Chenin Blanc "Le Chenière" *(leh shen ee air)*
- ✔ **Appellation:** Monterey
- ✔ **Price:** $11

Daniel Gehrs's winery is situated in Santa Barbara, California, but he purchases Monterey County grapes for his white wines, hence the Monterey appellation of this wine. One of his specialties is making characterful Chenin Blancs in the style he admires — such as the Chenins of France's Loire Valley. Gehrs's 1995 Chenin Blanc "Le Chenière" has quiet aromas of ripe apple and honey. It's round and creamy but has the crisp acidity typical of the Chenin Blanc grape, and it finishes dry. This is a wine of some substance and an excellent value. It does fine as an apéritif wine.

Ed: 86–88   **Mary:** 85–87

Estancia Sauvignon Blanc

- ♪ **Producer:** Estancia
- ♪ **Wine name:** Sauvignon Blanc
- ♪ **Appellation:** Monterey
- ♪ **Price:** $12

We can imagine a vicious rumor taking shape, and we want to head it off right now, before it builds steam: No, we're not on Estancia's payroll! Try a bottle of the terrifically flavorful 1995 Estancia Sauvignon Blanc, and you'll see for yourself that the wine has plenty to recommend it, without any outside influence needed. The lively aroma is herbal and *green*, like grass, and a little smoky. When you taste it, you discover flavors of lime and herbs on a dry but soft wine. If you're into gentle, discreet whites that don't have much flavor, however, you'll probably just conclude that we've been bought off.

Mary: 84–86

Flora Springs Soliloquy

- ♪ **Producer:** Flora Springs
- ♪ **Wine name:** Soliloquy
- ♪ **Appellation:** Napa Valley
- ♪ **Price:** $15

Soliloquy is a Sauvignon Blanc-based wine, but it's worlds apart from the lean, crisp grassy style of Sauvignon Blanc. In the 1994 vintage, Soliloquy has rich but understated aromas and flavors of lanolin, apple, and lemon, with a creamy, slightly oily texture. Full bodied and dry, this wine is rich without being excessive — quite an unusual and attractive take on Sauvignon Blanc.

Mary: 85–87

Foxen Vineyards Chenin Blanc

- ♪ **Producer:** Foxen Vineyards
- ♪ **Wine name:** Chenin Blanc
- ♪ **Appellation:** Santa Barbara
- ♪ **Price:** $15

Tired of Chardonnay? Take a chance on this California Chenin Blanc, which we think is a great alternative to the omnipresent Chardonnay. Foxen's 1995 Chenin Blanc has aromas and flavors of lanolin and honey with a vague suggestion of oak. It's a delightful Chenin Blanc: rich, round, and full bodied, yet crisp with acid. In your mouth, the wine's crispness and richness play off against each other, making this wine fascinating as well as delicious. Even though the wine is slightly sweet, it finishes dry. Try it while it's young and fresh, with a roast pork loin and some crispy, roast potatoes.

Ed: 87–89   **Mary:** 87–89

Handley Sauvignon Blanc

- ♪ **Producer:** Handley Cellars
- ♪ **Wine name:** Sauvignon Blanc
- ♪ **Appellation:** Dry Creek Valley
- ♪ **Price:** $11

The pickings are slim for U.S. Sauvignon Blancs in this section because, generally speaking, we don't think that this wine is being made successfully in this country. But we do make a few exceptions. We're big fans of Handley Cellars, in California, because Milla Handley makes our kind of white wines: crisp, lean, with real varietal character, and never over-oaked. The 1995 Handley Sauvignon Blanc has earthy, grassy, flowery aromas and is fairly flavorful, with a suggestion of pear and orange peel. This light- to medium-bodied wine with crisp acidity would make a perfect accompaniment to a platter of mixed shellfish.

Ed: 85–87

Hedges Vineyards Fumé/Chardonnay

- ♪ **Producer:** Hedges Vineyards
- ♪ **Wine name:** Fumé/Chardonnay
- ♪ **Appellation:** Oregon/Washington
- ♪ **Price:** $9

Except in Australia, where winemakers often blend Semillon and Chardonnay, little tradition exists for blending Chardonnay with other grapes. But in the realm of under-$10 wines, flavor and value count for more than tradition. The 1996 Hedges Fumé/Chardonnay, composed of 52 percent Sauvignon Blanc and 48 percent Chardonnay, scores on both counts. The wine has nutty, malty aromas almost like a New Zealand Sauvignon Blanc, rather subtle flavor, and a crisp texture. Although the wine seems to have been made with a delicate hand and its flavors are therefore not particularly assertive, it does give an impression of complexity.

Mary: 87–89

Lamoreaux Landing Dry Riesling

- ♪ **Producer:** Lamoreaux Landing
- ♪ **Wine name:** Dry Riesling
- ♪ **Appellation:** Finger Lakes
- ♪ **Price:** $8

New York's cool Finger Lakes region is one of the few places in the U.S. offering evidence of how good Riesling can be. The small but excellent Lamoreaux Landing winery in the Finger Lakes region has a fine 1996 dry Riesling. The wine has fresh aromas that are floral, appley, and spicy, and its flavors suggest citrus peel and earthiness. This Riesling is dry, light bodied, pleasant, and quite *pretty* (a highly technical word for a wine that tastes good in a charming, light-hearted, unimposing way). Because Riesling wines are somewhat out of favor in the U.S., they're usually wonderful buys, as is this one. Try it with a delicate fish entrée. If you have difficulty finding the wine, you can call the winery at 607-582-6011.

Ed: 84–86   **Mary:** 85–87

Lockwood Vineyard Pinot Blanc

- ? **Producer:** Lockwood Vineyard
- ? **Wine name:** Pinot Blanc
- ? **Appellation:** Monterey
- ? **Price:** $13

Lockwood Vineyard, in Monterey County, California, is one of only a handful of vineyards in the U.S. making a Pinot Blanc — which is unfortunate, because Pinot Blanc wine can be an excellent alternative to Chardonnay. Wines from the Pinot Blanc grape are usually lighter bodied than Chardonnays and have an understated fruitiness. The 1995 Lockwood has an aroma of ripe fruit and oak and flavors of citrus and caramel. It's medium to full bodied and quite intense in flavor, a rich, impressive wine for under $15. Drink this wine while it's young so that you capture its fresh flavors, accompanied, perhaps, with fish, seafood, or a salad.

Ed: 86–88

Ponzi Pinot Gris

- ? **Producer:** Ponzi Vineyards
- ? **Wine name:** Pinot Gris
- ? **Appellation:** Willamette Valley
- ? **Price:** $15

Oregon winemaking team Dick Ponzi and his daughter Luisa make their Pinot Gris in a similar style to their hallmark red wine, Pinot Noir — firm, full bodied, and long-lasting. Their 1995 Pinot Gris is crisp and lively, with a citrusy aroma and concentrated lemony flavors. It's rather full bodied and not as fruity as most Pinot Gris wines, and it has a lingering finish. (The 1996 version, by the way, is just as good as the 1995, if not better.) Try this wine with some Italian seafood, such as calamari or scungilli, or with any other seafood dishes.

Ed: 87–89   **Mary:** 86–88

Sanford Sauvignon Blanc

- ❧ **Producer:** Sanford Winery
- ❧ **Wine name:** Sauvignon Blanc
- ❧ **Appellation:** Central Coast
- ❧ **Price:** $12

Although we consider Richard Sanford a red-wine specialist (see our review of his Pinot Noir in Chapter 4), we've always been fond of his Sauvignon Blanc. Sanford's 1996 Sauvignon Blanc, from California's Central Coast district, has attractive peachy aroma and flavor that's quite unusual for Sauvignon Blanc wines. Soft, round, and flavorful, this wine does show typical varietal character in its dry, citrusy finish. Sanford's Sauvignon Blanc can take more flavorful food than other wines of its type; try it with a stir-fried beef or pork dish.

Ed: 86–88   **Mary:** 84–86

Trefethen Vineyards Dry Riesling

- ❧ **Producer:** Trefethen Vineyards
- ❧ **Wine name:** Dry Riesling
- ❧ **Appellation:** Napa Valley
- ❧ **Price:** $13

The only problem with the Trefethen Vineyards Dry Riesling is that the wine is produced in rather limited quantity; the fact that many critics consider it one of the best California Rieslings only compounds the difficulty of finding a bottle. What sets this wine apart from other California Rieslings is its relative dryness and its good concentration of Riesling character. In the 1996 vintage, Trefethen's Dry Riesling has delicate aromas and flavors of ripe apples, pears, flowers, honey, and candied grapefruit rind. It's firm and crisp, with good persistence of flavor in the finish. If more domestic Rieslings tasted this good, maybe Riesling would be much more popular than it is!

Ed: 88–90   **Mary:** 86–88

White Wines of Australia and New Zealand

Australia and New Zealand both make plenty of white wines from Chardonnay, Sauvignon Blanc, Semillon, Riesling, and other grapes, but Australia currently sends much more wine to the U.S. than New Zealand does.

Inexpensive Australian Chardonnays are popular with American wine drinkers because of their ripe fruit flavor and their pronounced oaky character, as well as their affordable prices. We tend to find white Australian wines from other grapes, such as Semillon, more interesting than Chardonnay, however, especially at the lower end of the price ladder. Our recommendations in this section reflect that personal preference. We list the wines alphabetically by producer.

Lindemans Semillon-Chardonnay "Bin 77"

- ✔ **Producer:** Lindemans
- ✔ **Wine name:** Semillon-Chardonnay "Bin 77"
- ✔ **Appellation:** South Eastern Australia (Australia)
- ✔ **Price:** $9

The personality of the Lindemans "Bin 77" Sem-Chard (as Semillon-Chardonnay wines are sometimes called for short) typifies the generous style of Australian wines. The 1996 "Bin 77" is full bodied and full flavored, with aromas of nuts, cream, and orange peel and flavors of ripe citrus fruit. The wine is more subdued than the Lindemans wildly popular "Bin 65" Chardonnay, however, probably because the Semillon component in the blended wine tones down the sweet ripeness of the Chardonnay component. Because the "Bin 77" has crisp acidity to balance its richness, it should work well with food.

Ed: 86–88

McGuigan Brothers Chardonnay "Bin 7000"

- ✔ **Producer:** McGuigan Brothers
- ✔ **Wine name:** Chardonnay "Bin 7000"
- ✔ **Appellation:** South Eastern Australia
- ✔ **Price:** $10

Winemakers in Australia are producing some discreet Chardonnays these days, but the dominant style of Australian Chardonnay on the U.S. market is still the full-blown, ripe, flavorful style. The 1996 McGuigan Chardonnay is exactly that. It has a heavy aroma of honey and tropical fruit and rich, intense flavors of tropical fruit and butter, cloaked in a creamy texture. This well-made wine's only flaw is a lack of finesse. If you don't enjoy big, full-blown Chardonnays, you probably won't like this wine. But if you do, you surely will!

Mary: 87–89

Penfolds Barrel-Fermented Semillon

- ♪ **Producer:** Penfolds
- ♪ **Wine name:** Barrel-Fermented Semillon
- ♪ **Appellation:** South Australia
- ♪ **Price:** $7.50

Australian Semillon is an exotic and unique type of wine. Take the 1994 Penfolds Semillon, for example. It has a rich, intense aroma of tangerine and rich flavor that suggests smoky orange marmalade. But the wine isn't sweet, the way many richly fruity wines are. It's dry, soft, and full bodied, with solid concentration of flavor. If you can't quite imagine what this wine tastes like, buy a bottle and find out; at only about $7.50, it's worth a gamble.

Ed: 86–88   **Mary:** 86–88

Seaview Semillon-Sauvignon Blanc

- ♪ **Producer:** Seaview
- ♪ **Wine name:** Semillon-Sauvignon Blanc
- ♪ **Appellation:** South Eastern Australia
- ♪ **Price:** $9.50

When we recently tasted 250 non-Chardonnay wines from around the world, the 1994 Seaview Semillon-Sauvignon Blanc turned out to be one of the top wines between $8.50 and $10. It has flavors of smoky oak and orange peel and a lovely, full aroma. The wine is dry, medium bodied, firm, concentrated, and intensely flavored. Even if you don't normally enjoy oaky wines, you might like this one due to the fascinating orange flavor.

Ed: 84–86   **Mary:** 84–86

Selaks Sauvignon Blanc/Semillon

> ♪ **Producer:** Selaks *(SEE laks)*
> ♪ **Wine name:** Sauvignon Blanc/Semillon
> ♪ **Appellation:** Marlborough (New Zealand)
> ♪ **Price:** $15

If you have never tasted a Sauvignon Blanc from New Zealand, we strongly urge you to try one because this type of wine offers a unique flavor experience. Sauvignon Blanc wines from New Zealand have a strong varietal personality, to say the least. Selaks makes a straight Sauvignon Blanc and this Sauvignon/Semillon blend, which we prefer. The 1995 blend has a pungent, aggressive, grassy, vegetal aroma and plenty of flavor, flavor, flavor (some call it "asparagus," and others say "green grass"). It's a rather rich, full-bodied wine with an oily texture and a finish that you won't forget. This wine is perfect with those big New Zealand mussels, but local mussels and some crusty bread will do just fine. We recommend consuming this wine in its first two or three years.

Ed: 86–88   **Mary:** 85–87

Stoneleigh Sauvignon Blanc

> ♪ **Producer:** Stoneleigh *(stone lee)*
> ♪ **Wine name:** Sauvignon Blanc
> ♪ **Appellation:** Marlborough (New Zealand)
> ♪ **Price:** $11

True, our tastes do sometimes run a bit toward the unusual. No sooner do we finish praising a wine that tastes like orange marmalade than we launch into a recommendation for a wine with asparagus-like flavor! Actually, asparagus is a common aroma and flavor descriptor for Sauvignon Blanc wines from New Zealand, and asparagus-flavored wine tastes better than it sounds (at least to us). This Stoneleigh wine provides an inexpensive way to experience true New Zealand Sauvignon Blanc. In the 1995 vintage, the wine is dry, medium to full bodied, with crisp acidity and yet richness of texture. Its aromas and flavors are vegetal and quite frank. Try it with goat cheese.

Ed: 84–86   **Mary:** 84–86

White Wines South African Style

South Africa's wines are better now than ever before, thanks to the explosion of knowledge in grape growing and winemaking technology there, plus the country's desire to compete successfully on the world wine market.

Chenin Blanc, often called *Steen* in South Africa, continues to be the dominant varietal wine locally (very little of this wine is exported to the U.S.), but more and more Sauvignon Blanc wines and Chardonnay wines are now being made. In South Africa, both types tend to have strong varietal character, and discreet oakiness in those cases when oak is used for the fermentation or aging of the wine. Sauvignon Blanc does particularly well in South Africa's warm, dry wine regions. The style of South African Sauvignon Blanc is assertive — but not quite so aggressive as New Zealand's intensely varietal Sauvignons.

In this section, we recommend mainly Sauvignon Blancs and Chardonnays because we believe that these are South Africa's best white wines. We list the wines alphabetically by producer, regardless of the grape variety of the wine. For more information on South Africa's white wines, see Chapter 12 in *Wine For Dummies.*

Boschendal Estate Sauvignon Blanc

- ⨍ **Producer:** Boschendal Estate
- ⨍ **Wine name:** Sauvignon Blanc
- ⨍ **Appellation:** Paarl
- ⨍ **Price:** $12

Boschendal is one of the oldest wine estates in South Africa — and one of the best. This winery has been especially consistent with its Sauvignon Blancs; Boschendal's is always ranked among the elite South African Sauvignons by critics. The 1995 version has a nutty, slightly oaky aroma, thanks to the inclusion of a small amount (9 percent) of oak-aged Sémillon in the blend. It's a lean, medium-bodied wine with crisp acidity and the classic, grassy, assertive flavors of South African Sauvignon Blanc. Its rather long finish suggests that you can keep this wine for a few years if you wish. Try it with mussels, clams, or oysters.

Ed: 85–87   **Mary:** 85–87

Groot Constantia Sauvignon Blanc

> ✻ **Producer:** Groot Constantia Estate
> ✻ **Wine name:** Sauvignon Blanc
> ✻ **Appellation:** Constantia
> ✻ **Price:** $10

South African wineries make Sauvignon Blanc wine in an array of styles, from figgy and fruity to lean and green. The style of the Groot Constantia Sauvignon veers in the same direction as our personal taste: more toward the herbal than the fruity. In the 1995 vintage, the wine has a pronounced, crisp, herbal scent and a malty character that we actually associate more with the Sauvignon Blancs of New Zealand than those of South Africa. Flavors of apple, some vegetal character, and even a hint of asparagus (which we enjoy) open up in your mouth. The wine is dry, crisp, and quite flavorful, with just a small amount of carbon dioxide giving it a slight spritzy character and enhancing the wine's freshness. We prefer to drink this wine when it's young.

Ed: 84–86   **Mary:** 84–86

Nederburg Chardonnay

> ✻ **Producer:** Nederburg *(KNEE da burg)*
> ✻ **Wine name:** Chardonnay
> ✻ **Appellation:** Paarl
> ✻ **Price:** $10

The beautiful Nederburg Estate in Paarl is one of South Africa's leading wine estates — renowned for both its white and red wines. And the wines are always reasonably priced. The 1996 Chardonnay has a very discreet touch of oak and suggestions of peach and tropical fruit in its aroma, plus attractive fruity flavors, including apple. It's soft and well balanced, within a medium-bodied frame, and has an earthy and appley finish. We love drinking clean, well-made Chardonnay such as this one, which is not dominated by oak flavors, as are so many Chardonnays today.

Ed: 84–86   **Mary:** 86–88

Neil Ellis Chardonnay, Elgin

> *!* **Producer:** Neil Ellis
> *!* **Wine name:** Chardonnay
> *!* **Appellation:** Elgin
> *!* **Price:** $15

Ace winemaker Neil Ellis makes two Chardonnays, from grapes grown in different parts of South Africa, each carrying a different appellation. The Chardonnay from the cool Elgin area is the finer, in our opinion, because the cool climate contributes a delicacy of aroma and flavor and a crispness of texture. The 1995 Chardonnay from Elgin has a lovely aroma of smoky oak, which isn't intense or overbearing, and a ripe lemon flavor. The wine is soft and yet crisp, with good depth of flavor and a tight finish that suggests that the wine will open somewhat with a year or two of age. Because this isn't a big, intensely flavored Chardonnay, your best bet is to serve it with foods that are relatively delicately flavored, such as simple preparations of chicken, veal, or turkey.

Ed: 85–87   **Mary:** 86–88

Chapter 7

The Best of Europe: Old World White Wines Over $15

*A*ll the world's great white wines are made from grape varieties that originated in Europe — such as Chardonnay, Riesling, and Sauvignon Blanc — and most of the great white wines of the world have a European prototype. The white wines of the Burgundy region of France, for example, inspired the development of California Chardonnay, even if California Chardonnay is now a very different wine from white Burgundy.

In this chapter, we tap the wellspring of great white wine, describing more than 60 classic European whites. We begin in France and then move on to Germany and Italy. We end with a few whites from Austria and Switzerland.

We list the vital information for each wine in the following way:

✔ **The producer:** The name of the producer (the company that makes the wine) is usually considered the brand name of the wine. Because this chapter deals with fine wine, most of the producers named here not only made the wine but also grew the grapes for the wine in their own vineyards.

✔ **The wine name:** For most of the wines in this chapter, the wine name is the place where the grapes for that wine grew. Occasionally in this chapter (for the wines of Alsace, for example, and some northeastern Italian wines), the wine name is a grape name, with or without a single-vineyard name attached.

✔ **The appellation of the wine:** *Appellations* are a necessary and legal part of the wine label, intended to tell you where the grapes for the wine were grown. For wines with place names, the appellation is repetitive: The appellation is the wine's name, and the wine's name is the appellation. For wines with grape names, the appellation gives you additional information about the wine.

✔ **The approximate retail price of the wine:** This price can vary quite a bit according to what part of the country you're in and the type of store where you buy your wine. We use the New York State full retail price, rounded to the nearest half dollar.

For most wines in this chapter, we each give a score based on a 100-point scale. (For some wines, only one of us gives a score.) Remember that this score indicates how much we like a wine, not necessarily the quality of the wine (although we don't tend to like poor wines!) or how much *you* might like the wine.

Great White Wines from France

We suspect that more diversity of great white wine exists in France than in any other country. When you put a glass of white Burgundy alongside a Sancerre, an Alsace Riesling, and a white Bordeaux, you have four dramatically different white wines.

In this section, we review some of our favorite wines from the regions of Alsace, Bordeaux, Burgundy, and the Loire Valley, in that order. Because of the number of reviews, we cover Burgundy in three parts, each part dealing with the wines of a separate district of the Burgundy region.

Alsace's finest

Almost all of Alsace's wines are white, and the region's serious winemakers thus devote their maximum energy to making great white wine. Nature gives them a big helping hand in the form of extremely varied soils and a fairly warm and dry climate during the grape-growing season.

Because the soils of Alsace are so varied, the region's wines don't come from a single grape variety but rather from several. Winemakers use each grape variety singly to make wines named for the grape variety. For the elite wines of Alsace, a vineyard name often appears on the label along with the grape name (and of course the appellation *Alsace*).

To enhance your enjoyment of Alsace wines, keep these three tips in mind:

- ✓ Alsace wines can age very well — especially Rieslings.
- ✓ The flavor of Alsace wines (especially the Rieslings) is easier to appreciate if you don't drink the wines too cold.
- ✓ Alsace wines seem to get better the longer that they sit in your glass. Try aerating the wine by swirling the glass several times, or pour the whole bottle into a decanter or pitcher to aerate the wine.

We list our recommended, over-$15 Alsace wines alphabetically by producer. For reviews of less expensive Alsace wines, turn to Chapter 5. For detailed information on Alsace wines, refer to *White Wine For Dummies,* Chapters 4 and 11.

Pinot Blanc, Clos St. Landelin

- ❧ **Producer:** Clos St. Landelin *(cloh san lahn deh lan)*
- ❧ **Wine name:** Pinot Blanc
- ❧ **Appellation:** Alsace
- ❧ **Price:** $18

The Clos St. Landelin is a large, walled vineyard owned by the Muré wine firm. Muré uses the grapes from this vineyard for its better wines, and labels those wines with the Clos St. Landelin name.The 1995 Clos St. Landelin Pinot Blanc has varied aromas of fruit, including banana, peach, and orange peel, and some chocolate; its flavors suggest ripe orange fruit and white chocolate. This is a rich, medium-bodied wine that you can drink now. Like most Pinot Blancs, it's a wine that's best consumed within three years of the vintage.

Ed: 86–88

Riesling Bennwihr, Marcel Deiss

- ❧ **Producer:** Marcel Deiss *(dice)*
- ❧ **Wine name:** Riesling Bennwihr
- ❧ **Appellation:** Alsace
- ❧ **Price:** $17

Marcel Deiss ships several Riesling wines to the U.S., and the wine designated Bennwihr — the name of a village, not of a grand cru vineyard — is the least expensive. Deiss's wines are generally rather rich, although dry and minerally, and his 1994 Riesling Bennwihr is no exception. The aroma suggests ripe apple, with some peach and mineral notes — all typical of Riesling — and the flavors are mainly ripe apple and peach skin. The wine is full bodied and soft in texture, but its crisp acidity and long finish indicate that it also has substance. I recommend drinking this wine while it's young. If you want a Deiss Riesling with more staying power, look for Deiss's Grand Cru Riesling Altenberg (about $40).

Mary: 86–88

Riesling Kastelberg, Marc Kreydenweiss

- **Producer:** Marc Kreydenweiss
- **Wine name:** Riesling Kastelberg
- **Appellation:** Alsace Grand Cru
- **Price:** $33

Marc Kreydenweiss is passionate about the soil differences from one vineyard to the next and about how these differences express themselves in his Riesling wines. The mineral notes in his Kastelberg vineyard Riesling, he explains, come from the deep layers of *schist* (a kind of rock) in the soil of the vineyard. In the 1993 vintage of Riesling Kastelberg, we notice this mineral character mainly in the finish of the wine. Starting at the beginning — the aroma — we find that the wine is quite closed, showing some quiet herbal notes. The wine is firm and steely in our mouths, with great, tight concentration of fruit character. It's rich, strong, and sleek (oh, that we all were!), and it has a long finish that tastes like minerals and slate. Clearly a great Alsace wine, it can live for a decade, no problem.

Ed: 88–90   **Mary:** 89–91

Riesling Herrenweg, Charles Schleret

- **Producer:** Charles Schleret (*shler ay*)
- **Wine name:** Riesling Herrenweg Turckheim
- **Appellation:** Alsace
- **Price:** $18

Charles Schleret is a relatively small producer whose wines are well regarded by the few people who know them. We like Schleret's wines for their vivid aromas and flavors and the way they develop over time — especially his Rieslings. His Riesling Herrenweg is a wine from the village of Turckheim. The 1994 Herrenweg has an amazing aroma that, on first whiff, suggests white truffles and then passes quickly to notes of mineral, wet stones, and citrus peel: Just smelling the wine makes us salivate! The wine is medium bodied and packed with flavors similar to its aromas. Its texture is fairly silky, making the wine very pleasurable now, but its concentration, depth of flavor, and excellent balance indicate that it has some developing yet to do — about three to five years worth, we estimate.

Ed: 89–91   **Mary:** 89–91

Riesling Kitterlé, Domaines Schlumberger

MARY'S CHOICE

- ♪ **Producer:** Domaines Schlumberger *(schlum bair jhay)*
- ♪ **Wine name:** Riesling Kitterlé *(kit ter lay)*
- ♪ **Appellation:** Alsace Grand Cru
- ♪ **Price:** $22.50

If you have any fear of heights (as I sometimes do), do not ride to the top of the beautiful, steeply terraced Kitterlé vineyard and walk down to road level on the steep, narrow steps dug out of the hillside by vineyard workers (as I did!). Although the experience would imbed the dramatic Kitterlé vineyard in your memory permanently, just tasting the rich wines of Kitterlé can deliver close to the same effect, and far less painfully. The 1991 Schlumberger Riesling from grapes grown on Kitterlé has a steely aroma with hints of fresh citrus and apricot, and its flavors are of tart apple, peach, and citrus. As flavorful and intense as the wine is, it's also dry. This full-bodied Riesling shows great concentration of flavor and is a truly refined, elegant wine. A terrific wine like this deserves a special dish, such as breast of pheasant (although it would go well with breast of chicken or turkey, too). Just don't drink it at the top of the vineyard.

Mary: 89–91

Riesling Cuvée Frédéric Émile, Trimbach

> ♪ **Producer:** Trimbach
> ♪ **Wine name:** Riesling, Cuvée Frédéric Émile
> ♪ **Appellation:** Alsace
> ♪ **Price:** $25

Trimbach's Cuvée Frédéric Émile Riesling has impressed us more often, and more dramatically, than any other Alsace wine. We remember, for example, the time that we pulled a 12-year-old bottle of the 1981 vintage from a forgotten place in our cellar and discovered, on opening it, that we had buried a treasure. Then there was our friend's 60th birthday dinner, when we served one of our finest Champagnes, a grand cru white Burgundy, a rare red Burgundy, and an aged Bordeaux — but the wine of the night for everyone was the 1983 Cuvée Frédéric Émile. (We rated it 96 points that night!)

This wine is the second tier of Riesling for Trimbach, occupying the middle ground between his normal Riesling bottling (reviewed in Chapter 5) and his monumental Clos Ste. Hune Riesling, perhaps the best Riesling wine of Alsace. The 1992 Cuvée Frédéric Émile has aromas and flavors that are (for now) minerally, steely, earthy, and slightly smoky, with some fruity character. The wine is dry, medium bodied, and lean, with a backbone of lively acidity that makes the wine taste succulent. If it follows the pattern of other vintages, you can expect this wine to develop a honeyed richness with age. But it's also delicious now, and would be especially wonderful with a stuffed veal roast.

Ed: 90–92   **Mary:** 90–92

Riesling Brand, Domaine Zind-Humbrecht

> ♪ **Producer:** Domaine Zind-Humbrecht
> ♪ **Wine name:** Riesling, Brand
> ♪ **Appellation:** Alsace Grand Cru
> ♪ **Price:** $37.50

The Zind-Humbrecht winery, with its opulent wines and stellar reviews, has done more than any other winery to lift the wines of Alsace from their relative obscurity among wine lovers. (And yet Alsace wines remain more obscure than they deserve to be.) As the result of Zind-Humbrecht's star status, the wines of this property are expensive.

One of our favorite Zind-Humbrecht wines is Riesling from the grand cru Brand vineyard. The 1992 vintage of this wine has an intense, penetrating aroma of lime and sweet melon and a pronounced intensity of ripe apple and melon flavor. The wine is full bodied and so rich that it doesn't taste completely dry. Based on our past tastings, we expect a stony flavor to emerge as this wine ages. Zind-Humbrecht makes about a dozen Riesling wines, as well as Tokay-Pinot Gris (the Alsace name for Pinot Gris) and other wines — and all of them are good. If you're a fan of serious white wines, don't let life pass you by without tasting a Zind-Humbrecht wine.

Ed: 87–89   **Mary:** 88–90

Bordeaux's best blancs

White Bordeaux (also known as *Bordeaux Blanc*) is primarily a blend of two grape varieties: Sauvignon Blanc and Sémillon. Sauvignon Blanc lends crispness and herbaceousness to the wine; Sémillon gives it the body, a viscous texture, and a honeyed character, especially as the wine ages. And the better white Bordeaux wines do age well — in some cases, as long as red Bordeaux.

The one problem with white Bordeaux is that hardly any good ones are available for under $25. (See Chapter 5 for a few under-$15 recommendations.) In this section, we describe three white Bordeaux wines ranging in price from $18 to $42. For more specific information on white Bordeaux, see Chapter 11 in *White Wine For Dummies* or Chapter 10 in *Wine For Dummies.*

Château de Fieuzal Blanc

 ✦ **Producer:** Château de Fieuzal *(fyu zahl)*

 ✦ **Wine name:** Château de Fieuzal Blanc

 ✦ **Appellation:** Pessac-Léognan *(pay sac lay oh nyahn)*

 ✦ **Price:** $42

Since 1985, a dramatic jump in quality has taken place at Château de Fieuzal, especially among its white wines. Since then, this property has been making one of the top three or four white Bordeaux wines each year. In fact, the Château's white wine is even better (and more expensive) than its red wine. The 1993 de Fieuzal Blanc, 50 percent Sauvignon Blanc and 50 percent Sémillon, has aromas and flavors of melons, lanolin, spice, and honey. It's a very young, crisp, full-bodied wine with complex flavors, terrific concentration, and a long finish. Its exquisite balance and lasting finish suggest that you can easily keep this wine for at least ten more years, when it should even be better than it is now.

Ed: 92–94   **Mary:** 91–93

Sauternes: glittering gold

Sauternes is a dessert wine that comes from the Sauternes/Barsac sub-district of Graves in southern Bordeaux, France. Sauternes is made primarily from two grape varieties: Sémillon and Sauvignon Blanc. In good vintages, the very best Sauternes, such as the famous Château d'Yquem *(dee kem),* can live over 100 years.

We like to drink Sauternes after they have lost some of their initial sweetness and have taken on secondary flavors, such as apricots, orange rind, toffee, and honey. This transformation usually begins after Sauternes are ten or more years old, when their color begins to resemble an old gold coin, with orange or amber highlights.

Most good Sauternes start at about $30 a bottle and go all the way up to $250 for Château d'Yquem. Half-bottles usually are about half the price. Barsac wines are typically a bit dryer and lighter-bodied than Sauternes. Recent good vintages for Sauternes have been 1990, 1989, 1988, 1986, and 1983. For more information about Sauternes, see Chapter 14 of *Wine For Dummies.*

The following is a list of our 15 recommended producers of Sauternes/Barsac. We list them in three categories, according to our own personal preferences:

Superb

Château d'Yquem

Château de Fargues

Château Climens (Barsac)

Château Coutet (Barsac)

Excellent

Château Suduiraut

Château Rieussec

Château Raymond-Lafon

Very Good

Château Lafaurie-Peyraguey

Château Guiraud

Château Latour Blanche

Château Rabaud-Promis

Château Doisy-Dubroca (Barsac)

Château Doisy-Daëne (Barsac)

Château Doisy-Védrines (Barsac)

Château Sigalas-Rabaud

Château La Louvière Blanc

> ❢ **Producer:** Château La Louvière, of André Lurton
> ❢ **Wine name:** Château La Louvière Blanc *(loo vee aire)*
> ❢ **Appellation:** Pessac-Léognan *(pay sac lay oh nyahn)*
> ❢ **Price:** $27.50

Château La Louvière's white wine (there's also a La Louvière *Rouge*) is consistently on our top-dozen white Bordeaux list, year after year. Having said that, Ed is not too thrilled with the 1994 La Louvière Blanc. Because we *both* enjoy the 1993 La Louvière Blanc, these notes apply to the wine from that year.

The 1993 La Louvière, 70 percent Sauvignon Blanc and 30 percent Sémillon, has smoky oak and pungent Sauvignon Blanc aromas (grassy and herbal); its flavors are intensely herbal, with earthy and minerally notes. It's a fullish-bodied wine with a rich texture and some sweet impression from its oak, and yet it has the zingy crispness of a high-acid wine. You can enjoy the 1993 La Louvière now, perhaps with scallops in a cream sauce, or hold on to it for four to six years. Older white Bordeaux wines do take on interesting flavors when the Sémillon portion of the wine develops and overtakes the Sauvignon Blanc vitality that the wine has when young.

Ed: 87–89   **Mary:** 87–89

Three great Bordeaux Blancs over $50

The three white Bordeaux wines generally acknowledged to be the finest all cost over $50 (in one case, well over!), are all made in small quantities, and are available only in wine shops dealing with fine French wines. (See *Wine For Dummies*, Chapter 16, for a few such shops.) We mention them to you just in case you want to experience the ultimate in great white Bordeaux wines; these three have the capacity to age 30 or more years in good vintages, just like red Bordeaux. All three wines are from the Pessac-Léognan subdistrict of Graves:

> ✔ Domaine de Chevalier
>
> ✔ Château Haut-Brion Blanc (rare; over $200)
>
> ✔ Château Laville-Haut-Brion

Vieux Château Gaubert Blanc

> *!* **Producer:** Vieux Château Gaubert
>
> *!* **Wine name:** Vieux Château Gaubert Blanc
>
> *!* **Appellation:** Graves
>
> *!* **Price:** $18

Vieux Château Gaubert is not a well-known Bordeaux property, but it should be. It's another discovery of importer Bobby Kacher, whose stable of fine French wines is second to none. The 1995 Vieux Château Gaubert Blanc (there's also a Vieux Château Gaubert *Rouge*), 65 percent Sémillon and 35 percent Sauvignon Blanc, has zingy citrus and oak aromas and rich, citrus fruit flavor that stands up to the wine's oaky character. It's a full-bodied, flavorful wine, done in a modern style (that is, with a pronounced expression of fruit). We recommend drinking the Château Gaubert Blanc now, or in the next two or three years, with a delicate fish entrée, such as Filet of Dover Sole or fresh trout.

Ed: 86–88   **Mary:** 87–89

White Burgundies from the Côte d'Or

The Côte d'Or district of France's Burgundy region — and particularly the southern part of the Côte d'Or, the Côte de Beaune — gets our votes as the greatest dry white-wine district anywhere (at least on the planet Earth). Almost all the fine white wines from this area are 100 percent Chardonnay.

But the Côte d'Or might also be the most frustrating wine district for wine drinkers. First of all, only a fairly small percentage of Côte d'Or white wine is great, or even very good. You really have to know the names of the best producers in order to find the best wines. (We recommend our favorite producers in a sidebar in this chapter.) Second, the best Côte d'Or white Burgundies are both expensive and scarce. And third, the most renowned Côte d'Or white Burgundies are usually sold only in wine shops that specialize in fine French wines. (See Chapter 16 in *Wine For Dummies* for a list of some of these stores.)

Finally, the whole nomenclature of Burgundy can be quite confusing. For example, Burgundies with the following labels are very different from each other:

- ✔ **Puligny-Montrachet:** A village-level wine that sells in the $30 to $40 range

- ✔ **Puligny-Montrachet Les Combettes:** A premier cru wine that sells in the $35 to $65 range

- ✔ **Chevalier-Montrachet:** A grand cru wine whose vineyard is located in the village of Puligny-Montrachet (This wine costs $75 and up.)

Are you still with us? For a clear explanation of white Burgundy nomenclature, see Chapter 10 in *White Wine For Dummies,* and, to a lesser extent, Chapter 10 in *Wine For Dummies.*

We list some of our favorite Côte d'Or white Burgundies in the $15 to $50 price range here, in alphabetical order according to the name of the producer.

Meursault-Charmes, Coche-Bizouard

- ! **Producer:** Alain Coche-Bizouard *(coshe bee zward)*
- ! **Wine name:** Meursault-Charmes Premier Cru
- ! **Appellation:** Meursault Les Charmes
- ! **Price:** $43.50

Alain Coche is one of the finest producers in the village of Meursault, and his name on a wine assures you of quality. Probably his best wine is his Meursault-Charmes, a premier cru. The 1994 Meursault-Charmes has complex aromas of herbs, citrus, and spicy oak, with vanilla, honey, and citrus fruit flavors. It's medium to full bodied, with good depth and concentration and a long finish. Alain Coche's wines are the opposite of "commercial"; they're made for the long haul. This is a fine Meursault, but I'd hold on to it for at least another four or five years to let it develop further.

Ed: 88–90

Saint Aubin en Remilly, Dominique & Catherine Derain

- ! **Producer:** Dominique et Catherine Derain
- ! **Wine name:** Saint Aubin en Remilly, Premier Cru *(san oh ban, on ray mee yee)*
- ! **Appellation:** Saint Aubin en Remilly
- ! **Price:** $21

Although the village of Saint Aubin and its vineyards are situated in the famous Côte de Beaune district of Burgundy (behind the villages of Meursault and Puligny-Montrachet), their wines are not well known — and therefore represent good value. We love this premier cru wine from the Derains for the very good quality it offers for (by Burgundy standards) an affordable price. In the 1995 vintage, the wine has a very quiet aroma that opens, with time in the glass, to mouth-watering scents of ripe apples with a glaze of honey, spice, and smoke on them. It's dry, full bodied, and creamy in texture. Because its acidity seems a bit low, the wine is soft and easy to like, but its good concentration of fruit character gives it substance that many soft wines don't have.

Use a large glass when you drink this wine so that it can open up with air, or hold the wine for a year or so to let it age a bit.

Ed: 86–88   **Mary:** 86–88

Beaune Grèves, Louis Jadot

    ! **Producer:** Louis Jadot

    ! **Wine name:** Beaune Grèves, Le Clos Blanc, Premier Cru

    ! **Appellation:** Beaune Grèves

    ! **Price:** $39

It's a pleasure to recommend a premier cru white Burgundy that you can find without too much difficulty. Because the firm of Louis Jadot is one of the largest in Burgundy, its wines are well distributed. Jadot produces several premier cru whites from Beaune, which are all good, but I'm especially fond of the Beaune Grèves. Le Clos Blanc is a portion of the Beaune Grèves vineyard that belongs to Jadot.

Jadot's 1993 Beaune Grèves has complex, earthy aromas with touches of butter and mushrooms, and its rich, developed flavors suggest citrus fruit, earth, and smoky oak. The flavors are evolved enough for you to enjoy this big wine now or in the near term, perhaps with a simple grilled chicken dish or with seafood.

Ed: 86–88

Trust these wine talent scouts

Many very fine European wines are made by small producers whose names are not exactly household words in the U.S. When you're considering buying a wine made by a producer whose name is unfamiliar to you, peruse the bottle for the name of the importer or broker who represents that brand, and consult the list below. Some small *importers* (companies holding a federal license to purchase wine abroad and resell it in the U.S.) and *brokers* (middlemen between the wine producer and the importer) specialize in finding very good wines from small wineries and making those wines available in the U.S. Their names can represent quality and reliability the way that the brand name of a wine from a larger producer can. Often these people are specialists in the wines of a particular region and are extremely skilled in finding and recruiting the top producers from that area.

We have come to trust numerous "wine talent scouts" (as we tend to think of them) and the wines they select. We list 12 of these companies and individuals here, alphabetically, and indicate their special areas of expertise. In some cases, we list a corporate name and an individual's name in parentheses next to it; one or both of these names can appear on a wine's label.

Importer / Broker	Wine Specialty
Classical Wines Of Spain	Spanish; German
European Cellars (Eric Solomon)	French
Fine Wines from Spain (Jorge Ordonez)	Spanish
Robert Kacher Selections	French
Louis Dressner Selections	French
Kermit Lynch Selection	French
Martine's Wines (Martine Saunier)	French
Select Vineyards (Neal Rosenthal Selection)	French; Italian
Terry Theise Selection	German; Austrian
Vinifera Imports	Italian
Rudy Wiest / Cellars International	German
Wines of France (Alain Junguenet)	French

Chassagne-Montrachet Les Caillerets, Louis Jadot

- **Producer:** Louis Jadot
- **Wine name:** Chassagne-Montrachet Les Caillerets, Premier Cru
- **Appellation:** Chassagne-Montrachet Les Caillerets *(kye yeh ray)*
- **Price:** $39

Les Caillerets is one of the best premier cru vineyards in the village of Chassagne-Montrachet. Jadot has done a terrific job with this cru in the 1994 vintage. The wine's color is a particularly vivid bright golden yellow. The 1994 Les Caillerets has broad, rich aromas and flavors of ripe pears, apples, and honey. This big, full-bodied, rich wine is crisp with acidity, has excellent balance, and shows a good depth of fruit, with a moderately long finish. Its creamy texture and its rich flavors are particularly strong points for this wine. We'd give this wine a year or two to develop further.

Ed: 90–92   **Mary:** 87–89

Puligny-Montrachet Clos de Vieux Château, Domaine Maroslavac

- **Producer:** Labouré-Roi (Domaine Maroslavac)
- **Wine name:** Puligny-Montrachet, Clos de Vieux Château *(clo deh v'yuh shah toe)*
- **Appellation:** Puligny-Montrachet
- **Price:** $36

Labouré-Roi *(lah boar ay wah)* is a large Burgundy firm that owns or manages many properties; among its best is the Domaine Maroslavac in Puligny-Montrachet. The 1995 Clos de Vieux Château, a single-vineyard wine, has subdued fruity aromas and flavors, primarily apple and lemon. It is medium to full bodied, and its ripe fruit character is balanced well with crisp acidity; we particularly appreciate the fact that this wine is not overblown from high alcohol, as so many white Burgundies are. You can enjoy this classy white Burgundy now or within the next two or three years; try it with grilled fish or a simple chicken entrée. Labouré-Roi wines are well distributed, so you should be able to find this wine without much difficulty.

Ed: 85–87   **Mary:** 86–88

Top producers of Côte d'Or white Burgundy

Good Burgundy, red or white, will always be scarce and expensive: Burgundy is just too small a region to satisfy the demands of the world's Burgundy lovers. If anything, good white Burgundy is even more difficult to find than red. And not all white Burgundies merit the very high prices that are the norm for white Burgundy; only the wines from the best producers deliver the quality you expect from prime vineyard sites such as premier cru and grand cru vineyards.

As a general guide to purchasing great white Burgundy, we list our favorite producers of Côte d'Or white Burgundies here. Most of the better wines from these producers sell for more than $50, and we therefore don't describe the wines individually. However, you might occasionally find a wine from one of these producers that costs less than $50 — including the wines we do review in our Côte d'Or Burgundy section. You can trust any wine from these producers, no matter how humble its status; even their village-level wines can be very good. We list the producers alphabetically. (Some producers bottle wines under two separate names.)

Domaine Guy Amiot & Fils (Amiot-Bonfils)
Domaine Jean-Marc Boillot
Domaine Bonneau du Martray
Domaine Boyer-Martinot
Domaine Louis Carillon & Fils
Domaine Alain Coche-Bizouard (or -Debord)
Domaine J. F. Coche-Dury
Domaine Michel Colin-Deléger
Domaine Jean-Noël Gagnard
Maison Louis Jadot
Domaine Patrick Javillier
Domaine François Jobard
Domaine des Comtes Lafon
Domaine Leflaive
Domaine (& Maison) Leroy
Domaine Bernard Morey
Domaine Marc Morey
Domaine Michel Niellon
Domaine Paul Pernot
Domaine Jacques Prieur
Domaine Ramonet
Domaine Étienne Sauzet
Maison Verget

Puligny-Montrachet, Olivier Leflaive

- ♪ **Producer:** Olivier Leflaive Frères
- ♪ **Wine name:** Puligny-Montrachet
- ♪ **Appellation:** Puligny-Montrachet
- ♪ **Price:** $36

Olivier Leflaive, nephew of the late Vincent Leflaive (of Domaine Leflaive fame), started his own business in 1984 and has been quite successful at it, producing a wide range of white and red Burgundy wines. A bonus for his wines is that they're generally in good distribution. The 1994 Puligny-Montrachet has reticent, floral aromas and an austere lemony flavor. It's a dry, full-bodied wine with good fruit concentration and a long finish. Still a young wine, it needs some time, perhaps a year, to develop. For now, this white Burgundy is a bit too austere to drink without food. Try it with grilled turbot or snapper.

Ed: 84–86   **Mary:** 84–86

Bourgogne d'Auvenay, Leroy

- ♪ **Producer:** Maison Leroy *(lay wah)*
- ♪ **Wine name:** Bourgogne d'Auvenay
  (boor guh nyuh doe ven ay)
- ♪ **Appellation:** Bourgogne Blanc
- ♪ **Price:** $18

No other name in Burgundy is a greater guarantee of quality on a bottle than that of Leroy. The indomitable Madame Lalou Bize-Leroy is one of France's — if not the world's — most respected winery proprietors. Mme. Leroy owns her own vineyards (for wines labeled Domaine Leroy) and also buys wine (for wines labeled Maison Leroy). Her legendary perfectionistic taste and her insistence on purchasing only the very highest-quality wine, no matter what the cost, set her apart from her fellow Burgundians. From her simplest, generic Bourgogne Blanc and Bourgogne Rouge (both called Bourgogne d'Auvenay) to her greatest grand cru Burgundies (costing hundreds of dollars), her wines are always among the best of their type.

The 1994 Leroy Bourgogne d'Auvenay has aromas of fresh, appley fruit, with some floral tones, and fruit flavors of ripe apple and apricot. It's a particularly well-balanced wine, despite its high alcohol, and it's fairly flavorful. For a simple Bourgogne Blanc, this wine is great. Although you normally should drink a simple Bourgogne Blanc within two years of the vintage, Leroy's wines, even the simplest, are so well made that they last for many years. You can drink the 1994 Leroy now, perhaps with a platter of seafood, or hold it for two or three years.

Ed: 87–89   **Mary:** 86–88

Chassagne-Montrachet Les Vergers, Marc Morey

- *!* **Producer:** Marc Morey
- *!* **Wine name:** Chassagne Montrachet Les Vergers Premier Cru
- *!* **Appellation:** Chassagne Montrachet Les Vergers
- *!* **Price:** $45

When you pay $45 or more for a bottle of white Burgundy — or any wine, for that matter — you want it to be sensational. Among Chassagne-Montrachet wines, if you stick to producers such as Marc Morey, Michel Niellon, Ramonet, or Bernard Morey, you can't go wrong. And Les Vergers is one of the most reliable premier cru Burgundy vineyards.

Marc Morey's 1995 Chassagne Montrachet Les Vergers has a near-perfect white Burgundy aroma: complex, with scents of smoky oak, flowers, and lemon, all quite subdued. The wine's flavors are similar, with tart apple and nuttiness adding a further note of complexity. Silky textured, full bodied, and flavorful, this intensely concentrated wine is quite seductive. Although it's still very young, you can enjoy this wine now, or you can hold it for a few years.

Ed: 88–90   **Mary:** 89–91

White Burgundies from the Côte Chalonnaise and Mâcon

Because most of the best white Burgundies from the Côte d'Or are expensive (from $35 to over $100 a bottle) and are often difficult to find, we frequently turn to the Côte Chalonnaise and Mâcon districts in southern Burgundy — the so-called bargain Burgundy area — for our "everyday" white wines.

The Côte Chalonnaise is Burgundy's least-known district; it lies directly south of the Côte d'Or and north of Mâcon. Most of the white Burgundies of the Chalonnaise are in the $12 to $25 price range.

The Mâcon district is directly south of the Chalonnaise and north of the Beaujolais district; its major city is Mâcon. Wines vary from light-bodied, inexpensive (under $15) Mâcon-Villages, to somewhat fuller-flavored St.-Véran wines, to the richer wines of Pouilly-Fuissé. For our recommendations of wines from the Mâcon district that cost $15 or less, see Chapter 5.

We list our white Burgundy recommendations from the Chalonnaise and Mâcon in alphabetical order by producer.

Pouilly-Fuissé La Roche, Daniel Barraud

> ♪ **Producer:** Daniel Barraud
>
> ♪ **Wine name:** Pouilly-Fuissé, La Roche *(poo ee fwee say)*
>
> ♪ **Appellation:** Pouilly-Fuissé
>
> ♪ **Price:** $26

Daniel Barraud is a respected grower who makes Pouilly-Fuissé and other wines of the Mâcon district from grapes grown in his own vineyards. His Pouilly-Fuissé La Roche comes from a single vineyard, but the vineyard is not a premier cru site; no vineyards for Pouilly-Fuissé are designated premier cru. In the 1995 vintage, the wine's aroma is smoky but quiet, and its flavors are orangey and lemony. The wine is dry and full bodied with a slightly bitter taste, possibly from the skins of the grapes or, more likely, from the soil in which the grapes grew. This wine seems austere now and should become more expressive with time. Because this wine is big and somewhat exotic, it's not easy to drink casually. Enjoy it slowly, with a mushroom risotto and good conversation.

Ed: 86–88   **Mary:** 85–87

Pouilly-Fuissé Vieilles Vignes, Château Fuissé

> ♪ **Producer:** Château Fuissé
>
> ♪ **Wine name:** Pouilly-Fuissé, Vieilles Vignes *(poo ee fwee say, vee ay vee nyeh)*
>
> ♪ **Appellation:** Pouilly-Fuissé
>
> ♪ **Price:** $45

This wine — made from the fruit of fairly old vines (that's what *vieilles vignes* refers to) by the unassuming but talented winemaker, Jean-Jacques Vincent — is the crème de la crème of Pouilly-Fuissé wines. It's an exotic, ageworthy wine that doesn't always show its stuff when it's young. The 1995 Vieilles Vignes is still extremely young, and we had difficulty evaluating it — until we tried what was left of a bottle that had been sitting half-full in the refrigerator for four days. Wow! (For some reason, aeration often mimics time in effecting changes in wine.)

The aromas of the 1995 are quiet at first, suggesting wildflowers and white pepper, but they turn lemony. The flavors are smoky and toasty from oak, and they also suggest some ripe but slightly (and attractively) bitter fruit. The wine is full bodied and dry, with a firm backbone of acidity and some soft, fleshy texture. With the capriciousness of youth, this wine comes on gentle and pretty one moment, and the next moment it's austere. Time will bring it all together.

Ed: 89–91 **Mary:** 89–91

Bourgogne Aligoté de Bouzeron, Domaine A. & P. de Villaine

- ☞ **Producer:** Domaine A. & P. de Villaine
- ☞ **Wine name:** Bourgogne Aligoté de Bouzeron
- ☞ **Appellation:** Bouzeron
- ☞ **Price:** $18

Aubert deVillaine is well known in Burgundy circles because he's co-proprietor of the most renowned red Burgundy firm, the Domaine de la Romanée-Conti. But he and his wife, Pamela, also produce three really fine, simpler wines on their home estate in Bouzeron, in the Côte Chalonnaise: a Bourgogne Rouge (called "La Digoine"), a Bourgogne Blanc (called "Les Clous"), and perhaps the finest example of Bourgogne Aligoté around. The Aligoté is a bit expensive for its type (most Aligotés are under $15), but it's worth the few extra dollars. Bourgogne Aligoté wines are best when they're young — they're so fresh and crisp that they really wake up the palate! The 1996 Aligoté of de Villaine has aromas and flavors of fresh herbs, spice, freshly cut pears, and figs. It's a rich, fairly full-bodied Aligoté with plenty of zingy acidity. This wine would be perfect with a platter of fresh mussels, clams, and oysters. Drink it within two years of the vintage to capture all its freshness.

Ed: 87–89   **Mary:** 87–89

Pouilly-Fuissé, Louis Jadot

- ♪ **Producer:** Louis Jadot
- ♪ **Wine name:** Pouilly-Fuissé
- ♪ **Appellation:** Pouilly-Fuissé
- ♪ **Price:** $21

Unlike many Côte d'Or white Burgundies that carry the Louis Jadot label, this wine does not come from vineyards owned by Jadot. It's a good wine, nonetheless — a solid expression of the character of Pouilly-Fuissé. In the 1995 vintage, the wine's aromas are subtle, suggesting mainly the nutty character that comes from letting the wine sit on its lees (fermentation deposits). The wine is full bodied and dry, with flavors of earthiness and smoky oak. These are subtle flavors, but the rest of the wine is not subtle: It's a big mouthful. Try it with food that's rich enough, like the wine, but not aggressively flavorful.

Ed: 85–87   **Mary:** 87–89

Rully Blanc, Château de Rully, of Antonin Rodet

- ♪ **Producer:** Château de Rully of Antonin Rodet
- ♪ **Wine name:** Rully Blanc *(roo yee blahnk)*
- ♪ **Appellation:** Rully
- ♪ **Price:** $20

The vineyards around the village of Rully now make more white wine than red, but enough red Rully exists that you have to specify when requesting the wine. The white wine from Château de Rully, an Antonin Rodet property, is particularly good and an excellent value. The aroma of the 1994 Rully Blanc is rich, smoky, and buttery, and the wine's moderately intense flavors suggest apples, nuts, mushrooms, and dry earth. This big, full-bodied, fairly rich wine has the earthiness that we expect from Rully, but it's more elegant than the wines of Mâcon, as Rully should be. Personally, we'd drink it with grilled chicken cutlets, but it could accompany all sorts of foods easily.

Ed: 85–87   **Mary:** 86–88

White Burgundy wines from Chablis

Although the Chablis district is technically a part of Burgundy, the wines are so different that they merit separate consideration. Like almost all other white Burgundies, Chablis wines are made entirely from Chardonnay grapes. However, the particular kind of limestone soil in the hills around the village of Chablis and a somewhat cooler climate result in a unique type of wine. In general, the wines of Chablis are the crispest and most minerally of all white Burgundies.

Just as for other Burgundy wines, various categories of Chablis exist, including premier cru Chablis and grand cru Chablis. (For an explanation of these categories, and the names of premier cru and grand cru Chablis vineyards, see *White Wine For Dummies,* Chapter 10.) Premier cru Chablis wines are generally considerably higher in quality than wines simply labeled *Chablis,* and grand cru Chablis is usually the fullest, richest, and most complex type of Chablis. However, as with other wines of Burgundy, *you must select the Chablis of a good producer* in order to experience Chablis at its finest.

Generally speaking, two styles of Chablis coexist:

- ✔ **Chablis fermented and aged in stainless steel tanks:** These wines tend to be lighter in body and quite austere in flavor. Winemakers of this style emphasize purity of fruit expression, without any extraneous flavors, such as oakiness.

- ✔ **Chablis fermented and aged in oak barrels:** These wines tend to be rounder, fuller bodied, and less austere than Chablis aged in stainless steel.

We list our recommendations of Chablis wines alphabetically by producer. One review of a less expensive Chablis appears in Chapter 5.

Chablis Montmains, Jean Dauvissat

- ❢ **Producer:** Jean Dauvissat *(doh vee saht)*
- ❢ **Wine name:** Chablis Premier Cru Montmains *(mon mahn)*
- ❢ **Appellation:** Chablis Premier Cru
- ❢ **Price:** $31

Jean Dauvissat, one of the five or six best producers in Chablis, has always been a proponent of aging his wines in stainless steel. These days, he makes two of his Chablis wines with partial oak-aging — but not the Montmains. The 1995 Chablis from the Montmains vineyard has aromas of fresh lemon and apple, with delicate touches of yeast, white chocolate, and flint, and rather intense mineral and lemony flavors. It's fairly light in body, dry, and crisp — a classic, unoaked Chablis with loads of flavor concentration. Mary describes it as "a wine of the earth and of the soil." The Montmains could use a year or two of additional aging. This leaner-styled Chablis would be perfect with shellfish or a delicate, grilled fish. (For an example of Jean Dauvissat's partially oak-aged Chablis, try his 1995 Vaillons Vieilles Vignes, a fuller, richer Chablis, priced at $41; we recommend them both, but the Montmains is the better buy.)

Ed: 86–88   **Mary:** 88–90

Chablis Forest, René et Vincent Dauvissat

ED'S CHOICE

- *! Producer:* Domaine René et Vincent Dauvissat
- *! Wine name:* Chablis Premier Cru Forest
- *! Appellation:* Chablis Premier Cru
- *! Price:* $34

The firm of René et Vincent Dauvissat is one of the leading proponents of oak-aged Chablis, and one of Chablis' best producers. This Domaine's grand cru Chablis Les Clos ($60) is consistently one of the finest wines in Chablis each year. The premier cru Forest (sometimes spelled Les Forêts, pronounced *lay for ay,* by other producers) is one of René and Vincent Dauvissat's best premier cru Chablis wines, probably because the Forest vineyard boasts a high percentage of old vines. The 1995 Chablis Forest has honeyed aromas, and flavors of ripe apples with rich lemony highlights. It's very concentrated and rich, but with enough acidity to balance the richness of the fruit. This Chablis could easily accompany chicken or a rich seafood dish. You can enjoy the 1995 Forest now, or hold it for a few years.

Ed: 89–91

The Chablis Hall of Fame

Of all the wine regions in the world, Burgundy is the one in which the greatest variation in quality exists among producers. To experience a really good Chablis (or any Burgundy wine), you must therefore seek out the wines of a top producer. We list our recommended producers alphabetically, in two groups. The wines of producers in the first group are of the very highest quality, but all the producers listed here make fine Chablis.

The crème de la crème:

> Domaine Jean Dauvissat
> Domaine René et Vincent Dauvissat
> Domaine Louis Michel et Fils
> Domaine François et J.M. Raveneau
> Maison Verget

Other top, reliable producers:

> Domaine Jean-Claude Bessin
> Domaine Billaud-Simon
> Domaine A. & F. Boudin
> Domaine Jean Collet
> Domaine Jean & Daniel Defaix
> Domaine Gérard Duplessis
> Domaine Jean-Paul Droin
> Domaine William Fèvre / Domaine de la Maladière
> Domaine Jean-Pierre Grossot
> Domaine Laroche
> Domaine A. Long-Depaquit
> J. Moreau et Fils
> Domaine Robert Vocoret et Fils

Chablis Vaillons, Louis Michel

> 🍷 **Producer:** Domaine Louis Michel
> 🍷 **Wine name:** Chablis Vaillons Premier Cru *(vay yon)*
> 🍷 **Appellation:** Chablis Premier Cru
> 🍷 **Price:** $30

When Ed was a raw youth of 20, he tasted his first great wine, which happened to be a grand cru Chablis. Years later, we rediscovered our love of Chablis together at Atwater's Restaurant in Portland, Oregon, over a bottle of Louis Michel's Chablis Vaillons. That last experience confirmed a growing belief of ours — that Louis Michel is the master of unoaked Chablis.

Michel's 1995 Vaillons has aromas and flavors of minerals, herbs, and tart apples, with a trace of licorice. It's a dry, crisp, full-bodied Chablis with plenty of flavor concentration and a long, complex finish. This substantial Chablis is delicious now — try it with baked oysters — or if you wish, you can keep it for many years, even ten or more. Louis Michel's well-balanced Chablis wines, which see only stainless steel in their production, prove that you don't have to make or age wines in oak in order for them to age well.

Ed: 89–91   **Mary:** 88–90

Chablis Vaudésir, Louis Michel

> ♪ **Producer:** Domaine Louis Michel
>
> ♪ **Wine name:** Chablis Vaudésir Grand Cru
>
> ♪ **Appellation:** Chablis Grand Cru
>
> ♪ **Price:** $45

Domaine Louis Michel makes three grand cru Chablis wines, all of them great: Les Clos, Grenouilles, and Vaudésir. The Les Clos is the most powerful; the Grenouilles, the most floral and perfumed; and the Vaudésir, perhaps the best balanced and most complex. All should keep for at least 10 to 15 years, if you choose to watch them develop.

The 1995 Vaudésir has powerful mineral aromas, along with touches of apples and herbs; its focused, concentrated flavors suggest minerals and apples. This full-bodied, rich, and complexly flavored wine has excellent balance, and its flavor carries through to a long, minerally finish. Despite how packed with character it is, this wine manages to remain very fine and elegant.

Ed: 91–93   **Mary:** 92–94

Chablis Vaudésir, J. Moreau et Fils

- **Producer:** J. Moreau et Fils *(jhee moh roe aye fees)*
- **Wine name:** Chablis Vaudésir Grand Cru *(voh deh zeer)*
- **Appellation:** Chablis Grand Cru
- **Price:** $48

J. Moreau et Fils, the largest and the oldest Chablis firm, is a very modern winery, with all of its Chablis fermented and aged in stainless steel only. The 1995 Chablis Grand Cru Vaudésir has intense aromas of tart citrus and smoky, damp earth, with very earthy and citrusy flavors. It's a dry, solid, young, tightly wound Chablis that obviously needs time to develop. For instance, we found that the wine remaining in a half-full bottle overnight tasted better the next day than the wine from the freshly opened bottle had. This wine is a classic, Moreau-style Chablis: relatively light bodied, very dry, in fact, almost austere, but with a core of stony, minerally flavor. Give this wine three to five years to open up and develop.

Ed: 86–88   **Mary:** 87–89

Chablis Montée de Tonnerre, Raveneau

- **Producer:** Domaine François et J. M. Raveneau *(rah veh noh)*
- **Wine name:** Chablis Montée de Tonnerre Premier Cru
- **Appellation:** Chablis Premier Cru
- **Price:** $45

The small Raveneau winery makes the most prestigious, sought-after, long-lived Chablis in the world — and also the most expensive. The 1992 vintage was the last in which any of Raveneau's premier cru Chablis wines cost under $50. (The current 1994 Raveneau premier cru Chablis wines are $65, and the 1994 Grand Cru Les Clos is $80!) Raveneau, along with René et Vincent Dauvissat, is the leading proponent of the oak-aged style of Chablis. But father and son François and Jean-Marie Raveneau seldom use new oak barrels; instead, they use the traditional, old oak barrels so that the wines are not overwhelmed by oakiness.

Raveneau's 1992 Montée de Tonnerre has rich, honeyed, minerally aromas and flavors. It's full bodied and concentrated, with an oily texture and excellent balance. The richness, unctuousness, and complexity of this wine is reminiscent of a grand cru white Burgundy from the Côte de Beaune. This unique, atypical Chablis will only improve with another six to eight years of aging. (Raveneau's Chablis takes at least ten years to develop fully.) We suggest a full-flavored meat dish, such as veal or pork, to accompany this wine.

Ed: 89–91   **Mary:** 89–91

The Loire Valley

Although the wine region known as the Loire Valley encompasses three distinct areas, each specializing in a different white grape variety, our recommendations of Loire Valley whites in this chapter are all wines from the eastern Loire Valley, where Sauvignon Blanc is the primary white grape variety. More specifically, we confine our reviews in this chapter to Sancerres and Pouilly-Fumés (wines from the vineyards around the town Sancerre and the town of Pouilly-sur-Loire, respectively), which happen to be our favorite Loire whites.

In Chapter 5, we review four Muscadets, from the westernmost part of the Loire Valley, as well as one less-expensive Pouilly-Fumé. We list our over-$15 Loire white wine recommendations alphabetically by producer.

Pouilly-Fumé, Cuvée de Boisfleury, A. Cailbourdin

> ♪ **Producer:** Domaine A. Cailbourdin *(kye bor dan)*
>
> ♪ **Wine name:** Pouilly-Fumé, Cuvée de Boisfleury *(bwah fleh ree)*
>
> ♪ **Appellation:** Pouilly-Fumé *(poo ee foo may)*
>
> ♪ **Price:** $18.50

Alain Cailbourdin has taken his young winery (founded in 1981) to the top rank of Pouilly-Fumé producers in a relatively short time. Cailbourdin makes three Pouilly-Fumés; the Cuvée de Boisfleury is the lightest and readiest to drink of the three. The 1995 Cuvée de Boisfleury has a quite herbal, grassy aroma, with lime accents, and its flavors suggest candied lime, minerals, and fresh grass. This crisp, medium-bodied wine is rather atypically fruity for Loire Sauvignon Blanc. We like its fresh, emphatic flavors. Drink it soon, with shellfish or a warm goat cheese salad.

Ed: 86–88   **Mary:** 84–86

Sancerre, Lucien Crochet

> ❧ **Producer:** Lucien Crochet *(loo see ahn cro shay)*
> ❧ **Wine name:** Sancerre
> ❧ **Appellation:** Sancerre
> ❧ **Price:** $18.50

Lucien Crochet is generally regarded by wine critics as one of the top three or four producers of Sancerre. We love his 1994 Sancerre! As Ed says, "It's the real McCoy." It has the classic Sancerre aromas of grassiness, intense minerals, and chalk, along with some smokiness, and has tons of minerally, lemony flavors. The wine is dry and very concentrated, with a long, deep finish. Unlike most Sancerres, which you can drink immediately, the Crochet could actually benefit from another year of aging because it's still a bit closed. It would be wonderful with fresh fish, such as snapper or turbot. And goat cheese always works with Sancerre. (Crochet makes three other, more expensive bottlings of Sancerre, which will be more difficult to find than this standard Sancerre.)

Ed: 88–90   **Mary:** 89–91

Pouilly-Fumé, En Chailloux, Didier Dagueneau

> ❧ **Producer:** Didier Dagueneau *(dee dee ay dag weh noh)*
> ❧ **Wine name:** Pouilly-Fumé, En Chailloux *(on shy you)*
> ❧ **Appellation:** Pouilly-Fumé
> ❧ **Price:** $27

Didier Dagueneau is *the* hot producer of Pouilly-Fumé. Although he resembles a child of the 1960s, he's definitely up-to-date and very intense about the care of his wines. In fact, *intense* is the operative word for Dagueneau because all his wines are so intensely flavored and concentrated that they need a few years of aging to soften and develop.

Dagueneau makes four different Pouilly-Fumé wines, but the En Chailloux is the only one that's not made in oak. The 1993 En Chailloux has piercing, stony, minerally aromas, with some nuttiness, and flavors that suggest earth, minerals, ripe fruit, and lime candy. Voluptuous, rich, and full bodied, this wine has a slightly creamy texture and the pure zappy-zinginess of Sauvignon Blanc. You can enjoy En Chailloux best when it has from four to eight years of age. Try it with chicken or a simple, light veal entrée.

Ed: 86–88   **Mary:** 86–88

Pouilly-Fumé, Vieilles Vignes, Régis Minet

> ♪ **Producer:** Domaine Régis Minet
>
> ♪ **Wine name:** Pouilly-Fumé, Vieilles Vignes
>
> ♪ **Appellation:** Pouilly-Fumé
>
> ♪ **Price:** $17

A good Pouilly-Fumé can offer the finest expression of the Sauvignon Blanc grape variety in the entire wine world. Domaine Régis Minet's 1995 Vieilles Vignes, selected by California importer Kermit Lynch, is such a wine. It has intense aromas and flavors of concentrated lime, smoke, and earth, along with the classic Pouilly-Fumé gunflint and minerally accents. The Vieilles Vignes is a medium-bodied, dry, crisp, vibrant wine. Have it with a simple salad or sandwich and enjoy its energy.

Ed: 85–87   **Mary:** 86–88

Sancerre, Michel Redde

> ♪ **Producer:** Michel Redde
>
> ♪ **Wine name:** Sancerre
>
> ♪ **Appellation:** Sancerre
>
> ♪ **Price:** $19.50

The 1995 Michel Redde Sancerre has an aroma that's steely and spicy and somewhat suggestive of grapefruit rind; the wine's flavors are grapefruity and tart with some mineral notes. This medium- to full-bodied wine has a roundness that's uncommon in Sancerre, as well as a very slightly sweet fruitiness — and yet it still shows the crispness characteristic of Sancerre wine. Redde's Sancerre carries the name

Les Tuilières across the top of the label; the wine is always trustworthy and is widely available. In 1995, though, Redde is at the top of his form. He also makes a good Pouilly-Fumé, by the way.

Ed: 91–93   **Mary:** 86–88

Sancerre, Clos de la Crèle, Lucien Thomas

> ♪ **Producer:** Lucien Thomas et Fils
>
> ♪ **Wine name:** Sancerre, Clos de la Crèle
>
> ♪ **Appellation:** Sancerre
>
> ♪ **Price:** $17

Three producers with the last name of Thomas happen to be making Sancerre (Claude, Lucien, and Paul), but because all of them are good, you can't go wrong. Lucien makes two Sancerres, the Clos de la Crèle, which is produced in stainless steel tanks, and the more expensive Cuvée Lucien Thomas, which is aged in small oak barrels. The 1995 Clos de la Crèle has subtle minerally and lemon-zest aromas and ripe peach and apricot fruit flavors, plus a suggestion of orange rind. It has terrific weight for a Sancerre, possibly a reflection of the very good 1995 vintage in the Loire region. You can enjoy this wine now with some chèvre (goat cheese) or hold it for one or two years.

Ed: 85–87   **Mary:** 86–88

Sancerre Chavignol "Les Comtesses," Paul Thomas

> ♪ **Producer:** Domaine Paul Thomas
>
> ♪ **Wine name:** Sancerre Chavignol Grande Réserve "Les Comtesses"
>
> ♪ **Appellation:** Sancerre Chavignol
>
> ♪ **Price:** $20

This wine has a double-barreled name, Sancerre Chavignol, because it comes from the hilly vineyards around the town of Chavignol (located in the Sancerre district), which is a well-regarded and historic area for Sancerre wines. In the 1995 vintage, Paul Thomas's Sancerre Chavignol "Les Comtesses" has terrific quality and exactly the sort of balance between flavor intensity and austerity that we like in Sancerre. The wine has a piercing aroma of herbs, citrus, and flintiness, and its fairly assertive (for Sancerre), well-concentrated flavors suggest citrus, herbs, and minerals. Medium bodied and crisp, the Sancerre Chavignol has a long, dry finish that's rich with mineral notes. Although definitely a wine with character, this wine is easy to appreciate because of its intense and complex flavors. Frankly, it's much more wine for $20 than you get elsewhere in the wine world!

Ed: 89–91   **Mary:** 90–92

Germany's Great White Wines

Germany's finer wines are rather confusing to understand and to purchase. The reason is twofold:

- Germany's best producers each make several wines, in small quantities. They segregate their production not only according to the vineyard where the grapes grow but also according to the ripeness level of the grapes when they were picked. (And sometimes they further segregate some wine for labeling as *dry* or *off-dry*.) When you buy a German wine, you must choose not only a producer and a vintage — as you would for any fine wine — but you must also select a specific vineyard (à la Burgundy) and a ripeness level. (Grapes of a higher ripeness level make fuller-bodied and richer, but not necessarily sweeter, wines.)

- All the details of the wine's identity are on the label, providing more information than a non-expert buyer usually wants.

For information on the ripeness designations that most of Germany's better wines carry — terms such as *kabinett, spätlese,* and *auslese* — and for information on Germany's wine regions, refer to *White Wine For Dummies,* Chapter 12, or *Wine For Dummies*, Chapter 11.

All of our recommended German wines over $15 a bottle are made from the Riesling grape. We review several wines from the Mosel-Saar-Ruwer region of Germany first, followed by wines from other German regions.

Wines of the Mosel-Saar-Ruwer region

The vineyards along the Mosel River and its tributaries, the Saar and Ruwer, are some of the finest vineyard sites in Germany for the Riesling grape. Even more importantly, the Mosel-Saar-Ruwer (pronounced *MOH sel zar ROO ver*) region has more than its share of serious producers, who sacrifice many an easy buck in the name of producing great wine.

Some of our favorite wines from this region follow, in alphabetical order by producer. Because these producers are all good, you can feel confident substituting another wine from the same producer if you can't find the exact wine that we recommend.

Graacher Himmelreich Riesling Spätlese, Friedrich Wilhelm Gymnasium

- ♪ **Producer:** Friedrich Wilhelm Gymnasium
- ♪ **Wine name:** Graacher Himmelreich Riesling Spätlese
- ♪ **Appellation:** Graacher Himmelreich Spätlese
- ♪ **Price:** $17.50

The Graacher Himmelreich vineyard is one of the many dramatic vineyards that rise steeply from the Mosel River as it twists and turns along its most scenic route, the part known as the Middle Mosel. The 1994 Riesling wine of the producer Friedrich Wilhelm Gymnasium, from the grapes of Graacher Himmelreich picked at spätlese-level ripeness, is a fine example of the delicious, fruity character of Mosel Rieslings. The aromas and flavors of this wine are lively with peach, lemon, and apple notes, as well as spicy white pepper and sweet cream. The wine is medium to full bodied, off-dry, firm, and packed with flavor. If we close our eyes, we can almost imagine being on a boat in the middle of the Middle Mosel — an instant vacation!

Ed: 86–88   **Mary:** 86–88

Erdener Treppchen Riesling Kabinett, Dr. Loosen

- ♪ **Producer:** Dr. Loosen
- ♪ **Wine name:** Erdener Treppchen Riesling Kabinett
- ♪ **Appellation:** Erdener Treppchen Kabinett
- ♪ **Price:** $19

The wines of young winemaker Ernst Loosen are consistently among my favorites in all of Germany because of their elegance and finesse. His 1995 Riesling Kabinett from the Erdener Treppchen vineyard has delicate, fairly subtle herbal aromas and flavors, with an underlying slatey character. The wine is unusually full and ripe for a kabinett-level wine, with terrific concentration of fruit character, and yet it's extremely elegant and fine. This wine is so intense and yet so delicate that it's sort of like a tightly coiled spring wrapped in a sheath of delicate lace — a corny and unorthodox way of saying that the wine is stunning. I would enjoy it with broiled fish, but it also has enough intensity to stand up to a richer dish, such as quail.

Mary: 89–91

Maximin Grünhäuser Herrenberg Riesling Spätlese

▶ **Producer:** Maximin Grünhaus, of C. Von Schubert

▶ **Wine name:** Herrenberg Riesling Spätlese

▶ **Appellation:** Maximin Grünhäuser Herrenberg Spätlese

▶ **Price:** $25

The Maximin Grünhaus estate is a famous property in the Mosel region, now owned by Carl von Schubert, a respected winemaker. The Riesling Spätlese from the Herrenberg vineyard in 1995 has a firm, minerally aroma with a slight hint of dry mustard, and its vivid flavors evoke apple, citrus fruit, earth, and tobacco. Although this wine is off-dry, it's definitely not soft: Its firm acidity and tight concentration of fruit character give this intense wine an impression of solidity and character. We would hold it for a few years because it will only become more interesting. For current drinking, we enjoy the Riesling QbA (QbA wines are made from grapes of less ripeness than kabinett or spätlese) of Maximin Grünhäuser, about $16.50; the 1994 Riesling QbA is delicious now and intensely flavored with fruit, fruit, fruit.

Ed: 85–87   **Mary:** 87–89

Ürziger Würzgarten Riesling Spätlese, Merkelbach

▶ **Producer:** Alfred Merkelbach

▶ **Wine name:** Ürziger Würzgarten Riesling Spätlese

▶ **Appellation:** Ürziger Würzgarten Spätlese

▶ **Price:** $17.50

The red sandstone and slate soils of the Ürziger Würzgarten vineyard grow some of the richest and most exotic Riesling wines in the Mosel region. Merkelbach's 1995 Riesling Spätlese from this vineyard is relatively restrained, however, at least now. It has a firm, steely aroma with a suggestion of damp earth, and it has flavors of mineral, grapefruit, and red berries. This wine is fairly dry, lean, and firm, all thanks to very high acidity — and yet it's very intense in its flavor concentration. Clearly, this wine is young and has yet to show its fullness of flavor. In the meantime, try pairing it with shellfish in a creamy but spicy sauce.

Ed: 86–88   **Mary:** 85–87

Erdener Treppchen Riesling Auslese, Meulenhof

> ♪ **Producer:** Weingut Meulenhof *(MEW len hof)*
>
> ♪ **Wine name:** Erdener Treppchen Riesling Auslese
>
> ♪ **Appellation:** Erdener Treppchen Auslese
>
> ♪ **Price:** $27

This wine, from the 1995 vintage, is from grapes of the same hillside as the Dr. Loosen wine we review earlier in this section, but this wine is an *auslese* rather than a *spätlese* — meaning that the grapes were riper at harvest. (And of course, it's made by a different producer.) As a result, this wine is richer and fuller bodied, with riper fruit flavors. The aroma suggests grapefruit rind, fresh peaches, and caramelized peaches, while the flavors include very ripe apple and peach notes, and a slatey character typical of the area where the grapes grow. This wine is somewhat sweet (although not as sweet as a dessert wine), very flavorful, and quite full blown in style. The wine's excellent balance of acidity keeps the wine from being too rich, however. Try it with duck breast in a fruit sauce.

Ed: 86–88   **Mary:** 86–88

Graacher Himmelreich Riesling Kabinett, Joh. Jos. Prüm

> ♪ **Producer:** Joh. Jos. Prüm
>
> ♪ **Wine name:** Graacher Himmelreich Riesling Kabinett *(GRAH ker HIM mel rike)*
>
> ♪ **Appellation:** Graacher Himmelreich Kabinett
>
> ♪ **Price:** $22

The wine estate that people usually refer to as "J.J. Prüm," to circumvent the difficult abbreviations in its name, is one of the most highly regarded properties of the Mosel-Saar-Ruwer region. Its 1995 Riesling Kabinett from the Graacher Himmelreich vineyard has a provocative aroma of damp earth, minerals, citrus rind, lime, and peaches. Although complex, this aroma is fairly tight and closed-in. In your mouth, however, the wine explodes with flavors that are similar to the aromas but much richer and more intense. Although this wine tastes completely agreeable now, the estate has a reputation for wines that develop magnificently with time. The winery's Riesling Spätlese from the same vineyard (from riper grapes than for the kabinett wine), for example, now has very tight flavors and so much intensely packed mineral character that we can imagine holding that wine for a decade before drinking. In the case of the kabinett, we recommend drinking it now or any time in the next five years.

Ed: 86–88   **Mary:** 87–89

Saarburger Rausch Riesling Spätlese, Zilliken

- ✦ **Producer:** Zilliken
- ✦ **Wine name:** Saarburger Rausch Riesling Spätlese
- ✦ **Appellation:** Saarburger Rausch Spätlese
- ✦ **Price:** $22.50

The aroma of this wine — a Riesling from grapes of spätlese-level ripeness, grown in the Saarburger Rausch vineyard — fascinates us with its notes of fresh herbs, such as thyme, rosemary, and tarragon, and its smoky character. We are no less impressed to taste it: a rich, medium- to full-bodied wine with flavors of fresh herbs and apple that are concentrated and carry through to the finish. Although the wine has sweetness, its crisp acidity balances the sweetness in such a way that the wine tastes solid rather than fat. Try it with roast pork or ham, and don't be afraid to let it age.

Ed: 86–88   **Mary:** 86–88

Wines from other German regions

Some of Germany's most exciting wines are made today by producers in regions such as the Pfalz, the Nahe, and the Rheingau. Even the Rheinhessen region, home to many inexpensive and forgettable wines, boasts serious winemakers who turn out top-quality wines.

We review a few wines from these regions in this section, organizing them alphabetically by producer. We indicate the region of each wine in parentheses next to the appellation.

Rüdesheim Estate Riesling, Georg Breuer

> ♪ **Producer:** Georg Breuer
>
> ♪ **Wine name:** Rüdesheim Estate Riesling
>
> ♪ **Appellation:** Rheingau QbA (Rheingau)
>
> ♪ **Price:** $16

If you prefer totally dry wines to wines that are mildly sweet, have we got a Riesling for you! The 1995 Georg Breuer Rüdesheim Riesling, made from grapes of various vineyards that the estate owns in the Rüdesheim area of the Rheingau, is so dry that it almost crackles in your mouth. Despite its dryness, this crisp, lean wine is not mean, however; it has a gentle aroma of flowers and white pepper spice and provocative flavors of smoke and grapefruit rind. It also has quite a bit of substance in the form of intense flavor concentration. This Riesling contrasts nicely with slightly sweet foods, such as crab or a creamy potato-leek soup.

Ed: 87–89   **Mary:** 85–87

Forster Ungeheuer Riesling Spätlese, Dr. Bürklin-Wolf

> ♪ **Producer:** Dr. Bürklin-Wolf
>
> ♪ **Wine name:** Forster Ungeheuer Riesling Spätlese
>
> ♪ **Appellation:** Forster Ungeheuer Spätlese (Pfalz)
>
> ♪ **Price:** $17

The wine estate known as Dr. Bürklin-Wolf is one of the more famous properties of the Pfalz region, a unique area with a climate that's warmer and drier than Germany's other famous wine zones. The 1995 Riesling Spätlese from the Forster Ungeheuer vineyard seduces you with aromas of honey-buttered apples and rich, thick flavors of honey and of butter-coated orange. The wine is full bodied and off-dry, with great flavor intensity. Although our words describe mainly the rich aspects of the wine, in fact the wine also has exciting energy and vitality, thanks to its crisp acidity. It's a baby that should age beautifully.

Ed: 87–89   **Mary:** 87–89

Nackenheimer Rothenberg Riesling Spätlese, Gunderloch

> ✔ **Producer:** Gunderloch
>
> ✔ **Wine name:** Nackenheimer Rothenberg Riesling Spätlese
>
> ✔ **Appellation:** Nackenheimer Rothenberg Spätlese (Rheinhessen)
>
> ✔ **Price:** $26

With every new vintage, we're increasingly impressed with the wines from the Gunderloch estate, which we now consider among Germany's finest. The 1995 Riesling from the Nackenheimer Rothenberg vineyard, harvested at spätlese-level ripeness, is fairly quiet in aroma, with just a bit of earthiness, smokiness, and peach-skin character. But when you taste the wine, you experience a real burst of flavor, like the first bite into a section of a very ripe orange (except that it tastes like peach as well as orange!). The wine is full bodied and full flavored, not dry but not sweet, and it has a lovely, light creaminess. Delicious enough to drink all by itself!

Ed: 87–89   **Mary:** 88–90

Münsterer Dautenpflänzer Riesling Spätlese, Kruger-Rumpf

MARY'S CHOICE

> ✔ **Producer:** Weingut Kruger-Rumpf
>
> ✔ **Wine name:** Münsterer Dautenpflänzer Riesling Spätlese
>
> ✔ **Appellation:** Münsterer Dautenpflänzer Spätlese (Nahe)
>
> ✔ **Price:** $16

Tasting the 1995 vintage of this wine is like watching a sci-fi movie — at least that's the way it performs in my mouth. The aroma is penetrating but quiet, with just a bit of apple, so I don't expect much flavor when I sip. But the wine is rich. It has lots of flavor. In fact, it's alive with an energy that zips through my mouth. The wine shoots off sparks of mineral, apple, and slatey flavor into the rich flesh that encircles its core of energy. Once the dust settles, the mundane attributes register in my brain: medium-bodied, fairly dry, crisp, and well concentrated in its fruit character.

Mary: 87–89

Hochheimer Herrnberg Riesling Kabinett, Franz Künstler

- *?* **Producer:** Franz Künstler
- *?* **Wine name:** Hochheimer Herrnberg Riesling Kabinett
- *?* **Appellation:** Hochheimer Herrnberg Kabinett (Rheingau)
- *?* **Price:** $19

This 1995 Riesling Kabinett from the Hochheimer Herrnberg vineyard is quite a bit sweeter than the Franz Künstler wines typically are — which is why Ed doesn't love it. But I find it not just sweet, but rich and succulent, with delicious flavors of orange, lemon, and apple. And it has enough of a backbone of minerally character to keep it from being just another Big Easy. Try it with smoked meats or a slightly sweet Asian stir-fry.

Mary: 86–88

Haardter Herzog Riesling Trocken Spätlese, Müller-Catoir

- *?* **Producer:** Müller-Catoir
- *?* **Wine name:** Haardter Herzog Riesling Trocken Spätlese
- *?* **Appellation:** Haardter Herzog Spätlese (Pfalz)
- *?* **Price:** $32

The Müller-Catoir winery might just be the hottest property in Germany at the moment, thanks to the praise and high scores that its wines have been racking up from critics. Frustration is in store for wine lovers, however, because this estate made very little wine in 1995 due to weather conditions in its vineyards. One of the 1995 wines from Müller-Catoir that we have been fortunate enough to enjoy is this dry (trocken) Riesling Spätlese from the Haardter Herzog vineyard. It's a racy and solid wine, definitely built to age. The aroma is quietly intense, with scents of smoke, grapefruit rind, and ripe lemon, and the flavor is concentrated, with fresh citrus notes and a stony character. This wine is only medium bodied, but it has great richness, nonetheless. We hear that Müller-Catoir's 1996 wines are terrific, by the way.

Ed: 85–87   **Mary: 87–89**

Italy's Better White Wines

Italy is *red* wine country. And yet Italy produces so much wine (in most years, more than any other country in the world) that Italian white wine production is greater than the total wine production of the U.S. — red and white combined.

The huge volume of white wine production in Italy comes from all 20 of the country's regions and encompasses a wide range of wine styles, prices, and quality gradations. The most important area of Italy for high-quality white wine production, however, is the northeast. We review wines from that area in one section and group the elite white wines from elsewhere in Italy in a separate section.

For more information on Italian white wines, refer to Chapter 13 of *White Wine For Dummies.*

Northeastern Italy

Two regions of northeastern Italy produce a disproportionate share of Italy's finest white wines:

- ✔ Friuli-Venezia Giulia, in the extreme northeast of Italy

- ✔ Trentino-Alto Adige, in north-central Italy, bordering Austria

Most of the white wines from these two regions are named for their grape variety, as well as the area where the grapes grow. Many of the best wines are made from the grapes of a single, favored vineyard and carry the name of that vineyard on their labels. Tradition dictates that the white wines are not oaked, but these days, many producers are making barrel-fermented or barrel-aged whites. Often, a producer makes a wine in two styles: oaked and unoaked.

In this section, we review several of our favorite white wines from northeastern Italy that sell for more than $15 a bottle. (For reviews of less expensive wines, see Chapter 5.) If you come across different wines from the producers that we mention in this section or if you find the same wines from different vintages, you can purchase them with confidence. (We caution against buying Italian white wines that are four years old or older, however, unless you know that they've been stored well.) We list our recommended wines alphabetically by producer.

Pinot Grigio, Borgo Conventi

- *!* **Producer:** Borgo Conventi
- *!* **Wine name:** Pinot Grigio *(PEE noh GREE jhee oh)*
- *!* **Appellation:** Collio
- *!* **Price:** $18

Borgo Conventi is one of the wineries responsible for demonstrating to the world what good quality wines the Friuli region can produce. The winery's 1995 Pinot Grigio, from grapes grown in the Collio district of Friuli, has one of the loveliest aromas that we've ever smelled in a Pinot Grigio: It's intense with lemon, lemon peel, and flint, and it suggests yet more scents huddled deep under the surface. The wine gives a similar impression of great depth in your mouth. It's dry and medium to full bodied, and it has a core of earthy and lemony flavor. We also like this winery's Chardonnay Colli Russian ($24), an oaked wine, but we prefer this Pinot Grigio because it's easier to enjoy now. Borgo Conventi Pinot Grigio is very flexible with food because it has enough weight to hold up to all those foods that occupy the middle ground between delicate, white-wine dishes and rich, red-wine dishes.

Ed: 90–92   **Mary:** 88–90

Tocai Friulano, Livio Felluga

- *!* **Producer:** Livio Felluga *(fel LOO gah)*
- *!* **Wine name:** Tocai Friulano *(toh KYE free oo LAH noh)*
- *!* **Appellation:** Colli Orientali del Friuli
- *!* **Price:** $18

Among the wines of the Friuli region, we find that those produced from the Tocai Friulano grape (a local specialty, as you might assume from its name) are particularly interesting. The Tocai Friulano from the Livio Felluga winery is consistently one of our favorites. In the 1995 vintage, this wine has fairly pronounced aromas and flavors of peach skins, dried apricots, and flower blossoms. The wine is dry, rather full bodied, round, and oily-textured — much fuller, bigger, and riper of fruit than most Italian whites. Try Livio Felluga's Tocai Friulano with darker fish, poultry, or seafood risotto.

(Another of this company's wines, named Terre Alte, combines Tocai Friulano, Sauvignon, and Chardonnay grapes; the result is an excellent, dry, full-bodied wine with broad flavors of almonds and dried fruits. It sells for $29.)

Ed: 88–90   **Mary:** 87–89

Sauvignon Lenenhof, Alois Lageder

> ♪ **Producer:** Alois Lageder *(AH loh is lah GAY der)*
> ♪ **Wine name:** Sauvignon, Lenenhof
> ♪ **Appellation:** Terlaner
> ♪ **Price:** $20

The Alois Lageder winery of Alto Adige is named for its founder and today is run by that man's great-great-grandson and namesake. Lageder makes a huge array of wines (including 16 different whites!); most of them are from single grape varieties, and the best of them are from single vineyards. Although we admire Lageder's wines in general, we're particularly impressed by his single-vineyard wines, such as this Sauvignon from the Lenenhof vineyard, for their good concentration of fruit character. Lageder's 1995 Lenenhof Sauvignon is a fairly flavorful (by Italian standards) and full-bodied dry wine with aromas and flavors of ripe apples, herbs, and grapefruit rind. The wine is crisp with high acidity — a real boon with food — and has an interesting, slightly oily texture; tart fruit and a mineral character come through on the wine's finish. We enjoy drinking this wine with goat cheese and with herb-seasoned vegetable dishes.

Ed: 86–88   **Mary:** 87–89

Ribolla Gialla, Walter Filiputti

> ♪ **Producer:** Walter Filiputti
> ♪ **Wine name:** Ribolla Gialla *(ree BOH lah JAH lah)*
> ♪ **Appellation:** Vino da Tavola della Venezia Giulia
> ♪ **Price:** $27.50

Walter Filiputti is one of the top winemakers in the Friuli-Venezia Giulia region. After spending much of his career working for renowned wine estates there, he now makes wine under his own label. His 1995 Ribolla Gialla, made from one of the more "characterful" grapes of the region, has aromas and flavors that suggest honey, tart fruit, earthiness, and stony or minerally character, with some spiciness and a touch of vanilla. The wine is full bodied and rather assertively flavorful, with a crispness of acidity that's offset by the impression that the wine is glazed in honey. This is a dry wine, but it's rich enough that some might call it slightly sweet. I call it lovely.

Mary: 88–90

Gewürztraminer Kolbenhof, Hofstätter

- **Producer:** Cantina J. Hofstätter *(HOF shtate ter)*
- **Wine name:** Gewürztraminer, Kolbenhof
- **Appellation:** Alto Adige
- **Price:** $20

The Hofstätter winery is one of those golden operations where every wine is of high quality, and some are sensational. The winery is in the town of Termeno, as the Italians call it, or Tramin, as the German-speaking natives call it. This town gave its name to a white grape called *Traminer,* which eventually mutated into the rosy-skinned grape known as *Gewürztraminer.* The Hofstätter Gewürztraminer doesn't rest on these historic laurels, however, to make its mark; it's as fine a Gewürztraminer as you can find anywhere. The 1995 Gewürztraminer from the Kolbenhof vineyard has an utterly seductive aroma of roses, and the typical Gewürztraminer flavors (lychee fruit and roses) manage not to be too perfumey. The wine is totally dry, full bodied, and soft — a really fetching wine. It is delicious all by itself but also goes well with flavorful, rich foods, such as dark-meat chicken, quail, or rabbit stew.

Ed: 88–90 **Mary:** 89–91

Vintage Tunina, Jermann

- **Producer:** Vinnaioli Jermann *(YER mahn)*
- **Wine name:** Vintage Tunina *(too NEE nah)*
- **Appellation:** Vino da Tavola di Friuli
- **Price:** $38

Silvio Jermann is a maverick among the wine producers of the Friuli region, making wines from unusual blends of grape varieties and giving them totally unorthodox names. His wine called Vintage Tunina happens to be on our short list for best white wine in all of Italy. It's a blend mainly of Sauvignon Blanc and Chardonnay, with some Ribolla Gialla and Picolit (the latter two being premium local grape varieties). Although Vintage Tunina is produced without using new oak barrels, it's as rich and complex as barrel-fermented white wines typically are — but its flavors are more subtle. The 1994 Vintage Tunina has a piercing, vivid aroma of spicy white pepper and flavors of lemon and exotic flowers. This full-bodied wine is dry and crisp, but it's also soft and fleshy, the two almost-opposite styles combining seamlessly when you taste the wine. In other vintages, we've noticed that this wine develops fascinating honey flavors as it ages in the bottle, evolving into a wine that's powerful but subdued, firm but rich.

We recommend drinking the 1994 Vintage Tunina beginning around 1999. If you want to try it sooner, be sure not to serve it too cold, give it about half an hour of aeration in a decanter, and drink it with food, such as grilled portobello mushrooms or fresh trout.

Ed: 91–93 **Mary:** 90–92

Tocai Friulano, Volpe Pasini

> ❧ **Producer:** Volpe Pasini
>
> ❧ **Wine name:** Tocai Friulano *(TOE kye free oo LAH noh)*
>
> ❧ **Appellation:** Colli Orientali del Fruili
>
> ❧ **Price:** $19.50

Volpe Pasini is one of the outstanding producers in the Friuli region, and its Tocai Friulano is one of the property's best wines. The 1995 Tocai has the classic peach-stone aroma of this variety, with sweet, ripe flavors suggestive of peaches and peach stone. It's dry and full bodied, with a viscous texture. This is a complete, well-balanced wine with great flavor intensity and a long, fruity finish that shows some attractive bitterness on the end. Enjoy it with some Italian seafood, such as calamari or scungilli.

Ed: 91–93 **Mary:** 89–91

Chardonnay Vigneto Zaraosti, Roberto Zeni

- ✦ **Producer:** Roberto Zeni *(ZAY nee)*
- ✦ **Wine name:** Chardonnay, Vigneto Zaraosti *(vee NYAY toh zah rah OHS tee)*
- ✦ **Appellation:** Trentino
- ✦ **Price:** $17

Roberto Zeni makes impressive white wines of real character and flavor in the Trentino area of the Trentino-Alto Adige region. His Chardonnay from a vineyard called Zaraosti is one of our favorites because it's an honest Chardonnay that expresses the fruit character of the grapes rather than oakiness. In the 1995 vintage, this wine has a broad aroma and a flavor of ripe apples. It's full bodied, dry, and fairly flavorful, with very precise appley character and a long, appley finish. This wine is flavorful enough to enjoy alone, without food, and yet discreet enough to work well at the table. Just be sure not to serve it very cold, or the wine's flavors will go into hiding.

Ed: 88–90   **Mary:** 90–92

Other premium Italian whites

We could easily have gotten carried away with this section, because Italy produces so many serious white wines these days. (A few good Chardonnays from Piedmont and from Tuscany immediately spring to mind.) The six wines we do review in this section are particular favorites. We organize the wines alphabetically by producer.

Cervaro della Sala, Antinori

- ✦ **Producer:** Marchesi Antinori
- ✦ **Wine name:** Cervaro della Sala
- ✦ **Appellation:** Vino da Tavola di Umbria
- ✦ **Price:** $31

In the white wine arena, the respected house of Antinori accommodates both tradition and innovation with Cervaro della Sala. This wine is predominantly Chardonnay, but also contains an Italian grape called Grechetto, and it is made in a traditional white-wine area of the region of Umbria. Now released in its tenth vintage, the 1995 Cervaro della Sala is at its best yet. The wine has smoky aromas and flavors from oak, along with lemony, minty, slightly vegetal, and floral notes. It's a big, full-bodied, and flavorful wine, but it also has the high-acidity crispness of an Italian white. Although we enjoy this wine now, while it's still youthful, it can be consumed over the next three or four years. Try it with simple herbed chicken cutlets so that the wine's nuances are easy to enjoy.

Ed: 86–88   **Mary:** 87–89

Vernaccia di San Gimignano, Vinea Doni, Falchini

 🍷 **Producer:** Riccardo Falchini *(fahl KEE nee)*

 🍷 **Wine name:** Vernaccia di San Gimignano, Vinea Doni *(vee NAY ah DOH nee)*

 🍷 **Appellation:** Vernaccia di San Gimignano *(ver NOTCH cha dee san gee me NYAH noh)*

 🍷 **Price:** $18

Riccardo Falchini makes two Vernaccia wines: an inexpensive ($9) one, called Vigna a Solatio, that has no oak aging, and the more interesting Vinea Doni, which is aged in small French oak barrels. The 1994 Vinea Doni has a deep gold color, with full, rich, honeyed, earthy aromas and flavors. It has loads of concentration, a good deal of flavor intensity, and a long finish. You can enjoy this full-flavored Vernaccia now, accompanied by a pasta dish with mushrooms and herbs.

Ed: 88–90

Chardonnay "I Palazzi," Lungarotti

 🍷 **Producer:** Cantine Lungarotti

 🍷 **Wine name:** Chardonnay, "I Palazzi" *(ee pah LAHTZ zee)*

 🍷 **Appellation:** Chardonnay di Torgiano

 🍷 **Price:** $19

Some of the red and white wines from the Lungarotti winery, in the Umbria region of Italy, are more exciting than others, but we've never had a single one that was less than good. This Chardonnay, from the wine district of Torgiano, is our favorite Lungarotti white. In the 1994 vintage, it has aromas and flavors of ripe lemon and ripe apple, along with a perfumey, floral character, probably from oak barrels. The wine's nuttiness probably results from holding the wine in contact with its *lees,* or fermentation deposits. This wine is fullish in body and dry, with some crisp acidity to balance its fullness — a proper Chardonnay by any standards. We like it with shellfish, especially baked oysters.

Ed: 86–88   **Mary:** 88–90

Greco di Tufo, Mastroberardino

> 🍷 **Producer:** Mastroberardino *(mah stro ber ar DEE no)*
>
> 🍷 **Wine name:** Greco di Tufo
>
> 🍷 **Appellation:** Greco di Tufo
>
> 🍷 **Price:** $18

The Mastroberardino winery and vineyards are off the beaten track of fine Italian wine, situated down south, in the region of Campania, the shin of the Italian boot. In the ancient soils of Campania, near the volcano Vesuvius, the family grows grape varieties that can be traced back to the days of the Greek empire, and elevates them to the high standards of modern winemaking. The fruity, perfumed, white grape called Greco, which makes the wine called Greco di Tufo, is in fact named for the Greeks.

Mastroberardino's 1995 Greco di Tufo wine has a rich nut-and-honey aroma and smoky, floral, appley and, especially, herbal flavors. Although the wine is full bodied and obviously made from very ripe grapes, it has crisp acidity to counterbalance the fullness, and it is dry. In fact, this wine is somewhat delicate in its aromas and flavors, and it leaves your mouth gently. Experience tells us that this wine can age nicely for several years if stored properly, but we can't say that we wouldn't drink it now.

Ed: 90–92   **Mary:** 87–89

Vernaccia di San Gimignano "Carato," Montenidoli

> 🍷 **Producer:** Montenidoli
>
> 🍷 **Wine name:** Vernaccia di San Gimignano, "Carato" *(cah RAH toh)*
>
> 🍷 **Appellation:** Vernaccia di San Gimignano *(ver NOTCH cha dee san gee me NYAH noh)*
>
> 🍷 **Price:** $20

The Montenidoli winery, under the tireless leadership of Elisabetta Fagiuoli, turns the simple Tuscan white wine, Vernaccia di San Gimignano, into a symphony in three parts — three Vernaccia wines, each made differently from the next and all of them quite good. The finest of the three, and perhaps the least traditional, is the Vernaccia designated "Carato," an Italian name for small oak barrels; it has a gold label, while the other two have white labels. In the 1995 vintage, this wine has a lovely smoke-and-vanilla aroma from its oak barrels, with a bit of honey. Toasted oak, honey, white peaches, orange peel, and lemon peel all emerge as flavors. The wine is creamy-textured but firm, and it's full bodied, with a gentle, slightly sweet impression from its ripe fruit and oak. Signora Fagiuoli believes that this wine will taste even better in the year 2000 than it does now — and we suspect that she's right. If you find a 1994 or 1993 bottle, rather than the 1995, by all means, try it.

Ed: 88–90 **Mary:** 89–91

Poggio alle Gazze, Tenuta dell'Ornellaia

- ♪ **Producer:** Tenuta dell'Ornellaia
  (te NOO tah dell or nell LIE ah)
- ♪ **Wine name:** Poggio alle Gazze
  (POH jee oh AH lay GAHTZ zay)
- ♪ **Appellation:** Vino da Tavola di Toscana
- ♪ **Price:** $18

The white wine called Poggio alle Gazze (which translates as "knoll of the magpies") is made entirely from Sauvignon Blanc grapes. We like this wine because, in the model of a Loire Valley Sauvignon Blanc, it relies only on the grapes for its flavor, without any helping hand from oak barrels. In the 1995 vintage, the wine has a smoky, almost flinty, pungent aroma; its flavors include a similar mineral note, but tart lemon fruit joins the team. This wine is medium bodied and very crisp, and yet it's not austere. Its most impressive characteristic to us is its very, very good concentration of fruit character, which not only is a mark of quality but also is an indication that the wine has the stuff to develop over time. Drink it now or in the next two years, with a mushroom pasta dish.

Ed: 86–88 **Mary:** 86–88

Switzerland's Svelte White Wines

The white grape variety that predominates for fine wine in Switzerland is the Chasselas (also called *Fendant* and *Neuchâtel,* in different regions). Although Chasselas *(chass lah)* is grown in France's Loire Valley, in Alsace and in Germany, it has emerged as a truly high-quality variety only in Switzerland, where it produces grapes with enough acidity to contribute to Switzerland's light and lively, delicate white wines.

We review three Swiss wines alphabetically by producer. For more information on Swiss white wines, refer to *White Wine For Dummies,* Chapter 14.

Pinot Gris, Château d'Auvernier

- **Producer:** Château d'Auvernier, of Thierry Grosjean
- **Wine name:** Pinot Gris, Château d'Auvernier *(doh ver nyay)*
- **Appellation:** Neuchâtel
- **Price:** $19.50

Thierry Grosjean's Château d'Auvernier is the leading winery in the Neuchâtel region. Grosjean makes arguably Switzerland's finest dry rosé wine, called Oeil de Perdrix (translates as "eye of the partridge"), from Pinot Noir grapes. We also like his statuesque white wine labeled, simply, Neuchatel, made from Chasselas grapes. Our favorite wine from this producer, however, is Pinot Gris. The 1995 Pinot Gris has a rich golden color, typical of the Pinot Gris grape. Its aromas are minerally, honeyed, and lemony, with a distinct peach-stone note that we find typical of Pinot Gris; its flavors are those of minerals and peach stone. This dry, full-bodied wine has a creamy texture; zingy, fresh acidity; good length; and a real concentration of true, ripe Pinot Gris flavors. Enjoy this wine soon, with a pork or veal entrée.

Ed: 88–90   **Mary:** 89–91

Fendant, Vétroz Les Terrasses, Germanier Balavaud

- **Producer:** Germanier Balavaud
- **Wine name:** Fendant, Vétroz Les Terrasses
- **Appellation:** Vétroz
- **Price:** $18

Germanier Balavaud is one of the leading producers in the Valais region; its winery and vineyards are in Vétroz, a hamlet adjacent to the town of Sion (the wine production center of the Valais). Germanier makes many different wines, but its most important one is the Fendant, Les Terasses. The 1995 Les Terrasses has a penetrating aroma that's minerally and slightly nutty, and its flavors suggest flowers, melon, earth, and minerals. It's dry, medium bodied, and richly flavorful, with a slightly oily texture and very good concentration of earthy, minerally character. A very interesting and unique wine, the Les Terrasses will go well with delicate freshwater fish, such as trout. Drink it now, while it's young and fresh.

Ed: 86–88   **Mary:** 87–89

St. Saphorin, Roche Ronde, Testuz

- **Producer:** Jean et Pierre Testuz
- **Wine name:** St. Saphorin, Roche Ronde
- **Appellation:** St. Saphorin
- **Price:** $27

St. Saphorin is a wine village on the shores of Lake Geneva in the Vaud region, and Roche Ronde is a single vineyard from which Testuz obtains the Chasselas grapes for this wine. (All the wines of the Vaud are made from the Chasselas grape variety unless their label specifies a different grape.) The 1995 Roche Ronde has rich, buttery, and minerally aromas and flavors. The wine is rich in texture, solid in weight, and yet crisp and firm. Despite its rather full body, it shows great finesse. You can enjoy the Roche Ronde now or within the next year or two, with a grilled lake trout or perch.

Ed: 86–88   **Mary:** 85–87

A Sampling from Austria

Austria's best wines come from small producers who generally own their own vineyards. These wines are in small production and are available mainly in specialty wine shops in major cities. But they're worth the effort to find them because not only are they high-quality, provocative wines, but they also are the first wave of what is bound to become a very important segment of the fine wine market.

For more information on Austrian white wines, refer to *White Wine For Dummies*, Chapter 14.

Sauvignon Blanc, Tement

- **Producer:** E & M Tement
- **Wine name:** Sauvignon
- **Appellation:** South Styria
- **Price:** $19.50

The Styria region of Austria is in the south of the country, bordering on Slovenia. Producers there claim that the district known as South Styria is a perfect area for growing Sauvignon Blanc — and judging from the several fine examples we've had, we suspect that they're right. Tement's 1995 Sauvignon Blanc has an intense aroma and flavors suggesting lemon, lime, vegetal notes, nuttiness, and malt. The wine is rather full bodied and dry, with crisp acidity and plenty of flavor. It offers just what we want in Sauvignon Banc: character and refreshment, side by side.

Ed: 86–88   **Mary:** 87–89

Ried Steinriegel Riesling Smaragd, Franz Prager

- **Producer:** Weingut Franz Prager
- **Wine name:** Riesling Smaragd, Ried Steinriegel
- **Appellation:** Wachau
- **Price:** $32.50

The Franz Prager winery makes impressive Rieslings and Grüner Veltliners from individual vineyards in the Wachau district of northern Austria. The richest wines are those designated *smaragd,* a term used locally in Wachau to indicate wines from riper grapes. Prager's 1995 Riesling Smaragd from the Ried Steinriegel vineyard has a piercing mineral aroma and citrus and peach fruit aromas, with mineral notes. It's medium to full bodied, rich, unctuous, and yet alive with freshness from its crisp acidity and succulent flavor. Still very young, this Riesling will improve for at least a year or two in the bottle. We enjoy it with smoked fish.

Ed: 88–90   **Mary:** 87–89

Chapter 8

The Best of the Rest: New World White Wines Over $15

*R*ed wines tend to be more expensive than white wines, and wines from the classic wine regions of Europe tend to cost more than wines from New World wine countries such as the U.S., Australia, and New Zealand. The wines we review in this chapter are exceptions to both rules, however: Although they are white and non-European, their prices range from just over $15 all the way up to $45 a bottle.

Many of the wines in this chapter are also exceptions to the rule that white wines are made to be consumed young. For many of the Chardonnay wines, in particular, we advise giving the wine a year or two of age between the time you buy it (assuming the wine is about two years old when you buy it) and the time you drink it. The reason for this suggestion is that most of these wines have absorbed some tannin from the oak barrels in which they aged, and the extra time enables their oaky character to quiet down.

We begin our reviews with white wines from the U.S., move to the wines of Australia and New Zealand, and conclude with white wines from South Africa.

For each wine, we list the following information:

- **The producer:** This is the company that makes the wine, and its name is often the brand name of the wine.

- **The wine name:** For New World wines, the wine name is usually a grape name.

✔ **The appellation of the wine:** A wine's *appellation* tells you the geographic area in which the grapes for that wine grew. Every wine must carry a geographic appellation. (When we review wines from two or more countries in the same section, we indicate each wine's country of origin in parentheses after the appellation.)

✔ **The approximate retail price of the wine:** This price can vary quite a bit according to what part of the country you're in and the type of store where you buy your wine. We use the New York State suggested retail price.

In this chapter, as in the rest of the book, we rate each wine on a scale of 100 according to how much we like it. Remember that taste is personal; no matter how high a wine ranks on our pleasure scale, you won't necessarily like it unless the particular style of that wine appeals to you. Let the description of each wine guide you in determining which wines might be your own favorites.

Elite U.S. White Wines

Chardonnay monopolizes the field of expensive domestic white wines even more than it does the less expensive category, because wines made from grapes other than Chardonnay usually sell at lower prices than Chardonnays do. (The grapes themselves are less expensive, for one thing; also, the wines are in less demand, thus inflating prices less.)

We discuss Chardonnay wines first and then review wines such as Sauvignon Blanc, Riesling, Gewurztraminer, and so forth. Nearly all our entries in this section are California wines, not because we overlooked the wines of other states, but because most of our choices from places such as New York State and Washington State fell into a lower price bracket; we cover those wines in Chapter 6.

Premium U.S. Chardonnay

We constantly rail against Chardonnay because (a) so much poor Chardonnay wine is out there; (b) variety really is more interesting than monotony; and (c) we tend to favor underdogs. But the Chardonnay grape is truly the finest white wine grape in the world. (Its only close competitor being Riesling.) The Chardonnay grape is capable of making extraordinary wines, and just about all the best white wines in the U.S. are made from Chardonnay. Within the $15-a-bottle-and-higher category of U.S. wines, Chardonnay is king.

All good Chardonnay wines are made entirely from the Chardonnay grape; nearly all expensive U.S. Chardonnays are also either fermented or aged in small barrels made of French oak. Naturally, no two Chardonnays are exactly alike, however, because of variations in the grapes' growing conditions and in the production of the wine.

But a family resemblance does exist among California Chardonnays. More than anything else, these wines tend to be quite high in alcohol, which makes for full-bodied, big wines with a slight impression of sweetness and/or a hard edge to the flavor, depending on how high the alcohol is and your personal threshold for detecting it. Many California Chardonnays also tend to be very flavorful. These big, flavorful wines can be delicious, but because they come on so strong, they're not easy to match with food.

In this section, we review our favorite U.S. Chardonnay wines costing from $15 to $50 — all of which happen to be from California. The wines we recommend tend to be rather restrained within the California Chardonnay idiom; they are likely to be less overtly flavorful and also lighter in alcohol than their fellow Chardonnays. That's our taste. (Because these Chardonnays are more subtle, you should be sure not to serve them very cold, or you'll wonder where the flavor is.)

We list our recommended wines alphabetically by producer.

Au Bon Climat Chardonnay, Talley Reserve

- ✔ **Producer:** Au Bon Climat
- ✔ **Wine name:** Chardonnay, Talley Reserve
- ✔ **Appellation:** Arroyo Grande Valley
- ✔ **Price:** $30

The Talley Reserve Chardonnay is one of five or six Chardonnay wines that owner-winemaker Jim Clendenen usually produces each year. These wines are made in the concentrated, minerally, somewhat austere style of a full-bodied white Burgundy. His Reserve Chardonnays, such as this one, usually benefit from a year or two of bottle aging because they're typically somewhat reticent when they're first released. The 1995 Talley Reserve — still a very young wine — has smoky oak, spice, and ripe fruit aromas and flavors. It has the crispness typical of all Au Bon Climat's Chardonnays, which helps to counter this wine's rich, full, voluptuous character.

The wine is well balanced, with good flavor concentration and a long finish. You can enjoy the 1995 Talley Reserve now, but I'd hold on to it for one more year to let it develop further.

Ed: 87–89

Beringer Private Reserve Chardonnay

- ☞ **Producer:** Beringer Vineyards
- ☞ **Wine name:** Chardonnay, Private Reserve
- ☞ **Appellation:** Napa Valley
- ☞ **Price:** $30

Each year, at the International Wine Center, we conduct a blind tasting of about 12 of the highest-rated, most elite California Chardonnays. Year after year, the Beringer Private Reserve is one of the tasters' favorites — sometimes even ranking first — and it's invariably one of the least expensive wines in the tasting. Typically, this wine shows aromas and flavors of ripe fruit, honey, and nuts, as well as definite oakiness; it's usually high in alcohol, but it also has enough acidity to balance the alcohol. The 1995 Private Reserve Chardonnay is still quite young and therefore is still dominated by an intense oaky character in both its aroma and flavor. Its rich texture, full body, and sweetness of high alcohol suggest that this wine has the right stuff to balance the oak, however.

Ed: 85–87   **Mary:** 86–88

Chalk Hill Winery Chardonnay

- ☞ **Producer:** Chalk Hill Winery
- ☞ **Wine name:** Chardonnay
- ☞ **Appellation:** Chalk Hill
- ☞ **Price:** $24

I've been a big fan of Chalk Hill Winery Chardonnay for years — despite my usual distaste for the rich, soft, and fleshy style of Chardonnay (which is what Chalk Hill Chardonnay is). I make an exception for Chalk Hill Chardonnay because it's so well made that its richness never gets out of hand; the rich, soft elements of the wine are always balanced by notes of firmness or restraint. The 1995 Chalk Hill Chardonnay, for example, has lovely, restrained aromas and flavors of toasty, smoky oak and nutty character; the high-alcohol hugeness of the wine and its soft richness of texture are offset not only by the subdued nature of the flavors, but also by the wine's tight concentration. As a result, the wine manages not to be flamboyant. The 1994 Chalk Hill shows the same artful balancing of richness and restraint: The full-bodied, smoky wine has a core of very concentrated lemony fruit character, creating a combined impression of come-on richness and stand-firm crispness. Because they're so well balanced, Chalk Hill Chardonnays tend to age nicely over about five years.

Mary: 91–93

Cronin Chardonnay, Stuhlmuller Vineyard

> *!* **Producer:** Cronin Vineyards
>
> *!* **Wine name:** Chardonnay, Stuhlmuller Vineyard
>
> *!* **Appellation:** Alexander Valley
>
> *!* **Price:** $22

Duane Cronin is a Chardonnay specialist whose wines are highly regarded by those in the know. Considering how good his Chardonnays are and how small their production is, the prices Cronin charges are unusually fair. We like Cronin's 1994 Alexander Valley Chardonnay from grapes grown in Stuhlmuller Vineyard for its knockout aroma of smoky oak and honey — the classic scent of a barrel-fermented Chardonnay. The wine's flavors suggest lemon and orange, even a bit of orange peel, but they're fairly subdued. This wine is fairly dry (not an automatic assumption for California Chardonnay), full bodied, smooth textured, and well balanced, and we believe that it has the right stuff to age nicely for a few years. Mary likes Cronin's Napa Valley Chardonnay ($23) even slightly more than this Alexander Valley wine.

Ed: 84–86   **Mary:** 87–89

Fisher Chardonnay, Whitney's Vineyard

> *!* **Producer:** Fisher Vineyards
>
> *!* **Wine name:** Chardonnay, Whitney's Vineyard
>
> *!* **Appellation:** Sonoma County
>
> *!* **Price:** $28

High up in the Mayacamas Mountains, just as you cross over the county line from Napa into Sonoma, lie Fred Fisher's winery and vineyards. Fisher Vineyards is one of those wineries that has been around for a while (since 1973) but has taken a big leap in quality in its wines — both red and white — during the 90s. The 1994 Whitney's Vineyard Chardonnay has rich lemony and mushroomy aromas, with ripe lemony flavors (almost like lemon drop candy) and some incipient honey, accented by oak and caramel. It's a lush, full-bodied, easy-to-drink Chardonnay that you can enjoy now or within the next two years. (If you have difficulty locating the Whitney's Vineyard wine, Fisher's Coach Insignia Chardonnay, at $18 to $20, is almost as good, just a little less intensely flavored, and is more readily available.)

Ed: 89–91   **Mary:** 90–92

Gallo-Sonoma Chardonnay, Laguna Ranch

- ♪ **Producer:** Gallo-Sonoma
- ♪ **Wine Name:** Chardonnay, Laguna Ranch
- ♪ **Appellation:** Russian River Valley
- ♪ **Price:** $16

Gallo's venture into the fine wine business has proved itself with this well-priced Chardonnay made from grapes grown at its Laguna Ranch vineyard in the cool Russian River Valley in Sonoma. Gina Gallo, granddaughter of the late Julio Gallo, is one of the winemakers here. The 1995 Laguna Ranch Chardonnay has concentrated citrusy and smoky oak aromas; its flavors suggest lemon, apple, and pear fruit, with smoky, nutty accents. It's a vibrant wine with lively acidity balancing the concentrated fruit flavors. An impressive Chardonnay, and a good value.

Ed: 88–90

Handley Cellars Estate Chardonnay

- ♪ **Producer:** Handley Cellars
- ♪ **Wine name:** Chardonnay "Estate Grown"
- ♪ **Appellation:** Anderson Valley
- ♪ **Price:** $16

Milla Handley makes two Chardonnay wines, one that carries a Dry Creek Valley appellation ($18) and this wine, which is made from grapes grown around her winery, in the cool Anderson Valley. The Dry Creek Valley wine is the richer of the two, but we prefer the Estate Chardonnay for its crisp, elegant, and restrained style. The 1995 Estate has a subdued, nutty aroma and a restrained but concentrated flavor of ripe lemon. Although it's creamy in texture and rather full bodied, its high acidity gives it an edge of crispness that's very appealing. This wine has plenty of substance in the form of its concentrated, tight lemony fruit character, and it should age beautifully, developing honeyed and spicy character. (In fact, Milla Handley says that this wine ages very slowly in the bottle.) In the meantime, enjoy it with lemon chicken, simple turkey, or Veal Piccata.

Ed: 88–90   **Mary:** 89–91

Hanzell Vineyards Chardonnay

> ! **Producer:** Hanzell Vineyards
> ! **Wine name:** Chardonnay
> ! **Appellation:** Sonoma County
> ! **Price:** $32

If we had to name the two U.S. wineries with the best track records for making world-class Chardonnays, we'd choose Hanzell Vineyards and the even more obscure Mount Eden Vineyards in the Santa Cruz Mountains (not to be confused with Villa Mt. Eden, a Napa Valley winery). We've had many memorable Chardonnays from these two wineries over the years. Mount Eden's been at it since 1972, but Hanzell traces its roots back to the mid-1950s. Its present winemaker, Bob Sessions, is carrying on the Hanzell tradition admirably.

The 1994 Hanzell Chardonnay has aromas of vanilla and caramel, with flavors of mango and ripe pears, accented with oak. Like most Hanzell Chardonnays, it's a big, firm, complex wine that will benefit from a few years of aging. We've enjoyed Hanzell Chardonnays with ten and more years of age that still were in great shape. Hanzell Chardonnays go well with flavorful poultry, such as duck, squab, or Cornish game hen.

Ed: 89–91   **Mary:** 88–90

Jordan Chardonnay

> ! **Producer:** Jordan Vineyards
> ! **Wine name:** Chardonnay
> ! **Appellation:** Sonoma County
> ! **Price:** $24

Jordan Chardonnay is like a trusted old friend to us. Sure, there are sexier Chardonnays, but you can't always find them when you need them. And sure, some Chardonnays are more thrilling, but you never know what you're going to get from vintage to vintage. And if playing the field of tiny-production, single-vineyard Chardonnays is fun, so is coming home.

The 1994 Jordan Chardonnay has a quiet, subtle aroma, toasty flavors of oak and *lees* (grape and yeast solids that contribute a nutty flavor to the wine during aging), and underlying mineral flavors. Full bodied but not full blown, this wine has a tight core of concentrated fruit character that will enable it to age nicely. And it's actually dry.

Ed: 88–90   **Mary:** 90–92

Kistler Chardonnay, Durell Vineyard

> ! **Producer:** Kistler Vineyards
> ! **Wine name:** Chardonnay, Durell Vineyard
> ! **Appellation:** Sonoma Valley
> ! **Price:** $38

Kistler is one of the hottest and most respected names in California Chardonnay; every one of the Chardonnays that this winery produces (each made from the grapes of a single vineyard) is excellent. We were recently bowled over by the 1994 Kistler Chardonnay from Durell Vineyard grapes. It's a full-throttle Chardonnay: full bodied, rich, voluptuous, flamboyantly oaky and sweet, and thick with presence in your mouth. And yet it's subtle in its actual flavors, with classic smokiness à la white Burgundy, some sour lemon, and other barely perceptible (at this young age) flavors giving an intriguing impression of complexity. If you're in the mood for something outrageous, look for this wine in better wine shops; if you come across a different vintage or vineyard of Kistler Chardonnay, rest assured that it's also good.

Ed: 87–89   **Mary:** 89–91

Matanzas Creek Chardonnay

- ♪ **Producer:** Matanzas Creek Winery
- ♪ **Wine name:** Chardonnay
- ♪ **Appellation:** Sonoma Valley
- ♪ **Price:** $30

Matanzas Creek makes the most expensive Chardonnay in the U.S., a wine called Journey that sells for $70 a bottle. That wine is blended from the best barrels of the winery's normal Chardonnay and is produced only in the best vintages. Although it's an excellent wine, Journey needs plenty of age in the bottle to show its stuff, and drinking it as soon as you buy it is a pity. Not so for the regular bottling of Matanzas Creek Chardonnay: Its rich flavors are ready when you are. The 1995 version has exotic aromas and flavors that suggest banana, ripe lemon, apples, honey, and coffee; something about the wine almost suggests apple pie, too — butter, apples, and burnt sugar. The wine is full bodied, rich, thickly textured, creamy, and opulent. Match it with an equally opulent dish, such as lobster.

Ed: 85–87   **Mary:** 86–88

Ravenswood Chardonnay, Sangiacomo Vineyard

ED'S CHOICE

- ♪ **Producer:** Ravenswood
- ♪ **Wine name:** Chardonnay, Sangiacomo Vineyard
- ♪ **Appellation:** Carneros
- ♪ **Price:** $26

The Sangiacomo Vineyard in Carneros has been a great source of grapes for Ravenswood's Merlots and, lately, also for some excellent Chardonnays. Talented winemaker Joel Peterson made his reputation with Zinfandel, but he seems to do well with every variety he handles. The 1995 Ravenswood Sangiacomo Chardonnay has exotic aromas of smoky oak, as well as flavors of citrus and green apple. It's a complex, lushly flavored wine with exquisite balance and a long finish. This wine is quite delicious right now, but Ravenswood Sangiacomo Chardonnays do age well, if you choose to keep the wine for a few years.

Ed: 91–93

Simi Chardonnay

- ♪ **Producer:** Simi Vineyards
- ♪ **Wine name:** Chardonnay
- ♪ **Appellation:** Sonoma-Mendocino-Napa
- ♪ **Price:** $19

Simi Chardonnay is one of the good old reliables of California Chardonnay, always decent and, compared with the cost of other Chardonnays, nearly a steal. Simi blends its Chardonnay from grapes grown in three counties to achieve complexity; hence, the wine carries an unusual three-part appellation.

The 1995 Simi Chardonnay has aromas of woody oak and lemon drops and flavors of ripe apples, earthiness, and candied lemon. The wine is full bodied and fairly flavorful, with attractive, crisp acidity. It's still a bit young; you can drink it easily now, but we suspect that it will continue to improve in the bottle for a year or so. Unlike many a California Chardonnay, Simi Chardonnay is not so huge that you can't enjoy it with a meal, such as fried chicken. If your taste runs more toward Chardonnays that are quite oaky, try the Simi Reserve Chardonnay, about $31.

Ed: 84–86 **Mary:** 85–87

Sonoma-Cutrer Chardonnay, Cutrer Vineyard

- ♪ **Producer:** Sonoma-Cutrer
- ♪ **Wine name:** Chardonnay, Cutrer Vineyard
- ♪ **Appellation:** Sonoma Coast
- ♪ **Price:** $27

Sonoma-Cutrer produces only Chardonnay, crafting three clean, crisp, well-made, single-vineyard wines in its state-of-the-art winery. After slipping a bit in quality during the late '80s, the wines have come back strong since the 1992 vintage. Of Sonoma-Cutrer's three Chardonnays, I tend to prefer the one made in the Cutrer Vineyard on the cool Sonoma Coast. The 1994 Cutrer Vineyard Chardonnay has subtle, citrusy aromas and flavors, with touches of burnt sugar. It's a big, complexly flavored wine with excellent balance and a long, crisp finish. Try it with monkfish or snapper. Welcome back, Sonoma-Cutrer!

Ed: 90–92

Wines from other grape varieties and blends

The landscape of the non-Chardonnay white wine scene in the U.S. changes dramatically after you cross the $15 line. Sauvignon Blanc, a common sight among inexpensive white wines, almost disappears from view, as do the delicate Semillon-based wines of Washington State and the dry Rieslings of New York. Meanwhile, Viognier wines, based on the white Viognier grape of the Rhône Valley in France, suddenly pop up all over the place.

Viognier is in fairly strong demand among wine lovers these days, but it's in short supply. And Viognier wines are sometimes (but not always) produced using oak barrels, which increases the cost of the wine. All of these factors explain why Viognier wines cost as much as Chardonnay. The perfumey, peachy character of the wine is quite different from Chardonnay, however; in fact, Viognier is different from everything. Maybe that's why it's in demand.

We review some of our favorite Viognier wines and other non-Chardonnays in this section, alphabetically by producer.

Alban Vineyards Estate Viognier

- ♪ **Producer:** Alban Vineyards
- ♪ **Wine name:** Viognier, Estate *(vee oh nyay)*
- ♪ **Appellation:** Edna Valley
- ♪ **Price:** $29

John Alban believes in Viognier. In the mid '80s, he planted 32 acres of Viognier on his property in the Edna Valley area of southern California. In fact, his is the only winery we know that specializes in this difficult-to-grow variety. Alban's gamble on a relatively unknown grape (on California soil, anyway) has already paid off, in a wine that is well regarded and commands a very high price. The 1995 Alban Estate Viognier (as opposed to his less expensive Central Coast bottling) has a persistent, concentrated lemon aroma and pronounced lemony flavor, along with some oaky notes. It's a dry, full-bodied, firm, solid wine that's less soft and opulent than many other wines from this grape. Match it with a fairly simple dish, such as grilled swordfish.

Ed: 89–91   **Mary:** 86–88

Arrowood Viognier

> ♪ **Producer:** Arrowood Vineyards
>
> ♪ **Wine name:** Viognier, Saralee's Vineyard
>
> ♪ **Appellation:** Russian River Valley
>
> ♪ **Price:** $30

Richard Arrowood attained renown as the winemaker for many years at Chateau St. Jean winery, where he specialized in white wines. Now that he has his own winery in Sonoma, he's rising to new heights with both his red and his white wines. Arrowood's 1995 Viognier has fascinating, complex aromas of cinnamon, ripe apple, white pepper, and oak, with trademark Viognier flavors of apricot and peaches. The crispness of the acidity and a bit of attractive bitterness nicely balance the soft, generous fruit flavors. This delicious wine ends with a long, concentrated finish. Try this Viognier with a delicate fish preparation.

A word of caution about all Viognier wines: They're at their best when they're young and fresh. About three years after the vintage, they start aging rapidly. The 1995 Arrowood, for example, will offer optimal enjoyment until about the end of 1998.

Ed: 91–93   **Mary:** 84–86

Cakebread Sauvignon Blanc

> ♪ **Producer:** Cakebread Cellars
>
> ♪ **Wine name:** Sauvignon Blanc
>
> ♪ **Appellation:** Napa Valley
>
> ♪ **Price:** $16.50

We often complain about the dearth of good Sauvignon Blanc wines in the U.S. However, the Cakebread Sauvignon Blanc stands out as a fine wine from this grape variety. The 1995 Cakebread is loaded with fairly intense aromas and flavors of fresh pears, herbs, and green grass. But the wine is not overly assertive; it has delicate, fresh, restrained flavors, plenty of personality, and good concentration. It's equally at home with a fillet of flounder, a simple grilled chicken, or a warm goat cheese salad. Drink it within three years of the vintage; Sauvignon Blancs are best when they're young.

Ed: 87–89   **Mary:** 87–89

Calera Viognier

- *?* **Producer:** Calera Wine Company
- *?* **Wine name:** Viognier
- *?* **Appellation:** Mount Harlan (San Benito County)
- *?* **Price:** $33.50

Calera owner Josh Jensen, with his sunbeaten, chiseled profile, looks as if he should be starring in Western films. Instead, this rugged individualist is turning out fine wines on remote Mount Harlan in central California. Calera winery was one of the very first in California to attain fame for extraordinary Pinot Noir wines, closer in quality to great red Burgundy than any other California Pinots. Not content with that difficult achievement, Jensen took on another "challenging" variety, Viognier. How's he doing? Critics generally acknowledge that, along with Alban Estate and Arrowood, Calera's is one of the three finest Viogniers in the U.S., and some critics put Calera at the very top of the pack.

Calera's Viognier, made from fruit grown in a low-yielding mountain vineyard, is clearly the fullest and most robust one that I've tried. The 1996 wine has delicate, attractive herbal and piney aromas, with flavors of peach skin and ripe apricot. It's a well-made, complex Viognier with tons of flavor intensity and a long finish. I'm pleased to see the 1996 vintage available for sale already, by the way, because Viognier wines need to be as young and fresh as possible in order to show their wonderful aromas and flavors.

Ed: 92–94

De Lille Cellars "Chaleur Estate White"

- *?* **Producer:** De Lille Cellars
- *?* **Wine name:** "Chaleur Estate White"
- *?* **Appellation:** Columbia Valley
- *?* **Price:** $18

The great white wines of Bordeaux are the inspiration for this excellent Washington wine blended from Sauvignon Blanc (about two-thirds of the blend) and Semillon. In the European style, "Chaleur Estate" is subtle and understated in its flavors, a gentle wine rather than a savory powerhouse. The 1995

"Chaleur Estate White" (we review the companion red in Chapter 4) has flavors of toasty oak and lime and a gently smoky aroma from the French oak barrels in which the wine was born. In our opinion, this full-bodied, dry, and above all, discreet wine is the best white wine in all of Washington. Considering its quality, we believe that "Chaleur" is a bargain at $18 — if you like the style, as we do.

Ed: 87–89   **Mary:** 88–90

Eyrie Pinot Gris

> *!* **Producer:** The Eyrie Vineyards *(EYE ree)*
> *!* **Wine name:** Pinot Gris
> *!* **Appellation:** Willamette Valley
> *!* **Price:** $16

For many years now, The Eyrie Vineyards has led the way in producing classic Oregon Pinot Gris. Winemaker-proprietor David Lett was, in fact, among the first to make a Pinot Gris wine in the U.S. The 1995 Eyrie Pinot Gris has a deep yellow-gold hue with a glint of copper; spicy pear and apple aromas, along with some earthy tones; and earthy, fruity flavors. It's dry, medium bodied, and well balanced, but its concentration of fruit makes it seem almost sweet. This is an excellent wine, perhaps the best Pinot Gris outside of Alsace. It's a fine accompaniment to grilled salmon or other full-flavored fish, as well as seafood entrées.

Ed: 89–91   **Mary:** 88–90

Martinelli Gewurztraminer

> *!* **Producer:** Martinelli Vineyards
> *!* **Wine name:** Gewurztraminer, Martinelli Vineyard
> *!* **Appellation:** Russian River Valley
> *!* **Price:** $16.50

With a handful of exceptions, the spicy, flower-scented Gewurztraminer grape has failed miserably in the hands of most U.S. wineries. Martinelli Vineyards is one of those exceptions. The Martinelli family, grape growers since the beginning of the century, started making its own wine about ten years ago. The winery is best known for its fine Zinfandels, but lately it's also gaining fame for Gewurztraminer. The 1996 Martinelli Vineyard Gewurztraminer has pure varietal expression of a sort that's seldom found outside of Alsace, France. The wine shows rich, intense aromas and flavors of roses and lychee fruit. The crisp acidity of this full-bodied wine counters the rich, exotic fruit character perfectly. We suggest that you try this wine soon (it's best when it's young) with Chinese food, other spicy Asian cuisine, or simply some flavorful cheeses.

Ed: 88–90

Preston Vineyards Viognier

- ✔ **Producer:** Preston Vineyards
- ✔ **Wine name:** Viognier *(vee oh nyay)*
- ✔ **Appellation:** Dry Creek Valley
- ✔ **Price:** $21

Two wineries named Preston exist on the West Coast. The California one, Preston Vineyards (whose wine we review here), is probably better known than Preston Wine Cellars in Washington State, although the Washington winery produces more wine. Lou Preston, of California, is a fan of grape varieties from the Rhône Valley of France, such as Syrah, and he makes several wines based on Rhône grapes, including this Viognier. Preston's 1995 Viognier is not the richest, most opulent Viognier going — in fact, its smoky, grassy, lemony aroma almost resembles austere Sauvignon Blanc fruit more than exotic Viognier. But the soft texture, full body, and ample weight of the wine in your mouth — all well balanced by crisp acidity — are typical Viognier. This well-made, dry wine also sports a little honey flavor. Serve it with a dish that's not weak in flavor but not aggressively flavorful, either; grilled sausages are a good companion.

Ed: 88–90   **Mary:** 87–89

J. Rochioli Sauvignon Blanc Reserve

- ❢ **Producer:** J. Rochioli Vineyards *(roke ee OH lee)*
- ❢ **Wine name:** Sauvignon Blanc Reserve Old Vines
- ❢ **Appellation:** Russian River Valley
- ❢ **Price:** $32

The name Rochioli appears on wine labels in two capacities: Sometimes *Rochioli* is the brand name for wine produced by the J. Rochioli winery from grapes grown in its own vineyards in the Russian River Valley section of Sonoma, and sometimes *Rochioli* is the vineyard source of grapes used by other wineries. (In the case of this Sauvignon Blanc, Rochioli is both the grape grower and the wine producer.) Rochioli does a great job with its Sauvignon Blanc, although there isn't much of it to go around. The 1995 Sauvignon Blanc Reserve has a strong aroma of pure, concentrated lemon and a slightly floral note; its flavor is intense, too, mainly suggesting sweet, ripe lemon. This rich, full-bodied wine has a slight sweetness due to its very concentrated fruit flavor and high alcohol. It's so big and flavorful that it needs a rich food; anything creamy makes a nice match.

Ed: 85–87   **Mary:** 86–88

Signorello Barrel-Fermented Semillon

- 🍷 **Producer:** Signorello Vineyards
- 🍷 **Wine name:** Semillon, Barrel Fermented
- 🍷 **Appellation:** Napa Valley
- 🍷 **Price:** $23

The Semillon grape and the wine it produces have had much less success in the U.S. than in such wine regions as Bordeaux in France or the Hunter Valley in Australia. But Signorello Vineyards is doing a good job with Semillon in California's Napa Valley. Signorello's successful 1994 Semillon has been followed by an equally good 1995 wine. The wine has complex aromas and flavors of ripe melon, figs, lemon, pear, and oak. A rich, well-balanced wine with unique aromas and flavors, Signorello Semillon deserves contemplation. But right now, it needs time to develop. Try this Semillon with some Greek cuisine; it's especially good with feta cheese.

Ed: 87–89

Australia and New Zealand

One thing that the Australian wine industry has accomplished so brilliantly is the production of truly delicious white wines. Furthermore, Australian wineries manage to sell these delicious wines at very affordable prices.

This section, however, deals with a different category of Australian white wine: elite wines. These wines, made by small producers or in small quantities, have a style and caliber to compete with the Really Serious White Wines of Europe and the U.S. Unfortunately, such wines are available rather spottily in the U.S., because American wine drinkers are still busy clamoring for more of Australia's delicious inexpensive wines.

We review a few of Australia's elite white wines in this section, along with the New Zealand Sauvignon Blanc that helped the northern world discover a whole new interpretation of that grape. We review the wines alphabetically by producer.

Cape Mentelle Chardonnay

- ❢ **Producer:** Cape Mentelle
- ❢ **Wine name:** Chardonnay
- ❢ **Appellation:** Margaret River (Australia)
- ❢ **Price:** $20

We've heard that unoaked Chardonnays are all the rage in Australia, but this wine isn't one of them. It goes in the other direction entirely: oaky and rich. The aromas of the 1994 Cape Mentelle Chardonnay suggest smoky, butterscotch scents (from oak) and ripe melon fruit. The flavor is similarly oaky, with some earthiness showing, but the fruity flavors are buried beneath the oakiness right now. The wine is fairly dry and fairly full bodied and has a refreshing crispness of acidity. Although all this oakiness might not sound appetizing, this wine is, in fact, a balanced, sophisticated Chardonnay. We recommend waiting a year or two before drinking it, however, so that its fruit flavors can emerge from behind the oak.

Mary: 86–88

Cloudy Bay Sauvignon Blanc

- ❢ **Producer:** Cloudy Bay
- ❢ **Wine name:** Sauvignon Blanc
- ❢ **Appellation:** Marlborough (New Zealand)
- ❢ **Price:** $16

Cloudy Bay Sauvignon Blanc is a sensation. This wine forced wine lovers all over the world to sit up and take notice. The 1996 Cloudy Bay Sauvignon Blanc has a wonderful aroma that could be called grassy, although the winery's literature describes the aroma as suggestive of "passion fruit and wild herbs." But to us, it smells a bit like scallions (wild herbs?), in the nicest way imaginable. The wine is full bodied and very flavorful, with good concentration of fruit character; crisp, piercing acidity; and no oakiness. The wine's lean characteristics and its full, rich characteristics play off each other in your mouth, creating a striking complexity in the wine. For some reason, we'd like to try this wine with a white bean salad or a thin piece of grilled veal; maybe we're inspired by the scallions.

Ed: 90–92   **Mary:** 90–92

Lindemans Chardonnay, Padthaway

> ❦ **Producer:** Lindemans
> ❦ **Wine name:** Chardonnay Padthaway
> ❦ **Appellation:** South Australia (Australia)
> ❦ **Price:** $15.50

Lindemans "Bin 65" Chardonnay, its under-$10 Chardonnay wine, is a big hit with wine drinkers. But Lindemans Padthaway Chardonnay, from grapes grown in a cooler area in South Australia, is the winery's best Chardonnay — and at a reasonable $15 and change. The Padthaway has a pronounced aroma of smoky oak and moderately subdued flavors of pineapple and pear beneath a mantle of smoky oak character. Creamy, soft, and rich, this wine is a fine value for the money. If you like the "Bin 65," why not step up to Lindemans Padthaway Chardonnay for your next special meal?

Ed: 86–88   **Mary:** 84–86

Mitchelton III White

> ❦ **Producer:** Mitchelton
> ❦ **Wine name:** Mitchelton III White
> ❦ **Appellation:** Goulburn Valley (Australia)
> ❦ **Price:** $16

The Mitchelton winery produces two wines named Mitchelton III, a white and a red, both blends of grapes from the Rhône Valley of France. The white is 60 percent Marsanne, with the balance split evenly between the Viognier and Roussanne grapes. The result of this blend is a fascinating dry white wine with fresh aromas and flavors that are slightly floral, slightly herbal, slightly spicy, and slightly smoky. Although the 1994 Mitchelton III is crisp with acidity, it has an unusual rich, oily texture and the full body typical of a Rhône Valley white. Try this wine with grilled portobello mushrooms.

Mary: 85–87

Rosemount "Show Reserve" Semillon

> *!* **Producer:** Rosemount Estate
>
> *!* **Wine name:** Semillon, "Show Reserve"
>
> *!* **Appellation:** Hunter Valley (Australia)
>
> *!* **Price:** $21.50

The Semillon grape, one of the major white grapes of Bordeaux, performs just as uniquely in Australia's Hunter Valley as Sauvignon Blanc, the other important white grape of Bordeaux, performs in New Zealand. The real magic of Australian Semillon lies in the way the wine develops with age. When this type of wine is more than about seven years old, even experienced wine lovers can confuse it with a white Burgundy, because of the honeyed richness and smokiness that the wine develops. The wine's apparent oaky character adds to the confusion — although no white Burgundy can boast the exotic orange marmalade and lime flavor of an Australian Semillon.

When Semillon is young, as the 1995 Rosemount Show Reserve Semillon is now, the wine has more subtle charms, such as an earthy, lemony aroma; smoky and fresh, lemony flavors; a rich, full body; and an unctuous texture. The wine is wonderful now and quite different from run-of-the-mill white wines, but its real beauty will prove itself in time. Until then, try it with a young goat cheese: fabulous!

Ed: 86–88   **Mary:** 87–89

South Africa's Top White Wines

The leading white grape variety in South Africa, in terms of quantity, is Chenin Blanc. But much of the Chenin Blanc production is relegated to inexpensive blends, sparkling wines, and an innocuous varietal wine called Steen. For fine white wines, the Chardonnay and Sauvignon Blanc grapes dominate.

Like New Zealand, South Africa has had even more success with Sauvignon Blanc so far than with the ever-popular Chardonnay, in terms of the wines' quality. But because of the worldwide popularity of Chardonnay wines, more and more South African wineries are concentrating on that variety. In this section, we recommend two Chardonnays and one Sauvignon Blanc that we believe are among the best white wines in South Africa today. We list them alphabetically by producer. For our recommendations of South African white wines that sell for less than $15 a bottle, see Chapter 6.

Hamilton Russell Chardonnay

- ♪ **Producer:** Hamilton Russell Vineyards
- ♪ **Wine name:** Chardonnay
- ♪ **Appellation:** Walker Bay
- ♪ **Price:** $16

Most of our favorite Chardonnays come from cool regions, which usually turn out the leaner, appley style of Chardonnay rather than the lush, tropical-fruit style of warmer regions. Hamilton Russell Vineyards is situated about as far south as you can go in Africa, in cool Walker Bay. Its 1996 Chardonnay has lemony, oaky aromas and flavors. It's a crisp, fresh Chardonnay, but it's also quite flavorful and rich, with complex fruit flavors and a long, dry finish. Based on the excellent staying power of previous Hamilton Russell Chardonnays we bet that you can hold on to this wine for quite a few years, if you're not in a hurry to drink it.

Ed: 87–89   **Mary:** 84–86

Plaisir de Merle Chardonnay

- ♪ **Producer:** Plaisir de Merle
- ♪ **Wine Name:** Chardonnay
- ♪ **Appellation:** Paarl
- ♪ **Price:** $19.50

Plaisir de Merle has been making wines for only a few years now (its first vintage was 1993), so you might not have heard of this winery. But we're so mightily impressed with its wines that we recommend all three of them in this book. (There's a Cabernet Sauvignon and a Sauvignon Blanc as well.) The 1995 Chardonnay has fresh, focused, lime fruit flavors and floral aromas with touches of vanilla and grapefruit. This well-balanced wine needs a bit more time to develop, but it's enjoyable even now. It reminds me somewhat of a white Burgundy in its style, but fortunately, the price doesn't approach the stratospheric level of most Burgundies. A winner!

Ed: 88–90

Plaisir de Merle Sauvignon Blanc

> ✔ **Producer:** Plaisir de Merle
> ✔ **Wine name:** Sauvignon Blanc
> ✔ **Appellation:** Paarl
> ✔ **Price:** $19.50

The five-year-old Plaisir de Merle winery has all the advantages of a privileged child in the wine world: a big-name wine consultant (Paul Pontallier, winemaker of Château Margaux in Bordeaux), an ultramodern facility, new French oak barrels, and some of the best vineyards in Paarl. Plaisir de Merle can thank its wealthy "daddy," the gigantic Stellenbosch Farmers Winery, South Africa's largest wine firm, for all the benefits. The money has been used to good advantage, because the Plaisir de Merle wines have been excellent from the first vintage. When Ed visited South Africa a few years ago, he returned frustrated that these fine wines weren't available in the U.S. Fortunately, that has changed.

The 1996 Sauvignon Blanc has subtle, smoky aromas with suggestions of lime and lanolin, and the crisp lime flavors are tinged with vanilla. It is well balanced and has good depth, and its flavor carries through well to the finish. Enjoy this Sauvignon now with grilled fish.

Ed: 86–88   **Mary:** 86–88

Recommended dry rosé wines

What do you do when the occasion calls for a light-bodied wine (at picnics, in warm weather, at large social functions, and so forth), but you don't feel like serving a white? At such times, we turn to a dry rosé wine as the perfect compromise — lighter than red, and redder than white.

Most of the rosé wines that we recommend here are on the dry side — not totally dry, like a red wine, but definitely not as sweet as blush wines or White Zinfandel. We find these wines refreshing and quaffable — the ideal warm-weather wine. Chill them in the fridge for a few hours before drinking. And drink them when they're young; rosé wines usually don't age well. We list ten rosé wines by country and then alphabetically by producer.

U.S. rosés:

- ✔ Cakebread Cellars, 1995 Rosé, Napa Valley: 76 percent Zinfandel; 24 percent Pinot Noir, 100 percent delicious. $15
- ✔ Étude, 1996 Rosé, Napa Valley: Made from 100 percent Pinot Noir, by one of California's top wineries. $11
- ✔ Swanson Vinyards, 1996 Rosato, Napa Valley: Made entirely from Sangiovese, totally dry, one of the best in the world. $11

French rosés:

- ✔ Fortant de France, 1993 Syrah Rosé, Vin de Pays d'Oc: From a reliable winery in southern France; made from the Syrah grape. $7
- ✔ Domaine Richaume, 1996 Rosé de Provence, Côtes de Provence: From Provence; absolutely delicious; very dry; one of the best. $12
- ✔ Chateau d'Acqueria, 1995 or 1996 Tavel Rosé: Consistently one of the top Rhône Valley rosés. $14

Italian rosé:

- ✔ Regaleali, 1996 Rosato, Vino da Tavola di Sicilia: One of our all-time favorite rosés; from a great winery in Sicily. $11

Spanish rosés:

- ✔ Bodegas Julian Chivite, 1996 Gran Feudo Rosado, Navarra: Navarra is a famous region for rosés; Chivite is an outstanding winery. $8
- ✔ Bodegas Montecillo, 1995 Rosado, Rioja: You won't believe how wonderful this is for the price! $6
- ✔ Conde de Valdemar, 1995 Rosado, Rioja: Another classy rosé from Rioja. $8.50

Part III
All Those Bubbles!

In this part . . .

*F*or us, life without Champagne and sparkling wine would be dreary indeed. No other wine perks us up quite like a bubbly wine. When one of us is feeling a bit out of sorts, the other suggests, "How about some Champagne?" We certainly don't wait around for special occasions to open a bottle of bubbly.

In this part, we share our passion for one of our favorite types of wine — Champagne. Chapter 9 includes reviews of dozens of specific wines from France's Champagne region. Then, in Chapter 10, we recommend some of our favorite sparkling wines from around the world, including the U.S., Italy, France, Australia, South Africa, and Spain. Here's to your health and happiness!

Chapter 9

Champagne: Only from France

. . . .

In This Chapter

▶ The region makes the wine

▶ Non-vintage versus vintage

▶ Rosé, blanc de blancs, and brut

▶ Great bubblies from $16 to $60

. . . .

*W*e love Champagne, and we suspect that we're not alone. Although Champagne is the beverage of celebration par excellence, we think that it's too good to save for special occasions.

Champagne wine is born in France's Champagne region, about 90 miles northeast of Paris. Most of the Champagne *houses,* as the wineries are called, are located either in the city of Rheims or in the town of Epernay.

Like any fine wine, Champagne expresses the particular climate and soil of its vineyards and the traditions of the people who make it. The Champagne tradition involves a specific production method that preserves bubbles in the wine and gives Champagne its unique quality and style. A cornerstone of this method is *blending.* Almost all Champagnes benefit from three levels of blending:

✔ **Blending of the wines from three different grape varieties:** Chardonnay, Pinot Noir, and Pinot Meunier. Although the last two are red grapes, their juice is vinified in such a way that their wine is white.

✔ **Blending of the wines from different vineyards:** For example, the wine of one vineyard can give power to the wine; the wine from another vineyard can give elegance; and so forth.

✔ **Blending of the wines of different years:** Eighty-five percent of all Champagne is classified as *non-vintage* — that is, not the product of a single year.

A few Champagnes (fewer than 5 percent) are made only from Chardonnay grapes. Such Champagnes, called *blanc de blancs,* are lighter bodied and usually more elegant than Champagnes blended from three grape varieties. Blanc de blancs Champagnes are ideal as apéritifs or for the first course in a meal. Rarer still is the *blanc de noirs* Champagne, made only from red (or, as they're known in the trade, "black") grapes.

Rosé Champagnes also make up a small but delicious part of the Champagne business. They're totally dry and usually more full bodied than other Champagnes. Rosé Champagne is especially suitable to serve with the main course during dinner.

Most Champagnes are dry and are labeled *brut* (which means "very dry" in Champagne language). *Extra brut, brut zero,* and *ultra brut* are all terms for even drier Champagnes, but these styles are rare. *Extra dry* Champagnes are slightly *less* dry than brut Champagnes. *Demi-sec* Champagnes are fairly sweet and should be enjoyed with desserts or on their own after dinner.

When "Champagne" is not Champagne

The French, especially those from the Champagne *(sham pahn yah)* region, get very upset when they see $3 to $6 bottles of undistinguished bubbly from California, New York, or Australia labeled as *Champagne.* And we don't blame them. The sparkling wine from the Champagne region of northeast France is special, and it deserves an identity that's different from that of other sparkling wines in the world.

European law permits the word *Champagne* to be used only for the sparkling wines from the Champagne region, but that law doesn't apply to wineries in non-European countries — and wineries outside of Europe have liberally "borrowed" the word for their own sparkling wines. Ironically, often the poorest examples of these non-European sparkling wines use the word *Champagne* on their labels, while the better sparkling wines refrain from using the word. *For the record, we believe that Champagne can only be made in one place: the Champagne region in France.* Everything else is sparkling wine, Sparkling Brut, Brut Spumante, Cava, Sekt, bubbly, or whatever else you want to call it, as long as you don't call it Champagne. (See Chapter 10 for our recommendations of sparkling wines from other parts of the world.)

We divide our Champagne recommendations into four categories:

- ✔ Non-vintage Champagnes
- ✔ Vintage Champagnes
- ✔ Blanc de blancs Champagnes (both non-vintage and vintage)
- ✔ Rosé Champagnes (both non-vintage and vintage)

Because all Champagnes are priced over $15, we don't divide our recommended wines into two price categories, as we do the other wines in the book. So many good Champagnes sell between $50 and $60, in fact, that we bend our own rules regarding the upper price limit and include Champagnes costing up to $60. (In any case, Champagne is one of the most heavily discounted wines on the market. Many stores seem to use them as *loss leaders* to lure customers.) Remember, the prices we're using are New York State *full-list* retail prices. Depending on where you shop, you might find lower prices.

We list the vital information for each wine in the following way:

- ✔ **The producer:** This is the company that makes the wine, and its name is usually considered the brand name of the wine.
- ✔ **The wine name:** For most of the wines in this chapter, the wine name is a fanciful name created to give a special cachet to the wine. This name usually incorporates a word such as *Brut* or *Rosé* that identifies the style of the wine.
- ✔ **The appellation:** The *appellation* is a necessary and legal part of a wine label, intended to tell you where the grapes that make up the wine came from and other technical information about the wine. Every wine in this chapter carries the appellation Champagne.
- ✔ **The approximate retail price of the wine:** This price can vary greatly according to where you live and the type of store where you buy your wine. We use New York State suggested retail prices.

Non-Vintage Brut Champagne

Non-vintage Champagnes are blends of wines from several vintages, usually three or more. Blending the wines of several vintages enables the winemaker to make a better sparkling wine than he would otherwise make. In most cases, blending evens out the weaknesses of any one vintage with the strengths of another and also creates complexity in the wine.

Non-vintage Champagne is the largest category of Champagne. Champagne producers often say that it's their favorite type of Champagne because it is the one type in which the winemaking style of each house is most evident. Almost all the non-vintage Champagnes we review in this section are made from a combination of Chardonnay, Pinot Noir, and Pinot Meunier, and are all white. (See the sections that follow for our recommendations of non-vintage rosé Champagnes and non-vintage blanc de blancs Champagnes.) We list our recommended wines in this section alphabetically by producer.

Paul Bara Brut Réserve

- ♪ **Producer:** Paul Bara *(ba rah)*
- ♪ **Wine name:** Brut Réserve
- ♪ **Appellation:** Champagne
- ♪ **Price:** $32.50

Have you ever served a full-bodied Champagne with dinner? The Paul Bara Brut Reserve is ideal with a meal because it's rich enough to stand up to moderately flavorful meats. This non-vintage Brut Réserve, made mainly with Pinot Noir grapes from the village of Bouzy, is a massive, concentrated beauty, dry and full flavored. If you have any difficulty finding the wine of this small producer, call a shop that always stocks Bara's Champagne: Kermit Lynch Wine Merchant, Berkeley, California, 510-524-1524.

Ed: 90–92   **Mary:** 88–90

Bollinger Special Cuvée Brut

- ♪ **Producer:** Bollinger
- ♪ **Wine name:** Special Cuvée Brut
- ♪ **Appellation:** Champagne
- ♪ **Price:** $36.50

Bollinger makes one of the driest, toastiest, fullest-bodied Champagnes available. It has a very deep gold color, with classic Bollinger yeasty, honeyed aromas and flavors, rather reminiscent of a brioche but much less sweet. Despite its richness and monumental fullness, Bollinger Champagne has a strong edge of austerity to it. Its dryness and austerity do not suit everybody, but this wine has many faithful devotees among those who enjoy dry, rich Champagnes. It's the ideal Champagne to serve with main courses, such as chicken with mushrooms, or quail.

Ed: 88–90 **Mary:** 88–90

Deutz Brut Classic

> ⚑ **Producer:** Champagne Deutz *(duhtz)*
> ⚑ **Wine name:** Brut Classic
> ⚑ **Appellation:** Champagne
> ⚑ **Price:** $27

The company known as Champagne Deutz is making some of the best value Champagnes today. And because the great Champagne house of Louis Roederer recently purchased a majority interest in Deutz, things promise to get only better for Deutz in the coming years. Deutz's non-vintage Champagne is called Brut Classic, and frankly, it's better than ever. It has lemony, nutty, creamy, and caramely aromas, and its rich flavors include yeast, toast, and nuts. Brut Classic stands out for its creamy texture, its rich flavors, its depth, and its complexity. It's a very approachable Champagne that's drinkable right now; there's no need to save it.

Ed: 90–92 **Mary:** 89–91

Charles Heidsieck Brut Réserve

> ⚑ **Producer:** Charles Heidsieck *(hide sick)*
> ⚑ **Wine name:** Brut Réserve
> ⚑ **Appellation:** Champagne
> ⚑ **Price:** $30

The Charles Heidsieck firm is clearly making one of the very finest non-vintage brut Champagnes today. Cellar master Daniel Thibault, one of Champagne's best, uses a particularly high percentage of reserve wines from earlier vintages in the Brut Réserve blend. This process creates more mature, toasty, complex aromas and flavors than most other brands have. It's a full, rich, very toasty Champagne with loads of flavor and really fine balance — our kind of Champagne! It's a good choice to accompany a flavorful fish or seafood dish.

Ed: 91–93 **Mary:** 87–89

Henriot Brut Souverain

- **Producer:** Henriot *(ahn ree oh)*
- **Wine name:** Brut Souverain
- **Appellation:** Champagne
- **Price:** $36

Henriot Champagne has had a very low profile in the U.S. for a number of years, but now that the dynamic Joseph Henriot has taken his firm out of the Moët-Hennessy corporate group and is running it independently again, Henriot Champagne is very much back in the U.S. market. The Henriot Brut Souverain is a big, flavorful Champagne that's toasty, austere, and very dry. It's rich and somewhat fleshy, with good concentration on the finish. Serve this Champagne with food, perhaps with a mushroom omelette at brunch.

Ed: 86–88   **Mary:** 88–90

J. Lassalle Brut Impérial Préférence

- **Producer:** J. Lassalle
- **Wine name:** Brut Impérial Préférence
- **Appellation:** Champagne
- **Price:** $34.50

J. Lassalle is a small, quality firm that is not generally well known, but that has a number of followers among Champagne devotees. The Brut Impérial Préférence has yeasty, bready aromas and flavors. It's an intensely flavored, complex Champagne, creamy and full, with good concentration on its long, full finish. J. Lassalle has been a consistently reliable producer of excellent Champagne for many years now. It's available in New York, at Neal Rosenthal Wine Merchants, 212-249-6650, and in California, at Kermit Lynch Wine Merchant, 510-524-1524.

Ed: 87–89   **Mary:** 87–89

Moët & Chandon Brut Impérial

- **Producer:** Moët & Chandon *(moh et eh shan don)*
- **Wine name:** Brut Impérial
- **Appellation:** Champagne
- **Price:** $39.50

We find it gratifying to recommend a Champagne such as Moët that we know is widely available. To its credit, Moët & Chandon, the largest Champagne house, has always maintained quality throughout its line, from the Brut Impérial to its top-of-the-line wine, Dom Pérignon. Moët's Champagne in the extra dry (slightly sweeter) style, White Star, is by far the largest-selling Champagne in the U.S., but we prefer the drier, fuller-bodied Brut Impérial. It has lots of the full, toasty aromas and flavors that we like in a Champagne, and it's invariably fresh because of its rapid turnover in the stores. If you prefer your Champagne a bit lighter bodied and not too dry, try Moët's White Star. (Our score below is for the Brut Impérial.)

Ed: 86–88   **Mary:** 85–87

Mumm Cordon Rouge Brut

 ❧ **Producer:** G.H. Mumm

 ❧ **Wine name:** Cordon Rouge Brut

 ❧ **Appellation:** Champagne

 ❧ **Price:** $30

Mumm is another large Champagne firm that has really upgraded its quality during the last five years. We like its non-vintage Cordon Rouge, and we especially enjoy its Mumm de Cramant (reviewed in the section "Blanc de blancs Champagnes"). The Cordon Rouge has very rich, toasty flavors of the sort that are really classic for Champagne. It's a big, full-styled Champagne. We suggest the Cordon Rouge with a full-flavored fish, such as salmon or swordfish, or even with roast chicken.

Ed: 86–88   **Mary:** 88–90

Perrier-Jouët Grand Brut

 ❧ **Producer:** Perrier-Jouët *(per re ay jhou et)*

 ❧ **Wine name:** Grand Brut

 ❧ **Appellation:** Champagne

 ❧ **Price:** $32

The value of tasting wines blind is that it removes the bias of preconceived opinions. We have had the popular Perrier-Jouët (note that you pronounce the last syllable as "et")

Grand Brut many times over the years and had concluded that it was "okay," but somewhat bland and a bit too soft and sweet. Well, we've changed our opinion (especially Ed) after tasting it blind on a couple of occasions. The Grand Brut has slightly nutty and vanilla aromas and flavors and has good flavor intensity. It's creamy and rich, yet crisp, with good length and complexity. No wonder it's one of the best-selling Champagnes in the U.S.!

Ed: 88–90 **Mary:** 85–87

Philipponnat Royale Réserve Brut

- **Producer:** Philipponnat *(fil ee poan nah)*
- **Wine name:** Royale Réserve Brut
- **Appellation:** Champagne
- **Price:** $24

Philipponnat is a fairly small house that has excellent prices for its entire line, including its outstanding prestige cuvée, Clos des Goisses *(gwahss)*, which is a reasonable $62.50. Philipponnat's basic non-vintage blend, the Royale Réserve Brut, has complex aromas and flavors that are primarily toasty and yeasty. It's a rich, fresh, elegant, very well-balanced Champagne with a delicious finish. It's clearly one of the best buys in Champagne today.

Ed: 87–89 **Mary:** 86–88

Piper-Heidsieck Cuvée Brut

- **Producer:** Piper-Heidsieck
- **Wine name:** Cuvée Brut
- **Appellation:** Champagne
- **Price:** $28

Cellar master Daniel Thibault oversees the production of Piper-Heidsieck Champagne as well as Charles Heidsieck Champagne. (Both houses are owned by Rémy Martin, the Cognac firm.) He has clearly improved the quality of Piper's non-vintage Brut, which is made in a softer, fruitier style than the drier Charles Heidsieck. The Piper-Heidsieck Cuvée Brut has nutty, yeasty aromas with very fresh, fruity, yeasty flavors. It's a full, round Champagne that is easy drinking right now and will appeal to you if you find most Champagnes too dry.

Ed: 85–87   **Mary:** 85–87

Pol Roger Extra Cuvée de Réserve

> ! **Producer:** Pol Roger *(pol ro jhay)*
> ! **Wine name:** Extra Cuvée de Brut Réserve
> ! **Appellation:** Champagne
> ! **Price:** $37.50

We like Pol Roger's entire line of Champagnes, including its prestige cuvée, called *Cuvée Sir Winston Churchill.* The Pol Roger non-vintage brut, the Extra Cuvée de Réserve, is a steady performer that often benefits from an extra year or two of aging after you purchase it. Firm and rich, this Champagne has aromas and flavors of nuts and a trace of rosemary, along with a bit of sweetness to balance its firmness. It's an elegant, medium-bodied Champagne that goes well with spicy Chinese food or other spicy Asian cuisine.

Ed: 87–89   **Mary:** 85–87

Pommery Brut Royal Apanage

> ! **Producer:** Pommery
> ! **Wine name:** Brut Royal Apanage *(ah pah nahj)*
> ! **Appellation:** Champagne
> ! **Price:** $36

The great Pommery house, which had been absent from the U.S. market for a while, is now back. This company has a brand-new non-vintage Champagne, called *Brut Royal Apanage.* (You can still buy Pommery's regular non-vintage Brut Royal, about $31, but we slightly prefer the Apanage.) The blend called Apanage has been aged about a year longer, is drier, and contains more Pinot Noir than the standard Brut Royal. The wine is complex and very flavorful, with citrusy and nutty aromas and delicate, floral, citrusy flavors. It's a rich but elegant Champagne with plenty of personality. (By the way, Pommery makes two of our very favorite Champagnes: Cuvée Louise and Cuvée Louise Rosé.)

Ed: 87–89   **Mary:** 87–89

Louis Roederer Brut Premier

- **Producer:** Louis Roederer *(roh der er)*
- **Wine name:** Brut Premier
- **Appellation:** Champagne
- **Price:** $42

The fact that we both come up with high ratings when we taste the Louis Roederer Brut Premier blind is no surprise to us. The Roederer Brut Premier has always been one of our very favorite non-vintage Champagnes. This great house is one of the top two or three Champagne firms, in our opinion. The Roederer Brut Premier is a big, full-bodied Champagne with classic toasty aromas and flavors. It's a very rich but understated wine with excellent balance, lots of complexity, and a fine, long finish. Mary notes that it "holds well in the glass," meaning that its bubbles and its crispness don't die out quickly, an important factor in enjoying Champagne.

Ed: 91–93

Mary: 89–91

Taittinger Brut La Française

- **Producer:** Taittinger
- **Wine name:** Brut La Française
- **Appellation:** Champagne
- **Price:** $36

Taittinger is another large Champagne house that has improved the quality of its non-vintage brut, called La Française. (Taittinger's vintage Champagne and its prestige cuvées, the Comtes de Champagne Blanc de Blancs and the Comtes Rosé, have always been superb.) The Taittinger house style stresses elegance rather than power. The La Française has toasty aromas and flavors, combined with some lemony fruit. It's light to medium bodied and not too dry. The La Française would be a good Champagne to serve with a first course, especially if you're having shellfish or mushrooms.

Ed: 86–88

Veuve Clicquot Brut

> - **Producer:** Veuve Clicquot Ponsardin
>   (*voov clee ko pohn sahr dan*)
> - **Wine name:** Brut (Yellow Label)
> - **Appellation:** Champagne
> - **Price:** $38

Veuve Clicquot Champagne has taken the U.S. by storm. Ten years ago, the brand was far back in the ranks in sales; today, Veuve Clicquot is second only to Moët & Chandon in U.S. sales. Its non-vintage Brut (which for some strange reason is called *Yellow Label,* when everyone can see that the label is orange!) is made in a rich, full-bodied style; in fact, it's always among the biggest in weight of the non-vintage Champagnes. It has biscuity and fresh citrus aromas and flavors, with perhaps a touch of orange peel. This Champagne is complex in flavor, with really good length, excellent depth, and a long finish — all signs of very good quality. We'd serve this wine with game birds, such as pheasant or quail, or with chicken fillets covered with mushrooms.

Ed: 87–89   **Mary:** 87–89

Vintage Champagnes

Most Champagne houses make a *vintage* Champagne (a Champagne whose grapes come only from the year indicated on the label) — but only in years when the weather has been especially good. Four or five years in a decade, on the average, merit the production of vintage Champagne.

Vintage Champagnes usually cost $10 to $15 more than their non-vintage counterparts. Is vintage Champagne worth that extra money? That depends on how much you love Champagne. For us, the answer is an emphatic "Yes," for two major reasons:

- The best grapes from the choicest vineyards (and from the best years) are used for vintage Champagnes; as a result, the wines are typically more intensely flavored and fuller bodied than non-vintage wines.
- Vintage Champagnes age in the cold Champagne cellars for at least two years longer than non-vintage Champagnes, giving them more complexity.

Other good Champagne producers

As we scan through all of our Champagne reviews, we realize that some fine Champagne houses are not included among our recommendations because we haven't tasted their wines recently, although we have enjoyed them in the past. We list ten such houses here, in alphabetical order. You can buy these brands with confidence.

- ✔ Champagne de Castellane
- ✔ Champagne Cattier
- ✔ Champagne Charles de Cazanove
- ✔ Champagne Delamotte Père et Fils
- ✔ Champagne Drappier
- ✔ Champagne Gosset
- ✔ Champagne Alfred Gratien
- ✔ Champagne Heidsieck & Co. Monopole
- ✔ Champagne Bruno Pailliard
- ✔ Champagne Joseph Perrier

Two additional Champagne houses, Krug and Salon, deserve particular mention. (Because their wines sell for more than $60, we don't include them in our reviews but merely list the wines in our $60-and-over sidebar.) Champagne Krug is high on the list of outstanding producers in every Champagne lover's book. All of Krug's Champagnes, from the Grande Cuvée to the sublime vintage Champagne (1985 is the current release) to the Clos de Mesnil Blanc de Blancs to the extraordinary Rosé, are uniquely Krug — great, dry, complex wines that happen to have bubbles. They all will provide you with an incredible Champagne experience.

Champagne Salon is a small house that makes only one Champagne — and then only in good vintage years. That wine is a blanc de blancs called Le Mesnil. The style is different from other blanc de blancs Champagnes: Le Mesnil is a rich, powerful Champagne that ages extremely well and, in fact, needs time to develop. The last two vintages for Salon have been 1982 and 1983; the 1982 vintage is the better of the two.

We list our vintage Champagne recommendations (applying an upper price limit of $60) alphabetically by producer.

Bollinger 1988 Grande Année Brut

> - **Producer:** Bollinger
> - **Wine name:** 1988 Grande Année Brut
> - **Appellation:** Champagne
> - **Price:** $60

1989 is the current vintage for Champagne Bollinger, but we both prefer the more powerful 1988 vintage, which is more in the classic Bollinger style. The 1988 Grande Année has really toasty, biscuity aromas and intense flavors of spice, mushrooms and toasted bread. It's almost as good as the glorious Bollinger 1985 Grande Année, which was one of the stars of that superb vintage. We expect the 1988 Grande Année to be long-lived; you can enjoy it now, with a full-flavored poultry or game entrée, or allow it to develop for another three to five years. (By the way, for a truly extraordinary experience, try the Champagne that brought tears to Mary's eyes: the 1986 Bollinger Vieilles Vignes, one of the few existing blanc de noirs Champagnes. Its flavor and complexity are otherworldly, but so is the price — $200.)

Ed: 91–93   **Mary:** 92–94

Deutz 1990 Brut

> - **Producer:** Champagne Deutz
> - **Wine name:** 1990 Brut
> - **Appellation:** Champagne
> - **Price:** $40

The 1990 Deutz bears witness to the greatness of this vintage in Champagne. The wine is so lively, delicious, and full flavored that you want to drink it right now, although it might even be better in a couple of years. It's a medium-bodied, rich, elegant Champagne with lemony, toasty, and yeasty aromas and flavors. The 1990 Deutz has exquisite balance, complex flavors, and a long finish. It'd be a perfect match with oysters or mussels.

Ed: 90–92   **Mary:** 86–88

Laurent-Perrier 1990 Vintage Brut

- **Producer:** Laurent-Perrier
- **Wine name:** 1990 Vintage Brut
- **Appellation:** Champagne
- **Price:** $49.50

Laurent-Perrier is one of the largest — and finest — Champagne houses, and yet it's not well known in the U.S. This house produces elegant, delicate, exquisitely balanced Champagnes. (Its prestige cuvée wine, called *Grand Siècle*, is particularly outstanding.) Among Laurent-Perrier's vintage Champagnes, both the 1990 and the 1988 Brut are excellent. The 1990 Vintage Brut is lively and complex and still quite young, with earthy, yeasty, lemony, and spicy aromas and flavors. It's so delicious that it's difficult not to drink it now, although it might even improve with two or three years of aging.

Ed: 89–91

Mary: 88–90

Moët & Chandon 1992 Vintage Brut

- **Producer:** Moët & Chandon
- **Wine name:** 1992 Vintage Brut Impérial
- **Appellation:** Champagne
- **Price:** $48

Although 1992 is not regarded as a very good vintage in Champagne (most houses did not make a 1992 Champagne), the huge Moët firm, with so many vineyards at its disposal, did manage to produce a surprisingly fine 1992 wine. It has austere, fresh, lemony, toasty aromas, along with flavors of green apple, citrus, and freshly baked bread. The quality of this wine shows in its good concentration and pleasant, lively finish. The 1992 Moët is obviously quite young, but you can enjoy it now. A vintage such as 1992 is not for aging.

Ed: 87–89

Mary: 84–86

Piper-Heidsieck 1985 or 1989 Vintage Brut

> ✔ **Producer:** Piper Heidsieck
> ✔ **Wine name:** 1985 or 1989 Vintage Brut
> ✔ **Appellation:** Champagne
> ✔ **Price:** $42.50

Perhaps the biggest surprise for us in our recent blind tastings of Champagne was how well the Piper-Heidsieck wines did. Not that we thought poorly of this fine, old house; we just didn't realize how much its wines had improved during the past several years. Both the 1985 (current vintage) and 1989 (just coming on to the market) Piper-Heidsieck Vintage Champagnes earn our approval; we prefer the 1985 vintage (Ed gives it a 90-92 rating), and we urge you to look around for it. This very toasty and full-bodied Champagne, with mature, honeyed flavors is definitely a Champagne to have with dinner.

The 1989 Piper-Heidsieck Vintage Brut has fresh, complex aromas that suggest bread dough, toast, and nuts; it has flavors of ripe lime and apple. This wine is very well balanced and has a long finish. Because the 1989 vintage generally produced delicious but not long-lasting Champagnes, we recommend drinking the 1989 Piper-Heidsieck in the near future. (The following ratings are for the 1989 Vintage Brut.)

Ed: 86–88   **Mary:** 85–87

Pommery 1989 Brut Millésimé

> ✔ **Producer:** Pommery
> ✔ **Wine name:** 1989 Brut Millésimé *(broot mee lay see may)*
> ✔ **Appellation:** Champagne
> ✔ **Price:** $36

Having Pommery back in the U.S. market again, after a ten-year absence, is like welcoming an old friend home. Pommery's Brut Millésimé (a word that basically means *vintage*) is selling for a particularly attractive price, making the welcome-back party all the more celebratory. The 1989 Pommery has citrusy, smoky aromas; its complex, rich, mature flavors are in the toasty, smoky, chocolatey vein. The wine is fresh, crisp, and well balanced, with a long, lively finish. Although the 1989 Brut Millésimé is still a bit young, we'd drink this wine within two years. It would go well with snapper, monkfish, or a seafood entrée.

Ed: 88–90   **Mary:** 86–88

Louis Roederer 1990 Vintage Brut

- *Producer:* Louis Roederer
- *Wine name:* 1990 Vintage Brut
- *Appellation:* Champagne
- *Price:* $54

Louis Roederer's Vintage Brut is always its most powerful Champagne, even more so than its famous prestige cuvée, Cristal (a wine that emphasizes elegance and balance rather than power). The 1990 Vintage Brut is a rich, assertive, full-bodied Champagne with an intense, floral, nutty, toasty scent and spicy, honeyed flavors. It's a lively, delicious Champagne with excellent balance and ultra-fine bubbles. You can enjoy it now, but it should even get better with a few years of aging.

Ed: 89–91   **Mary:** 88–90

Taittinger 1991 Brut Millésimé

- *Producer:* Taittinger
- *Wine name:* 1991 Brut Millésimé
- *Appellation:* Champagne
- *Price:* $48.50

The 1991 vintage did not get too much acclaim among wine critics, but we are impressed with most of the 1991 Champagnes that we try. Taittinger's success with its 1991 Brut Millésimé follows two strong showings with its 1988 and especially its 1990 Brut. If you see either of those two vintages around, we suggest that you buy them. The 1991 Brut Millésimé has Taittinger's characteristic strong lemony and baked bread aromas, with ripe, lemony fruit flavors and notes of chocolate. It is well balanced and has lots of character and a nice, long finish. This elegant Champagne would be perfect for a first course in a dinner, especially if the first course is shellfish, such as oysters or mussels, or crab.

Ed: 88–90   **Mary:** 88–90

Veuve Clicquot 1989 Vintage Brut

- **Producer:** Veuve Clicquot Ponsardin
- **Wine name:** 1989 Vintage Réserve Brut (Gold Label)
- **Appellation:** Champagne
- **Price:** $50.50

Veuve Clicquot makes rich, full-bodied Champagnes, and the 1989 Vintage Brut, or Gold Label, is an excellent representative of this house style. The wine has a rich aroma of yeast and toasted bread, with earthy and lemony flavors. The 1989 Vintage Brut is a generous, round Champagne with good concentration and excellent fruit character. You can drink this voluptuous Champagne now or during the next two or three years. It's really a good value when you compare it with Veuve Clicquot's magnificent prestige cuvée, the slower-to-develop La Grande Dame, which is twice the price of the Gold Label. (By the way, if you come across any 1985 Gold Label Brut, we strongly suggest that you buy it; it's still superb!)

Ed: 89–91   **Mary:** 90–92

Blanc de Blancs Champagne

We place blanc de blancs Champagne in a section of its own because it's quite different in style from other types of Champagne. While almost all Champagnes are blends of one or two black grapes (Pinot Noir, Pinot Meunier) with Chardonnay, blanc de blancs Champagnes are always made entirely from Chardonnay. The result is a lighter-styled, more elegant Champagne that's ideal as an apéritif or as an accompaniment to the first course of a dinner.

Not all Champagne houses make a blanc de blancs Champagne; some of the more traditional firms, such as Moët & Chandon, Veuve Clicquot, Laurent Perrier, Piper-Heidsieck, and Pommery, do not believe in this "new-style" Champagne (which only really became popular after World War II). To them, Champagne can be made only from a blend of grape varieties. But blanc de blancs Champagne, which represents only a very small part of the Champagne market, does have its devotees. Personally, we like them quite a bit and are glad that they exist.

We list our recommended blanc de blancs Champagnes alphabetically by producer. Most of these wines are also technically vintage bruts because they are dry and carry a vintage year; one of them is a non-vintage brut Champagne.

Billecart-Salmon 1988 Blanc de Blancs

- **Producer:** Billecart-Salmon *(bil lay cart sal mohn)*
- **Wine name:** 1988 Brut Blanc de Blancs
- **Appellation:** Champagne
- **Price:** $59

You might not have heard of Billecart-Salmon, because it's a fairly small house. But we believe that it's one of the very best of all Champagne firms, especially for its blanc de blancs and rosé Champagnes. Through the years, we've had so many great bottles of Billecart-Salmon Blanc de Blancs that this wine has become one of our very favorites. And it ages amazingly well; a 1983 Billecart-Salmon Blanc de Blancs we recently drank was completely fresh, with no deterioration, even at 14 years old.

The 1988 Billecart Salmon Blanc de Blancs is a lively, flavorful, rather assertive Champagne for a blanc de blancs. (1988 produced dry, austere, powerful, long-lasting Champagnes.) It has a lemony, yeasty, spicy aroma and delicious baked bread, ripe pear, and lemon flavors. Firm and concentrated, with a very long finish, this wine is absolutely fabulous with caviar! You can enjoy it now or save it for five or six years, or more. It will still be fine if stored properly.

Ed: 95–97   **Mary:** 93–95

Deutz 1989 Blanc de Blancs

- **Producer:** Champagne Deutz
- **Wine name:** 1989 Brut Blanc de Blancs
- **Appellation:** Champagne
- **Price:** $49

Deutz always makes a great blanc de blancs Champagne, and its 1989 is even better than usual. Deutz's blanc de blancs wines typically have really zesty, lemony, yeasty aromas and flavors, along with a touch of hazelnuts, and this 1989 version is no exception. The 1989 Deutz Blanc de Blancs is a lively, delicious Champagne with excellent balance and a long, honeyed finish. You can enjoy it now or within the next year or two. It's an excellent apéritif Champagne to sip before a meal.

Ed: 91–93   **Mary:** 84–86

Jacquesson 1990 Blanc de Blancs

- **Producer:** Jacquesson & Fils
- **Wine name:** 1990 Brut Blanc de Blancs
- **Appellation:** Champagne
- **Price:** $30

Jacquesson & Fils is a very fine, small Champagne firm that does not receive enough recognition in the U.S. Its prices are among the best of any in the Champagne region; its excellent prestige cuveés, Signature and Signature Rosé, at $45 and $50 respectively, are two of the very few prestige cuvée Champagnes available for under $60.

Jacquesson's Blanc de Blancs Brut is one of the house's best Champagnes and a great value. In the 1990 vintage, this wine is particularly good, with full, rich, toasty aromas and flavors of butter and yeast. Despite the richness of its flavor, this is a delicate Champagne with lots of finesse, excellent balance, good concentration, and a long, complex finish. Enjoy it now, or soon, as an apéritif Champagne, accompanied by smoked oysters, smoked mussels, or stuffed mushrooms.

Ed: 89–91   **Mary:** 87–89

Mumm de Cramant Blanc de Blancs

- **Producer:** G.H. Mumm
- **Wine name:** Mumm de Cramant Brut Blanc de Blancs (non-vintage)
- **Appellation:** Champagne
- **Price:** $42.50

The vineyards around the village of Cramant *(crah mahn)* are among the very best sites for the Chardonnay grape. Mumm's non-vintage blanc de blancs, Mumm de Cramant, is made entirely of Chardonnay grapes from Cramant; not surprisingly, this wine is consistently Mumm's best Champagne. Mumm de Cramant has aromas and flavors that suggest smoke, toast, lemon, and minerals. This is a medium-bodied Champagne with a complex, medium-long finish. The fairly delicate style of this wine suggests that it would be fine with a delicately flavored fish, such as Dover sole.

Ed: 87–89   Mary: 86–88

Pol Roger 1988 Brut Chardonnay

- ✔ **Producer:** Pol Roger
- ✔ **Wine name:** 1988 Vintage Brut Chardonnay
- ✔ **Appellation:** Champagne
- ✔ **Price:** $59

The excellent blanc de blancs Champagne that the house of Pol Roger labels Brut Chardonnay is consistently one of this firm's very best Champagnes. The 1988 Brut Chardonnay aged in the bottle for seven years before being released, an unusually long time; as a result, it is less austere than many other Champagnes from the 1988 vintage. This wine has delicate, complex aromas and flavors of lemon and bitter chocolate. It's medium bodied, fresh, dry, and lively, with a lengthy, austere finish. Like other Pol Roger Brut Chardonnays, the 1988 Chardonnay Brut should develop and improve with a few more years of aging, but it's also delicious right now.

Ed: 90–92   Mary: 86–88

Louis Roederer 1990 Blanc de Blancs

- ✔ **Producer:** Louis Roederer
- ✔ **Wine name:** 1990 Brut Blanc de Blancs
- ✔ **Appellation:** Champagne
- ✔ **Price:** $55

Louis Roederer is one of the Champagne houses whose entire line of Champagnes we unhesitatingly recommend. Roederer's 1990 Blanc de Blancs is a lively Champagne with yeasty, toasty, nutty aromas and flavors. This extremely well-balanced Champagne is richer and fuller than most blanc de blancs, with lots of flavor. You can enjoy the 1990 Roederer

Blanc de Blancs now, perhaps with a seafood entrée, or keep it for a few years: Roederer Champagnes age well.

Ed: 88–90   **Mary:** 87–89

Rosé Champagnes — Pretty in Pink

Rosé Champagnes are pretty to look at, delicious to drink, and go remarkably well with food. They're the one type of Champagne that really accompanies main courses well, especially full-flavored fish, poultry, or ham, and even rare lamb chops.

Rosé Champagnes range in color from pale onion skin to salmon to rosy pink. They do suffer from a slight image problem in the U.S. because some people confuse them with sweet, inexpensive blush wines. But rosé Champagnes are definitely dry, and they're certainly not inexpensive; those we review are mainly in the $40 to $60 price range.

Our reviews of rosé Champagne do not include over-$60 prestige cuvée rosés, such as Dom Pérignon or Cristal. (Prestige cuvée rosés are, in fact, among the most expensive Champagnes.) Those wines are mentioned in the sidebar "Great over-$60 Champagnes," later in this chapter. In this section, we list our recommended rosé Champagnes, both vintage and non-vintage, alphabetically by producer. For information about rosé Champagne and how it's made, see Chapter 13 of *Wine For Dummies*.

Billecart-Salmon Brut Rosé

> ✔ **Producer:** Billecart-Salmon
> ✔ **Wine name:** Brut Rosé (non-vintage)
> ✔ **Appellation:** Champagne
> ✔ **Price:** $49

Billecart-Salmon makes one of the best rosé Champagnes available; in fact, rosé is a house specialty of this excellent Champagne firm. (Recently, Billecart-Salmon released its first prestige cuvée rosé, Cuvée Elisabeth Salmon Rosé 1988.) Billecart-Salmon's non-vintage Brut Rosé has a delicate salmon pink color, in part because only 6 percent Pinot Noir wine is added to this Champagne to make it rosé, about half as much as is typically used for rosé Champagnes. *Delicate,* in fact, describes not just the color, but everything about this

Champagne. This wine has delicate aromas and flavors of cherries and raspberries. It is a gentle but lively Champagne with exquisite balance. It's absolutely delicious — a real crowd pleaser. You can enjoy this rosé as an apéritif; in fact, this wine is often referred to as "the blanc de blancs of rosé Champagnes."

Ed: 90–92   **Mary:** 90–92

Bollinger 1988 Grande Année Rosé

>   ♪ **Producer:** Bollinger
>   ♪ **Wine name:** 1988 Grande Année Brut Rosé
>   ♪ **Appellation:** Champagne
>   ♪ **Price:** $60

Bollinger makes its rosé Champagne in the same style that it makes all of its Champagnes — dry, austere, and full bodied. The only other rosé Champagnes that we know of that are as dry as Bollinger's are Krug, which is very expensive, and Gosset, which is difficult to find in the U.S. The 1988 Grande Année Rosé has a striking coppery pink-gold color, with aromas and flavors of toasted bread and citrus. It's a full-bodied, dry, lively, assertive Champagne with lots of complex, mature flavors, good concentration, and a lengthy finish. It's the perfect Champagne to have with a full-flavored main course at dinner. We suggest lobster as a tasty companion to this excellent rosé, for a truly special occasion meal.

Ed: 89–91   **Mary:** 88–90

Piper-Heidsieck NV Brut Rosé

>   ♪ **Producer:** Piper-Heidsieck
>   ♪ **Wine name:** Brut Rosé (non-vintage)
>   ♪ **Appellation:** Champagne
>   ♪ **Price:** $34

Piper-Heidsieck Brut Rosé is a deeper rose-pink than most other rosés; it's also a bit fruitier than most other rosé Champagnes. I like this full-bodied, assertively flavored rosé because of the richness its redness brings; Ed thinks it's a bit coarse and lacks elegance, but what does he know? This rosé would be a good choice to serve when you're entertaining, because it's a fun Champagne that doesn't require much contemplation. Try it and see if you agree with Ed's taste or mine.

Mary: 87–89

Pol Roger 1988 Brut Rosé

- ✔ **Producer:** Pol Roger
- ✔ **Wine name:** 1988 Brut Rosé
- ✔ **Appellation:** Champagne
- ✔ **Price:** $52.50

Pol Roger has been making excellent rosé Champagnes lately. The 1988 Brut Rosé has a deep salmon pink color with glints of copper-orange; spicy, nutty aromas; and rich strawberry and peach flavors. Quite dry, fine, and delicate, this Champagne has good balance and lots of flavor. Despite the typical austerity and ageworthiness of Champagnes from the 1988 vintage, we suggest that you drink this delicious rosé soon; it would be perfect with a shellfish dinner.

Ed: 88–90   **Mary:** 87–89

Pommery NV Brut Rosé

- ✔ **Producer:** Pommery
- ✔ **Wine name:** Brut Rosé (non-vintage)
- ✔ **Appellation:** Champagne
- ✔ **Price:** $32

All of the Pommery Champagnes have been showing strongly recently; they seem to be drier and more complexly flavored than they were a couple of years ago. A case in point is the very dry Pommery Brut Rosé, which is also an excellent value. It has the austerity of a white Champagne but the red-fruit flavors of a rosé. It's a spirited, spunky Champagne, a little bit wild, that's fun to drink right now. Because it's light and delicate in style, the Pommery Rosé is a good choice as an apéritif Champagne to enjoy with hors d'oeuvres.

Ed: 86–88   **Mary:** 86–88

Louis Roederer 1991 Brut Rosé

- **Producer:** Louis Roederer
- **Wine name:** 1991 Brut Rosé
- **Appellation:** Champagne
- **Price:** $56

Louis Roederer might just be making the best rosé Champagne in existence, judging from its consistently strong performance in blind group tastings that we conduct. The color of the 1991 Brut Rosé is gorgeous; one of us described it as topaz or pale onion skin, the other as pale pink-gold. It has a wonderfully complex, yeasty aroma, with strawberry and citrusy flavors, along with some suggestion of chocolate. This is a very elegant, medium-bodied Champagne with excellent balance, lots of complexity, and a long, delicious finish. The quality here is almost beyond words — just outstanding. We suggest that you enjoy this delicious Champagne now or in the near future, with something simple, such as mushroom tarts.

Ed: 98–100   **Mary:** 92–94

Taittinger Cuvée Prestige Rosé

- **Producer:** Taittinger
- **Wine name:** Cuvée Prestige Brut Rosé (non-vintage)
- **Appellation:** Champagne
- **Price:** $44.50

A few years ago, Taittinger introduced its non-vintage brut rosé, called Cuvée Prestige, as a less expensive alternative to its prestige cuvée Rosé, the magnificent Comtes de Champagne Rosé. The current version of the Cuvée Prestige is much improved over the debut wine, which in our opinion was not dry enough. The current blend has a beautiful "eye of the partridge" light pink hue, with red berry fruit aromas and flavors. It's a lively, dry, well-balanced, delicate rosé Champagne with good concentration of red-fruit flavors. For its delicacy, the Cuvée Prestige Rosé makes an ideal apéritif Champagne.

Ed: 86–88   **Mary:** 88–90

Veuve Clicquot 1988 Rosé Réserve

- **Producer:** Veuve Clicquot Ponsardin
- **Wine name:** 1988 Brut Rosé Réserve
- **Appellation:** Champagne
- **Price:** $60

Veuve Clicquot's Rosé Champagne has been getting better and better during the last ten years, to the point that it's now one of the very best rosés made. The 1988 Rosé Réserve is the finest rosé we've ever tasted from Veuve Clicquot. It has a deep topaz-pink color, with red-fruit aromas and flavors (a blend of cherries and berries). This is a full-bodied, very dry Champagne with rich, developed flavors, great balance, and a long finish. The 1988 Rosé Réserve is perfect for drinking now and makes an ideal accompaniment to a full-flavored main course, such as ham or lamb chops.

Ed: 92–94   **Mary:** 91–93

Great over-$60 Champagnes

Champagne is the one type of wine in which we indulge ourselves with a special, expensive bottle every now and then. Almost all the very expensive Champagnes that we recommend here are classified as *prestige cuvées*, meaning that they are each the finest Champagne of the particular house that makes them. (Prestige cuvées are made from the best grapes of the finest vineyards, receive longer aging, and enjoy other production advantages over normal Champagnes.) Some houses make a prestige cuvée rosé, which is often even more expensive than the white prestige cuvée from the same house. We list our recommended over-$60 Champagnes alphabetically by producer:

Champagne House	Prestige Cuvée Wines
Champagne Billecart-Salmon	Cuvée Elisabeth Salmon Rosé
Champagne Bollinger	Cuvée Vieilles Vignes Françaises
Champagne de Castellane	Cuvée Florens de Castellane
Champagne Cattier	Clos du Moulin
Champagne Charles de Cazanove	Stradivarius

(continued)

(continued)

Champagne House	Prestige Cuvée Wines
Champagne A. Charbaut & Fils	Certificate Blanc de Blancs; Certificate Rosé
Champagne Deutz	Cuvée William Deutz; Cuvée William Deutz Rosé
Champagne Gosset	Celebris; Grand Millésimé; Grand Millésimé Rosé
Champagne Alfred Gratien	Cuvée Paradis
Champagne Charles Heidsieck	Blanc des Millénaires
Champagne Heidsieck & Co Monopole	Diamant Bleu; Diamant Bleu Rosé
Champagne Henriot	Cuvée des Enchanteleurs
Champagne Krug	Grande Cuvée; Vintage Krug; Rosé; Clos du Mesnil (Blanc de Blancs)
Champagne Laurent-Perrier	Cuvée Grand Siècle; Cuvée Grand Siècle Alexandre Rosé
Champagne Moët & Chandon	Cuvée Dom Pérignon; Cuvée Dom Pérignon Rosé
Champagne Joseph Perrier	Cuvée Joséphine
Champagne Perrier-Jouët	Fleur de Champagne ("Cuvée Belle Epoque"); Fleur de Champagne Rosé
Champagne Philipponnat	Clos des Goisses
Champagne Piper-Heidsieck	Champagne Rare
Champagne Pol Roger	Cuvée Sir Winston Churchill; Réserve Speciale PR
Champagne Pommery	Cuvée Louise; Cuvée Louise Rosé
Champagne Louis Roederer	Cristal; Cristal Rosé
Champagne Ruinart	Dom Ruinart Blanc de Blancs; Dom Ruinart Rosé
Champagne Salon	Le Mesnil (Blanc de Blancs)
Champagne Taittinger	Comtes de Champagne (Blanc de Blancs); Comtes de Champagne Rosé
Champagne Veuve Clicquot Ponsardin	La Grande Dame; La Grande Dame Rosé

Chapter 10

Sparkling Wines from around the World

In This Chapter

▶ Great sparklers from the U.S.

▶ France moves to California

▶ Around the world in sparkling wine

▶ Italian delicacy for dessert

*A*lthough we do love Champagne, we often find ourselves
drinking a good sparkling wine from California, New York,
Spain, Italy, or elsewhere. Price is one consideration: When we're
dining in a fine restaurant, we don't always want to spend the
money for a costly bottle of Champagne. But even more than that,
we like diversity in our wines. A California brut, for example, is so
different from Champagne — and sometimes it goes better with
the food we're eating.

In this chapter, we recommend some of our favorite U.S. dry
sparkling wines, and then we tour the world, recommending a few
of our favorite dry sparklers from France, Spain, Italy, Australia,
and South Africa. We end with two reviews of a special type of
dessert sparkling wine from Italy: Asti.

We list the vital information for each wine in the following way:

✔ **The producer:** This is the company that makes the wine, and
its name is usually considered the brand name of the wine.

✔ **The wine name:** For most of the wines in this chapter, the
wine name is a fanciful name created to give a special cachet
to the wine. This name usually incorporates a word, such as
Brut or *Rosé,* that identifies the style of the wine.

✔ **The appellation:** The *appellation* is a necessary and legal
part of a wine label, intended to tell you where the grapes
that make up the wine came from and other technical information about the wine. In the case of sparkling wines, the

appellation often implies a particular production process for the wine. (We include the country of origin in parentheses when we group the wines of several countries in the same section.)

✔ **The approximate retail price of the wine:** This price varies greatly depending on where you live and the type of store at which you buy your wine. We use New York State suggested retail prices.

U.S. Sparkling Wines

The U.S., especially California, is the best source in the world for quality sparkling wines (after Champagne, of course). Although Spain and Germany — and even other regions in France, outside Champagne — produce a great deal more sparkling wine than the U.S. does, the quality level for sparkling wines in these countries is not as high.

Most of the better California sparkling wines come from Napa and Sonoma, but three excellent producers (Roederer Estate, Scharffenberger Cellars, and Handley Cellars) are in cool Mendocino County, and one (Maison Deutz) is down south in San Luis Obispo. The other region in the U.S. that has proved to be a good source for sparkling wines is the Finger Lakes district in western New York State.

We don't like to compare U.S. sparkling wines with those of Champagne, because the two types of wine are so different. Sparkling wines from the U.S. tend to be fruitier than Champagne wines, which are toastier and more earthy. Good sparkling wines come from both places, and we enjoy both styles.

We review our recommended U.S. sparkling wines alphabetically by producer.

S. Anderson Vintage Blanc de Noirs

- ✔ **Producer:** S. Anderson
- ✔ **Wine name:** Vintage Blanc de Noirs
- ✔ **Appellation:** Napa Valley
- ✔ **Price:** $22

Although S. Anderson also makes *still* (non-sparkling) wines in the Stags Leap District of Napa Valley, the company is a sparkling wine specialist. Of the several different sparkling wines it makes, the Blanc de Noirs, made from Pinot Noir, is our favorite. The 1991 Blanc de Noirs is a big, fruity, full-bodied sparkler with lots of tart cherry fruit flavor. We find it terrific as an apéritif wine, with smoked oysters on sourdough bread. Other S. Anderson sparkling wines are almost as good as the Blanc de Noirs, which says something for the consistency of this Napa Valley winery.

Ed: 86–88   **Mary:** 85–87

Chateau Frank Vintage Brut Champagne

- **Producer:** Chateau Frank
- **Wine name:** Vintage Brut Champagne
- **Appellation:** Finger Lakes
- **Price:** $18.50

Chateau Frank is the sister winery of Dr. Konstantin Frank's Vinifera Wine Cellars in the Finger Lakes region of New York State. Willy Frank founded Chateau Frank more than 15 years ago, and is now making two of the best sparkling wines in New York, a blanc de blancs (all Chardonnay) and what he calls Brut Champagne. (Unlike European Union countries, the U.S. has no laws prohibiting the use of the word *Champagne* on sparkling wine labels.) Chateau Frank Brut is made from the same three grape varieties that are used in the Champagne region: Pinot Noir, Pinot Meunier, and Chardonnay.

The 1989 Chateau Frank Brut, which we slightly prefer to the Frank Blanc de Blancs, has ripe lemon and lime aromas and flavors. This dry, very crisp, fruity sparkler is big, firm, and rich. It would be a good accompaniment to freshwater fish or to oysters. And it's also a very good value.

Ed: 85–87   **Mary:** 85–87

Domaine Carneros Vintage Blanc de Blancs

- **Producer:** Domaine Carneros
- **Wine name:** Blanc de Blancs
- **Appellation:** Carneros
- **Price:** $26

Domaine Carneros is owned by the great Taittinger Champagne firm. Its sparkling wines, made in the cool Carneros district of southern Napa, have a similar style to the wines of the parent company: The wines stress elegance and finesse rather than power and weight. Domaine Carneros makes a vintage-dated brut sparkling wine from a blend of four grape varieties and, since the 1988 vintage, a blanc de blancs, which is primarily Chardonnay, with a small amount of Pinot Blanc. We believe that the Domaine Carneros Blanc de Blancs is one of California's best of its kind.

The 1991 Blanc de Blancs has rich, toasty, developed aromas, with accents of apple and pear, and toasty flavors reminiscent of Champagne, but with a lemony, New World component — New World fruit made in an Old World style. It's a dry, crisp, fresh, light- to medium-bodied sparkler that holds its bubbles and freshness well in the glass.

Ed: 86–88   **Mary:** 86–88

Domaine Chandon Reserve

> ❧ **Producer:** Domaine Chandon
> ❧ **Wine name:** Reserve Cuvée 490
> ❧ **Appellation:** Napa County
> ❧ **Price:** $21

The establishment of Domaine Chandon by the Moët & Chandon Champagne house in 1973 marked the beginning of a wave of French sparkling-wine migration to California. Today, Champagne houses own most of the better sparkling wine firms in California.

Domaine Chandon makes five different sparkling wines, but the Reserve Cuvée is our clear favorite. (We also like the Chandon Blanc de Noirs.) Dawnine Dyer, winemaker since 1976, puts aside special lots of wine and earmarks them for the Reserve Cuvée, which receives extra aging. The Reserve Cuvée 490 (technically a non-vintage wine, but based mainly on wines from 1990) is about two-thirds Pinot Noir, with some Chardonnay and Pinot Meunier. It has toasty, biscuity aromas and flavors and a rich, creamy texture. This wine is quite dry, complex, and full of character, with good length. Considering the quality of this wine, we believe it's very fairly priced.

Ed: 87–89   **Mary:** 86–88

Maison Deutz Brut Cuvée

- ❦ **Producer:** Maison Deutz
- ❦ **Wine name:** Brut Cuvée
- ❦ **Appellation:** San Luis Obispo
- ❦ **Price:** $17

Maison Deutz started out life as a joint venture between Deutz Champagne (of France) and Beringer Estates, but when Deutz Champagne was acquired by the Louis Roederer company in 1993, Beringer completely took over Maison Deutz. Based in San Luis Obispo, in southern California, Maison Deutz has always made very good sparkling wines at decent prices, and that trend continues. We like both its Brut Cuvée and Blanc de Noirs, both non-vintage wines, but give the slight edge to the Brut Cuvée. Predominantly derived from Chardonnay and Pinot Blanc, along with some Pinot Noir, Maison Deutz Brut Cuvée has yeasty aromas, with lemon, melon, pear, and red berry fruit flavors. It's an elegant sparkling wine — ideal for serving in warm weather.

Ed: 87–89   **Mary:** 88–90

Fox Run Blanc de Blancs

- ❦ **Producer:** Fox Run Vineyards
- ❦ **Wine name:** Blanc de Blancs
- ❦ **Appellation:** Finger Lakes
- ❦ **Price:** $14

Fox Run Vineyards is a winery to watch. The Fox Run non-vintage Blanc de Blancs, entirely from Chardonnay grapes, is one of the best sparkling wines of its kind that we've had from the U.S. The wine is totally dry, with lemony fruit and some attractive earthiness but not a bit of toastiness; it's also fairly delicate in style. This sparkler confirms our notion that the Finger Lakes district has excellent potential for blanc de blancs bubblies. We like the Fox Run Blanc de Blancs with salade niçoise. If you have difficulty finding this wine (it is produced in small quantities), call the winery at 800-963-8376 or 800-636-9786.

Ed: 85–87   **Mary:** 86–88

Iron Horse Vintage Blanc de Blancs, Late Disgorged

> ♪ **Producer:** Iron Horse Vineyards
> ♪ **Wine name:** Vintage Blanc de Blancs, Late Disgorged
> ♪ **Appellation:** Green Valley (Sonoma)
> ♪ **Price:** $45

In Green Valley, the coolest wine region in Sonoma, wine-maker and part-owner Forrest Tancer makes some of the finest sparkling wines in the U.S. Iron Horse's best-known sparkling wine is undoubtedly its very good blanc de noirs, called Wedding Cuvée; better yet is the wine called Vrais Amis, similar to the Wedding Cuvée, but with more aging. (Both sell for around $25.) The two top-of-the-line sparkling wines of Iron Horse are its excellent Brut Late Disgorged and its Blanc de Blancs Late Disgorged. (*Late-disgorged* wines age longer in the bottle than the company's other sparklers, to gain more complex, mature flavors.) Of the two, we slightly prefer the Blanc de Blancs Late Disgorged.

Even the few California sparkling wines that cost over $50 can't match the quality of the 1990 Blanc de Blancs, Late Disgorged of Iron Horse, in our opinion. In addition to its rich, mature, toasty aromas and flavors, what sets this wine apart are its concentration, its balance, its very long finish, and the complexity and depth of its flavors. This is one of the three greatest sparkling wines that we've ever tasted outside of Champagne. Bravo, Forrest Tancer and Iron Horse!

Ed: 94–96   **Mary:** 91–93

"J" Vintage Sparkling Wine

> ♪ **Producer:** Jordan Sparkling Wine Company
> ♪ **Wine name:** "J"
> ♪ **Appellation:** Sonoma County
> ♪ **Price:** $29

Tom Jordan has the Midas touch; not only does his Jordan Winery produce one of the most popular Cabernet Sauvignons in the U.S., but his Jordan Sparkling Wine Company (a separate operation, headed by daughter Judy Jordan) makes one of the best domestic bubblies. Jordan's sparkling wine comes in a stunning dark green bottle, with a dramatic yellow "J" painted on it. But what's inside the bottle counts more, and sparkling "J" delivers.

The 1993 "J," made from Chardonnay and Pinot Noir grapes grown in the cool Russian River Valley, has yeasty, toasty aromas with touches of apples and pears, plus citrus and apple fruit flavors. It has a fresh, assertive character, lots of flavor, and a breathtakingly gentle finish. Since its first sparkling wine (the 1987), "J" has been getting better with each vintage; it's already a classic California sparkling wine.

Ed: 88–90   **Mary:** 87–89

Mumm Cuvée Napa Blanc de Noirs

> **Producer:** Mumm Napa Valley
>
> **Wine name:** Mumm Cuvée Napa Blanc de Noirs
>
> **Appellation:** Napa Valley
>
> **Price:** $17

Mumm Napa Valley, whose wines carry the brand name Mumm Cuvée Napa, is one of the most successful of the wineries with a Champagne parent (G.H. Mumm Champagne), possibly because it also has a Canadian godfather (Seagram's, the owner of G.H. Mumm). Mumm Napa Valley makes about seven or eight different sparkling wines, all ranging from very good to excellent, and its blanc de noirs has consistently been one of our favorites. The non-vintage Mumm Cuvée Napa Blanc de Noirs, medium pink in color, is primarily made from Pinot Noir, which accounts for its cherry aromas and candied cherry flavors (that remind Mary of red Life Savers). It has good fruit flavors and some character, plus a nice dry finish — an impressive sparkling wine for the price.

Ed: 88–90   **Mary:** 86–88

Roederer Estate Brut

> **Producer:** Roederer Estate
>
> **Wine name:** Roederer Estate Brut
>
> **Appellation:** Anderson Valley (Mendocino County)
>
> **Price:** $18

When it comes to quality, perhaps no producer of sparkling wine has been as successful in the U.S. as Roederer Estate. Owned by the house of Louis Roederer, this was the only Champagne-owned winery in the cool Anderson Valley in Mendocino County, until Pommery Champagne purchased

Scharffenberger Cellars. Roederer Estate is still the only French-owned winery in California to grow all of its own grapes. Its winemaker, Michel Salgues, is French and produced Champagne for Roederer before launching Roederer Estate in 1986.

Roederer Estate Brut is a non-vintage wine blended 70 percent from Chardonnay and 30 percent from Pinot Noir. It has smoky, toasty (very Champagne-like) aromas and complex fruit flavors, suggestive of pears; although the wine is reminiscent of Champagne, it's actually fruitier than a typical Champagne. Roederer Estate Brut is a very dry, fresh, lively, well-balanced sparkling wine with fine, persistent bubbles — a good tasting sparkler with lots of character.

Ed: 88–90   **Mary:** 87–89

Roederer Estate Vintage L'Ermitage

> ♪ **Producer:** Roederer Estate
>
> ♪ **Wine name:** Vintage L'Ermitage Brut
>
> ♪ **Appellation:** Anderson Valley
>
> ♪ **Price:** $34

With the 1989 vintage, Roederer Estate introduced its prestige cuvée, L'Ermitage, which is 56 percent Chardonnay and 44 percent Pinot Noir. The 1991 L'Ermitage has rich, toasty aromas and toasty, hazelnut flavors. It is very firm and flavorful, with excellent balance and a rich finish. You can enjoy it now, perhaps with a fish entrée, but this complex beauty will develop even further with two or three years of aging. The 1991 L'Ermitage is probably closer in style to a fine Champagne than any other sparkling wine made outside of the Champagne region.

Ed: 92–94   **Mary:** 93–95

Roederer Estate Brut Rosé

> ♪ **Producer:** Roederer Estate
>
> ♪ **Wine name:** Brut Rosé
>
> ♪ **Appellation:** Anderson Valley
>
> ♪ **Price:** $19

Roederer Estate Rosé, made from equal parts of Pinot Noir and Chardonnay, is the newest child of winemaker Michel Salgues; he believes that even a rosé needs quite a bit of Chardonnay to give the finesse and elegance he seeks in his sparkling wines. This rosé is the most subtle, understated rosé sparkler that we've ever tasted. It's a very pale coppery pink in color, and it's very dry. This wine has fascinating herbal and toasty aromas, which Mary describes as "fresh as a sea breeze," and concentrated cherry fruit flavors. The Roederer Estate Rosé is a very fine, delicate sparkling wine — a well-bred child, Monsieur Salgues!

Ed: 89–91   **Mary:** 90–92

Scharffenberger Vintage Blanc de Blancs

> ♪ **Producer:** Scharffenberger Cellars
> ♪ **Wine name:** Vintage Blanc de Blancs
> ♪ **Appellation:** Mendocino County
> ♪ **Price:** $21

Of the four Scharffenberger Cellars sparkling wines, its Blanc de Blancs, which is all Chardonnay, receives the most critical acclaim and, in fact, is our favorite. The 1991 Blanc de Blancs has delicate, toasty aromas and subtle, lemony flavors. It's a firm, relatively light-bodied, crisp blanc de blancs that has the elegance you want from this type of sparkler. It would be ideal as an apéritif wine or as an accompaniment to some light, fishy hors d'oeuvres.

Ed: 86–88   **Mary:** 88–90

Other Dry Sparkling Wines of the World

Besides the Champagne region of France, the U.S., and the Asti district of Italy — all of which we cover separately — good sparkling wine comes from Australia, South Africa, Spain, throughout France, parts of Italy, Germany, and Austria. We don't review wines from all these areas in this section, because we don't have favorite sparkling wines from all of them. (We admit to being so in love with Champagne that our taste in sparkling wines is skewed heavily away from other areas.) But we do review sparkling wines from around the world that offer either great value or a different style, or both.

We organize our recommended wines in this section alphabetically by producer, intermingling wines of various prices, color, and origin.

Bouvet Rosé Excellence

> ♪ **Producer:** Bouvet-Ladubay *(boo vay lah du bay)*
> ♪ **Wine name:** Bouvet Rosé Excellence
> ♪ **Appellation:** France
> ♪ **Price:** $13

The Bouvet-Ladubay winery in the Loire Valley region of France produces a range of sparkling wines under the Bouvet label. Although these wines are made in the classic method of the Champagne region, they are made from locally important grape varieties (not traditional Champagne grapes). The non-vintage Rosé Excellence, our favorite Bouvet wine, is made primarily from Cabernet Franc grapes, along with 10 percent of Groslot, a local red grape. The wine has a salmon pink color, a rather quiet aroma, and subtle but clear flavors of red berry; it's quite full bodied and dry, with some complexity. Bovet Rosé tastes fine when you sip it without food, but we plan to pair our next bottle with pasta in cream sauce.

Ed: 85–87   **Mary:** 88–90

Ferrari Brut

> ♪ **Producer:** Ferrari-Fratelli Lunelli
> ♪ **Wine name:** Ferrari Brut
> ♪ **Appellation:** Trento (Italy)
> ♪ **Price:** $18

Ferrari is one of the largest producers of *traditional-method* sparkling wines in all of Italy, and it's certainly one of the very finest. The non-vintage Ferrari Brut is made almost entirely from Chardonnay grapes, with only 5 percent Pinot Noir in the blend. This rather straightforward sparkling wine is medium bodied, fairly dry, and crisp, with some elegance. Like so many nonsparkling Italian white wines, this wine doesn't have much richness or complexity of aroma or flavor, but it is fresh, refreshing, and easy to drink. Precisely because of its lack of rich flavor, Ferrari Brut works very well on the table, accommodating itself to all sorts of foods.

Ed: 84–86   **Mary:** 84–86

Bruno Giacosa Vintage Extra Brut

> ♪ **Producer:** Cantine Bruno Giacosa
>
> ♪ **Wine name:** Bruno Giacosa Vintage Extra Brut
>
> ♪ **Appellation:** Neive (Italy)
>
> ♪ **Price:** $28.50

We still remember how casually Bruno Giacosa asked us if we'd like to try a new wine of his, just a little something he was playing around with. Then he popped a cork and poured us the best Italian sparkling wine we've ever had. We were stunned, not because we didn't expect great things from this remarkable winemaker, but because Giacosa specializes in rich red wine, and the process of making a sparkling wine (let alone a great one) is a world apart from red wine production. But such is his talent. Years later, we still consider Giacosa's bubbly the finest sparkling wine of Italy—and one of the best in the world, outside of Champagne.

Bruno Giacosa makes his sparkling wine (he makes only one) entirely from Pinot Noir grapes that grow in the Oltrepò Pavese district of Lombardy, in the region adjacent to his home region of Piedmont. The wine is made in the traditional method, as practiced in Champagne. Bruno Giacosa Extra Brut is a full-bodied, dry sparkling wine with richly toasty and smoky aromas and flavors, and a creamy texture. Its production is small, but the wine is available in the U.S. The current vintage is 1991.

Ed: 92–94   **Mary:** 89–91

Juve y Camps Reserva de la Familia Vintage Extra Brut

> ♪ **Producer:** Juve y Camps *(hoo vay ee cahmp)*
>
> ♪ **Wine name:** Reserva de la Familia Vintage Extra Brut
>
> ♪ **Appellation:** Cava (Spain)
>
> ♪ **Price:** $17

Cava is the term for Spanish sparkling wines made in the traditional method (the method of France's Champagne region); the grapes are usually local Spanish varieties, principally Maccabeo, Parellada, and Xarel-lo (pronounced *cha REL loh*). Compared with many other Cava wines that sell for less than $10 a bottle, the wines of Juve y Camps cost a small fortune — but this company is one of the better Cava producers.

The 1992 Juve y Camps Reserva de la Familia has a typical Cava aroma, which we can only describe as a little rubbery (far more appetizing than it sounds!). The wine is full bodied and relatively dry, with earthy and mushroomy flavors. If you enjoy the inexpensive Spanish bubblies, step up to this wine for your next special occasion.

Ed: 84–86   **Mary:** 84–86

Pierre Jourdan Cuvée Belle Rose

- ♪ **Producer:** Cabrière Estate
- ♪ **Wine name:** Pierre Jourdan Cuvée Belle Rose
- ♪ **Appellation:** Franschhoek (South Africa)
- ♪ **Price:** $21

The Cabrière Estate winery in the Franschhoek region of South Africa produces numerous sparkling wines under the Pierre Jourdan label (the name of the person who founded this winery 300 years ago). The wines vary according to the grape variety from which they are made or their style. We like the Cuvée Belle Rose, a non-vintage wine that is a light salmon pink color and is made entirely from Pinot Noir. The aroma of this wine suggests strawberries and a slight toastiness, and the flavors are quite fruity, particularly cherry and red berries. These flavors are exquisitely re-strained, and the general style of the wine is delicate and refined. The delicacy of this wine would make a nice counter-point to a light fish prepared in a cream sauce.

Ed: 89–91   **Mary:** 84–86

Seaview Vintage Brut

- ♪ **Producer:** Seaview
- ♪ **Wine name:** Vintage Brut
- ♪ **Appellation:** South Eastern Australia (Australia)
- ♪ **Price:** $10

If we wanted to quibble, we could note that the 1995 vintage of Seaview Brut is already on the U.S. market, barely two years after the grapes were harvested — a rather truncated aging period for a classic-method sparkling wine. If the wine had aged longer, it would have gained all those toasty-smoky-caramely aromas and flavors that we love. But this wine is shooting for a different style. One taste of the wine tells us that youthful fruitiness, rather than developed flavors, is the goal of Seaview Brut, and the wine achieves that goal remarkably well. Fresh flavors of lemon, melon, and peach accent this full-bodied, rich, relatively dry sparkler and carry through to the wine's finish. We urge you to try this wine because, if you like it, you can probably afford to enjoy it often.

Ed: 85–87　　　　　　　　　　　　　　**Mary:** 86–88

Villiera Estate Tradition Brut "Carte Rouge"

- 🍷 **Producer:** Villiera Estate
- 🍷 **Wine name:** Tradition Brut "Carte Rouge"
- 🍷 **Appellation:** Paarl (South Africa)
- 🍷 **Price:** $13.50

This non-vintage sparkling wine is produced in the classic Champagne method, and two of its grapes (Pinot Noir and Chardonnay) are classic Champagne grape varieties. But about 40 percent of the blend for this wine derives from South Africa's local Pinotage grape and the locally important Chenin Blanc grape. The Chenin Blanc component is particularly evident in the wine's rather pungent aroma, although the aroma also has the typical toasty notes of a classic-method bubbly. The "Carte Rouge" has earthy and fruity flavors, and a crisp acidity gives it liveliness.

Ed: 85–87

Asti, the Italian Original

If you want to be cool, turn your nose up at Asti, the Italian sparkling wine formerly known as *Asti Spumante*. Plenty of wine drinkers dismiss it with just two words: "Too sweet."

Well, Asti *is* sweet. It's also delicate and delicious, with the precise flavor of the Muscat grapes from which it is made. We love it.

Asti is made from Muscat grapes grown around the town of Asti, in the Piedmont region. The Asti production process is completely different from that of Champagne. Fresh fruit character is the winemaking goal for Asti, whereas Champagne producers seek complex, mature flavors. The word *Spumante,* which simply means "sparkling," was recently dropped from the official name of Asti because so many wineries now make cheap Asti imitations called Spumante. These imitations have flavors similar to Asti, but they tend to be heavy-handed and lack the delicacy of the real thing.

Because freshness is so important for Asti, and because you have no way of knowing how fresh a bottle of Asti is (the wine is always non-vintage), we suggest that you shop for Asti in a store that has a regular turnover of this wine. If the wine feels heavy — rather than delicate and light — in your mouth, the wine is too old.

Fontanafredda Asti

- **Producer:** Fontanafredda
- **Wine name:** Asti
- **Appellation:** Asti
- **Price:** $13

Fontanafredda is a huge operation, situated in the picturesque hills of the Barolo production zone in Italy's Piedmont region. Besides producing good red and white wines, Fontanafredda makes about 3.5 million bottles of Asti every year. Fontanafredda Asti has fabulous fruity aromas and flavors — everything from grapefruit to melon to apples to peaches. It's fairly soft in texture, and it leaves your mouth with a fresh, clean finish. Warm apple tarts with real whipped cream on top are our idea of a perfect match for this wine; of course, the wine is also delicious all by itself.

Ed: 89–91   **Mary:** 85–87

Martini & Rossi Asti

- **Producer:** Martini & Rossi
- **Wine name:** Asti
- **Appellation:** Asti
- **Price:** $13

Martini & Rossi is one of the best-known names in the Asti business. Martini & Rossi Asti is a bit subdued and understated in aroma, but it still shows the classic peachy and floral notes of the Muscat grape. The wine has delicate and delicious fruity flavor (peaches and melon) and a very fine carbonation. Because of its delicacy, we personally appreciate this wine more without food than with food.

Ed: 88–90   **Mary:** 86–88

Part IV
Appendixes

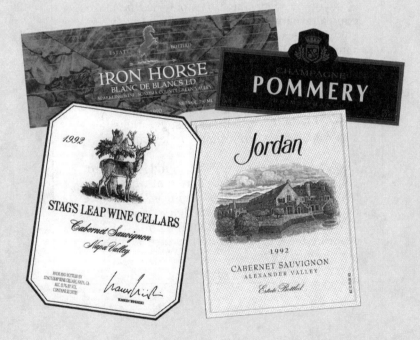

In this part . . .

In this part, we try to inspire the adventurer in you by suggesting types of wine that make good alternatives to wines that you already enjoy — because life's too short to drink the same thing all the time! Appendix A is where you'll find ideas for branching out.

When you know what's for dinner but you're uncertain what to drink with it, Appendix B comes to the rescue with wine suggestions for all sorts of foods, from simple to lavish.

And when a wine we describe sounds terrific to you, but you want to make sure that what you think we mean is really what we mean, Appendix C is the place to turn. Here, we define most of the terms that we use throughout the book to describe the aromas, flavors, texture, and taste of the wines we review.

Appendix A

Branching Out

*F*inding a wine you enjoy is great, but sometimes it pays
to push your boundaries a little and experiment with new
wines. Use the following table to move from wines that you
already know you enjoy to wines that you may end up enjoying
even more!

If You Like This	Try This	Because
Red Wines		
Cabernet Sauvignon or Merlot	Bordeaux	Cabernet Sauvignon and Merlot are the two main grape varieties in Bordeaux.
Pinot Noir	Burgundy (French)	French Burgundy is 100 percent Pinot Noir.
Syrah or Shiraz	Hermitage, Côte Rôtie, Cornas, Crozes-Hermitage, or St.-Joseph	All these wines from the Northern Rhône Valley are made from the Syrah grape.
Sangiovese	Chianti or Brunello di Montalcino	Chianti and Brunello are made from the Sangiovese grape variety.
Red Zinfandel	Petite Sirah	Although different grape varieties, Red Zinfandel and Petite Sirah share similar styles — full bodied, rustic, and a little wild.
Bordeaux	Rioja	Both wines are usually made in a style that stresses elegance rather than power.
Beaujolais	Bardolino	Although a bit drier and less fruity, Italian Bardolino resembles French Beaujolais in style — light bodied and not too tannic.

(continued)

If You Like This	Try This	Because
Red Wines *(continued)*		
Pinot Noir	Barbera (Italian)	Both wines stress fruitiness (cherry) and are low in tannin.
Barolo	Barbaresco or Gattinara	All these wines are made from the Nebbiolo grape; all are dry and full bodied.
White Wines		
Chardonnay	Pouilly-Fuissé, Saint-Véran, Mâcon-Villages, Meursault, Puligny-Montrachet (white Burgundies)	Although white Burgundies are leaner than Californian or Australian Chardonnays, all come from the Chardonnay grape.
Sauvignon Blanc (Fumé Blanc)	Sancerre; Pouilly-Fumé	Sancerre and Pouilly-Fumé are livelier, more intensely flavored wines from France's Loire Valley, and both are made from the Sauvignon Blanc grape variety.
Soave or Pinot Grigio	Muscadet	Although all three are different grape varieties, they are similar in style — light bodied, lively, and rather neutral in flavor.
Sémillon	White Bordeaux or Tocai Friulano	Most white Bordeaux wines contain some Sémillon; all three share a similar viscous style.
Pinot Grigio	Verdicchio or Bianco di Custoza	All three are Italian wines that share similar styles — light bodied, lively, with an appealing fruitiness.
Chardonnay	Pinot Blanc	These grape varieties make similar wines, but Pinot Blancs are usually lighter bodied and fruitier.

Appendix B

What's for Dinner?

· ·

*W*e can't help it, any of us. It's human nature. We want to drink The Right Wine with our meal, especially if company is coming.

But in reality, even if there were such a thing as the single perfect wine for any one dish, finding that perfect combination would be nearly impossible. There are simply too many variables: the number of different foods, the number of different preparations, and the number of different wines in the world! The perfect match in the world of wine and food pairing is extremely elusive.

Fortunately, several kinds of wine are likely to taste good with several different dishes. As long as the weight of the food and wine and their relative intensities of flavor are compatible, the combination is likely to work — provided, of course, that you personally *like* the wine and the food.

Our wine suggestions for various types of food appear in the following table. Try a few of our recommendations to see whether you like these combinations. We believe that they're good matches, but never forget that, in the end, *you* are the only judge of what tastes right to you.

Food and Preparation	Wine Suggestion
Beef	
Barbecue	Richer Zinfandel
Burgers	Australian Cabernet; Chilean Cabernet; lighter U.S. Cabernet; U.S. Merlot; lighter Zinfandel; Côtes du Rhône
Cheeseburgers	St.-Joseph; Zinfandel
Chili, moderately spicy	California Cabernet; richer Zinfandel; Gigondas; Rosso di Montalcino
Filet mignon	Barolo; red Bordeaux; St.-Joseph

(continued)

Food and Preparation	Wine Suggestion
Beef *(continued)*	
Pot roast	California Cabernet; Chilean Cabernet; Vacqueyras
Roasted	Argentinean red; Barolo; Chianti Rufina Riserva; red Bordeaux; red Burgundy; Crozes-Hermitage; Portuguese red
Steak, plain	Australian Cabernet; California Cabernet; South African Cab/Merlot blend; Zinfandel; Bordeaux; Chianti Classico; Rioja Reserva
Steak, with barbecue sauce or ketchup	Australian Cabernet; U.S. Cabernet; Crozes-Hermitage; Zinfandel
Stew	Cornas; Côtes du Ventoux; Argentinean Cabernet; Chilean Cabernet; Barbaresco; Rioja Gran Reserva
Stir-fry, with vegetables	Bardolino; dry rosé; U.S. Sauvignon Blanc; Zinfandel
Veal Parmesan	Lighter Chianti; Salice Salentino
Lamb	
Chops	Chilean Cabernet; red Bordeaux; Chianti Classico; rosé Champagne
Roasted	Australian Shiraz; Bordeaux; Brunello di Montalcino; South African Cabernet
Shish kebab	Greek red; any Chianti
Stew	South African Cab/Merlot blend; Chianti Classico; Cornas; Côtes du Ventoux; Hermitage
Pork	
Baked ham	Australian Shiraz; Corbières; German Riesling; dry rosé; rosé Champagne
Chops	Australian Shiraz
Ham steak with fruit	German Riesling; rosé Champagne
Roasted	Alsace Gewurztraminer; Alsace Riesling; California Syrah; Chenin Blanc; German Riesling; Malbec; rich white Burgundy
Salami	Bardolino; Dolcetto
Sausages	Australian Cabernet; California Cabernet; Viognier; Zinfandel

Food and Preparation	Wine Suggestion
Chicken	
Asian, spicy	German Riesling; Gewürztraminer; NV brut Champagne; U.S. Chardonnay
Barbecued	Australian Shiraz; California Cabernet; richer Zinfandel
Breast fillets, with cream sauce	Alsace Riesling; Italian white; Pouilly-Fuissé; Tokay-Pinot Gris
Breast fillets, with herbs and butter	Lighter California Chardonnay; St.-Véran; Washington Semillon
Cacciatore or stewed	Barbera d'Alba; NV brut Champagne; Salice Salentino; Valpolicella
Curry	Alsace Pinot Blanc; Gewürztraminer; Pinot Grigio
Fried	Beaujolais; Côtes du Rhône; U.S. Chardonnay; Australian Chardonnay
Grilled	U.S. Chardonnay; white Burgundy; Tuscan Sangiovese; U.S. Chardonnay; U.S. Pinot Noir
Roasted	Beaujolais; Cahors; California Cabernet; red Burgundy; Rioja Reserva; Zinfandel; Côte Rôtie; NV brut Champagne
Salad	U.S. Pinot Noir
Stir-fry with vegetables	Lighter Zinfandel; Pouilly-Fumé; Traminer or dry Gewürztraminer
Turkey	
Boneless fillets, sauteed	Lighter Chianti; U.S. Chardonnay
Burgers	Beaujolais; Chianti Classico; Dolcetto; dry rosé
Roast, dark meat	Dry Gewürztraminer; red Burgundy; U.S. Pinot Noir
Roast, white meat	Alsace Riesling; Australia Semillon; South African Chardonnay; white Burgundy
Duck	
Confit	Crozes-Hermitage
Roast	Cahors; Provence red; California Cabernet

(continued)

Food and Preparation	Wine Suggestion
Duck (continued)	
With fruit sauce	California Syrah; German Riesling; richer Zinfandel; Spanish red
Game birds	
Roasted	Barbaresco; Brunello di Montalcino; Cannonau di Sardegna; Côte Rôtie; red Bordeaux; Rioja Reserva; Spanish red from Penedés; California Cabernet; German Riesling; Sémillon; NV brut Champagne
Venison and Other Game	
Any preparation	Barolo; Chianti Classico Riserva; Lagrein; Minervois; Gigondas; hearty Provence red; California Syrah; U.S. Cabernet
Fish and Other Seafood	
Any fried fish	Blanc de blancs sparkling wine; Soave; Verdicchio
Darker fish, grilled or broiled	Australian Semillon; U.S. Chardonnay; Viognier; white Burgundy; U.S. Pinot Noir; lighter Zinfandel; NV brut Champagne
Darker fish, with tomato-based sauce	Tocai Friulano; U.S. Pinot Gris
Light fish, broiled, with lemon and butter	Blanc de blancs Champagne; Chablis; Mâcon; Pinot Blanc; Soave; white Bordeaux
Light fish, with cream sauce	German Riesling; Sylvaner; vintage Champagne
Salmon, grilled or baked	NV brut Champagne; red Burgundy; U.S. Pinot Noir
Salmon, smoked	Blanc de blancs Champagne
Crab cakes	German Riesling; U.S. Pinot Noir; vintage Champagne
Lobster, broiled or steamed	Rich Pinot Grigio; rich U.S. Chardonnay; rosé Champagne
Lobster, grilled	U.S. Pinot Noir
Shrimp salad	Soft Spanish white

Food and Preparation	Wine Suggestion
Fish and Other Seafood *(continued)*	
Scallops ceviche	Muscadet
Scallops, in cream sauce	Richer white Bordeaux
Shellfish, cooked with mild flavors	Bourgogne-Aligoté; Provence white; rosé Champagne; South African Sauvignon Blanc; U.S. Chardonnay; U.S. Pinot Noir; U.S. Sauvignon Blanc; vintage Champagne
Shellfish, in spicy sauce	New Zealand Sauvignon Blanc; Tocai Friulano
Paella	Albariño
Raw shellfish	Chablis; Muscadet; NV brut Champagne; NV brut Sparkling wine
Pasta	
Cream sauce	Rosé sparkling wine; Tocai Friulano
Lasagna	Salice Salentino
With spicy tomato sauce	Chianti Classico; Chianti Classico Riserva; lighter Zinfandel; Barbera d'Alba
With tomato and meat sauce	Dolcetto d'Alba; Barbera d'Alba; Barolo; Chianti Classico; California Sangiovese
With vegetables and cheese	Lighter Zinfandel; Italian Sauvignon Blanc; Vernaccia di San Gimignano
Pizza	
Spicy	Australian Shiraz
Tomatoes and cheese	Barbera d'Alba; Côtes du Rhone; Valpolicella; Zinfandel
Risotto	
With wild mushrooms	Barolo; Pouilly-Fuissé; richer Italian white
Salads	
Chef	German Riesling
With warm goat cheese	California Sauvignon Blanc; Italian Sauvignon; Pouilly-Fumé
Niçoise	Provence white
Spinach, with eggs and bacon	German Riesling

(continued)

Food and Preparation	Wine Suggestion
Vegetables	
Stuffed mushrooms	Rosé Champagne
Casserole	California Syrah
Eggplant parmesan	Salice Salentino; Dolcetto d'Alba
Grilled	California Cabernet; California Chardonnay
Ratatouille	Côtes du Ventoux; Zinfandel
Eggs	
Cheese omelette	Moscato d'Asti
Eggs Benedict	German Riesling
Mushroom omelette	NV brut Champagne; rosé Champagne
Soup	
Hearty	Vacqueyras
Veal stew	California Merlot; lighter Australian Shiraz; Provence red
Vegetable	German Riesling
Cheese	
Aged goat cheeses	Australian Semillon
Fresh goat cheese	New Zealand Sauvignon Blanc; Sancerre
Hard, aged (cheddar, Gouda)	Argentinean red; Barbaresco; Chilean Cabernet; Lagrein Dunkel; red Bordeaux; Zinfandel
Mild cow cheeses (Monterey Jack)	Alsace Gewurztraminer
Soft, ripened (Brie, Camembert)	Mâcon-Villages; Pouilly-Fuissé
Strong-tasting	St.-Chinian

Glossary of Wine-Tasting Terms

*U*nfortunately for all of us, the words people use to describe the taste of wine are often very personal, and don't mean the same thing (if they mean anything at all!) to the next person. A few basic words, whose meanings wine experts generally agree on, do exist, and we stick to those terms as much as possible in our wine descriptions throughout this book.

In this glossary, you can find our definitions for these basic terms, such as *body, tannin, crispness, fruitiness,* and so forth. You can also find our definitions for other wine descriptors that are a little more personal. With the help of this glossary, you can at least fathom what we *think* we're saying when we use these wine-tasting terms.

acidic: A term used to describe wines that you perceive to be too high in acidity.

ample: A descriptor for wines that give the impression of being full and expansive in your mouth.

angular: A term for wines that give the impression of having sharp edges in your mouth, as opposed to being round.

aroma: The smell of a wine. Some purists use the term *aroma* only for the straightforward, youthful smells of a wine and use the term *bouquet* for the more complex smells of an aged wine. But we use *aroma* as a general term for all wine smells.

aromatic: A descriptor for a wine that has a pronounced smell, used particularly in reference to fruity and floral smells. Some white grape varieties also are dubbed *aromatic* because the wines made from them tend to be extremely strong in aroma.

aromatic compounds: Those substances in wine — derived from the grapes, from winemaking, or from aging — that are responsible for a wine's aromas and flavors.

attack: The first impression a wine gives you when you taste it. A wine's attack is usually related to sensations gathered in the front of your mouth, especially the tip of your tongue, which is usually the first place the wine touches.

balance: The interrelationship of a wine's alcohol, residual sugar, acid, and tannin. When no one component stands out obtrusively on the palate, a wine is said to be well balanced. Balance is a prized characteristic in wines.

big: A general descriptor for wines that are either very full or very intense.

black fruits: A general term for wine aromas and flavors that suggest blackberries, blueberries, black cherries, black currants, and so forth.

blousy: A word used to describe a wine that seems to be imbalanced in favor of high alcohol or sweetness.

body: The impression of a wine's weight in your mouth. A wine's body is generally described as light, medium, or full.

brambly: A descriptor for aromas and flavors that suggest brambly or thorny bush fruits such as raspberries or black-berries.

bright: Indicates a wine whose characteristics are perceived vividly by the senses. A wine can be visually bright, or it can have bright aromas and flavors; in both cases, the opposite is *dull.*

cedary: Having aromas or flavors that resemble the smell of cedar wood.

character: An anthropomorphic attribution for wines that give the impression of being solid and having substance and integrity.

charry: Having aromas or flavors that suggest burnt or charred wood.

chocolatey: Having aromas or flavors that suggest chocolate.

compact: A descriptor for wines that give the impression of being intense but not full.

complex: Not simple. A complex wine has many different aromas and flavors, and "has a lot going on."

concentrated: A descriptor for aromas and flavors that are dense rather than dilute.

concentration: A characteristic of wines whose flavors or fruit character are tightly knit as opposed to being dilute or watery.

crisp: A wine that feels clean and slightly brittle in your mouth. It's the opposite of *soft.* Crispness is usually the result of high acidity.

depth: A characteristic of fine wines. Wines with depth give the impression of having underground layers of taste rather than being flat and one-dimensional.

dilute: A descriptor for wines whose aromas and flavors are thin and watery, as opposed to concentrated.

dry: A wine that is not sweet. The word *dry* can also be used to describe the texture of a wine that feels rough in your mouth, as in "dry texture" or "dry mouth-feel." But when *dry* is used alone, it refers specifically to lack of sweetness.

dull: A wine whose expression is muddled and unclear. This term can apply to a wine's appearance, to its aromas and flavors, or to its general style.

earthy: Having aromas and flavors that suggest earth, such as wet soil, dry earth, certain minerally aromas, and so forth. This term is sometimes used as a general descriptor for wines that are rustic and lack refinement.

elegance: An attribute of wines that express themselves in a fine or delicate manner, as opposed to an intense or forceful way.

finish: The final impressions a wine gives after you have swallowed it or spat it out.

firm: A descriptor for wines that are not soft, but are not harsh and tough; generally relates to the tannic content of red wines and oaky white wines.

flabby: A term used to describe wines that are too soft.

flavors: Aromatic constituents of a wine that are perceived in the mouth.

fleshy: A descriptor for a rich textural or tactile impression of some wines.

fruit character: Those characteristics of a wine that derive from the grapes, such as a wine's aromas and flavors, its grape tannin, natural acidity, and extract.

fruity: Having aromas and flavors suggestive of fruit. This is a broad descriptor; in some cases, the fruity aroma or flavor of a wine can be described more precisely as suggestive of fresh fruit, dried fruit, or cooked fruit, or even more precisely as a specific fresh, dried, or cooked fruit, such as fresh apples, dried figs, or strawberry jam.

full: A descriptor for wines that give the impression of being large in your mouth. A wine's fullness can derive from high alcohol or from other aspects of the wine.

generous: A descriptor for wines whose characteristics are expressive and easy to perceive.

harmonious: A descriptor of wines that are not only well balanced but also express themselves in a particularly graceful manner.

herbal: Having aromas and flavors that suggest herbs, such as fresh herbs, dried herbs, or specific herbs (rosemary, thyme, tarragon, and so forth).

intense: A descriptor for wines that express themselves strongly. When used in reference to a wine's aromas and flavors, this word describes the volume of those aromas or flavors — how strong the smell of lemon is in the wine, for example. When used in reference to a wine's total expression, this word describes an impression of general forcefulness that the wine gives.

lead-pencil: Having aromas or flavors that suggest a combination of graphite and wood.

lees: Grape solids and dead yeast cells that precipitate to the bottom of a white wine following fermentation.

length: A sustained sensory impression across the tongue, characteristic of some fine wines.

minerally: Having aromas or flavors that suggest minerals (as opposed to organic substances such as plants or animals). This is a broad descriptor; in some cases, the minerally aroma or flavor of a wine can be described more precisely as suggestive of chalk, iron, steel, and so forth.

nutty: Having aromas or flavors that suggest nuts. This is a broad descriptor; in some cases, the nutty aroma or flavor of a wine can be described more precisely as suggestive of roasted nuts, toasted nuts, nut butter, cashews, almonds, hazelnuts, and so forth.

oaky: A wine that has characteristics deriving from oak, such as toastiness, smokiness, a charry smell or taste, vanilla aroma, or a higher tannin level than the wine might ordinarily have. Usually, these oaky characteristics occur as the wine ages in oak barrels, but in very inexpensive wines, they might have been added as an actual flavoring.

off-dry: A generalized term for wines that are neither fully dry nor very sweet.

petrol: Aromas or flavors that suggest diesel fuel.

plummy: Having aromas or flavors that suggest ripe plums.

plush: A textural or tactile descriptor for wines that feel luxurious in your mouth.

powerful: An anthropomorphic descriptor for wines that convey an impression of strength and intensity.

pretty: An anthropomorphic descriptor for wines that are attractive for their delicacy and finesse.

restrained: A descriptor for wines whose characteristics are not particularly expressive.

rich: A descriptor for wines that offer an abundance of flavor, texture, or other sensory perceptions.

round: A descriptor for wines that are perceived to be neither flat nor angular. Roundness relates to the wine's structure — that is, its particular make-up of acid, tannin, sweetness, and alcohol.

silky: Having a supple, smooth texture.

smoky: Having aromas or flavors that suggest smoke or smoked wood.

soft: Textural descriptor for a wine whose sugar (if any) and alcohol dominate its acidity and tannin, resulting in a lack of hardness or roughness.

steely: Having aromas or flavors that suggest metal or steel.

stony: Having aromas or flavors that suggest stones. In some cases, the stony aroma or flavor of a wine can be described more precisely as suggestive of wet stones.

structure: That part of a wine's expression that derives from the wine's basic elements (mainly alcohol, acid, tannin, and sugar).

stuffing: A synonym for a wine's essential substance.

style: The set of characteristics through which a wine manifests itself.

supple: A descriptor for wines that seem fluid in texture in the mouth, without roughness or sharpness.

sweaty: Having aromas or flavors that suggest sweat.

tannic: A word used to describe wines that seem to be high in *tannin* (a substance in red wines and oaked white wines that causes the wine to seem firm or, in the extreme, astringent).

tastes: The three basic tastes that you perceive in wine: sweetness, sourness (acidity), and bitterness. We also use the word *taste* for the complete impression a wine gives in your mouth.

tarry: Having aromas or flavors that suggest fresh tar.

tart: A descriptor for aromas or flavors of under-ripe fruit. This term can also apply to a wine that is too high in acid.

thin: A word used to describe wines that are lacking in substance.

tight: A descriptor for wines that seem to be inexpressive. This term can apply to a wine's aromas and flavors or to its structure.

underbrush: Aromas or flavors that suggest wet leaves, dampness, and slight decay.

vegetal: Having aromas or flavors that suggest vegetation or vegetables.

well-balanced: A term used to describe wines whose acid, alcohol, tannin (if any), and residual sugar (if any) relate to each other in such a way that none of the four components seems too dominant.

Index

Notes

Notes